Phraseology and Multiword Expressions

Series editors

Agata Savary (University of Tours, Blois, France), Manfred Sailer (Goethe University Frankfurt a. M., Germany), Yannick Parmentier (University of Lorraine, France), Victoria Rosén (University of Bergen, Norway), Mike Rosner (University of Malta, Malta).

In this series:

ISSN: 2625-3127

Representation and parsing of multiword expressions

Current trends

Edited by

Yannick Parmentier
Jakub Waszczuk

language
science
press

Parmentier , Yannick & Jakub Waszczuk (ed.). 2019. *Representation and parsing of multiword expressions*: *Current trends* (Phraseology and Multiword Expressions 3). Berlin: Language Science Press.

ISBN: 978-3-96110-145-0 (Digital)
      978-3-96110-146-7 (Hardcover)

ISSN: 2625-3127
DOI:10.5281/zenodo.2579017
Source code available from www.github.com/langsci/202
Collaborative reading: paperhive.org/documents/remote?type=langsci&id=202

Cover and concept of design: Ulrike Harbort
Typesetting: Felix Kopecky, Jakub Waszczuk, Yannick Parmentier
Proofreading: Alexandr Rosen, Amir Ghorbanpour, Aniefon Daniel, Brett Reynolds, Carlos Ramisch, Daniela Schroeder, Ikmi Nur Oktavianti, Jakub Waszczuk, Jeroen van de Weijer, Jean Nitzke, Lachlan Mackenzie, Phil Duncan, Timm Lichte, Valentin Vydrin, Valeria Quochi, Vasiliki Foufi
Fonts: Linux Libertine, Libertinus Math, Arimo, DejaVu Sans Mono, ScheherazadeRegOT, UMing
Typesetting software: XƎLATEX

Language Science Press
Unter den Linden 6
10099 Berlin, Germany
langsci-press.org

Storage and cataloguing done by FU Berlin

Freie Universität Berlin

Contents

Preface

Yannick Parmentier
University of Orléans
University of Lorraine

Jakub Waszczuk
University of Tours
University of Düsseldorf

In this introductory chapter, we first present the topic and context of this volume. We then summarize its contributions, which have been collected through an open call for submissions and a peer-reviewing process.

1 Introduction

While Multiword Expressions (MWEs), i.e. sequences of words with some unpredictable properties such as *to count somebody in* or *to take a haircut*, have been attracting attention for a long time because of these idiosyncratic properties which go beyond word boundaries, they remain a challenge for both linguistic theories and natural language (NL) applications.

Indeed, most of these theories and applications admit an (explicit or implicit) division of language phenomena into clear-cut levels: (i) tokens (indivisible text units, roughly words), (ii) morphology (properties of words e.g. number, gender, etc.), (iii) syntax (structural links between words, e.g. number/gender agreement), (iv) semantics (meaning of words and sentences). However, human languages frequently show a high degree of ambiguity and fuzziness with respect to this layer-oriented model. In particular, MWEs are placed on the frontier between these levels due to their idiosyncratic properties on the one hand, and their morphological, syntactic and semantic variations on the other hand. For instance, their meaning is often non-compositional as in *to take a haircut* (i.e. *to suffer a*

Yannick Parmentier & Jakub Waszczuk. 2019. Preface. In Yannick Parmentier & Jakub Waszczuk (eds.), *Representation and parsing of multiword expressions: Current trends*, iii–ix. Berlin: Language Science Press. DOI:10.5281/zenodo.2579031

serious financial loss), although they admit some syntactic variation similarly to many other expressions (*take/takes/have taken/has taken/took a serious/70% haircut*). Strictly layer-oriented language models fail to reflect this specificity, and thus yield erroneous text processing results (e.g. word-to-word translations of idioms). Although the quantitative importance of MWEs is well known (they cover up to 30% of all words in human language utterances, and are much more numerous in lexicons than single words), the achievements in their formal representation and automatic processing are still largely unsatisfactory.

In this context, an international and multilingual consortium of researchers recently took part in the European PARSEME COST Action[1] (2013–2017), which aimed at better understanding the nature of MWEs in order to improve their support in natural language applications. Two main challenges were considered: LINGUISTIC PRECISION (how to account for the highly heterogeneous nature of MWEs in linguistic resources and treatments?) and COMPUTATIONAL EFFICIENCY (how to deal with MWEs' idiosyncratic properties within reliable applications?).

To contribute to meeting these two challenges, PARSEME was based on four Working Groups (WGs):

- WG1 focused on the Grammar/Lexicon interface and the design of interoperable MWE lexicons,

- WG2 aimed at developing parsing techniques for MWEs,

- WG3 studied hybrid (e.g. symbolic and/or statistical) NL applications dealing with MWEs (e.g. MWE detection, machine translation, etc.),

- WG4 was concerned with the annotation of MWEs within treebanks.

This book has been created within WG2. It consists of contributions related to the definition, representation and parsing of MWEs. These contributions were collected via an open call for chapters. Each Chapter proposal was reviewed by 2 members of the editorial board. Out of this reviewing, 10 proposals were selected. They reflect current trends in the representation and processing of MWEs. They cover various *categories* of MWEs such as verbal, adverbial and nominal MWEs, various *linguistic frameworks* (e.g. tree-based and unification-based grammars), various *languages* including English, French, Modern Greek, Hebrew, Norwegian), and various *applications* (namely MWE detection, parsing, automatic translation) using both symbolic and statistical approaches.

---

[1]http://www.cost.eu/COST_Actions/ict/IC1207

2 Outline of the book

The book is organized as follows.

Part 1: MWE representations

The first part of the volume (Chapters 1 to 5) is dedicated to the study of MWE properties and representations.

In Chapter 1, Lichte et al. (2019 [this volume]) discuss the representation of MWEs within lexicalised formalisms. In particular, they show how the eXtensible MetaGrammar (XMG2) formalism offers a natural encoding of MWEs, which allows us to account for the fact that irregularities exhibited by MWEs are a matter of scale rather than binary properties.

In Chapter 2, Sheinfux et al. (2019 [this volume]) study a specific type of MWEs (namely verbal MWEs), focusing mostly on Hebrew, and show that unlike what previous work suggests, flexibility of verbal MWEs is not a discrete concept but rather a continuous property. They propose a new classification of MWEs which is based on semantic notions.

In Chapter 3, Dyvik et al. (2019 [this volume]) present the analysis of MWEs in an LFG grammar for Norwegian, NorGram, which is used in the construction of NorGramBank, a treebank of parsed sentences. The chapter describes how classes of MWEs are analysed by means of LFG templates, which capture the lexical and syntactic properties of MWEs in a succinct way.

In Chapter 4, Markantonatou et al. (2019 [this volume]) present a grammar of Modern Greek in the LFG formalism. Their grammar has been implemented with the Xerox Linguistic Engine (XLE), a grammar editor which also includes a parsing engine. In their Chapter, the authors pay a particular attention to the use of a pre-processor to detect and annotate MWEs prior to parsing.

In Chapter 5, Angelov (2019 [this volume]) presents the Grammatical Framework, a description language for developing NLP multilingual resources, and its application to some classes of MWEs. In particular, the author shows how to define MWE-aware multilingual grammars, which can be used for instance for in-domain machine translation.

Part 2: MWE parsing

The second part of the volume (Chapters 6 to 8) focuses on MWE parsing, that is, on the automatic construction of deep representations of the syntax of MWEs. Two main approaches to parsing coexist: the data-driven approach aims at extracting syntactic information from corpora using Machine Learning techniques and is discussed in Chapter 6. The knowledge-based approach relies on the en-coding of linguistic properties of MWEs within lexical entries, which are used by a parsing algorithm to compute the expected syntactic structure. The impact of MWE detection on such parsing algorithms is discussed in Chapters 7 (for a categorial parser) and 8 (for an attachment-rule-based parser).

In Chapter 6, Constant et al. (2019 [this volume]) give a detailed overview of various ways to extend statistical parsing with MWE identification, either during parsing or as a pre- or post-processing step. These extensions are compared and their evaluation discussed.

In Chapter 7, de Lhoneux et al. (2019 [this volume]) extend a CCG parsing architecture for English with a module for detecting MWEs and pre-process them. The effect of this pre-processing is evaluated in terms of parsing accuracy when (i) the parser is trained on pre-processed data (so-called training effect) and (ii) the parser uses information from pre-processed data (so-called parsing effect).

In Chapter 8, Foufi et al. (2019 [this volume]) investigate the extension of a knowledge-based parser with collocation identification. They apply this exten-sion to the description of MWEs for various languages (including English and Greek), and show how it improves parsing efficiency in terms of percentages of complete analyses.

Part 3: Multilingual NL applications for MWEs

Finally, in the third part of the volume (Chapters 9 and 10), multilingual MWE acquisition techniques are presented.

In Chapter 9, Semmar et al. (2019 [this volume]) present three techniques for word alignment between parallel corpora and their application to MWEs. The bilingual MWE lexicons built using these techniques are then evaluated accord-ing to their effect on phrase-based statistical machine translation. The authors empirically show that MWE-aware lexicons improve translation quality.

Finally, in Chapter 10, Jacquet et al. (2019 [this volume]) present an architecture which allows for the identification of multiword entities (organizations, medical terms, etc.) within large collections of texts, together with the linking of mono-lingual variants of a given multiword entity, and of groups of variants accross multiple languages. Their architecture is evaluated against data from *Wikipedia*.

3 Acknowledgments

We are grateful to the COST framework of the European Union for their support for the PARSEME Action.

We would like to warmly thank Agata Savary and Adam Przepiórkowski, respectively chair and vice-chair of PARSEME, for their commitment to this action. They made it a dynamic environment, where researchers can have fruitful discussions and exchange ideas, leading to long-term collaborations.

We are grateful to Manfred Sailer, who, as a member of the editorial board of the *Phraseology and Multiword Expressions* series, accompanied us throughout the publication process.

We would like to thank the reviewers of this volume:

- Doug Arnold, University of Essex, UK

- Gosse Bouma, University of Groningen, the Netherlands

- Svetla Koeva, Bulgarian Academy of Sciences, Bulgaria

- Cvetana Krstev, University of Belgrade, Serbia

- Ana R. Luís, University of Coimbra, Portugal

- Stella Markantonatou, Institute for Language and Speech Processing/Athena RIC, Greece

- Petya Osenova, Bulgarian Academy of Sciences, Bulgaria

- Carla Parra Escartín, Dublin City University, ADAPT Centre, Ireland

- Victoria Rosén, University of Bergen, Norway

- Michael Rosner, University of Malta, Malta

- Manfred Sailer, University of Frankfurt am Main, Germany

- Agata Savary, University of Tours, Blois, France

- Veronika Vincze, University of Szeged, Hungary

- Shuly Wintner, University of Haifa, Israel

We are grateful for their valuable evaluations, comments and feedback, and to the proofreaders for their thorough work. Without their help, this book would not exist.

Special thanks go to Language Science Press (especially Sebastian Nordhoff and Stefan Müller for their continuous help and their engagement in the promotion of high-quality peer-reviewed open-access publication).

Yannick Parmentier and Jakub Waszczuk, Feb. 2019

References

Angelov, Krasimir. 2019. Multiword expressions in multilingual applications within the Grammatical Framework. In Yannick Parmentier & Jakub Waszczuk (eds.), *Representation and parsing of multiword expressions: Current trends*, 127–146. Berlin: Language Science Press. DOI:10.5281/zenodo.2579041

Constant, Mathieu, Gülşen Eryiğit, Carlos Ramisch, Mike Rosner & Gerold Schneider. 2019. Statistical MWE-aware parsing. In Yannick Parmentier & Jakub Waszczuk (eds.), *Representation and parsing of multiword expressions: Current trends*, 147–182. Berlin: Language Science Press. DOI:10.5281/zenodo.2579043

de Lhoneux, Miryam, Omri Abend & Mark Steedman. 2019. Investigating the effect of automatic MWE recognition on CCG parsing. In Yannick Parmentier & Jakub Waszczuk (eds.), *Representation and parsing of multiword expressions: Current trends*, 183–215. Berlin: Language Science Press. DOI:10.5281/zenodo.2579045

Dyvik, Helge, Gyri Smørdal Losnegaard & Victoria Rosén. 2019. Multiword expressions in an LFG grammar for Norwegian. In Yannick Parmentier & Jakub Waszczuk (eds.), *Representation and parsing of multiword expressions: Current trends*, 69–108. Berlin: Language Science Press. DOI:10.5281/zenodo.2579037

Foufi, Vasiliki, Luka Nerima & Eric Wehrli. 2019. Multilingual parsing and MWE detection. In Yannick Parmentier & Jakub Waszczuk (eds.), *Representation and parsing of multiword expressions: Current trends*, 217–237. Berlin: Language Science Press. DOI:10.5281/zenodo.2579047

Jacquet, Guillaume, Maud Ehrmann, Jakub Piskorski, Hristo Tanev & Ralf Steinberger. 2019. Cross-lingual linking of multi-word entities and language-dependent learning of multi-word entity patterns. In Yannick Parmentier & Jakub Waszczuk (eds.), *Representation and parsing of multiword expressions: Current trends*, 269–297. Berlin: Language Science Press. DOI:10.5281/zenodo.2579049

Lichte, Timm, Simon Petitjean, Agata Savary & Jakub Waszczuk. 2019. Lexical encoding formats for multi-word expressions: The challenge of "irregular" regularities. In Yannick Parmentier & Jakub Waszczuk (eds.), *Representation and parsing of multiword expressions: Current trends*, 1–33. Berlin: Language Science Press. DOI:10.5281/zenodo.2579033

Markantonatou, Stella, Niki Samaridi & Panagiotis Minos. 2019. Issues in parsing MWEs in an LFG/XLE framework. In Yannick Parmentier & Jakub Waszczuk (eds.), *Representation and parsing of multiword expressions: Current trends*, 109–126. Berlin: Language Science Press. DOI:10.5281/zenodo.2579039

Semmar, Nasredine, Christophe Servan, Meriama Laib, Dhouha Bouamor & Morgane Marchand. 2019. Extracting and aligning multiword expressions from parallel corpora. In Yannick Parmentier & Jakub Waszczuk (eds.), *Representation and parsing of multiword expressions: Current trends*, 239–268. Berlin: Language Science Press. DOI:10.5281/zenodo.3264764

Sheinfux, Livnat Herzig, Tali Arad Greshler, Nurit Melnik & Shuly Wintner. 2019. Verbal multiword expressions: Idiomaticity and flexibility. In Yannick Parmentier & Jakub Waszczuk (eds.), *Representation and parsing of multiword expressions: Current trends*, 35–68. Berlin: Language Science Press. DOI:10.5281/zenodo.2579035

Chapter 1

Lexical encoding formats for multi-word expressions: The challenge of "irregular" regularities

Timm Lichte
University of Düsseldorf

Simon Petitjean
University of Düsseldorf

Agata Savary
University of Tours

Jakub Waszczuk
Université of Tours
University of Orléans

This chapter contributes a general overview and discussion of lexical encoding formats for multi-word expressions (MWEs) that can be used in NLP systems, in particular with large-scale grammars. The presentation is kept general in the sense that we will try to elicit basic aspects of lexical encoding and then elaborate on the specific sorts of challenges encountered when dealing with MWEs, especially the "irregular" regularities mentioned in the title. These insights will eventually be used to classify and evaluate different approaches to encoding. Even though this kind of evaluation cannot be conclusive given the diversity of languages and tastes, we will nevertheless argue in favor of fully flexible encoding formats exemplified with PATR-II and XMG, as opposed to the fixed encoding formats of DuELME and Walenty.

Timm Lichte, Simon Petitjean, Agata Savary & Jakub Waszczuk. 2019. Lexical encoding formats for multi-word expressions: The challenge of "irregular" regularities. In Yannick Parmentier & Jakub Waszczuk (eds.), *Representation and parsing of multi-word expressions: Current trends*, 1–33. Berlin: Language Science Press. DOI:10.5281/zenodo.2579033

Timm Lichte, Simon Petitjean, Agata Savary & Jakub Waszczuk

1 Introduction

In this chapter, we seek to answer a seemingly simple question: what is it that makes an encoding format suitable for encoding multi-word expressions (MWEs) as part of an electronic resource? One quick answer could be: the encoding must be both machine- and human- readable, it must be factorized, and, last but not least, it must be able to cope with the specific irregularities of these objects. But what does this exactly mean? In fact, we claim that the casual use of "irregularity" actually threatens to cover a great deal of regularity, even though it is often a regularity that might look uncommon. In this chapter, we therefore aim to provide a more precise understanding of the underlying notions and concepts, and to apply this to a selection of formats which have a potential of encoding large classes of MWEs, including notably verbal ones, namely DuELME, Walenty, PATR-II and XMG. Thus, we are not aiming at the presentation of a comprehensive list of encoding formats ever proposed for MWEs, but rather want to elicit general aspects and typical examples thereof.

The chapter is structured as follows. We will first sort out general notions and principles of lexical encoding, starting with the notion of regularity in Section 2 and the notion of encoding in Section 3, and then turn to general virtues of lexical encoding formats in Section 4. Following this, in Section 5, we will go into more specific aspects, or rather challenges, that are to be dealt with when encoding MWEs. With this in view, we will then analyze existing formats by dividing them into two groups: fixed encoding formats will be treated in Section 6, and fully flexible ones in Section 7. In Section 8, we will finally compare the encoding formats and summarize the chapter.

2 On the notion of regularity

Regularity in the sense we are concerned with refers to the way properties are shared between the members of a set of objects. For now, we take a property to be just some atomic name and assume that every object is assigned exactly one subset of a given set of properties. We then say that a property p is REGULAR with respect to a set of objects E, iff p is shared by at least two members in E. Otherwise p is IRREGULAR (or IDIOSYNCRATIC). If p is regular but is shared only by a proper subset of E, we call p NON-TRIVIALLY REGULAR. By contrast, in the TRIVIALLY REGULAR case, p is regular and shared by all the objects in E. Here, p can be removed without harm because it does not distinguish any two objects in E. Sets of properties can be treated accordingly, hence a property set P is regular, if it is a subset of property sets of at least two objects in E. We then extend the notion of regularity to objects by calling an object regular, if it only has regular properties and property sets, and otherwise irregular. Finally, this simplistic formalization allows for a straightforward characterization of the DEGREE OF REGULARITY, for example, in terms of likelihood (how likely is the property set of an object given a property distribution in the underlying object set) and diversity (how many property sets are found in an object set).

This notion of (ir)regularity implies that it is impossible to determine once and for all whether the properties of certain objects are regular or irregular, simply because the set of conceivable properties and objects is unbounded. In other words, the whole business of telling apart regularity from irregularity hinges on the selection of properties along with a specific set of objects.

Applying this to linguistics, the traditional view on the division of labor between syntax and lexicon is only valid for a specific set of linguistic objects, namely words, phrases and sentences, and a specific set of "syntactic" properties. Only on these premises is it valid to say that syntax is the realm of regularity whereas the lexicon is the collecting point for irregular aspects. To give an example, one could consider phrase structure rules as properties of words, phrases and sentences, depending on whether the phrase structure rules can be used to derive them. According to this set of properties, the words would be derived only by idiosyncratic rules that cannot be used to derive any other word. Hence, the set of words (= the lexicon) would not be fully regular, other than the sets of phrases and sentences (= the syntax). However, when taking other properties into account such as semantic, morphological and phonological ones, this division becomes blurred quite easily.

Similarly, if an MWE (or some property of it) is called "irregular", this can have at least one of three possible reasons: (i) the set of objects is sufficiently restricted (e.g., by contrasting the MWE with non-MWEs only), or (ii) the set of properties is sufficiently extended (e.g., by taking into account very specific properties of the MWE), or (iii) the property set of the MWE is relatively unlikely and "irregular" is assigned a likelihood related meaning. In all three cases, there is actually a high risk of overlooking or neglecting some regularities, even more since we are dealing with objects that have not been in the center of interest in most of the mainstream grammar theories. This gives a hint of how we want "irregular regularities" from the title to be understood: as regularities that concern unusual properties. The assumption throughout this chapter will be that the irregularity of MWEs can be attributed to very few properties concerning the syntax-semantics interface, while there is a great deal of non-trivially regular properties that are shared across MWEs and permeate all levels of linguistic descriptions.

Timm Lichte, Simon Petitjean, Agata Savary & Jakub Waszczuk

3 The most basic encoding format

Given what has been said in the last section, it should be fairly easy to see that the most basic encoding format of the properties of an MWE is via PROPERTY NAME SETS. Two examples for *kick the bucket* and *spill beans* are shown in (1):

(1) a. kick-the-bucket : =
$\{NP_0 \text{ V } NP_1, NP_1.\text{Det.the}, NP_1.\text{N.bucket}, \text{V.kick}, \text{meaning=die}\}$

b. spill-beans : =
$\{NP_0 \text{ V } NP_1, NP_1.\text{N.beans}, \text{V.spill}, \text{passive}, \text{meaning=divulge}\}$

Even if the property names seem to have some compositional structure (NP_1.Det.the means that the determiner of the object NP is *the*), they are chosen here for purely mnemonic reasons – one could have equally written something alphabetically innocent like p_{23}. So, in order to proceed, what is needed is an INTERPRETATION FUNCTION from property names to objects of whatever target formalism is chosen. Essentially, this is the characteristic of any encoding format, even the more sophisticated ones. Of course, there is some variance as to how close the encoding format is related to the target formalism. Daelemans & van der Linden (1992) refer to this aspect as notational adequacy. But be aware that, in our view, the adequacy of a lexical encoding format is multi-aspectual (see Figure 1 on page 6) and ultimately *user-oriented*. We will elaborate more on this in Section 4.

Speaking of the adequacy of property name sets, there are, in fact, some attractive properties of this very simple way of encoding: (i) it is very flexible in terms of adding and removing property names and adapting the interpretation function to some target formalism; (ii) it makes empirically largely neutral descriptions available; (iii) it is conceptually lean and inviting for formal novices because the main data structures are just ordinary sets. On the other hand, it is obvious that nobody would seriously make use of property name sets when encoding a large electronic lexicon – at least not without a tool that helps to ensure correctness by accounting for, and therefore encoding underlying generalizations, that is, patterns of co-occurrence among properties. Furthermore, one would need tools to specify and carry out the interpretation function. In our view, this does not only hold for pure property name sets; the actual encoding format is *always* surrounded by tools mediating towards the human user, the target formalism or the electronic resource – to what degree depends on the encoding format in question (see Section 4).

A closely related but more transparent encoding format is based on tables in which the rows correspond to lexical entries, or any other sort of object, and

4

Table 1: Table encoding of the property name sets in (1)

ID	NP$_0$ V NP$_1$	NP$_1$.det	NP$_1$.N	V	passive	meaning
kick-the-bucket	+	the	bucket	kick	–	die
spill-beans	+		bean	spill	+	divulge

the columns to properties. Binary cell values then indicate whether a property holds for an object or not. This format has gained some popularity, for example, through the extensive work of Maurice Gross (and colleagues) within his lexicon-grammar framework (Gross 1994). While lexicon-grammar matrices are binary, at least for the most part, a larger range of cell values helps to yield a more succinct matrix. This is shown in Table 1 which translates the property sets from (1). Needless to say, for any such non-binary matrix, there is an equivalent binary one with a larger number of columns or properties.

The table format makes the presentation of property name sets more readable, but apart from this, it comes with very similar methodological implications: it is suitable for collecting observations, but it cannot express recurring patterns within these observations, that is, a theory. For this, and thus also for ensuring correctness and completeness, additional tools are needed.

4 General virtues of lexical encoding formats

The preceding section showed that certain encoding formats stand out in terms of simplicity and accessibility, but also manifest critical drawbacks as to usability and expressivity. This section tries to sort out more systematically the diverse and sometimes contradicting virtues an encoding format can have. The cause of diversity is not hard to pinpoint: it is the interface status of encoding formats, as illustrated in Figure 1, with similarly diverse conjugates, namely a human user, a lexical object and a lexical resource.

4.1 Encoding virtues with respect to a lexical object

We already learned in Sections 2 and 3 that the simplest conception of a lexical object and an encoding format is a set of properties or property names. Let P_i be the property set of a lexical object. An encoding of P_i is a property name set P_i^e together with an encoding function which maps P_i onto P_i^e. Hence, the encoding examples given in (1) on page 4 are actually accompanied by an imagined lexical

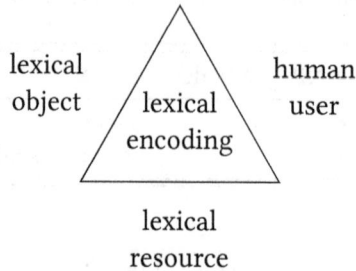

lexical
object

lexical
encoding

human
user

lexical
resource

Figure 1: Interface aspects of lexical encoding

object and an encoding function. It is furthermore important to keep in mind that, for now, we ignore inferential means of encoding formats that help to express generalizations, that is, we assume that encodings are fully resolved.

Based on this understanding of encoding, the encoding virtues are easy to see and capture, namely, the encoding of a property set P_i should be complete and concise. An encoding (function) is COMPLETE *iff* every property of P_i is mapped onto a property name of P_i^e. Thus the encoding function is injective. On the other hand, an encoding is CONCISE *iff* for every encoding property p_i^e there is a source property p_i such that p_i^e is the encoding of p_i. Here, the encoding is surjective. In other words, no property name is added unmotivatedly. Of course, an encoding should be both complete and concise, and consequently the encoding function should be bijective. This implies that distinctions made in P_i are minimally preserved in the encoding of P_i.

To give an example, Table 1 is a complete encoding of the property sets in (1). Yet it is not perfectly concise: the property set of *kick-the-bucket* does not have a passive feature, while there is a passive cell in the table encoding. Similarly, the NP$_1$.det cell in the encoding of *spill-beans* does not have a corresponding property in the source set. Still, the encoding in Table 1 appears to be only slightly less concise than the original property sets in (1), and moreover the table encoding is (in most cases) more accessible for the human eye. This teaches us two things: (i) the validity of some encoding virtues can be a matter of degree, and (ii) they may conflict with other encoding virtues.

But before turning to possibly conflicting encoding virtues having to do with other aspects of encoding, let us finally have a look at the encoding of *sets* of lexical objects. Here, it is clearly desirable for an encoding to be CONSISTENT, simply meaning that the relation between the properties appearing in all the lexical objects under consideration and the target properties of the encoding is functional as well. This clearly holds for the encoding in Table 1 where identical properties are encoded as identical cell values within the same row.

4.2 Encoding virtues with respect to a human user

When it comes to the human user, a lexical encoding should be transparent, flexible and sufficiently powerful to capture generalizations.

By TRANSPARENT we mean that the human user should be able to map the encoding back to the source set of lexical properties. Needless to say, the degree of transparency very much depends on the taste and reading habits of the user in question. It could well be, although it is rather unlikely, that some users will feel more comfortable with plain property sets also when dealing with larger lexicons. Depending on the degree of training, it is even imaginable that users become fluent in rather opaque encoding languages that make use of property names such as p_{23}. This is, of course, not what we consider desirable: lexical encodings should not come with notational idiosyncrasies that keep novices away or are prone to lead to encoding errors (e.g., by misremembering p_{23}). Thus, since we are dealing with computational lexicons, we conceive an encoding language as transparent *iff* it is (i) mnemonic as to the property names and their denoted properties and (ii) precise by means of a rigorous denotational semantics to avoid vagueness and thus inconsistencies.

Since transparency is so important to the human user, but at the same time human users and also lexical objects can differ to a great deal, another crucial virtue of encoding formats is FLEXIBILITY. Lexical encoding usually is an incremental process where unforeseen properties can be encountered or the denotation of a property may change over time. A flexible encoding format allows the user to freely choose property names and to include new properties on the fly.[1]

Closely related to flexibility is the POWER TO GENERALIZE. With an increasing number of lexical objects that are encoded in a lexicon, usually also the desire to factorize the property sets increases in order to avoid redundancy. In other words, one would like to group properties and assign them collectively. Again, the human encoder should be free to choose the content and name of property subsets, or, more technically speaking, the parts of encodings should be reusable at any level of representation and detail. What may sound like a nice add-on is in fact a necessary prerequisite to express any non-trivial lexical generalization, such as that a passive construction does not include an accusative object.

Finally, we can consider an encoding format to be IMPLEMENTATION-FRIENDLY *iff* there exist tools that assist a human user with encoding large sets of lexical objects, or with verifying these encodings. This virtue already touches upon one aspect that will be also dealt with in the next section, which is the existence of software tools that help to convert lexical encodings into a lexical resource.

---

[1]Of course, flexibility also helps to keep the encoding complete in the sense of Section 4.1.

4.3 Encoding virtues with respect to a lexical resource

A lexical resource is an electronic representation of lexical encodings that can be (more or less) directly used in NLP applications. Accordingly, the virtue of ELECTRONIC VERSATILITY assigned to lexical encoding formats describes the relative ease with which a corresponding lexical encoding can be converted into a lexical resource. This easiness can allude to at least two different aspects; either the properties of existing conversion tools or the engineering task to produce them. Ultimately, what really matters when mapping a lexical encoding to an electronic resource is the mere existence of software tools to achieve this. Obviously, this is not a property of the encoding format itself, but a property of its interface with the specific format of an intended lexical resource. Thus, in this view, an encoding format would be electronically versatile whenever there exist many (and among them the desired) conversion tools. From the perspective of the programmer, however, electronic versatility has a different implication: it is rather related to the efforts it takes to implement such a conversion tool from scratch.

Even worse, it's certainly hard to say something conclusive about electronic versatility in global terms, as there is no true one-to-one relation. NLP applications can vary distinctively in their interface specifications, and therefore there is rather a one-to-many relation between a particular lexical encoding and the lexical resources that one might wish to derive from it. In the simplest case, the lexical encoding can act as the lexical resource proper. Yet, presumably in the majority of cases, the lexical encoding will be preprocessed and converted into something *less* user-friendly. This is most obvious in graphically enhanced encoding methods where the lexical resource is derived from the underlying, non-graphical representation. But, of course, this also holds for interchange formats such as LMF (Francopoulo et al. 2006), which are meant to provide a mediating standard and rely on cumbersome XML or the like.

Another relevant property of the interface between the lexical encoding and the lexical resource seems to be whether the generalizations expressed in the lexical encoding are preserved during conversion, or whether only fully resolved entries are included. From the point of view of the encoder, the availability of generalizations seems to be preferred, but this is a virtue of the lexical resource proper, and also depends on the targeted NLP application.

Summing up, electronic versatility is an important but also complex virtue that covers orthogonal, or even conflicting, aspects of the interface between lexical encodings and lexical resources. Moreover, given the heterogeneity of the latter ones, a general verdict is often difficult to obtain.

5 Challenges posed by MWEs

From a general point of view, MWEs are in no way different from any other lexical object: they can be encoded using property name sets as in (1) or using the table format from Table 1. But what is then so challenging about MWEs? On the one hand, it is the peculiarity of the affected properties, for example, the property $NP_1.Det.the$ in the property set of *kick the bucket*. This is challenging with respect to the flexibility of an encoding format. On the other hand, the interactions between these and other properties pose a challenge to the power of an encoding format to generalize. In this section, we will go through some of these challenging properties and interactions, confining ourselves mainly to syntax and morphology.

Let us first examine a multilingual set of MWE examples[2] together with their peculiarities, which the MWE-related literature often calls irregularities or idiosyncrasies. In what follows, each property is either DEFECTIVE or RESTRICTIVE. In the former case, it excludes a literal interpretation of a given object. In the latter, it reduces the number of possible surface realizations of a given object with respect to the corresponding literal interpretation.

1. defective agreement, e.g. in (FR) *grands-mères* 'grandmothers' the adjective does not agree with the noun in gender, unlike most regular adjectival modifiers;

2. restrictive agreement, e.g. (EN) *to cross one's fingers* imposes agreement in person, number and gender between the possessive pronoun and the subject: #*I cross his fingers*

3. restrictive paradigm, e.g. (PL) *zjadłbym konia z kopytami* (lit. *I would eat a horse with its hooves*) 'I am very hungry' can only occur in conditional mood: #*zjem konia z kopytami* 'I will eat a horse with its hooves';

4. defective subcategorization, i.e. imposing a subcategorization frame which the MWE headword does not admit outside MWEs, e.g. (PL) *dobrze mu z oczy patrzy* (lit. *well him looks from eyes*) 'he looks like a good person' prohibits a subject: *uczciwość dobrze mu z oczy patrzy* (lit. *honesty well him looks from eyes*), while *patrzy* 'looks' as a standalone verb always requires one;

---

[2]Each example is preceded by its language code in parentheses. The hash (#) character signals the loss of the idiomatic reading due to a missing property, while the asterisk (*) means ungrammaticality.

5. restrictive diathesis, e.g. (EN) *to kick the bucket* does not allow passiviza- tion: *#the bucket was kicked*, while (FR) *les carottes sont cuites* (lit. *the carrots are cooked*) 'the situation is hopeless' only allows passive voice: *#on cuit les carottes* (lit. *one cooks the carrots*) ';'

6. restrictive choice of determiners and modifiers, e.g. (FR) *avoir raison* (lit. *to have reason*) 'to be right' allows neither a determiner nor a modifier of the nominal component: *#avoir (une) raison évidente* 'to have an obvious reason';

7. restrictive dependencies between determiners and modifiers: (FR) *avoir en- vie* (lit. *to have desire*) 'to feel like' admits no determiner for the predicative noun *envie* 'desire', if it takes no argument or modifier, or if it takes an in- finitival argument governed by the preposition *de* 'of': *j'ai envie de le faire* (lit. *I have desire of to do it*) 'I feel like doing it'; but if the noun is modified by an adjective, the determiner is compulsory: *j'ai une   envie folle de le faire* (lit. *I have a crazy desire of to do it*) 'I feel a lot like doing it';

8. restrictive modification, e.g. (FR) *mener une vie (de riche)* 'to live a life (of a rich)' imposes an adjectival or a prepositional modifier on the nominal: *#il mène une vie* 'he leads a life';

9. restrictive linearization, e.g. (EN) *drink and drive* requires the strict order of its coordinated verbs, violating this constraint leads to the loss of the idiomatic reading: *#drive and drink*;

10. restrictive lexical selection, i.e. imposing particular lexical realizations of certain syntactic arguments, e.g. (EN) *to pull someone's leg* requires the head verb *pull* with a direct object headed by *leg*: *#to pull one's arm/mem- ber*.

Note that while the above properties are perceived as unexpected or unpredict- able, they are most often shared with other MWEs, therefore, in our understand- ing (cf. Section 2), they are regular. To make this more precise, recall that reg- ularity of a property is not absolute but relative to a given set of objects E. In linguistic modeling, we tend to group objects into sets based on their similari- ties rather than their discrepancies. For instance, in valence-oriented modeling (such as Walenty or PART-II described in Sections 6.2 and 7.1, respectively, or ID- ION and the MWE lexicon of NorGram discussed in Markantonatou et al. (2019 [this volume]) and Dyvik et al. (2019 [this volume]) respectively), verbal construc- tions are grouped according to the lemma of their head verb, whereas in more constructionist approaches (like DUELME and XMG, introduced in Sections 6.1 and 7.2), they are grouped by the syntactic structure of their subcategorization frames. Such properties used to group objects become trivially regular properties of these groups (since they are shared by all objects of a group). Most other properties have a varying degree of regularity and are only rarely truly idiosyncratic.

As an example, let us consider a set of English verbal expressions, each of which is headed by a verb, taking a subject and a direct object, and admitting modifiers, e.g. (EN) *John pulled the heavy door*. In this set, the property of allowing any head verb with the proper subcategorization frame is much more regular than restricting it to the verb *kick*. Furthermore, the property of allowing passivization is more regular than prohibiting passive voice, like in *John kicked the bucket* 'John died'. Also, allowing a possessive determiner of the object, as in *John pushed the/my door* is more regular than imposing it, as in *John broke his/ her/our fall* 'John made his/her/our fall less forceful', which itself is more regular than imposing a possessive which agrees with the subject, as in *John crossed his fingers*. This last property is, however, still regular. In order for it to be idiosyncratic, *John crossed his fingers* 'John wished luck' and *John held his tongue* 'John refrained from expressing his view' could not co-occur in the same object set, which would hinder the usability of such a set for linguistic modeling. Without resorting to such artificial choice of object sets, Property 10 is one of the rare truly idiosyncratic properties, since it is usually specific to one MWE only, except in case of truly ambiguous MWEs like *to go on* 'to continue, to happen'.

Note finally that one MWE usually exhibits different properties of varying degrees of regularity. For instance, while the components of (FR) *grands-mères* 'grandmothers' do not agree in gender, they do agree in number. While (PL) *zjadłbym konia z kopytami* (lit. *I would eat a horse with its hooves*) 'I am very hungry' requires conditional mood, it has a highly regular inflection for person and number. While the object in (EN) *to pull someone's leg* is partly lexicalized, the subject is not. While (EN) *to kick the bucket* cannot be passivized, it does admit a restricted number of internal modifiers as in *to kick the proverbial bucket*, etc.

As a conclusion, the challenging nature of MWE is manyfold: (i) regularity of properties of MWEs is scale-wise, (ii) properties of different degrees of regularity co-occur in each MWE, (iii) truly idiosyncratic properties are rare (under the usual similarity-oriented grouping strategies), (iv) shared properties can be unforeseen (cf. Property 7), so listing them all in advance is hard. A general-purpose encoding format should possibly face all these challenges simultaneously. Note also the similarity of observations (i) and (ii) with the notion of a *flexibility continuum* in idioms, discussed in Sheinfux et al. (2019 [this volume]).

6 Fixed MWE encoding formats

While lexical approaches dedicated to a large variety of MWEs have a relatively long linguistic tradition, notably with Gross (1986) and Mel'čuk et al. (1988), NLP-oriented work on lexical encoding of MWEs has mainly dealt with continuous instances (Savary 2008). More recently, proposals have been put forward which also take verbal MWEs into account whose components are discontinuously linearized. Here, we study two instances of such approaches tailored to specific languages: DuELME (Grégoire 2010) for Dutch and Walenty (Przepiórkowski et al. 2014) for Polish. They stand out as: (i) having been designed with a (relative) theory-neutrality in mind, (ii) having resulted in MWE lexicons of several thousands of entries, (iii) having been coupled with real-size grammars, so as to test their usability for parsing. At the same time, DueLME and Walenty can be characterized as fixed encoding formats in the sense that their encoding language (basically the set of property names and their interpretation) cannot be freely chosen or extended.

6.1 DuELME

DuELME (Dutch Electronic Lexicon of Multiword Expressions, Grégoire 2010) is an electronic lexicon comprising roughly 5,000 Dutch multiword expressions.[3] It distinguishes two sorts of descriptions, pattern descriptions and MWE descriptions, which are composed of non-intersecting sets of predefined fields. Patterns, also called *parameterized equivalence classes*, represent mainly the syntactic structures of MWEs and the part-of-speech tags of their leaves. MWE descriptions express MWE-specific lexical and morpho-syntactic constraints.

Figure 2 shows a sample pattern (Lines 1–5), called ec1, and a MWE entry (Lines 7–11) assigned to it: (NL) *zijn kansen waarnemen* (lit. *one's chances perceive*) 'to seize the opportunity'.

The pattern describes expressions headed by a verb, taking a direct object consisting of a fixed determiner and a modifiable noun. The POS-entitled Line 3 lists the parts of speech of MWE components. The PATTERN-entitled Line 4 shows the syntactic structure, roughly, as a dependency tree where syntactic categories (VP, NP, D, N1[4], V) and dependency labels (obj1, det, hd) are marked explicitly, and some of the leaves are indexed (1, 2, 3) so as to be matched with components of a

---

[3]http://duelme.clarin.inl.nl/
[4]The N1 category denotes an NP of which some elements are lexically fixed, but which is still subject to standard grammar rules such as agreement

```
 1  % Pattern description
 2  PATTERN_NAME ec1
 3  POS d n v
 4  PATTERN  [.VP [.obj1:NP [.det:D (1) ] [.hd:N1 (2) ]] [.hd:V (3) ]]
 5  DESCRIPTION Expressions headed by a verb, taking a direct object
        consisting of a fixed determiner and a modifiable noun.

 6
 7  % MWE description
 8  EXPRESSION zijn kansen waarnemen
 9  CL zijn kans[pl] waar_nemen[part]
10  PATTERN_NAME ec1
11  EXAMPLE hij heeft zijn kansen waargenomen
```

Figure 2: DuELME pattern description ec1 (from Grégoire 2007b) and MWE description of (NL) *zijn kansen waarnemen* (lit. *one's chances perceive*) 'to seize the opportunity' (from Grégoire 2010)

particular MWE. Thus, the components *zijn* 'one's', *kansen* 'chances' and *waarnemen* 'perceive' of the MWE in Lines 8–9 are implicitly co-indexed with the det:D, hd:N1 and hd:V nodes in the ec1 pattern. Moreover, the component list (CL) in Line 9 lists the MWE-specific values of the "parameters" for the pattern, i.e. the lemmas of all components, as well as some morphosyntactic constraints, here: *kans* 'chance' must be in plural (pl), and *waarnemen* 'perceive' is a separable particle verb (part).

This approach is constructionist in the sense that MWEs are grouped into sets based on their structure (rather than their headword). While the syntax of patterns seems theory-specific, they might be seen rather as identifiers of equivalence classes, allowing to group MWEs of the same structure, whatever the syntactic formalism used to express this structure.[5] DuELME's view of the regularity is binary, which is reflected by its two-level description paradigm. Namely, it is assumed that each type of a syntactic structure has some "generally regular" properties covered by general grammar rules. These properties are not described in the lexicon but symbolized by patterns. Conversely, the MWE-specific properties are described in MWE entries. For instance, while the number of *kans* 'chance' is restricted to plural in Line 9, its other grammatical features are not specified since they are supposedly governed by grammar rules. This principle avoids some grammar vs. lexicon redundancy. Note, however, that the choice of properties to be included in patterns is rather arbitrary and in most cases leads

---

[5] Jan Odijk, personal communication 21 September 2015. Odijk, Jan@Odijk, Jan

to partly redundant descriptions. For instance, the part property in Line 9 is shared with other MWEs containing separable particle verbs, and has to be specified for each of them. This redundancy at the level of MWE descriptions could be avoided, if the ec1 pattern were restricted to d-n-v constructions containing separable particle verbs only. This would, however, require a new pattern with the same structure but a different verb type selection, in order to cover e.g. (NL) *zijn debuut maken* (lit. *to make one's debut*), which would lead to redundancy at the level of patterns. Since there is no notion of reference, or reuse, among the 141 pattern descriptions that DuELME comprises (Grégoire 2007b), such redundancy could not be avoided.

As a conclusion, the distinction between patterns and MWE descriptions introduces a limited degree of factorization. While some syntactic constraints, e.g. dependencies, are mentioned more or less explicitly in patterns, some other syntactic properties are implicit (supposed to be covered by the grammar and known to the NLP system). Some specific constraints, e.g. restrictive agreement, diathesis, determination, modification and linearization, discussed in Points 2 and 5–9 in Section 5, seem not possible to express. The interpretation of the encoding is led partly by the syntax of patterns and entries, and partly by textual documentation (Grégoire 2007a), where it is sometimes hard to distinguish formal properties and inference rules from methodological strategies and recommendations, i.e. the transparency level of the format is relatively low. Lastly, the format is not flexible, i.e. extending the set of describable properties can only be done ad hoc rather than within an established framework with a clear denotational semantic.

It is worth noting that DuELME benefits from a standard LMF format (Odijk 2013), which makes it more electronically versatile, even if it does not seem implementation friendly in the sense that tools supporting lexicographic encoding in this format do not seem publicly available.

6.2 Walenty

A quite different encoding style is found in Walenty, a Polish large-scale valence dictionary that includes an elaborate phraseological component (Przepiórkowski et al. 2014; 2016). It contains over 100,000 syntactic frames, 14,000 of which are verbal frames with lexicalized arguments, i.e. verbal MWEs. An entry in Walenty contains a headword (here a verb), followed by a list of argument descriptions (separated by +).

Figure 3 shows a (slightly simplified) sample MWE entry of (PL) *dobrze [KO-MUŚ] z oczu patrzy* (lit. *well someone.DAT from eyes looks*) 'someone looks like a

```
patrzeć: np(dat)+advp(misc)+lex(prepnp(z,gen),pl,'oko',natr)
```

Figure 3: Description of *dobrze [KOMUŚ] z oczu patrzy* (lit. *well some-one.DAT from eyes looks*) 'someone looks like a good person' in Walenty

good person', which exhibits several interesting constraints. Firstly, the syntactic subject is prohibited here, which is expressed simply by omitting the subj argument in the valence frame. Secondly, the indirect object in dative is compulsory (np(dat)). These two properties are unusual, since *patrzeć* 'look', as a stand-alone verb, does take a subject and it only admits an indirect object with prepositional complements headed by *na* 'on' and *w* 'in'. Thirdly, the adverb *dobrze* 'well' can have some variations, e.g. *źle [KOMUŚ] z oczu patrzy* (lit. *evilly someone.DAT from eyes looks*) 'someone looks like an evil person', therefore it is encoded by a more generic, non lexicalized, advp(misc) requirement of a "true" adverbial clause.[6] Finally, within the lexicalized prepositional group (lex(prepnp(…))), which does not admit modification (natr), the preposition *z* 'from' governing the genitive case ((z,gen)) requires its nominal complement to be a plural form of the lemma *oko* 'eye' (pl,'oko').

This approach is valence-based, i.e. MWEs are seen as particular syntactic frames of their head verbs, in which some arguments happen to be (at least partly) lexicalized. Regularity is implicit: "generally regular" properties are supposed to be covered by grammar rules and only MWE-specific properties are expressed in lexicon entries. E.g., while the plural number of *oko* 'eye' is specified, its case is not, since it is supposed to regularly agree with its governing preposition (which requires genitive case). This principle is similar to the one admitted in DuELME (cf. Section 6.1), here however, no equivalence classes are used, so the syntactic structure, understood as the list of arguments (possibly structured themselves) required by the head verb, is encoded in each entry (similarly to the IDON lexicon discussed in Markantonatou et al. (2019 [this volume])), which leads to redundancy in the lexicon. For instance, entries for all MWEs taking a non-lexicalized subject, direct object and indirect object, and a partly lexicalized prepositional complement, contain the same sequence: subj{np(str)} + obj{np(str)} + {np(inst)} + {lex(prepnp(…))}[7]. Some redundancy can, however, be avoided due to macros which encode some repetitive substructures. For

---

[6] A "true" adverbial clause cannot be realized by a prepositional nominal group.

[7] The str feature stands for a structural case. For the subject, it is usually nominative, but it turns to genitive when the expression is nominalized. For the direct object, it is accusative but it turns to genitive when it occurs under the scope of negation.

instance, the `possp` macro encodes all possible realization of a possessive phrase, including nominal phrases with genitive and possessive determiners like *mój, czyjś, własny, …* 'my, one's, one's own, …'.

Some additional syntactic properties can be expressed on the level of the whole MWE, e.g. the fact that the head verb is perfective or imperfective, that the MWE must always contain negation, or that it can or cannot be passivized. Some other types of constraints, e.g. restrictive agreement, paradigm, determination, or linearization (cf. Points 2–3, 6–7 and 9 in Section 5), exceed Walenty's expressive power. Therefore, one cannot express the fact that, in (PL) *dobrze [KOMUŚ] z oczu patrzy* (lit. *well someone.DAT from eyes looks*) 'someone looks like a good person', the head verb *patrzeć* 'look' is always in the 3rd person singular (any tense or mood), although it has a complete inflection paradigm as a stand-alone verb.[8] Also, there is no means to specify that the adverb *dobrze* 'well' should usually precede the prepositional complement and the verb.[9] Note, however, that a conservative extension of the formalism to include some of these constraints was proposed by Przepiórkowski et al. (2016).

The interpretation of the encoding is led partly by the syntax of entries and explicit macro extensions, and partly by the accompanying textual documentation. Some inferences remain unclear, e.g., some macros contain non-documented shortcuts, and some codes have no clear denotational semantics. The format is rather inflexible, that is, extending the set of describable properties can only be done ad hoc. Walenty does benefit from a standard interchange XML metaformat, namely TEI[10], but does not provide its precise instantiation in terms of a DTD, RelaxNG or XML schema. Finally, it has a rather elaborate lexicographical support, with several user roles, where the existing entries can be browsed together with their corpus examples, and new entries can be added, corrected, compared, assigned to users, etc. (Nitoń et al. 2016). Recent developments couple Walenty with a Polish wordnet so as to enrich valency data with semantic frames.

7 Fully flexible encoding formats

What we mean by fully flexible is that properties, property names and inference rules (or macros) can be freely chosen – one consequence being that there are

---

[8]Impersonal (i.e. allowing no subject) finite verbs typically occur in the 3rd person singular in Polish, so the expression of this fact is probably left to the grammar. If so, then this fact seems implicit.

[9]A different word order would be considered as marked.

[10]Text Encoding Initiative: http://www.tei-c.org/Guidelines/P5/

usually many ways to implement an object within such an encoding format. In this section, we will show two exemplars of fully flexible encoding formats: the venerable PATR-II and the more recent XMG. The motivation for choosing these two encoding formats is twofold. On the one hand, both engage different notational means with a different denotational semantics; on the other hand, two extremes of modeling argument structure can be covered that were the focus of some debate recently, namely the lexical versus the phrasal approach (Müller & Wechsler 2014). In doing so, we will again, as in the preceding section, restrict ourselves to the tentative encoding of (NL) *zijn kansen waarnemen* 'to seize the opportunity' and (PL) *dobrze [KOMUŚ] z oczu patrzy* 'someone looks like a good person'. The presentation will, we think, strengthen the view that MWEs should be better encoded with fully flexible encoding formats in order to obtain and maintain the virtues mentioned in Section 4.

7.1 PATR-II

A true classic, PATR-II (Shieber 1984; 1986) dates back to the early 80s and has greatly influenced the development of later encoding formats, for example LKB (Copestake 2002: 6), thanks to its notational transparency and conceptual rigor.[11] The basic idea is simple: to enhance CFG rules with descriptions of untyped feature structures, which are then unified during rule applications. Hence, the models of PATR-II descriptions are just directed acyclic graphs with labeled nodes and edges. But the means of description are more elaborate and do also include templates, lexical rules and sometimes – depending on the PATR-II implementation – default inheritance.[12] The encoding examples that we will give do not, however, make use of the full non-monotonic power of PATR-II, as lexical rules and default inheritance will be left out. On the other hand, we will follow the head-driven perspective of PATR-II in that MWEs will be encoded in their head only, that is, MWEs headed by a verb will essentially emerge from the encoding of their verbal component.[13]

---

[11] A superficially similar encoding framework is DATR (Evans & Gazdar 1996). See Kilbury et al. (1991) for a comparison with PATR-II that also highlights the considerable differences between the two.

[12] Default inheritance is available, for example, in PC-PATR (McConnel 1997), which is a parser for PATR-II grammars developed at the Summer Institute of Linguistics (SIL).

[13] The only previous work on encoding MWEs with PATR-II that we are aware of is found in Habert & Jaquemin (1995). There, the focus is on French nominal compunds like *verre à vin* ('wineglass').

All this is exemplified for (NL) *zijn kansen waarnemen* in Figure 4. Templates are headed by `Define-as` constructs. The body of a template may either contain template names (or disjunctions thereof as in Line 33), from which the template inherits, or feature structure descriptions. Word entries such as the one of *waarnemen* at the bottom are similiar to templates but define the terminals of CFG rules. Keep in mind that *waarnemen* acts as the verbal head of the MWE, hence the templates in this example all describe the feature structure of *waarnemen* only. Also note that the features are chosen to keep the example as simple as possible – typically one would find subcategorization lists in PATR-II implementations.

In Figure 4, the first five templates (`Verb`, `Subject`, `Object`, `Intransitive`, and `Transitive`) just act as an example of how general properties, like being a transitive verb, *could* be factorized into even more general properties. Finally, the sixth template, `SubjectPossObjectAgreement`, is more immediately relevant to the MWE (NL) *zijn kansen waarnemen* since it captures the agreement of the subject with the possessive pronoun at the object. This is achieved by using the shared variable `$1`. Crucially, this template could be reused in many other MWEs such as (EN) *to do one's best*. Again, this is not to say that this sort of agreement should be treated in this way, but that it is *possible* to do so, choosing here just one of the many available options. In other words, the template `SubjectPossObjectAgreement` is an instance of one of such MWE-specific regularity that PATR-II is flexible enough to encode directly. Finally, in Figure 4, the template `ZijnKansenWaarnemen` inherits from the templates `Transitive` and `SubjectPossObjectAgreement`, and it adds further information on the shape and modifiability of the object and on the idiomatic semantics of the whole MWE.

Comparing the PATR-II encoding with the DuELME encoding from Figure 2, it becomes evident that PATR-II is more flexible at defining properties or factorizing what are called "patterns" in DuELME. The reason for this divergence of flexibility also lies in the fact that PATR-II descriptions come with a clear denotational semantics, which does not seem to be fixed for DuELME encodings. In fact, one could see this as an advantage of DuELME, taking it as a sign of desired neutrality. But then one must also accept intransparency and inflexibility, at least to some degree.

A tentative PATR-II encoding of (PL) *dobrze [KOMUŚ] z oczu patrzy* is presented in Figure 5. As explained in Section 5, the challenge with this MWE is a mixture of particular constraints regarding the subcategorization frame of the verb (*patrzy* 'looks' is used as an impersonal transitive) and the sentence initial linearization of the adverb. The encoding example in Figure 5 takes care of this by stipulating special features that would trigger the right CFG rules at the right

```
 1  Define Verb as
 2      [cat: v]
 3
 4  Define Subject as
 5      [subject: [cat: np]]
 6
 7  Define Object as
 8      [object: [cat: np]]
 9
10  Define Intransitive as
11      Verb
12      Subject
13
14  Define Transitive as
15      Intransitive
16      Object
17
18  Define SubjectPossObjectAgreement as
19      [subject: [agr: $1]
20      object: [poss: [agr: $1]]]
21
22  Define ZijnKansenWaarnemen as
23      Transitive
24      SubjectPossObjectAgreement
25      [lex: waarnemen
26       object: [lex: kans
27               agr: [num: pl]
28               modifiable: -]
29      sem: [paraphrase: seize_the_opportunity]]
30
31  Word waarnemen:
32      Verb
33      {[WaarnemenLiteral] [ZijnKansenWaarnemen]}
34      [lex: waarnemen]
```

Figure 4: PATR-II description (with PC-PATR notation) of (NL) *zijn kansen waarnemen* 'to seize the opportunity'

```
 1  Define ImpersIntransitive as
 2      [cat: v
 3       pers: 3
 4       num: sg
 5       subject: -
 6       object: -]
 7
 8  Define IndirectObject as
 9      [iobject: [cat: np
10                 case: dat]]
11
12  Define PrepositionalObject as
13      [pobject: [cat: pp]]
14
15  Define DobrzeZOczuPatrzy as
16      ImpersIntransitive
17      IndirectObject
18      PrepositionalObject
19      Adverb
20      [pobject: [lex: z
21                 object: [cat:np
22                          case: gen
23                          num: pl
24                          lex: oko
25                          modifiable: -]]
26       adverb: [word: dobrze
27                position: initial]]
28       sem: [paraphrase: someone_looks_like_a_good_person]
29
30  Word patrzy:
31      Verb
32      {[PatrzecLiteral] [DobrzeZOczuPatrzy]}
33      [lex: patrzeć]
```

Figure 5: PATR-II description (with PC-PATR notation) of (PL) *dobrze [KOMUŚ] z oczu patrzy* 'someone looks like a good person'

time. Remember that the constraints on the occurrence of certain arguments can be encoded by using subcategorization lists in the usual way. This is left out in the example. Now, compared to the Walenty encoding in Figure 3, the corresponding PART-II template `DobrzeZOczuPatrzy` is much more verbose, not only because it contains more information. But this should not be taken as a general disadvantage, as it can help to promote transparency.

Summing up, the examples provided here demonstrate that PATR-II does many important things right: it makes available a transparent, flexible enough encoding language; it has a well-defined denotational semantics; it includes means to arbitrarily factorize properties and to express generalizations even beyond strict monotonicity. In our view, this makes PATR-II better suited to encode MWEs than DuELME and Walenty *in the long run*, since it can integrate unforeseeable properties, regularities or encoding styles much easier.

Yet at the same time, encoding with PATR-II is subject to some severe restrictions:

- PATR-II does not seem to allow for templates to be embedded. Hence, templates can only be applied to the root of a feature structure description.

- Feature structures are untyped in PATR-II which makes them harder to be checked for consistency or to encode representations that rely on types.

- PATR-II allows one to describe full word forms as terminals of CFG rules, but it is not possible to analyze them further, that is, describe the underlying morphemes and how they combine. Consequently, it is at least tedious to describe morphological paradigms. This is something that, for example, DATR (Evans & Gazdar 1996) is better suited for.

- In PATR-II, word order constraints are accounted for by filtering CFG rules via features. Thus, it is not possible to state these constraints in just one place, but one has to think of which features prohibit or trigger the application of which CFG rules in which situation of a derivation.

Furthermore, as we said before, PATR-II chooses a lexical approach to argument structure in the sense of Müller & Wechsler (2014) where the argument structure emerges from lexical units and crucially determines the syntax. The other extreme, namely the phrasal approach to argument structure, rather puts emphasis on the syntactic side, assuming phrasal representations of argument structure that exist independently of lexical anchors. This latter approach better fits into the encoding format of XMG, which will be presented next.

7.2 eXtensible MetaGrammar

The framework of eXtensible MetaGrammar (XMG, Crabbé et al. 2013 and XMG2, Petitjean et al. 2016) most obviously differs from the ones of PATR-II, DuELME and Walenty in that it can be used to generate a wide range of linguistic resources. The variety of these resources is made possible by XMG's modularity and extensibility, allowing to create new dedicated compilers using adapted description languages. XMG is a multi paradigm language, as it manipulates programs (metagrammars) which make intensive use of logic (such as Prolog programs) and constraints. XMG also borrows some aspects from object-oriented programming, whose advantages in the context of linguistic knowledge description are discussed in Daelemans & De Smedt (1994). The most obvious example of such an aspect is that XMG descriptions are organized into CLASSES, which have encapsulated name spaces. Inheritance relations may hold between classes, and the scope of the identifiers is explicitly controlled, thanks to export statements. The crucial elements of a class are DIMENSIONS. Each of them is equipped with a description language, which is specifically adapted to the kind of structures needed in the dimension (trees, predicates, ...). Dimensions are compiled independently, thereby enabling the grammar writer to treat the levels of linguistic information separately. In the following, we will be using the dimension <syn> for the syntax and the more recent <frame> dimension for frame-semantic descriptions, skipping over other available dimensions. Note that <syn> contains tree descriptions where nodes may carry untyped feature structures, while <frame> comprises *typed* feature structure descriptions (Lichte & Petitjean 2015).

Figure 6 shows a part of a tentative XMG encoding of (NL) *zijn kansen waarnemen*. The first thing to notice when comparing the XMG description to the DuELME counterpart in Figure 2 is that there is no principled distinction between "patterns" and "MWE descriptions" (similarly to the PATR-II encoding in Figure 4). Rather, they are equally represented as classes, yet of varying specificity. Crucially, the classes stand in inheritance relations, here marked with the import statement. For example, the most basic class shown in Figure 6, intransitive[], imports two other classes, subject[] and verb[] (cf. Line 2). On the other hand, intransitive[] is further handed down to transitive[], just adding object[]. Finally, transitive[] is imported into subject_poss_object_agreement[] to add the compulsory agreement between the subject and the possessive pronoun of the object, and, in turn, this class is further imported into zijn_kansen_-waarnemen[], which is the class of the MWE proper. Hence, subject_poss_object_agreement[] contains the more regular properties of the MWE, and zijn_-kansen_waarnemen[] the less regular ones. The corresponding inheritance hier-

```
 1  class intransitive
 2  import subject[] verb[]
 3  { <syn> { ?Subj >>+ ?V }}
 4
 5  class transitive
 6  import intransitive[] object[]
 7  { <syn> { ?Subj >>+ ?Obj;
 8            ?Obj >>+ ?V } }
 9
10  class subject_poss_object_agreement
11  declare ?Subj ?Obj ?NUM ?PERS ?GEND
12  export ?Subj ?Obj
13  { <syn> {
14      ?Subj[num=?NUM,pers=?PERS,gend=?GEND];
15      ?Obj [] {
16        [cat=d,num=pl,possnum=?NUM,pers=?PERS,gend=?GEND] "zijn"}}}
17
18  class zijn_kansen_waarnemen
19  import transitive[] subject_poss_object_agreement[]
20  declare ?I
21  { <syn> {
22      ?Subj[i=?I];
23      ?Obj [] {
24        [cat=n,modifiable=-,num=pl] "kans"};
25      ?V[] "waar_nehmen" };
26    <frame> {
27      [using-event,
28        actor:?I,
29        theme:chance]}}
```

Figure 6: XMG encoding of *zijn kansen waarnemen* ('to seize the opportunity')

archy of the used classes is shown in Figure 7, in which the MWE shows up as leaf, i.e. as the most specific class. Note that this inheritance hierarchy mirrors the one of the PATR-II encoding in Figure 4.

In general, classes that correspond to irregular or weakly regular properties of lexical entries appear as leaves, whereas more regular aspects are assigned to dominating classes. Hence, "patterns" can be arbitrarily factorized, which is in sharp contrast to the DuELME encoding format. Another difference is the general availability of variables in XMG, which are commonly prefixed with a question mark. This is exploited in subject_poss_object_agreement[] when expressing

```
subject[]   verb[]
        \      /
         \    /
   intransitive[]   object[]
            \        /
             \      /
           transitive[]
                |
                |
  subject_poss_object_agreement[]
                |
                |
     zijn_kansen_waarnemen[]
```

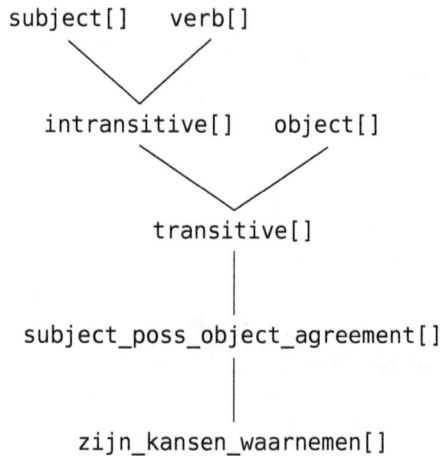

Figure 7: Inheritance hierarchy of XMG classes according to the code in Figure 6

agreement between the subject and the possessive determiner using the variables ?NUM, ?PERS, and ?GEND (cf. Lines 14 and 16). Variables are also used for sharing information between dimensions, for example between <syn> and <frame>, which holds the idiomatic meaning of the MWE, in class zijn_kansen_waarnemen[]: the unification variable ?I here is the frame referent of the subject, and consequently appears both in the syntactic node ?Subj and as the value of the feature actor in the semantic frame. Finally, features and variables can be freely added to XMG, for example, features to indicate constraints on modification (modifiable) or passivization.

Remember that the descriptions in <syn> are tree descriptions, which are able to express the usual, potentially underspecified node relations regarding dominance and precedence. For example, >>+ (cf. Lines 3, 7 and 8 in Figure 6) expresses the transitive, non-reflexive precedence relation between two nodes of a tree. As the tree descriptions can be underspecified in this way, the denotation can be a set of trees. XMG comes with a solver for these descriptions, and a viewer, both of which are available online.[14] Hence, the solutions can be inspected independently of a specific application belonging to some specific framework.

The preliminary XMG encoding of (PL) *dobrze [KOMUS] z oczu patrzy* is presented in Figure 8.[15]

---

[14]http://xmg.phil.hhu.de/
[15]We owe the frame semantic representation in Figure 8 to Rainer Osswald.

```
 1  class impers_intransitive
 2  export ?VP ?V
 3  declare ?VP ?V
 4  { <syn>{
 5      ?VP [cat=vp] { ?V [cat=v,pers=3,num=sg] }}}
 6
 7  class dobrze_z_oczu_patrzy
 8  declare ?I ?A ?P
 9  import impers_intransitive[] ind_object[] pp_object[] adverb[]
10  { <syn> {
11      ?IndObj [i=?I];
12      ?AdvP [] { ?A [] "dobrze"};
13      ?PP [] { [case=gen] "z"
14        [] {
15          [num=pl,modifiable=-] "oko"}};
16      ?V "patrzeć";
17      ?VP -> ?PP;
18      ?VP -> ?IndObj;
19      ?AdvP >>+ ?PP;
20      ?AdvP >>+ ?V };
21    <frame> {
22    [impression-about,
23      perceiver: ?P,
24      theme: ?I,
25      content:[has-prop,
26              theme: ?I,
27              prop: good]
28      ]}
29  }
```

Figure 8: XMG encoding of *dobrze* [KOMUŚ] *z oczu patrzy* ('someone looks like a good person')

Again, the class that corresponds to the MWE, dobrze_z_oczu_patrzy[], inherits from more abstract (and "regular") classes, which can be also seen from the inheritance hierarchy in Figure 9.

Here, the impers_intransitive[] class encodes the fact that the subject is absent (as only the verb phrase and its subordinate verb are listed), and that the (impersonal) verb must occur in the third person singular. Finally, the dobrze_-z_oczu_patrzy[] class reuses the previous class and adds the compulsory adverb. Moreover, certain nodes, identified by shared variables, are further specified for lemmas (in double quotes) and all weakly regular morphological constraints are

Timm Lichte, Simon Petitjean, Agata Savary & Jakub Waszczuk

```
impers_intransitive[]   ind_object[]   pp_object[]   adverb[]



                      dobrze_z_oczu_patrzy[]
```

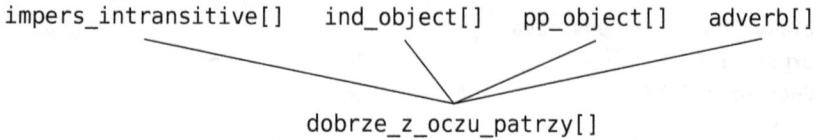

Figure 9: Inheritance hierarchy of XMG classes according to the code in Figure 8

listed. Notably, the noun governed by the preposition *z* 'from' is restricted to the lemma oko 'eye' and to plural, and its modification is prohibited. Note that the genitive case of *oko* is not specified in this class, as it is already part of the agreement rules which were inherited from the pp_object[] class. Linearization constraints on the adverb appear in Lines 19–20. The example also includes dominance constraints in Lines 17–18 that use -> to describe an immediate dominance relation. Finally, we use unification variable once again to express the fact that the semantic referent of the syntactic subject (?I) is the theme of the semantic frame of the MWE. This frame can be read as follows: a perceiver ?P, left unspecified, has an impression about ?I, and this impression is that ?I has the property of being a good person. Thus, all the necessary constraints imposed on this MWE can be covered at various abstraction levels, while factorizing information in such a way that the dobrze_z_oczu_patrzy[] class only contains the constraints which are specific to the MWE or at least weakly regular.

By way of conclusion, let us compare the presented encoding examples for PA-TR-II and XMG in more detail. Despite their large commonalities when contrasting them with fixed encoding formats such as DuELME and Walenty, PATR-II and XMG can differ considerably in some of their properties.

- In the given examples, XMG is constructionist in the sense that it models phrasal units, whereas PATR-II assumes a head-driven (or "lexicalist", Müller & Wechsler 2014) approach to representing argument structure. However, this is not to say that XMG cannot be also used in a head-driven way.

- XMG supports type inferences, hence the unification of typed feature structures. In PATR-II, feature structures are strictly untyped.

- XMG comes with different description languages as well as different types of models, namely trees, typed feature structures, expressions of predicate logic and even strings. PATR-II is restricted to the description of feature structures and CFG rules.

- XMG allows for directed inheritance in the sense that inherited descriptions can be added to any part of the description, not just the root part as with PATR-II.

- XMG is more verbose than PATR-II because it is designed to implement a truly object-oriented programming style with encapsulated namespaces etc. When considering just toy examples, it is admittedly just a matter of taste whether this is something worthwhile. In large-scale grammars and lexicons, however, the advantage can be more substantial by helping to ensure consistency due to the extra checking done by the solver.

In sum, XMG seems to be generally more powerful than PATR-II, but also more cumbersome in the way of encoding.

8 Summary

Table 2 shows a comparison of the encoding formalisms presented in Sections 6 and 7 with respect to the encoding virtues described in Sections 4.2 and 4.3. We omit the encoding virtues with respect to a lexical object (cf. Section 4.1). They are mostly related to a particular lexical encoding and not to the underlying formalism.

Table 2: Ranking of encoding formats in different categories – lexical encoding virtues – with special focus on MWEs. The range of values is from 1 to 4, where 1 means that we judge the corresponding format as relatively the best in the given category.

	human user oriented				lexical resource oriented
	TRANSPARENCY	FLEXIBILITY	POWER TO GENERALIZE	IMPLEMENTATION FRIENDLINESS	ELECTRONIC VERSATILITY
DuELME	4	4	3	2	1
Walenty	3	3	3	1	1
PATR-II	1	2	2	4	4
XMG	1	1	1	3	3

Descriptions in PATR-II and XMG come with clear denotational semantics, which makes these two formalisms stand out as highly transparent in comparison with their less flexible counterparts. Transparency of the Walenty's encoding format is relatively high. Due to its conciseness, it is possible to read, analyze and write new entries relatively quickly. However, this requires some experience, since interpretation of certain syntactic constructions (e.g., positions in lexically restricted phrase descriptions) is implicit. More importantly, interpretation of the meaning of symbols used in Walenty descriptions is often implicit as well. Certain patterns – for instance, a prepositional noun phrase (PREPNP) – are defined as atomic constructions, and the recommended way to model new phenomena – for instance, agreement between the subject and the possessive determiner of the direct object – is to add new symbols to the alphabet of the formalism.[16] This can be seen as a flexible solution, but it may also lead to proliferation of atomic symbols with encoding-specific semantics, not defined within the formalism itself. This in turn may harm transparency of the individual Walenty-based encodings and decrease its overall electronic versatility. Finally, there seems to be no clear denotational semantics defined for DuELME descriptions (except, maybe, in its LMF standard export format). Their interpretation is based partially on formal properties and inference rules, partially on methodological recommendations, and the borderline between the two is hard to determine, which severely harms the clarity of the format.

Not very surprisingly, XMG and PATR-II are also more flexible than Walenty or DuELME. In comparison to XMG, PATR-II exhibits certain restrictions (see Section 7.1 for details) which limit, among others, its power to express word order constraints.[17] Walenty is flexible enough to account for most of the MWE-related properties. Yet, the need to introduce new symbols to express previously unforeseen phenomena (already mentioned w.r.t. the virtue of transparency) may stem from the insufficient flexibility of the formalism. As for DuELME, we see its relatively low transparency as the main cause of its relatively low flexibility – it is hard to define complex constructions when clear foundations are not established.

The restrictions enforced by PATR-II diminish also its power to express certain factorizations – notably, by not allowing templates to apply to feature structure nodes other than roots. Due to the untyped nature of feature structures, representation of certain properties based on types – and, therefore, the related generalizations – may be hindered as well. The power to generalize of DuELME is limited by the distinction between patterns and MWE descriptions. Moreover, DuELME provides no way to express any kind of sharing between the individual patterns. As to Walenty, a hierarchy of macros (in the sense that a macro can

---

[16]In fully flexible formalisms such new syntactic phenomena can be factored through the use of dedicated classes whose semantics remains explicit.

[17]Note, however, that while word order constraints are supposed to be expressed in PATR-II through filtering CFG rules via features, these constraints could be also expressed directly as feature structure values.

refer to other macros) can be used to account for repeating patterns. However, it is not clear to what extent macros constitute a part of the formalism itself and it seems that the mechanism of macros is too simple to account for more complex patterns (for example, the abovementioned subject/possessive agreement restriction).

Both DuELME and Walenty seem to be more electronically versatile than XMG. DuELME supports the standard LMF format, while one of the formats supported by Walenty is TEI – based on XML, less concise than the default Walenty's format but more explicit and application-friendly. While XMG encodings can be compiled and stored in an XML format which directly represents all the resolved property names, it does not necessarily contain all the underlying generalizations (i.e., those encoded in the class inheritance hierarchy). One could imagine parsing and interpreting XMG descriptions themselves, and not the resulting compiled encodings, as a first step of converting XMG descriptions to a particular lexical resource. However, this solution would require certain knowledge about the formal principles and mechanisms underlying XMG. Thus the additional flexibility and power to generalize of XMG come with additional cost in terms of the preprocessing work that needs to be done to obtain a particular resource from XMG descriptions. As to PATR-II, there seem to be very few actively maintained software tools for it. While a parser of this formalism can still be downloaded, its further development has been discontinued as of 2006.[18] We therefore estimate the electronic versatility of PATR-II as being rather low due to the current unavailability of dedicated software tools.

Implementation friendliness of DuELME and Walenty has been already confirmed in practice. DuELME has been used to encode a lexicon of 5,000 Dutch MWEs, while Walenty underlies The Polish Valence Dictionary which, in particular, contains around 8,000 MWE entries. Moreover, a dedicated tool Slowal (http://zil.ipipan.waw.pl/Slowal) has been designed for creating, editing and browsing Walenty dictionaries. Thus, Walenty comes with an implementation friendly environment, editing tools and, on top of that, provides conversion between several dictionary formats adapted for different needs. In XMG, MWEs are defined as terminal classes and are encoded directly in the source code. At the moment, there is no dedicated tool which would assist a human user with encoding large sets of MWEs. At the same time, encoding MWEs directly in the source code can be seen as a flexible solution which allows the user to adopt his or her own organization of MWE-related classes. High factorization capabilities of XMG should also facilitate handling large sets of lexical objects, heterogeneous yet often showing

---

[18]http://software.sil.org/pc-patr/

common patterns. On top of that, the process of compiling XMG descriptions provides a verification mechanism which allows to check the correctness of the individual XMG-based lexical entries. For PART-II, again, we found no readily available software tool that is designed to support the implementation process.

As a general conclusion, lexical encoding of MWEs is a highly challenging task, as also stressed in Dyvik et al.; Markantonatou et al. (2019; 2019 [this volume]), due to the complexity and versatility of the regular and idiosyncratic phenomena exhibited by the linguistic objects. The four encoding formats examined here show complementary strengths and weaknesses. We believe that transparency, flexibility and the power to generalize[19] are the fundamental virtues to promote in lexical encoding of MWEs, and in this respect XMG seems to stand out as a particularly appropriate framework. These qualities have to be confirmed, however, in large-scale lexicographic efforts, which call for enhancing its implementation friendliness via developing a lexicographic framework to automate the encoding and validation process. Note finally that relatively few considerations have been made here on semantic properties of MWEs. Maybe the most outstanding feature of many MWEs is their semantic non-compositionality, and addressing it in a lexical encoding framework remains one of the most challenging perspectives.

Acknowledgements

This work has been supported by the IC1207 PARSEME COST action, by the Deutsche Forschungsgemeinschaft (DFG) within the CRC 991 "The Structure of Representations in Language, Cognition, and Science", and by a doctoral grant from the French Ministry of Higher Education and Research.

References

Copestake, Ann. 2002. *Implementing typed feature structure grammars.* Stanford: CSLI Publications.

Crabbé, Benoît, Denys Duchier, Claire Gardent, Joseph Le Roux & Yannick Parmentier. 2013. XMG: eXtensible MetaGrammar. *Computational Linguistics* 39(3). 591–629. DOI:10.1162/COLI_a_00144

Daelemans, Walter & Koenraad De Smedt. 1994. Default inheritance in an object-oriented representation of linguistic categories. *International Journal of Human-Computer Studies* 41(1). 149–177.

---

[19]We believe that the latter property – the power to generalize – should be particularly helpful in modeling the varying degrees of flexibility exhibited by MWEs, discussed in Sheinfux et al. (2019 [this volume]).

Daelemans, Walter & Erik-Jan van der Linden. 1992. *Evaluation of lexical representation formalisms.* ITK Research Memo. Tilburg: Institute for Language Technology & Artificial Intelligence, Tilburg University.

Dyvik, Helge, Gyri Smørdal Losnegaard & Victoria Rosén. 2019. Multiword expressions in an LFG grammar for Norwegian. In Yannick Parmentier & Jakub Waszczuk (eds.), *Representation and parsing of multiword expressions: Current trends*, 69–108. Berlin: Language Science Press. DOI:10.5281/zenodo.2579037

Evans, Roger & Gerald Gazdar. 1996. DATR: A language for lexical knowledge representation. *Computational Linguistics* 22(2). 167–216.

Francopoulo, Gil, Monte George, Nicoletta Calzolari, Monica Monachini, Nuria Bel, Mandy Pet & Claudia Soria. 2006. Lexical markup framework (LMF). In *Proceedings of the international conference on Language Resources and Evaluation (LREC 2006)*, 233–236.

Grégoire, Nicole. 2007a. *MWE Lexicon for Dutch: Encoding protocol.* http://duelme.clarin.inl.nl/documentation.php.

Grégoire, Nicole. 2007b. *MWE Lexicon for Dutch: Overview of pattern descriptions.* http://duelme.clarin.inl.nl/documentation.php.

Grégoire, Nicole. 2010. DuELME: A Dutch electronic lexicon of multiword expressions. *Language Resources and Evaluation* 44(1–2). 23–39.

Gross, Maurice. 1986. Lexicon-grammar: The representation of compound words. In *Proceedings of the 11th coference on Computational Linguistics* (COLING '86), 1–6. Bonn, Germany: Association for Computational Linguistics.

Gross, Maurice. 1994. Constructing lexicon-grammars. In B.T.S. Atkins & A. Zampolli (eds.), *Computational Approaches to the Lexicon*, 213–263. Oxford: Oxford University Press.

Habert, Benoît & Christian Jaquemin. 1995. Construction nominales à contraintes fortes et grammaires d'unification. *Lingvisticae Investigationes* 19(2). 401–427.

Kilbury, James, Petra Naerger & Ingrid Renz. 1991. DATR as a lexical component for PATR. In *Proceedings of the fifth conference of the European Chapter of the Association for Computational Linguistics (EACL-91)*, 137–142.

Lichte, Timm & Simon Petitjean. 2015. Implementing semantic frames as typed feature structures with XMG. *Journal of Language Modelling* 3(1). 185–228.

Markantonatou, Stella, Niki Samaridi & Panagiotis Minos. 2019. Issues in parsing MWEs in an LFG/XLE framework. In Yannick Parmentier & Jakub Waszczuk (eds.), *Representation and parsing of multiword expressions: Current trends*, 109–126. Berlin: Language Science Press. DOI:10.5281/zenodo.2579039

McConnel, Stephen. 1997. *PC-PATR Reference Manual.* Summer Institute of Linguistics. Dallas, TX. http://www.sil.org/pcpatr/manual/pcpatr.html. Version 0.99b5.

Mel'čuk, Igor, Nadia Arbatchewsky-Jumarie, Louise Dagenais, Léo Elnitsky, Lidija Iordanskaja, Marie-Noëlle Lefebvre & Suzanne Mantha. 1988. *Dictionnaire explicatif et combinatoire du français contemporain: Recherches lexico-sémantiques*. Vol. II (Recherches lexico-sémantiques). Presses de l'Univ. de Montréal.

Müller, Stefan & Stephen M. Wechsler. 2014. Lexical approaches to argument structure. *Theoretical Linguistics* 40(1–2). 1–76.

Nitoń, Bartłomiej, Tomasz Bartosiak & Elżbieta Hajnicz. 2016. Accessing and elaborating Walenty – a valence dictionary of Polish – via Internet browser. In *Proceedings of the 10th edition of the Language Resources and Evaluation conference (LREC)*, 1352–1359. Portorož, Slovenia.

Odijk, Jan. 2013. DUELME: Dutch electronic lexicon of multiword expressions. In Gil Francopoulo (ed.), *LMF: lexical markup framework*, chap. 9, 133–144. Wiley-ISTE.

Petitjean, Simon, Denys Duchier & Yannick Parmentier. 2016. XMG2: Describing description languages. In Maxime Amblard, Philippe de Groote, Sylvain Pogodalla & Christian Retoré (eds.), *Logical aspects of computational linguistics: Celebrating 20 years of LACL (1996–2016)*, 255–272. Berlin & Heidelberg: Springer.

Przepiórkowski, Adam, Jan Hajič, Elżbieta Hajnicz & Zdeňka Urešová. 2016. Phraseology in two Slavic valency dictionaries: Limitations and perspectives. *International Journal of Lexicography* 29.

Przepiórkowski, Adam, Elżbieta Hajnicz, Agnieszka Patejuk & Marcin Woliński. 2014. Extended phraseological information in a valence dictionary for NLP applications. In *Proceedings of the workshop on Lexical and Grammatical Resources for Language Processing (LG-LP 2014)*, 83–91. Dublin, Ireland.

Savary, Agata. 2008. Computational inflection of multi-word units: A contrastive study of lexical approaches. *Linguistic Issues in Language Technology* 1(2). 1–53.

Sheinfux, Livnat Herzig, Tali Arad Greshler, Nurit Melnik & Shuly Wintner. 2019. Verbal multiword expressions: Idiomaticity and flexibility. In Yannick Parmentier & Jakub Waszczuk (eds.), *Representation and parsing of multiword expressions: Current trends*, 35–68. Berlin: Language Science Press. DOI:10.5281/zenodo.2579035

Shieber, Stuart M. 1984. The design of a computer language for linguistic information. In *Proceedings of the 10th international conference on Computational Linguistics and 22nd annual meeting of the Association for Computational Linguistics (ACL 1984)*, 362–366. Stanford, CA. http://www.aclweb.org/anthology/P84-1075.

Shieber, Stuart M. 1986. *An introduction to unification-based approaches to grammar* (CSLI Lecture Notes Series 4). Stanford, CA: CSLI.

Chapter 2

Verbal multiword expressions: Idiomaticity and flexibility

Livnat Herzig Sheinfux
University of Haifa

Tali Arad Greshler
University of Haifa

Nurit Melnik
The Open University of Israel

Shuly Wintner
University of Haifa

Verbal multiword expressions are generally characterized by their formal rigidity, yet they exhibit remarkable diversity in their flexibility. Our primary research question is whether the behavior of idioms is an idiosyncratic property of each idiom or a consequence of more general constraints. We challenge Nunberg et al.'s (1994) proposal, attributing decomposability as the determining factor regarding idioms' flexibility/rigidity, first due to the fuzziness of the notion of decomposability, and second, in light of empirical investigations in English and in other languages that revealed flexibility within idioms previously classified as non-decomposable. We propose an alternative classification that builds on the notions of TRANSPARENCY and FIGURATION. We hypothesize that the more transparent and figurative an idiom is, the more likely it is to be "transformationally productive". We put this hypothesis to the test by conducting an empirical corpus-based study of a set of idioms of varying degrees of transparency and figuration, using a large corpus of Modern Hebrew.

Livnat Herzig Sheinfux, Tali Arad Greshler, Nurit Melnik & Shuly Wintner. 2019. Verbal multiword expressions: Idiomaticity and flexibility. In Yannick Parmentier & Jakub Waszczuk (eds.), *Representation and parsing of multiword expressions: Current trends*, 35–68. Berlin: Language Science Press. DOI:10.5281/zenodo.2579035

Livnat Herzig Sheinfux, Tali Arad Greshler, Nurit Melnik & Shuly Wintner

1 Introduction

Multiword expressions (MWEs) are lexical items that consist of multiple words. They form a heterogeneous class of constructions which include, among others, compounds (e.g., *hot dog*), verb-particle constructions (e.g., *take off*), complex prepositions (e.g., *on top of*), adverbials (e.g., *by and large*) and verbal phrases (e.g., *spill the beans*). MWEs are characterized by their idiosyncratic behavior. The most prominent type of idiosyncrasy ascribed to MWEs is their semantic idiomaticity; their meaning cannot be systematically derived from the meanings that their parts have when they are used independently. For example, there is nothing about the meaning of the words *spill* and *beans* which is necessarily related to the meaning of the idiom *spill the beans*. MWEs may also display idiosyncrasy in other linguistic domains. At the lexical level, MWEs may contain components which are not part of the conventional lexicon (*ad hoc*). Morphologically, they may undergo idiosyncratic processes (*still lifes* and not *still lives* when referring to paintings). Some MWEs have an internal structure which is not accounted for by standard syntax (*by and large*).

MWEs are extremely prevalent: the number of MWEs in a speaker's lexicon is estimated to be of the same order of magnitude as the number of single words (Jackendoff 1997). This may even be an underestimate, as 41% of the entries in WordNet (Fellbaum 1998), for example, are multiwords (Sag et al. 2002). Erman & Warren (2000) found that over 55% of the tokens in the texts they studied were instances of PREFABS (defined informally as word sequences preferred by native speakers due to conventionalization). However, while MWEs constitute significant portions of natural language texts, most of them belong to the long tail in terms of frequency: specific MWEs tend to occur only rarely in texts.

In this chapter we focus on *verbal* MWEs, often referred to as "verbal idioms" or simply "idioms". Unlike syntactically idiosyncratic expressions such as *by and large*, the structure of verbal idioms is more often than not governed by productive syntactic rules: they contain a verbal head which combines with one or more complements (and possibly adjuncts) to form a verb phrase.[1] Nevertheless, verbal idioms impose stringent selectional restrictions on their lexical components. Moreover, they are known to exhibit "transformational deficiencies" (Chafe 1968: 111), such as resistance to passivization, modification and topicalization. Not all idioms, however, are equally rigid, as some maintain their idiomatic meaning even when they do not appear in their canonical form. The versatile behavior of verbal MWEs raises a question regarding the speakers' knowledge of idioms.

---

[1]The internal structure of some idioms can be syntactically idiosyncratic (e.g., *find fault, close up shop*).

Is information regarding their flexibility encoded for each idiom individually, or can the behavior of idioms be predicted from general principles?

2 Decomposability and flexibility

The groundbreaking work of Nunberg et al. (1994) opened up the possibility of considering the behavior of idioms not as idiosyncratically specified for each idiom individually, but rather as determined by the semantics of the idioms. In this section we first present Nunberg et al.'s (1994) proposal regarding the correlation between the semantic decomposability of idioms and their flexibility/rigidity. We then consider the notion of decomposability and its coherence, and present a number of studies which assessed whether this correlation holds in English and in other languages.

2.1 Decomposability and flexibility: A correlation

The contribution of Nunberg et al. (1994: 503) is set against the background of what they refer to as "well-established assumptions in generative grammar" which is that idioms are non-compositional. In contrast, the authors argue that most idioms do have identifiable parts with assigned interpretations. They distinguish between two types of idioms: DECOMPOSABLE IDIOMS ("idiomatically combining expressions" in their terminology) and NON-DECOMPOSABLE IDIOMS ("idiomatic phrases"). The former are idioms whose meaning, once known, can be distributed among their parts. A typical example is *spill the beans*, where *spill* roughly means 'reveal' and *beans* roughly means 'secrets'. The meaning of non-decomposable idioms is associated with the *entire* expression; no meanings are assigned to individual words. The often-cited example of this type is *kick the bucket*, for which the meaning 'to die' is carried by the phrase in its entirety.

Nunberg et al. (1994) take their analysis a step further by suggesting that there is a correlation between the semantic type of idioms and their behavior. They propose that the semantic distinction between decomposable and non-decomposable idioms accounts for the difference between "transformationally productive" and "transformationally deficient" idioms. The fact that parts of decomposable idioms are assigned interpretations allows them to undergo different "transformations" similarly to ordinary verb phrases.[2] These parts can be passivized, modified by adjectives or relative clauses, quantified, elided, topicalized/focalized and be antecedents to anaphora. Non-decomposable idioms, on the other hand, only allow verbal inflection.

---

[2]We adopt the cover term "transformation" for ease of exposition, with no commitment to its theoretical implications.

2.2 Identifying decomposability

Nunberg et al. (1994) do not provide precise definitions for the two categories, or a specific procedure for distinguishing between them. They do however explicitly warn against confusing decomposability with transparency, which they define as the relation between the literal and idiomatic meaning. Thus, although the idiom *saw logs* is transparent – there is an obvious relation between the sound made by sawing logs and the sound of snoring – it is non-decomposable, since there is no meaning that can be assigned to *logs* in this context. An additional distinction is made between decomposability and paraphrasability. The fact that the meaning of an idiom can be paraphrased using a phrase of a similar argument structure does not necessarily indicate that it is decomposable. For example, although the transitive idiomatic phrase *kick the bucket* could be paraphrased as the transitive phrase *lose one's life* there is nothing about the role of *bucket* in the idiom which suggests that it denotes 'life'.

The coherence of this classification has been put to the test in a number of psycholinguistic experiments. In one experiment Gibbs et al. (1989) compiled a set of idioms which they categorized, based on their own intuitions, into three groups: NORMALLY DECOMPOSABLE IDIOMS for which a part of the idiom is used literally (e.g., *pop the question*), ABNORMALLY DECOMPOSABLE IDIOMS (e.g., *carry a torch*, which refers to the metaphorical extension of torches as warm feelings), and SEMANTICALLY NON-DECOMPOSABLE IDIOMS (e.g., *shoot the breeze*). They presented these idioms along with a paraphrase of their figurative meaning to subjects and asked them to decide whether the individual words in an expression made some unique contribution to its idiomatic meaning, thus testing their intuitions regarding decomposability. As a second step the subjects were instructed to distinguish among the decomposable idioms between those which "have words which are closely related to their individual figurative meaning" (i.e., normally decomposable idioms such as *pop the question*) and those "whose individual words have a more metaphorical relation to their figurative meanings" (i.e., abnormally decomposable idioms such as *spill the beans*).

Gibbs et al. (1989) found that with the exception of three idioms, there was at least 75% agreement among subjects regarding the classification of 36 idioms into one of the three categories. The mean proportion of subject agreement was 86% for those idioms which were initially labeled by the researchers as normally decomposable idioms, 79% for those identified as abnormally decomposable idioms and 88% for semantically non-decomposable idioms. In contrast, Titone & Connine (1994) did not find reliable agreement regarding decomposability in their study. Of the 171 idioms which they examined, only 40% were classified into one of the three categories (normally decomposable, abnormally decomposable non-decomposable) with at least 75% agreement among subjects. The authors suggest that grouping idioms into these categories may rely on a type of linguistic knowledge that is not easily accessed.

2.3 Empirical assessments of the correlation

Under the assumption that the decomposable/non-decomposable classification is indeed valid, various studies have attempted to assess whether the correlation between decomposability and flexibility holds. Gibbs et al. (1989) presented subjects with idioms in which a lexical item was replaced with a semantically related alternate and with paraphrases of the interpretation of the original idioms. The subjects were asked to judge the similarity between the distorted idiom and the original interpretation. Gibbs et al. found that decomposable idioms were judged by native speakers to be less disrupted by lexical changes. For example, *burst the ice* was found to be more related in meaning to the interpretation of *break the ice* than *kick the pail* was to the interpretation of *kick the bucket*. Similar results were obtained in a set of experiments which focused on syntactic variations (Gibbs & Nayak 1989). Non-decomposable idioms were found to be more limited in terms of the syntactic changes that they can undergo and still retain their figurative meaning. Differences were found also between normally decomposable and abnormally decomposable idioms, where the latter were relatively more constrained in their syntactic behavior. Importantly, not all syntactic operations produced similar results. Some syntactic changes such as adjective insertion and passivization were successful only with normally decomposable idioms. Other changes, such as present participle and adverb insertion, which influence the entire idiom phrase, and not only parts of it, were successful with all types.

A different research method was adopted by Riehemann (2001), who conducted an extensive study of verbal idioms using a 350 million token corpus. She examined four sets of data: (i) idioms that have been discussed in the literature, (ii) idioms that have interesting properties (e.g., passive, negation, adjuncts, no verbal head, more than one idiomatic noun), (iii) idioms with "non-independent words" (or "cranberry expressions", see Section 3.1 below), and (iv) a random sample of frequent V+NP idioms. Riehemann classified the idioms as decomposable or non-decomposable by attempting to match them with a similarly structured paraphrase. She classified those for which she found an appropriate paraphrase as decomposable. Nevertheless, she observed that the boundary between the two categories is fuzzy. This notwithstanding, her findings show a clear distinction between the decomposable and non-decomposable idioms with respect to their variability. On average, the canonical forms of idioms account for about 75% of the occurrences of decomposable idioms and 97% of the occurrences of non-decomposable idioms. Moreover, she found that decomposable idioms constitute a majority, with only 27% of the random sample of V+NP idioms classified as non-decomposable.

Nunberg et al.'s (1994) proposed correlation between decomposability and flexibility predicts that non-decomposable idioms would exhibit complete "transformational deficiency". Nevertheless, Webelhuth & Ackerman (1999) identified a number of German idioms which appear to be non-decomposable yet maintain their idiomatic meaning under topicalization. Bargmann & Sailer (2015) noted similar observations with passivization. Schenk (1995) showed that non-decomposable idioms in German can participate in a verb-second configuration. Verb-second with non-decomposable idioms was also found in Dutch by Grégoire (2007).

Abeillé (1995) argued against the clear bifurcation between fixed and flexible idioms and questioned the validity of the concept of the distribution of the meaning of an idiom among its parts. She examined a sample of 2,000 French verbal idioms and found that most of them did not behave as predicted by Nunberg et al.'s (1994) theory. For example, she showed that a non-decomposable idiom can undergo clefting, provided that a contrastive interpretation, which is a general licensing condition of clefting, is possible.

2.4 Summary

Instances of flexible non-decomposable idioms challenge the all-or-nothing view of transformational deficiencies proposed by Nunberg et al. (1994). Moreover, findings regarding the behavior of idioms in German, Dutch and French cast doubts on the cross-linguistic validity of Nunberg et al.'s (1994) proposal, which was mostly concerned with English idioms. We follow Bargmann & Sailer (2015) in hypothesizing that further research of the flexibility of idioms, especially in languages that differ from English, would reveal language-specific variations that are dependent on language-specific constraints on different transformations.

3 Deconstructing idiomaticity and flexibility

In this chapter we challenge the validity of the hypothesized correlation between decomposability and flexibility. As previously mentioned, decomposability is a fuzzy notion which is difficult to apply when classifying idioms. Although it was proposed by Nunberg et al. (1994) to be the semantic property of idioms which predicts their behavior, at times this hypothesis is turned around and idiom flexibility is used as a defining property of non-decomposable idioms. Moreover, empirical investigations of the above-mentioned correlation in languages other than English have revealed flexibility within idioms that were classified as non-decomposable. Thus, we argue that decomposability is not a primitive semantic property of idioms, nor can it be used to predict idioms' behavior.

As a first step we picked the quintessential non-decomposable idiom *kick the bucket* to serve as a test case. While this idiom is one of the most frequently cited idioms in the literature, it is scarcely attested in corpora. Moon (1998) did not find any instances of this idiom in the 18 million word corpus that she consulted. Riehemann (2001), using a 350 million word corpus, retrieved only twelve instances, of which one did not appear in the canonical form.

In order to verify that the idiom's common characterization as a rigid idiom is not an epiphenomenon of its low frequency, we consulted a much larger corpus: *enTenTen13* (Baroni et al. 2009), a 20 billion word English corpus, available on SketchEngine (Kilgarriff et al. 2004). Following are examples of determiner variation (1a–1b), modification (1c) and passivization (1d–1e).

(1) a. When I kick my bucket, Cecelia's yarn can find a new good home.
     b. So what if consuming the foods therein might make us kick that bucket a tad earlier?
     c. My faithful old Samsung i730 PDA phone was starting to kick the battery bucket.
     d. Constantine is a weary, dapper, neo-noir demon-hunting chainsmoker who carries the unfortunate burden of knowing that, when his bucket's kicked, he's going down, not up.
     e. Then Melanie says her last words to Scarlett and falls back onto the starched pillows, her bucket finally kicked.

This preliminary mini-study has shown that given a large enough corpus, even *kick the bucket* can be found to exhibit variations. Consequently, we suggest that the answer to what determines the flexibility or rigidity of idioms is not whether they are decomposable or not. Moreover, we hypothesize that idioms cannot be categorically classified as either flexible or rigid. Rather, we envision a continuum with idioms exhibiting varying degrees of flexibility, possibly dependent on their semantic properties. In an effort to uncover the logic behind the behavior of idioms we reconsider the notions of idiomaticity and flexibility, and propose an alternative classification, which we then empirically examine by consulting a large corpus of Modern Hebrew.

3.1 Dimensions of idiomaticity

Idiomaticity is often characterized by CONVENTIONALITY; the meaning of idioms cannot be entirely predicted from the meaning of their parts when they appear in isolation from one another. There are, however, a number of other semantic dimensions according to which idioms can be characterized. The dimension which Nunberg et al. (1994: 498) assume plays a crucial role in determining the behavior of an idiom is its decomposability. Nevertheless, as was previously mentioned, determining whether an idiom is decomposable or not is rather impressionistic, and is prone to circularity, where its flexibility is taken as evidence for its decomposability.

In this chapter we consider an alternative categorization of idioms. More precisely, we cross-classify idioms according to two dimensions: FIGURATION and TRANSPARENCY. Figuration reflects the degree to which the idiom can be assigned a literal meaning. Transparency (or opacity) relates to how easy it is to recover the motivation for an idiom's use, or, in other words, to explain the relationship between its literal meaning and its idiomatic one. Idioms are FIGURATIVE if their literal meaning can conjure up a vivid picture in the speaker's mind. Within the figurative idioms we distinguish between two types. In TRANSPARENT FIGURATIVE idioms the relationship between the literal picture and the idiomatic meaning is perceived to be motivated. English examples include *saw logs* ('snore') and *the cat's out of the bag* ('previously hidden facts were revealed'). Conversely, OPAQUE FIGURATIVE idioms portray a picture whose relationship to the idiomatic meaning is not perceptible. English examples include *shoot the breeze* ('chat') and *chew the fat* ('talk socially, gossip'). Idioms which are not figurative do not have a comprehensible literal meaning, and as such are necessarily opaque. Among these idioms we find what are referred to as "cranberry idioms" (Moon 1998; Trawinski et al. 2008), which, similarly to "cranberry morphemes", have parts which have no meanings (e.g., *run amok* 'behave in an unrestrained manner' and *take umbrage* 'take offense'). These idioms may have been figurative and transparent once, but synchronically they contain a word whose meaning is not accessible to contemporary speakers.[3]

---

[3]Opaque non-figurative idioms are not necessarily cranberry idioms. One Hebrew example is *natan ba-kos ʃein-o* 'gave in the cup his eye' → 'got drunk'. Although all the words in this idiom are common "everyday" words, it does not conjure up any type of image. Such idioms seem to be rare.

In what follows we present a sample of Hebrew idioms representing each of the three categories, namely transparent figurative, opaque figurative and cranberry idioms. Each idiom is illustrated with a corpus example taken from the *heTenTen 2014* corpus (see Section 4.1). We use boldface to highlight the canonical parts of the idioms.[4] This set of idioms serves as the dataset for our corpus-based investigation of idiom flexibility presented in Section 4.

3.1.1 Transparent figurative idioms

3.1.1.1 *yarad me-ha-ʕec* 'descended from the tree' → 'conceded'

This idiom is part of a more complex expression. To get to a state where a person is required to concede they first need to adopt an unrealistic stance by idiomatically climbing a tall tree: *tipes ʕal ʕec gavoha* ('climbed on tree tall'). Once there, they may need to eventually climb down, or in other words – to concede.

(2) ʔulai mi ʃe-be-ʕemdat ha-koaħ carix *laredet*
maybe who that-in-position.CS the-power should *to.descend*
me-ha-ʕec.
from-the-tree
'Maybe whoever is in a position of power should concede.'

3.1.1.2 *hosif ʃemen la-medura* 'added oil to the bonfire' → 'aggravated the situation'

This metaphorical idiom describes the act of making a situation worse than it already is. A similar English idiom is *add fuel to the fire*.

(3) beit ha-miʃpat ha-meħozi *hosif* *ʃemen la-medura*: gam hu
house.SM.CS the-court the-district *added.3SM oil* *to.the-bonfire* also he
lo haya muxan liʃmoʕa ʔet ha-mevaqeʃ.
not was ready to.hear ACC the-petitioner
'The district court added fuel to the fire: it also wasn't willing to hear out the petitioner.'

---

[4]The citation form of Hebrew verbs is the third person singular masculine, past tense. Consequently idioms are presented in past tense, and translated as such. When verbs are referred to in isolation their translation is given in the standard English citation form (bare infinitive).

3.1.2 Opaque figurative idioms

3.1.2.1 *ṭaman yad-o ba-calaḥat* 'buried his hand in the plate' → 'refrained from acting'

The origin of this idiom is from the *Book of Proverbs* 19:24, where it describes a person who is so lazy that he leaves his hand in the plate instead of bringing it back into his mouth.[5]

(4)   *ṭaman*   ʕacel   *yad-o*   *ba-calaḥat* gam ʔel pi-hu   lo
       buried.3sm sluggard.sm *hand-his in.the-plate* also to mouth-his not
       yaʃiv-ena.
       return-it
       'A sluggard buries his hand in the dish; he will not even bring it back to his mouth.'

    Most Hebrew speakers are not familiar with the original text and use the idiom in its truncated form. However, without the explicit mention of the actor – the sluggard – and out of context, the idiom is completely opaque, and even more so, it is confusing since it describes an action (i.e., the burying of the hand in the plate), while denoting inaction. Ironically, it is mostly used negatively, to describe someone who does not sit idle.

(5)   gam be-yaḥasei   ʔenoʃ *lo ṭaman*   *yad-o*   *ba-calaḥat,*
       also in-relations.cs human *not buried.3sm hand-his in.the-plate*
       pineq   ve-ʔirgen   lanu micraxim la-piqniq.
       spoiled.3sm and-organized.3sm to.us supplies   to.the-picnic
       'Also with regards to interpersonal relations, he did not sit idle; he spoiled us and prepared supplies for the picnic.'

3.1.2.2 *heʃela ḥeres (be-yad-o)* 'brought up a shard (in his hand)' → 'tried in vain, failed'

This idiom is figurative since it is possible to imagine someone picking up a shard of clay with their hand. However, it is also opaque since there does not seem to be an obvious relationship between this act and failure. Similarly to the previous idiom, this idiom introduces a paradox: it literally describes the situation of finding something, but it is used to describe an unsuccessful attempt. The original context, unknown to most speakers, is of pearl retrievers who dove in search of

---

[5]The translation is taken from http://www.biblestudytools.com/proverbs/19.html.

pearls, but only came up with a piece of clay (or a pearl-less shell, according to a different interpretation) instead.

(6) ha-ʔemet hi ʃe-ħipasti   gam ʔani ʔax *heʃeleti*   *ħeres*
the-truth is that-searched.1s also I   but *brought.up.1s shard*
be-yad-i.
in-hand-my
'The truth is that I also searched, but I failed.'

3.1.2.3 *yaca me-ha-kelim* 'came out from the tools' → 'became upset'

Evidence regarding the opacity of this idiom is found in the ambiguity of the word *kelim*, which could mean 'tools', 'dishes' or 'instruments'. There is no consensus among speakers as to which of the meanings applies to this idiom, since none of them seems appropriate. Nevertheless, regardless of the chosen meaning, it is possible to conjure up an image associated with the literal meaning of this expression.

(7) hu nirʔa   keʔilu hu *yoce*   *me-ha-kelim.*
he looked.3sm as.if   he *coming.out.sm from-the-tools*
'He looked as if he was becoming upset.'

3.1.3 Opaque non-figurative idioms (cranberry idioms)

3.1.3.1 *ʔavad ʃal-av (ha-)kelaħ* '(the-)KELAH was lost on him' → 'became outdated'

The cranberry word in this idiom is *kelaħ*, which has no known literal meaning. It appears three times in the Old Testament, twice as a name of a place, and once as part of this idiom (Book of Job 30:2). Nevertheless, this idiom is an established part of the Hebrew lexicon. Interestingly, although the noun *kelaħ* is indefinite in the original Biblical idiom, in Modern Hebrew it is mostly used with a definite prefix.

(8) ʔatem ʕosqim be-vikuaħ   ʃe-*ʔavad*   *ʃal-av ha-kelaħ.*
you engaged in-argument.sm that-*lost.3sm on-him the-KELAH.SM*
'You are engaged in an argument that has become outdated.'

Apart from the cranberry word, one idiosyncracy exhibited by this idiom is its argument structure. Outside the context of this idiom, the head verb *ʔavad* 'lose' does not appear with a PP complement headed by the preposition *ʃal* 'on'. In addition, unlike the rest of the idioms presented here, this idiom is a full clause, with *kelaħ* functioning as the subject. Although it is clausal, the complement of the PP is an open slot, and the property of being outdated is predicated on it. Consequently, it is mostly used as a relative clause in which the open slot is occupied by a resumptive pronoun (see also 56).

3.1.3.2 *yaʃav ʃal ha-meduxa* 'sat on the MEDUXA' → 'deliberated'

The original meaning of the word *meduxa* is 'mortar', yet it is not used outside the context of this idiom and its meaning is not known to most Hebrew speakers.

(9) ha-cevet   yaʃav   ʃal ha-meduxa   ve-qiyem   kama   yeʃivot.
     the-team.SM *sat.3SM on the-MEDUXA.SF* and-held.3SM several meetings
     'The team deliberated and held several meetings.'

3.1.3.3 *higdiʃ ʔet ha-seʔa* 'overfilled the SEAH' → 'exaggerated'

The word *seʔa* is originally a biblical unit of measurement, usually of grain, but it is rarely used outside of this idiom (exceptions are texts which deal with religious laws). Interestingly, the verb *higdiʃ* is hardly used outside of this context as well, although the consonantal root *g-d-ʃ* is productive in a different verbal template (*gadaʃ* 'fill').[6] The original literal meaning of the verb *higdiʃ* was 'to gather wheat sheaves', and the literal meaning of the phrase was to overfill a set measure with wheat. The idiom can be used with an agentive subject (10) who "overdoes it", or an abstract noun (11) which in itself is "too much".

(10) bronil   liʃʕamim *magdiʃ*   ʔet ha-seʔa   be-kama   ʃe-hu
     Bronil.SM sometimes *overfills.SM* ACC *the-SEAH.SF* in-how.much that-he
     meruce me-ʃacmo.
     pleased from-himself
     'Bronil sometimes overdoes it in how much he is pleased with himself.'

(11) ʕikuv   ze *higdiʃ*   ʔet ha-seʔa.
     delay.SM this *overfilled.3SM* ACC *the-SEAH.SF*
     'This delay was too much.'

---

[6]Semitic morphology is largely based on roots-and-patterns. Roots are sequences of (typically) three consonants. Patterns are sequences of vowels and possibly consonants with open slots for the roots consonants, indicated by capital Cs. For example, *higdiʃ* and *gadaʃ* are formed by combining the same consonantal root *g-d-ʃ* with two different templates: hiCCiC and CaCaC.

3.1.3.4 *lo yesula be-paz* 'will not be SULA in gold' → 'priceless'

Unlike the other idioms in this category, the cranberry word in this case is a verb: *sula*. The verb is formed in a passive morphological template (CuCaC) and is never used in the active template (CiCeC). Its original (Biblical) meaning is 'was measured', but it is not used out of this context in Hebrew. The noun *paz* 'gold' is a very rare synonym of the commonplace *zahav*; its distribution is mostly restricted to fixed phrases (e.g., *hizdamnut paz* 'golden opportunity') and the current idiom.

(12)   kenut   tihiye   kan, ve-ze   davar   ʃe-lo   yesula
       honesty.SF will.be.3SF here and-this thing.SM *that-not will.SULA.3SM*
       be-paz.
       in-gold
       'There will be honesty here, and that's priceless.'

3.2 Types of flexibility

Section 3.1 described semantic dimensions of idiomaticity. In this section we present the formal aspect of this phenomenon, namely the set of lexical, morphological and syntactic transformations that verbal idioms can potentially undergo. We distinguish between four types of transformations: SYNTACTIC VARIATIONS, ARGUMENT STRUCTURE VARIATIONS, LEXICAL INSERTIONS and LEXICAL SUBSTITUTIONS.

3.2.1 Syntactic variations

Syntactic variations are those which preserve the lexical material of the idiom, as well as the grammatical function of the constituents which make up the idiom, but which vary the syntactic configuration of the expression. The occurrence of syntactic variations constitutes evidence against analyses of idioms as fixed phrases ("words with spaces") which are entered in the lexicon as complete phrases, and which are inserted "as is" into the sentence.

Syntactic variations range from what could be considered as superficial argument shuffling within the VP to extra-phrasal operations such as argument fronting and relativization. One type of syntactic variation that we find is order alternations within the VP. The order of complements in Hebrew is fairly free. Thus, for example, with ditransitive verbs, the position of the two complements can be interchanged with no change of meaning or register.

(13)   a.   dan natan matana le-dana.
             Dan gave present to-Dana

> b. dan natan le-dana matana.
> Dan gave to-Dana present
> 'Dan gave a present to Dana.'

A different case of word order alternation is verb-second. Although the unmarked word order of Hebrew is SVO, subject–verb inversion may be triggered by the occurrence of a clause-initial element, similarly to verb-second constructions. The V2 configuration splits the VP and inserts the subject between the verb and its complements (14b).

(14) a. * natan dan matana le-dana.
          gave Dan present to-Dana

     b. ʔetmol natan dan matana le-dana.
          yesterday gave Dan present to-Dana
          'Yesterday Dan gave a present to Dana.'

In addition, we include in the category of syntactic variation two types of long-distance dependencies: topicalization/focalization and relativization. Information structure considerations motivate the fronting of VP-internal material to a clause-initial position. A fronted constituent can be a focal element (15a) or a topicalized element (15b).

(15) a. [gam le-sara] dan natan matana.
          also to-Sarah Dan gave present
          'Dan gave a present also to Sarah.'

     b. [ʔet ha-matana ha-zot] dan natan le-dana.
          ACC the-present the-this Dan gave to-Dana
          'This present, Dan gave to Dana.'

An additional long-distance dependency involves relativization. When NP complements are relativized in Hebrew a resumptive pronoun can optionally occur in the relativization site (16a). Oblique complements are obligatorily resumed by a pronoun, and the language does not allow preposition stranding (16b).

(16) a. lo raʔiti ʔet ha-matana$_i$ [ʃe-dan natan (ʔota$_i$) le-sara].
          not saw.1s ACC the-present that-Dan gave (it) to-Sarah
          'I didn't see the present that Dan gave to Sarah.'

     b. lo raʔiti ʔet ha-yalda$_i$ [ʃe-dan natan l-a$_i$ matana].
          not saw.1s ACC the-girl that-Dan gave to-her present
          'I didn't see the girl that Dan gave a present to.'

3.2.2 Argument structure variations

Argument structure variations involve a change in the mapping of arguments to grammatical functions (e.g., passive) as well as valence changing operations (e.g., causativization, reflexivization). Passivization, a primary example of argument structure variation, was found to be a feature that sets decomposable idioms apart from non-decomposable ones (Nunberg et al. 1994), but not in all languages (Bargmann & Sailer 2015).

Hebrew presents an interesting case in this respect, since argument structure variations are associated with the combination of one consonantal root with different morphological templates (Doron 2008; 2003). Thus, the following examples illustrate the root *l-b/v-ʃ* in four different templates: active (17a), reflexive (17b), causative (17c), and passive (17d).

(17) a.   dan **lavaʃ** ħulca.
          Dan wore shirt

          'Dan wore a shirt.'

      b.   dan **hitlabeʃ**.
          Dan dressed

          'Dan got dressed.'

      c.   dan **hilbiʃ** ʔet ha-yeled be-ħulca.
          Dan dressed ACC the-child in-shirt

          'Dan dressed the child with a shirt.'

      d.   ha-yeled **hulbaʃ**   be-ħulca.
          the-child was.dressed in-shirt

          'The child was dressed in a shirt.'

3.2.3 Lexical insertions

Lexical insertions refer to the inclusion of non-selected lexical material within the idiom. This material includes adverbials, quantifiers and different types of noun modifiers. The ability to modify only a part of the meaning is taken by Nunberg et al. (1994) to be a key property of decomposable idioms. They assume that only idiom parts that have individual idiomatic meanings can be modified. However, Ernst (1981) proposed that not all idiom-internal modifiers are equal. He distinguished between INTERNAL and EXTERNAL MODIFICATION, which differ in the semantic scope of their modification. Internal modifiers modify only the element to which they are adjoined (18a). External modifiers, which attach to the object but are semantically associated with the entire verb phrase, are not indicators of decomposability. The semantically external modifier in (18b) is a "domain delimiter" (Ernst 1981), which specifies the domain to which the idiom applies.

(18) a. Dan *pulled* some **important** *strings*. (= Dan used some important connections.)

   b. Dan *pulled* some **economic** *strings*. (= In the domain of economics, Dan pulled some strings.)

The question of whether a modifier is internal or external relates to the issue of decomposability, but not to the question of flexibility. When idiom parts are syntactically modified in an idiom this is certainly an instance of variation; the idiom does not appear in its canonical form. Thus, modifications of all types are variations. The semantic scope of the modifier can provide evidence with respect to whether idiom parts are assigned individual idiomatic meanings or not. For a modifier to be internal the modified part must have its own meaning. For example, *spill royal beans* is acceptable and comprehensible due to the fact that *beans* means 'secrets' in the context of this idiom, and royal beans refer to 'secrets of the royal family'. Conversely, the modifier in *kick the battery bucket* does not attribute any property to the bucket, but rather provides information regarding the domain or cause of death. Nevertheless, the two cases attest to the flexibility of their respective idioms.

3.2.4 Lexical substitutions

Although idioms are known to impose rigid selectional restrictions, there are idioms that maintain their idiomatic meaning even when some of their lexical components are substituted with others. Moon (1998) found verb variation to be the most common type (e.g., *bend/stretch the rules*). Interestingly, the interchangeable verbs are not necessarily synonymous but in that particular context their co-substitution does not alter the idiomatic meaning. As Moon (1998: 50) noted, "searching for verbal variation is the hardest part of corpus-based investigations, and ultimately a matter of serendipity". For this reason, it is impossible to conduct exhaustive searches of this phenomenon. Nevertheless, with manual inspection of the results of very general queries valuable findings can be gleaned.

4 Corpus findings

In the previous section we proposed an alternative semantic classification of idioms, which builds on the notions of TRANSPARENCY and FIGURATION. In addition,

we distinguished between four types of transformations which idioms can potentially undergo. We hypothesize that the more transparent and figurative an idiom
is, the more likely it is to be "transformationally productive".

To put this hypothesis to the test we conducted an empirical corpus-based
study of the behavior of the set of idioms presented in Section 3.1. In light of
our preliminary examination of the flexibility of the idiom *kick the bucket*, we
chose to consult a very large corpus of Modern Hebrew, which increased the
likelihood of finding variations even for relatively infrequently used idioms. The
corpus search revealed evidence for variability across the different dimensions
of idiomaticity and flexibility. We did not find any idiom which exhibited no variation at all. In what follows we present selected examples of our corpus findings.

4.1 Method

We used *heTenTen 2014* (Baroni et al. 2009), a billion-token web-crawled Hebrew
corpus, available on SketchEngine (Kilgarriff et al. 2004), to search for different
types of variations that occur with representative MWEs from the three semantic
classes we outlined in Section 3.1. We focused on fifteen specific verbal MWEs,
and annotated 400 examples overall. Nine of the fifteen MWEs are presented in
Section 3.1.

SketchEngines's Corpus Query Language (CQL) provides a way of defining
complex queries which target morphological features of words (e.g., POS, lemmas, clitics) and which make use of logical operators (AND/OR/NOT). These features are particularly important when our goal is to cast a wide net to retrieve
variations in general, and in particular non-canonical word orders, discontinuous
elements and various morphological inflections. Nevertheless, a wide net comes
at a cost; not all the retrieved results are necessarily instances of the idiom. Often,
only a manual inspection of each result can weed out the false positives. For this
reason we do not present quantitative data with regard to the distribution of the
canonical idiom and its variations. We did, however, verify the occurrence of all
types of variation for each idiom.

In what follows we present our findings regarding the idioms described in Section 3.1. The presentation is first divided into the four flexibility categories (i.e.,
syntactic variation, argument structure variation, lexical insertions, and lexical
substitutions), and within each category, by the three idiom types (i.e., transparent figurative idioms, opaque figurative idioms, and cranberry idioms). We use
boldface to highlight the canonical parts of the idioms, and underline the parts
which exhibit the variation under discussion (when possible).[7]

---

[7]Note that some example sentences exhibit more than one variation, yet in the text we refer
only to the one under discussion.

4.2 Syntactic variations

4.2.1 Word order

Verb second configurations are found with all types of idioms. In what follows are examples of transparent figurative idioms (19–20), opaque figurative idioms (21–22), and cranberry idioms (23–24). Note that in all these examples, the clause-initial "trigger" is not part of the idiom. The fronting of idiom parts is discussed in Section 4.2.2.

(19)   ha-ʃavuʕa *yarad*   kanirʔe misrad   ha-datot
      the-week *descended.3SM* probably ministry.SM.CS the-religions
      me-ha-ʕec   ve-biṭel   ʔet roʕa   ha-gzera.
      from-the-tree and-cancelled.3SM ACC evil.CS the-decree
      'This week it seems as if the ministry of religions conceded and cancelled the harsh decree.'

(20)   yeter   ʕal ken, *mosifa* ha-ʃmuʕa   *ʃemen la-medura*   mispar
      remainder on thus *adds.SF* the-rumor.SF *oil*   to.the-bonfire few
      yamim lifnei qrisat   beit   ha-haʃqaʕot   liman   braders.
      days   before downfall.CS house.CS the-investment Lehman brothers
      'Moreover, the rumor adds fuel to the fire a few days before the downfall of the investment firm Lehman Brothers.'

(21)   legabei danela *heʕelu*   ha-maʔamacim *ħeres.*
      about   Danella *brought.up.3PM* the-efforts.PM   *shard*
      'As for Danella, the efforts were unsuccessful.'

(22)   be-mahalax reʔayon   be-yoman   ha-caharayim
      during   interview in-daily.news.broadcast.CS the-noon
      yaca   profesor yosef ʔagasi *me-ha-kelim*   ve-amar...
      came.out.3SM professor Yosef Agasi *from-the-tools* and-said.3SM
      'During the daily news broadcast at noon, Prof. Yosef Agasi became upset and said ...'

(23)   be-yamim ʔelu *yoʃevet vaʕadat*   german ʕal ha-meduxa.
      in-days   these *sitting.SF* committee.SF.CS German on *the-MEDUXA.SF*
      'These days, the German committee is deliberating.'

(24) be-ʃavuʕa ʃe-ʕavar   *higdiʃ*   fridman   ʔet ha-seʔa.
     in-week   that-passed *overfilled.3sm* Friedman.sm ACC the-SEAH.SF
     'Friedman overdid it last week.'

A different type of word order variation involves an alternative ordering of VP-complements. This, of course, can only occur with ditransitive verbs. Instances of complement ordering with the transitive idiom *hosif ʃemen la-medura* 'added oil to the bonfire' → 'aggravated the situation' with its canonical lexical parts were not found. Examples (25–26) illustrate this variation, as attested with the opaque figurative idioms *heʕela ħeres (be-yad-o)* 'brought up a shard in his hand' → 'tried in vain, failed' and *ṭaman yad-o ba-calaħat* 'buried his hand in the plate' → 'refrained from acting', respectively.[8]

(25) haʃavti   ʃe-ʔulai be-ʔarxion qaqal ʔemca   tʃuvot, ʔax gam
     thought.1s that-maybe in-archive.cs JNF   will.find.1s answers but also
     ʃam heʕeleti   be-yad-i   ħeres.
     there brought.up.1s in-hand-my shard

     'I thought that maybe I'd find answers in the JNF archive, but I was unsuccessful there as well.'

(26) ʔanoxi baħanti   dark-a, ki lo ṭov, *ve-lo* ṭamanti ba-calaħat
     I   inspected.1s way-her that not good *and-not buried.1s in.the-plate*
     yad-i.
     hand-my

     'I inspected her behavior, realized it wasn't good, and did not sit idle (regarding this matter).'

One can note that the canonical form of the cranberry idiom *ʔavad ʃal-av (ha-)kelaħ* '(the-)KELAH was lost on him' → 'became outdated' is in a marked VOS order, which is used when the O argument is more topical than the S argument (Melnik 2016). In the following example the idiomatic clause appears in an SVO word order. The placement of a cranberry word in this clause-initial position suggests that it is more topical, which is surprising due to its lack of meaning.

(27) *ha-kelaħ*   *ʔoved*   gam ʃal ha-tfisa   ʃe-lefi-ha   kol
     the-KELAH.SM is.lost.SM also on the-view.SF that-according.to-her every
     ma   ʃe-lo   racyonali hu ṭipʃi.
     thing that-not rational   is silly

     'The view that anything that isn't rational is silly is becoming outdated.'

---

[8]The style of (26) belongs to a high/literary register.

In the following example the PP, which canonically appears between the verb and the subject, appears postverbally, most likely due to "heavy PP shift".

(28) ha-ʔiʃa   hivhira ʃe-ʔavad   kelaħ   [ʃal ha-tguvot
      the-woman clarified *that-lost.*SM KELAH.SM *on*   the-responses
      ʃe-ʃolelot   ʔet ha-nituħim   ha-ʔestetiyim mi-kol va-xol].
      that-denounce ACC the-operations the-aesthetic from-all and-all

      'The woman clarified that the responses that denounce plastic surgery
      altogether have become outdated.'

4.2.2 Topicalization/focalization of idiom-internal material

Instances of fronting of idiom parts were found across the three semantics types. Following are examples of transparent figurative idioms (29–30), opaque figurative idioms (31), and cranberry idioms (32–34). Note that the fronted part is within square brackets.

(29) ʔaval levasof   [gam *me-ha-ʃec*   ha-ze] hu *yarad.*
      but   eventually also *from-the-tree* the-this he *descended.3*SM

      'However, eventually he abandonded this stance as well.'

(30) [*ʔet ha-ʃemen le-medurat* ha-geruʃim] *mosif*   ʃorex   ha-din
      ACC *the-oil*   *to-bonfire.*CS the-divorce *adds.*SM editor.SM.CS the-law
      ʃe-lo   tovat   ha-laqoħot ke-neged ʃein-av ʔela tovat   ħeʃbon
      that-not good.CS the-clients as-against eyes-his but good.CS account.CS
      ha-banq ʃelo.
      the-bank his

      'The lawyer, who is interested in his bank account more than in his
      clients' interest, adds fuel to the divorce fire.'

(31) [gam *yedei-hem*] *lo tamnu   ba-calaxat.*
      also *hands-their* *not buried.3*P *in.the-plate*

      'Also, they did not sit idle.'

(32) [*ʃal meduxa   ħaʃuva   zo*]   *yoʃvim*   horim rabim.
      on MEDUXA.SF important.SF this.SF *sitting.*PM parents many

      'Many parents are deliberating on this important issue.'

(33) [*ʔet ha-seʔa*]   *higdiʃ*   *ʃadar*   radio populari...
     ACC *the-SEAH.SF overfilled.3SM* announcer.SM radio popular.SM
     'A popular radio announcer overdid it...'

(34) ʕerk-o   ʕacum u-muflag   [*ve-be-paz*] *lo yesula.*
     value.SM-its great.SM and-immense.SM *and-in-gold not will.SULA.3SM*
     'Its value is great, immense and priceless.'

As is evident from these examples, fronted idiom parts do not usually appear in their canonical form. The fronted constituents in (29) and (31) are modified with the focal marker *gam* 'also'. In (29) the demonstrative *ha-ze* 'the-this' further emphasizes the contrastive interpretation. The topicalized idiom parts in (30) and (32) include modifiers. In fact, in (30) both idiomatic complements are fronted. In examples (32) and (33) the topicalized elements are cranberry words. In (32) the modifier *ħaʃuva* 'important' reveals that *meduxa* is interpreted in this context as the issue on which the parents are deliberating (see more about this in Sections 4.4 and 4.5).

4.2.3 Relativization

When idiom parts are relativized, they surface as the head of the relative clause, which is modified by it. Instances of relativization were found for transparent figurative idioms and cranberry idioms. Examples are given in (35–36) and (37–38), respectively, with the relative clause in square brackets. No instances of relativization were found for opaque figurative idioms. Note that in (36), (37) and (38) a resumptive pronoun inside the relative clause is anaphoric, with an idiom part which functions as the head of the relative clause as its antecedent.

(35) ve-nesayem   be-mila   qtana ʕal *ha-ʃemen* [*ʃe-hosifu*
     and-will.conclude.1P with-word small on *the-oil*   *that-added.3PM*
     ha-ciyonim *la-medura*].
     the-zionists *to.the-bonfire*
     'And we'll conclude by mentioning the fuel that the Zionists added to the fire.'

(36) ze lo ʕec   gavoha [*ʃe-nitan*   *laredet*   *mime-no*].
     this not *tree.SM* tall.SM   *that-possible to.descend from-him*
     'This is not an unrealistic stance that it is possible to withdraw from.'

(37) po ʕadayin lo heqimu   ʔet *ha-meduxa*   [ʃe-ʔeʃʃar   *laʃevet*
     here yet   not established.3P ACC *the-MEDUXA.SF* that-possible *to.sit*
     ʕalei-ha ve-ladun   ʔeix niftarim me-ha-ħevra   le-meʃeq
     on-her and-discuss how get.rid.PM from-the-society to-economy
     ve-kalkala].
     and-economy
     'Here they haven't yet figured out how to deliberate on the issue of how to get rid of Local Government Economic Services.'

(38) hu miher   la-liʃka,   mosad.SM geriyatri.SM *ʃe-ha-kelaħ*
     he hurried to.the-bureau institution geriatric   *that-the-KELAH.SM*
     [*ʃe-ʔavad*   *ʕal-av*] kvar   hiħlid   mizman.
     that-lost.3SM on-him already rusted.3SM long.ago
     'He hurried to the bureau, a geriatric institution that had become outdated long ago.'

The cranberry words in these examples are clearly functioning outside their idiomatic context. In (37) the cranberry word *meduxa* serves as the complement of the verb *heqimu* 'established' in a unique and innovative yet comprehensible combination. In (38) *kelaħ* is the head of a relative clause, yet it also functions as a subject of predicate: *kvar hiħlid mizman* 'rusted long ago'. The speaker in this case attributes to this cranberry word physical properties which are related to aging. In doing so, s/he emphasizes his/her assessment of the bureau as an old and outdated institution.

4.3 Argument structure variations

4.3.1 Mapping variations

Variations with respect to the mapping of idiom parts to grammatical functions were found with transparent figurative idioms. Consider examples (39) and (40). In these examples *ʃemen* 'oil', which is the complement of the verb in the canonical idiom, functions as the subject.

(39) be-xol ʔofen **niʃpax**   *ha-ʃemen* ʕaxʃav kmo ʃe-ʔomrim
     in-all way **was.spilled.3SM** *the-oil.SM* now   as   that-they.say
     la-medura.
     to.the-bonfire
     'Anyway, fuel was now added, as they say, to the fire.'

(40) nitan   lehosif le-kax ʔet ha-gzerot ʃel ʔadriʔanus ke-*ʃemen*
      possible to.add to-that ACC the-decrees of Adrianus   as-*oil*.SM
      ʃe-hidliq   ʔet *ha-medura* ʃel ha-mered.
      that-ignited.3SM ACC *the-bonfire* of the-rebellion
      'It is possible to add to that the decrees of Adrianus as fuel which ignited
      the fire of the rebellion.'

In (39) the passive verb *niʃpax* 'was.spilled' is used instead of the canonical
transitive verb *hosif* 'added'. The agent is not expressed. In (40) the oil is the
causer which lights the idiomatic bonfire. Here, too, a different verb is used. This
idiom was found to be particularly prone to lexical substitutions (see Section 4.5).

None of the opaque figurative idioms were found to be passivized. Nevertheless, (41) illustrates a different type of argument realization pattern. Indeed, the
hand, which is realized as oblique in the canonical idiom (*heʕela ħeres be-yad-o*
'brought up a shard in his hand' → 'tried in vain, failed') is realized in this case
as the subject.

(41) zar   ha-mefaʃpeʃ   be-maʔagarei hasfarim
      outsider.SM that-rummaging.SM in-stock.CS   the-books
      yufta   legalot   ki *yad-o*   *maʕala*   *ħeres*.
      will.be.surprised.3SM to.discover that *hand.SF-his brings.up.SF shard*
      'An outsider rummaging in the stock of books would be surprised to find
      himself unsuccessful.'

In the cranberry idiom *higdiʃ ʔet ha-seʔa* 'overfilled the SEAH' → 'exagger-
ated' the cranberry word *ha-seʔa* functions as the complement of the verb. There
are, however, instances of this idiom where *ha-seʔa* functions as the subject and
the verb is a morphological variant of the canonical verb: the passive *hugdeʃa*
'was.overfilled' in (42) and the middle *nitgadʃa* 'was.overfilled' in (43).

(42) ha-paʕam **hugdeʃa**   *ha-seʔa*.
      the-time **was.overfilled.3SF** *the-SEAH.SF*
      'This time things went overboard.'

(43) ʕata **nitgadʃa**   *ha-seʔa*   ve-higiʕa   ha-ʕet letaqen ʔet
      now **was.overfilled.3SF** *the-SEAH.SF* and-arrived the-time to.fix   ACC
      ha-meʕuvat.
      the-wrong
      'Now that things went overboard, it is time to fix the wrongdoing.'

4.3.2 Causativization

The verbs *yarad* 'descend', *yaca* 'come out' and *yaʃav* 'sit', which head a transparent figurative, opaque figurative and cranberry idiom, respectively, are also used in their causative form in the same idioms. The causee argument, indicated by square brackets, is an "open slot". This is illustrated in (44), (45) and (46).

(44) ʔein kmo ʕilot biṭħoniyot **lehorid** [ʔet ʃnei ha-cdadim]
no like reasons security **to.bring.down** ACC both.cs the-sides
me-ha-ʕec.
from-the-tree

'There is nothing like security reasons to cause the two (opposing) sides to concede.'

(45) ha-ʔofanayim ha-ʔele yexolim **lehoci** [ʔafilu baħur ʃaqeṭ kamoni]
the-bicycle.PM the-these can.PM **to.take.out** even guy quiet like.me
me-ha-kelim.
from-the-tools

'This bicycle can make even a quiet guy like me upset.'

(46) higiʕa ha-zman **lehoʃiv** *ʃal ha-meduxa* [kalkelanim
arrived the-time **to.cause.sit** on the-MEDUXA.SF economists
ve-aqtuʔarim].
and-actuaries

'It's time to make economists and actuaries deliberate (on some issue).'

The following example exhibits a neologism. The verb *heʔevid* is created by combining the consonantal root of the original verb *ʔavad* 'lose' (*ʔ-b/v-d*) with the causative template HiCCiC to create a verb whose meaning is 'cause to be lost'.[9] The cranberry word *kelaħ* serves as the causee and surfaces as a direct object (marked with the accusative case marker *ʔet*). This suggests that it is interpreted (at least in this case) as some property, perhaps relevance, whose absence makes something outdated. Although this neologism is attested only once in the corpus, it is comprehensible in the context of this idiom, due to the transparent morphological relationship between it and the canonical verbal form.

---

[9]The original Biblical meaning of *heʔevid* is 'demolish, destroy'.

(47) sifro ha-riʃon doħe ʔet ha-haʃqafa ha-rovaħat ʃe-qant
his.book the-first rejects ACC the-view the-common that-Kant.SM
heʔevid **ʔet** *ha-kelaħ* ʃal ha-meṭafiziqa.
cause.be.lost.3SM ACC *the-KELAH.SM* on the-metaphysics

'His first book rejects the common view that Kant made metaphysics outdated.'

4.4 Lexical insertions

Transparent figurative idioms were found to be amenable to different types of modifications. Consider the following examples with the idiom *yarad me-ha-ʃec* 'descended from the tree' → 'conceded'.

(48) hi crixa *laredet* *me-ha-ʃec* **ha-cadqani**
she needs.SF *to.descend* *from-the-tree.SM* **the-righteous.SM**
ve-ha-baxyani **ʃe-ʃal-av** hi ṭipsa.
and-the-whiny.SM **that-on-him** she climbed.3SF

'She needs to abandon the righteous and whiny stance which she adopted.'

(49) ʔoto ʃef mesaper ʃe-hu himci ʔet ha-ʕuga ha-popolarit. yeʃ
same chef tells that-he invented ACC the-cake the-popular there.are
kaʔelu ʃe-ħolqim ʃal-av ve-menasim lehorid ʔoto **qcat**
those.PM that-disagree.PM on-him and-try.PM to.bring.down him **bit**
me-ha-ʃec **ha-ʃoqoladi.**
from-the-tree.SM **the-chocolaty.SM**

'The same chef claims that he invented the popular (chocolate) cake. There are those who disagree and try to make him slightly abandon his stance re. chocolate.'

In example (48) the idiomatic tree is modified by two adjectives, and with a relative clause which includes the associated idiom *ṭipes ʃal ʃec gavoha* 'climbed on a tall tree' → 'adopted an unrealistic stance'. In the canonical idiom the adjective *gavoha* 'tall' modifies *ʃec* 'tree' by relating to its literal sense, yet in this example the adjectives modify the assumed idiomatic meaning of *ʃec* 'tree' → 'stance'. The modifier *ʃoqoladi* 'chocolaty' in (49) also modifies *ʃec* 'tree', but in this case it is an external "domain delimiter" (Ernst 1981), which specifies the domain to which the idiom applies.

A different type of variation is exhibited by the following example, where the idiomatic tree is both quantified and pluralized. In addition, the adverb *befeqet* 'quietly' externally modifies the entire phrase.

(50) kulam   *yordim*   **beʃeqeṭ** mi-kol   *ha-ʕecim.*
      everyone *descending*.PM **quietly** from-all *the-trees*
      'Everybody is quietly abandoning all of their stances.'

Opaque figurative idioms exhibit less variation in terms of different types of modification. Following are two examples.

(51) gam gugel   *lo   ṭomenet*   *ʔet yad-a*   **ha-virṭuʔalit** *ba-calaħat.*
      also Google.SF *not burying*.SF ACC *hand*.SF-*her* **the-virtual**.SF *in.the-plate*
      'Google also isn't sitting idle.'

(52) *heʕeleti*   *be-yad-i*   *ħeres*   **muħlaṭ.**
      brought.up.1s *in-hand-my* *shard*.SM **absolute**.SM
      'I absolutely failed.'

The adjective *virṭuʔalit* 'virtual' in (51) is a domain delimiter, similarly to *ʃo-qoladi* 'chocolaty' in (49) above. The modification of *ħeres* 'shard' in (52) is also external: the speaker describes a situation where she searches for something and finds *absolutely* nothing.

The occurrence of modification in cranberry idioms is especially surprising due to their opaqueness and lack of figuration. Nevertheless, as the following examples show, cranberry words are compatible with different types of modifications. In (53) the cranberry word *meduxa* is modified by an adjectival phrase and with a demonstrative, in (54) by a relative clause and in (55) *meduxa* is the head of a construct state NP which is modified by its complement. In all three instances, the modification suggests that the speakers perceive the interpretation of *meduxa* to be 'issue'. A similar case was presented in (32) above.

(53) miʃʔala codeqet ve-nexona zo   ha-meqanenet be-lev   kol
      wish   justified and-right this that-lies   in-heart.CS every
      ha-yoʃvim   *ʃal meduxa*   qaʃa   ve-ṭragit   zo...
      that-sitting.PM on MEDUXA.SF **difficult**.SF **and-tragic**.SF this.SF
      'This justified and right wish, that lies in the heart of all those deliberating on this difficult and tragic issue...'

(54) notnim le-ʃofeṭ *laʃevet ʃal meduxa* **ʃe-lo** **qayemet**, ve-lehaxliṭ
      give to-judge *to.sit* *on* MEDUXA.SF **that-not** **exists.SF** and-to.decide
      ʃe-yeʃ latet lahem ʔet ʔadmot ha-negev ʃelanu.
      that-must to.give to.them ACC plots.CS the-negev ours

      '(They) assign a judge to deliberate on a non-existing issue, and decide
      that our plots in the Negev should be given to them!'

(55) *ʃal meduxat* **heter ʃimuʃ be-neʃeq** le-naʃim kvar *yaʃvu*
      on MEDUXA.SF.CS **license use.CS in-weapon** to-women already *sat.3PM*
      posqei dorenu.
      adjudicators.PM.CS our.generation

      'The adjudicators of our time have already deliberated on the issue of
      women using weapons.'

Instances of lexical insertions with the other cranberry idioms were also found.
In (56) the cranberry word *kelaħ* appears with an indefinite quantifier and an adjective, although it is not clear what it denotes, neither literally nor idiomatically.
In (57) the cranberry word *seʔa* is modified with a relative clause, which refers
to its literal meaning as a measure.

(56) hem ħoqrim ʃe-miʃtamʃim be-ṭexniqot ve-tfisot ʃolam
      they researchers that-use in-techniques.PF and-views.PF.CS world
      ʃe-ʔavad *ʃalei-hem* **ʔeize** *kelaħ* **qaṭan.**
      that-lost.3SM *on-them* **some** KELAH.SM **small.SM**

      'They are researchers who use techniques and world-views that are a bit
      outdated.'

(57) be-caʃad ze *higdaʃtem* *ʔet* *ha-seʔa* **ha-meleʔa gam kax**
      in-step this *overfilled.2PM* ACC *the-SEAH.SF* **the-full.SF also this.way**
      be-piguʃei ṭeror.
      in-attacks.CS terror

      'With this step you overdid a situation that was already too much with
      respect to the terror attacks.'

4.5 Lexical substitutions

4.5.1 Transparent figurative idioms

Note that transparent figurative idioms exhibit lexical substitution of both verbs and nouns. In (58) the verb *yarad* 'descend' is replaced with the more active *qafac* 'jump', without loss of idiomatic meaning.

(58) hu hevin   ʃe-cadaqnu   ve-maca   derex mavriqa
      he understood.3SM that-were.right.1P and-found.3SM way   brilliant
      liqpoc *me-ha-ʃec.*
      to.jump *from-the-tree*

      'He understood that we were right and found a brilliant way to concede.'

The idiom *hosif ʃemen la-medura* 'added oil to the bonfire' → 'aggravated the situation' exhibits lexical substitutions of both the verb and the noun. The verb *hosif* 'add' is substituted by different verbs whose meaning approximates 'adding something (mostly liquid) to something else'. One such case is exemplified in (59). Other examples are *niʃpax* 'be spilled' in (39) and *hidliq* 'ignite' in (40).

(59) wiqipedia   **yoceqet**   ʃemen la-medura   ʃel ħiluqei
      Wikipedia.SF **pouring.SF** *oil*   *to.the-bonfire* of disagreements.CS
      ha-deʃot   ha-beinleʔumiyim.
      the-opinions the-international

      'Wikipedia is seriously aggravating the situation of international disagreements.'

More creative variations are found with the substitution of nouns. In (60) *ʃemen* 'oil' is substituted by the more general *ħomer nafic* 'explosive material', still within the semantic domain of the literal meaning. In (61) it is replaced with an abstract noun which refers to its idiomatic interpretation.

(60) ʔanaħnu lo crixim leħapes ʃod **ħomer nafic**   *lehosif*
      we   not need to.search more **material explosive** *to.add*
      la-medura.
      to.the-bonfire

      'We don't need to search for additional ways to aggravate the situation.'

(61) mazuz ʕacmo *hosif*   *la-medura* ʔet **ha-hitnaḥalut**
Mazuz.SM himself *added.3SM to.the-bonfire* ACC **the-conduct**
ha-ʃaʕaruriyatit be-tiq   qacav.
the-outrageous in-case.CS Katsav

'Mazuz himself aggravated the situation, with the outrageous conduct in Katsav's case.'

4.5.2 Opaque figurative idioms

Lexical substitutions are also found in the category of opaque figurative idioms. In (62) the idiom is exploited to describe not the act of bringing up a piece of shard, but rather the end result: remaining with it in your hand. This change of verb and perspective does not disrupt the meaning of the idiom.

(62) ʔazai kʃe-tagiʕa   kvar le-bḥinat   ha-hitqadmut
then when-will.arrive.2SM already to-examination.CS the-step
ha-hamcaʔatit **tivater**   ʕim ḥeres be-yad-xa.
the-inventive **will.remain.2SM with** *shard in-hand-your*

'When you finally get to the examination of inventive step you will have failed.'

In (63) and (64) the hand which in the canonical idiom is buried (or not) in the plate, is replaced with other instruments: a camera and a sting. These expressions can only be understood provided that the canonical idiom is known.

(63) gam nadav *lo ṭaman*   **maclema-to** *ba-calaḥat*
also Nadav.SM *not buried.3SM* **camera-his** *in.the-plate*
ve-cilem   ba-mozeʔon lelo heref.
and-photographed.3SM in.the-museum without stop

'Nadav also didn't refrain from using a camera, and took pictures in the museum without stopping.'

(64) gam ha-cirʕa *lo ṭomenet* ʔet **ʕoqc-a** *ba-calaḥat.*
also the-wasp.SF *not bury.SF* ACC **sting-her** *in.the-plate*

'The wasp also does not refrain from using its sting.'

4.5.3 Cranberry idioms

Cranberry idioms are also subject to lexical substitutions. There are a few instances of the idiom *lo yesula be-paz* 'will not be SULA in gold' → 'priceless' where the cranberry verb *sula* is replaced with a Hebrew synonym *heʕerix* 'evaluate'. One such example is given in (65).

(65) ze   mifgaʃ   hevrati   ʃe-leʕolam lo yahzor   ve-ʔein
      this get.together.SM social.SM that-never not will.return.3SM *and-not*
      lehaʕarix-o   *be-paz.*
      to.evaluate-him *in-gold*

      'This is a social get-together that will never return and should be considered priceless.'

In (66) the verb *yaʃav* 'sit' is substituted by the verb *hitqabec* 'gather', yet the idiomatic meaning is maintained.

(66) *ʕal meduxa*   zo   **hitqabcu**   harbe melumadim.
      on MEDUXA.SF this.SF **gathered.P** many scholars

      'Many scholars have deliberated on this issue.'

4.6 Discussion

Verbal MWEs in Hebrew turned out to be consistently more flexible than would be expected given Nunberg et al.'s (1994) categorical bifurcation. All the idioms we investigated in this study exhibited flexibility to a certain extent. The variations exhibited by the transparent figurative idioms refer to both the literal and the figurative meanings of the expressions. Thus, speakers can relate to the tree in *yarad me-ha-ʕec* 'descended from the tree' → 'conceded' in its literal meaning as an entity with physical properties (e.g., 'tall' in 36) which can be physically manipulated, either by climbing down from it (in the canonical form) or by jumping down from it (58). The height of the tree or the manner with which one descends from it transfer metaphorically to the idiomatic meaning of the phrase. Conversely, speakers can also attribute to the tree in the idiom abstract properties which are only appropriate in the context of the idiom (e.g., *cadqani ve-baxyani* 'righteous and whiny' in 48).

Even more flexibility is found with the transparent figurative idiom *hosif ʃemen la-medura* 'added oil to the bonfire' → 'aggravated the situation'. The vivid picture which this idiom conjures allows speakers to describe it in different terms, while still maintaining the idiomatic meaning. Thus, we find lexical substitutions for both the verb *hosif* 'add' and the noun *ʃemen* 'oil', which refers to the material added to the bonfire (both literal as in (60) and idiomatic as in (61)). As far as we can tell, the word *medura* 'bonfire' cannot be substituted.

On the other side of the flexibility continuum are the opaque figurative idioms. While different types of variations were found to be compatible with these idioms, this class exhibited a more constrained behavior. We did not find any evidence for instances of relativization, and only a handful of cases of lexical insertions. Lexical substitutions, too, were rare. The two examples given for *ṭaman yad-o ba-calaḥat* 'buried his hand in the plate' → 'refrained from acting' in (63) and (64) are instances of what could be considered as "word play". Furthermore, the opacity of this idiom is especially evident in light of attested instances where its use reflects a wrong/alternative interpretation of the idiom, one in which the burying of the hand indicates involvement in something. This is illustrated in (67).

(67) ʔarbaʕim ḥavarot   beinleʔumiyot ṭomnot ʔet yad-an
      forty   companies.PF international.PF *bury.*PF ACC *hand-their*
      be-calaḥat   ha-zihum   ha-gduʃa ʃel sin.
      *in-plate.*SF.CS the-pollution the-full.SF of China

      'Forty international companies are involved in heavily polluted China.'

We suggest that the combination of figuration and opacity emphasizes the idiosyncracy of these idioms, and consequently speakers are more conservative in the way that they use them.

We were especially surprised by the behavior of the cranberry idioms. Our initial expectation was that the lack of transparency and figuration would render these idioms more rigid. Our corpus findings, however, reveal a different picture. The usage patterns exhibited by these idioms suggest that speakers attribute to the meaningless cranberry words some semantic content, or to put it more idiomatically – breathe new life into them. As was illustrated and discussed above, the usage patterns of these idioms suggest that speakers are imposing some interpretation on cranberry words. The word *meduxa* in *yaʃav ʃal ha-meduxa* 'sat on the MEDUXA' → 'deliberated' is interpreted as denoting the issue which is under deliberation (see 32, 53 and 55). A similar situation is found with respect to *kelaḥ*. From the examples, we can see that in spite of its lack of meaning it is conceptualized as a physical object which can be small (56) and can become rusty (38). Moreover, it can function as the topic of a clause (27 & 38). It would seem that the meaninglessness of cranberry words frees speakers to apply their own interpretation to them, and to provide idioms which are opaque and non-figurative with transparency and figuration.

4.7 Conclusion

In this chapter we challenged the predictive ability attributed to the notion of decomposability by Nunberg et al. (1994). We argued that this notion is too fuzzy to be used as a principle for reliably categorizing idioms, and, moreover, that it cannot be used to predict their flexibility or rigidity. On the contrary, we hypothesized that idioms cannot be categorically classified as either flexible or rigid, rather, that they occupy a continuum, with different idioms exhibiting varying degrees of flexibility.

We questioned the validity of the assumption that some idioms are completely rigid (modulo verbal inflection) and demonstrated that even the quintessential non-decomposable idiom *kick the bucket* can undergo transformations. However, since this idiom is used relatively rarely and idiom variations in and of themselves are relatively infrequent, non-canonical instances of it and other infrequent idioms can only be empirically attested in very large corpora. This, we believe, is an important methodological finding, which at this point in time, with the availability of large annotated corpora, cannot be overlooked.

Rather than focusing on decomposability as a defining property of idioms, we considered two distinct semantic dimensions: FIGURATION and TRANSPARENCY. We hypothesized that the more figurative and transparent an idiom is, the more amenable it is to various transformations. Our corpus-based investigation and subsequent comparison of idioms associated with three semantic types (transparent figurative, opaque figurative and opaque non-figurative) revealed that the usage patterns of opaque figurative idioms are the most conservative among the three.

Opacity, however, was found not to be the sole "culprit", since cranberry idioms which contain meaningless words were found to be relatively flexible. Thus, we propose that neither transparency nor figuration alone can account for the behavior of idioms. Our findings suggest that there is an interaction between the two dimensions. Figurative idioms are flexible dependent on their transparency: when transparent they are relatively amenable to various transformations. Conversely, the flexibility of opaque idioms depends on their figuration: when opaque idioms are not figurative due to the inclusion of meaningless cranberry words speakers can ascribe to these meaningless words content which renders the idioms more figurative and less opaque, and consequently – more flexible. Naturally, this generalization, which is based on our work on only a limited set of Hebrew verbal idioms, requires further investigation.

Abbreviations

1/2/3	person	ACC	accusative case
S/P	number	CS	construct state
F/M	gender		

Acknowledgements

This research was supported by The Israel Science Foundation (grant No. 505/11).

References

Abeillé, Anne. 1995. The flexibility of French idioms: A representation with lexical tree adjoining grammar. In M. Everaert, E. van der Linden, A. Schen & R. Schreuder (eds.), *Idioms: Structural and psychological perspectives*, chap. 1, 15–42. Hillsdale: Lawrence Erlbaum Associates.

Bargmann, Sascha & Manfred Sailer. 2015. *Syntactic flexibility of non-decomposable idioms.* Poster at the 4th General PARSEME Meeting, Valletta, Malta.

Baroni, Marco, Silvia Bernardini, Adriano Ferraresi & Eros Zanchetta. 2009. The WaCky wide web: A collection of very large linguistically processed web-crawled corpora. *Language Resources and Evaluation* 43(3). 209–226. DOI:10.1007/s10579-009-9081-4

Chafe, Wallace L. 1968. Idiomaticity as an anomaly in the Chomskyan paradigm. *Foundations of language* 4(2). 109–127.

Doron, Edit. 2003. Agency and voice: The semantics of the Semitic templates. *Natural Language Semantics* 11(1). 1–67.

Doron, Edit. 2008. The contribution of the template to verb meaning. In Galia Hatav (ed.), *Modern linguistics of Hebrew*, 57–88. Jerusalem: Magnes Press. In Hebrew.

Erman, Britt & Beatrice Warren. 2000. The idiom principle and the open choice principle. *Text* 20(1). 29–62.

Ernst, Thomas. 1981. Grist for the linguistic mill: Idioms and 'extras' adjectives. *Journal of Linguistic Research* 1(3). 51–68.

Fellbaum, Christiane (ed.). 1998. *WordNet: An electronic lexical database* (Language, Speech and Communication). MIT Press.

Gibbs, Raymond W. & Nandini P. Nayak. 1989. Psycholinguistic studies on the syntactic behavior of idioms. *Cognitive psychology* 21(1). 100–138.

Gibbs, Raymond W., Nandini P. Nayak, John L. Bolton & Melissa E. Keppel. 1989. Speakers' assumptions about the lexical flexibility of idioms. *Memory & Cognition* 17(1). 58–68.

Grégoire, Nicole. 2007. Design and implementation of a lexicon of Dutch multi-word expressions. In *Proceedings of the workshop on a Broader Perspective on Multiword Expressions*, 17–24. Prague, Czech Republic: Association for Computational Linguistics. http://www.aclweb.org/anthology/W/W07/W07-1103.

Jackendoff, Ray. 1997. *The architecture of the language faculty.* Cambridge, MA, USA: MIT Press.

Kilgarriff, Adam, Pavel Rychly, Pavel Smrz & David Tugwell. 2004. The Sketch engine. In *Proceedings of EURALEX*, 105–116. Lorient, France.

Melnik, Nurit. 2016. *The development of the VOS construction.* Paper presented at the "Language contact, language continuity and change, and the emergence of Modern Hebrew" workshop, Hebrew University, Jerusalem.

Moon, Rosamund. 1998. *Fixed expressions and idioms in English: A corpus-based approach.* Oxford: Oxford University Press.

Nunberg, Geoffrey, Ivan Sag & Thomas Wasow. 1994. Idioms. *Language* 70(3). 491–538.

Riehemann, Susanne. 2001. *A constructional approach to idioms and word formation.* Stanford University dissertation.

Sag, Ivan, Timothy Baldwin, Francis Bond, Ann Copestake & Dan Flickinger. 2002. Multiword expressions: A pain in the neck for NLP. In *Proceedings of the 3rd international conference on Computational Linguistics and Intelligent Text Processing* (Lecture Notes in Computer Science 2276), 1–15. Springer.

Schenk, André. 1995. The syntactic behavior of idioms. In M. Everaert, E. van der Linden, A. Schen & R. Schreuder (eds.), *Idioms: Structural and psychological perspectives*, 253–272. Hillsdale: Lawrence Erlbaum Associates.

Titone, Debra A. & Cynthia M. Connine. 1994. Descriptive norms for 171 idiomatic expressions: Familiarity, compositionality, predictability, and literality. *Metaphor and Symbol* 9(4). 247–270.

Trawinski, Beata, Manfred Sailer, Jan-Philipp Soehn, Lothar Lemnitzer & Frank Richter. 2008. Cranberry expressions in English and in German. In *Proceedings of the LREC workshop Towards a Shared Task for Multiword Expressions (MWE 2008)*, 35–38.

Webelhuth, Gert & Farrell Ackerman. 1999. A lexical-functional analysis of predicate topicalization in German. *American Journal of Germanic Linguistics and Literatures* 11(01). 1–61.

Chapter 3

Multiword expressions in an LFG grammar for Norwegian

Helge Dyvik
University of Bergen

Gyri Smørdal Losnegaard
University of Bergen

Victoria Rosén
University of Bergen

This chapter describes the analysis of multiword expressions in NorGram, an LFG grammar of Norwegian. All multiword expressions need to be accounted for in the lexicon, but in different ways depending on the flexibility of the expression. Each multiword expression is provided with a lexical entry that has a special predicate name incorporating the lexical items that the multiword consists of and that specifies the argument structure of the predicate. In this way, analyses are provided for a wide range of multiword types, including fixed expressions, phrasal verbs, verbal idioms, and others.

1 Introduction

In this chapter we[1] show how multiword expressions (MWEs) are represented in NorGram, a hand-written computational grammar of Norwegian (Dyvik 2000). The grammar is couched in the Lexical-Functional Grammar (LFG) formalism (Bresnan 2001; Dalrymple 2001). It was first developed in the context of the Parallel Grammar Project (ParGram), an international cooperative effort to develop

---

[1]The authors have contributed equally and are listed in alphabetical order.

Helge Dyvik, Gyri Smørdal Losnegaard & Victoria Rosén. 2019. Multiword expressions in an LFG grammar for Norwegian. In Yannick Parmentier & Jakub Waszczuk (eds.), *Representation and parsing of multiword expressions: Current trends*, 69–108. Berlin: Language Science Press. DOI:10.5281/zenodo.2579037

parallel LFG grammars for a number of languages (Butt et al. 2002). The Xerox Linguistic Environment (XLE) is the platform we use for grammar development and parsing (Maxwell & Kaplan 1993).

NorGram contains about 380 complex syntactic rules, corresponding to a transition network with more than 160,000 states and more than 4.7 million arcs. The lexicon comprises approximately 180,000 lemmas for Norwegian Bokmål and 110,000 lemmas for Norwegian Nynorsk. NorGram uses not only the grammar rules and the lexicon but also templates to efficiently encode linguistic generalizations. As noted in Dalrymple et al. (2004: 207), templates in LFG grammars "can play the same role in capturing linguistic generalizations as hierarchical type systems in theories like HPSG". Templates are for instance used to express generalizations about subcategorization frames for verbs; there are more than 200 such verbal templates.

NorGram analyzes several types of MWEs, including fixed and flexible expressions. The classification of MWEs according to their relative flexibility was initially proposed for English (Sag et al. 2002; Baldwin & Kim 2010), presupposing that MWEs with the same degree of flexibility may receive the same or similar treatment in NLP systems. The distinction between fixed, semi-fixed and syntactically flexible MWEs may thus be useful also for other languages than English, although the criteria for distinguishing between the classes may vary.

Fixed MWEs are found in most languages with MWEs and in basically every part of speech. These are expressions that are completely invariable, with no morphosyntactic variation or internal modification, such as the adverb *by the way* and the determiner *each and every*. Semi-fixed MWEs, as defined for English, allow some lexical and morphological variation such as limited internal modification and inflection, while the relative word order of the components does not change. Examples are compound nominals (*chicken soup*), proper names, such as *Donald Duck*, and the subset of verbal idioms with fixed word order, such as *shoot the breeze* 'chat' and *kick the bucket* 'die'. Syntactically-flexible expressions display a wider range of flexibility, allowing some or all types of syntactic variation including passivization, relativization and other operations that are not possible in semi-fixed MWEs. All flexible MWEs are verbal. They include verb-particle constructions, light verbs, and the subset of verbal idioms whose word order is less restricted than semi-fixed expressions. Table 1 illustrates how common types of English MWEs distribute over these classes.

The syntactic variation in verbal MWEs in English has given rise to a theory of semantic decomposability (Nunberg et al. 1994) which has led to increased interest in the relation between the syntax and semantics of verbal MWEs. Semantic decomposability is a measure of whether the meaning of the expression

Table 1: Classes of flexibility

Flexibility class	Type	Example MWE
Fixed		*by the way*
Semi-fixed	compound nominals	*chicken soup*
	proper names	*Donald Duck*
	non-decomposable idioms	*kick the bucket*
Flexible	verb-particle constructions	*give up*
	light verbs	*give a speech*
	decomposable idioms	*spill the beans*

distributes over the MWE components or only relates to the expression as a whole. It may explain why individual parts of an expression may be fronted, topicalized, and relativized, and may also in other ways contribute meaningfully to the information structure of the sentence. On the other hand, semantic non-decomposability blocks compositional interpretations, which again explains why semi-fixed MWEs are not subject to operations that would normally indicate that their components are associated with some independent meaning.

While a distinction between semantically decomposable and nondecomposable verbal idioms may also hold for Norwegian, the correlation between syntactic flexibility and semantic decomposability seems less conspicuous than for English. In particular, Norwegian has subject-verb inversion in interrogative main clauses, so that the word order will vary in MWEs that are otherwise highly restricted. Most verbal idioms may also undergo at least some modification (e.g., impersonal passives). Furthermore, the mechanisms for representing restrictions and variation in NorGram are technically the same for semi-fixed and flexible MWEs. Since no distinction is reflected in the way verbal MWEs are represented in the lexicon and grammar, all such MWEs are considered flexible, and MWEs with similar morphosyntactic properties are accounted for with templates which are in effect mini-grammars for subsets of MWEs.

With respect to subtypes of MWEs, the types of MWEs analyzed by NorGram more or less correspond to the types in Table 1, with a few exceptions. As in many other Germanic languages, compound nominals in Norwegian form single graphical words. These are thus not considered multiword expressions. In addition to prepositional verbs, NorGram analyzes nouns and adjectives with selected prepositions as MWEs. Expressions that are completely regular on the morphological and syntactic levels, such as light verb constructions, are analyzed composition-ally by the grammar and are not represented in the lexicon as MWEs. A special case is complex numerals such as *hundre og to* 'one hundred two' and *to og nitti* 'ninety two', which may also be considered a subtype of MWE. The particular syntax and semantics of such expressions is accounted for with a special set of lexical entries and syntactic rules.

NorGramBank, a large parsebank for Norwegian, has been created by parsing a corpus with NorGram (Dyvik et al. 2016). Because of lexical and syntactic am-biguity, parsing with NorGram often results in many analyses for each sentence, and efficient disambiguation is therefore necessary. The INESS project[2] has de-veloped a treebanking infrastructure for parsing, disambiguating, storing, and searching the texts in NorGramBank (Rosén et al. 2012). The parsebank currently consists of about 60 million words of analyzed text, of which sentences covering 350,000 words have been manually disambiguated by computer-generated dis-criminants (Rosén et al. 2007). The remainder of the corpus has been stochasti-cally disambiguated. INESS Search is a tool for searching in LFG and other tree-banks in the treebanking infrastructure (Meurer 2012). MWEs are analyzed by NorGram in such a way that the different types may be searched for.

The original lexical resource used for the NorGram lexicon, NorKompLeks, contained a small number of fixed expressions (Nordgård 2000). The main design of the treatment of MWEs in NorGram was developed during ParGram (Butt et al. 2002) and especially during the LOGON machine translation project (Lønning et al. 2004). A large number of MWEs have been added to NorGram's lexicon dur-ing the construction of NorGramBank. When disambiguators discovered MWEs that did not receive an analysis or that received an incorrect analysis, they con-structed new lexical entries or edited existing lexical entries as needed in order to cover the MWEs (Losnegaard et al. 2012; Rosén et al. 2016).

This chapter is organized as follows. In Section 2 an overview of the basics of LFG is given, showing how constructions without MWEs are analyzed in Nor-Gram as a background for the treatment of MWEs in the following sections. Sec-tion 3 illustrates the NorGram analysis of MWEs, both fixed expressions and flexible expressions such as phrasal verbs, verbal idioms, and nonverbal flexible expressions. Section 4 shows how various syntactic modifications are handled, in-cluding intervening words, long-distance dependencies and passive alternations. Section 5 discusses numerous complex complementation patterns that are cov-ered by NorGram for Norwegian MWEs. Section 6 presents our conclusions.

---

[2]http://clarino.uib.no/iness

2 Syntactic analysis in LFG

LFG analyses have two distinct levels of syntactic representation: constituent structure (c-structure) and functional structure (f-structure). The c-structure is a phrase structure tree that represents precedence and dominance relations. The f-structure is an attribute-value matrix with information about grammatical functions such as subject and object and grammatical features such as tense, gender and number. An example of a NorGram analysis of the sentence in (1) is given in Figure 1.[3]

(1) Hun tenkte   på buss-en.
     she thought on bus-DEF.SG

     'She was thinking (while) on the bus./She thought about the bus.'

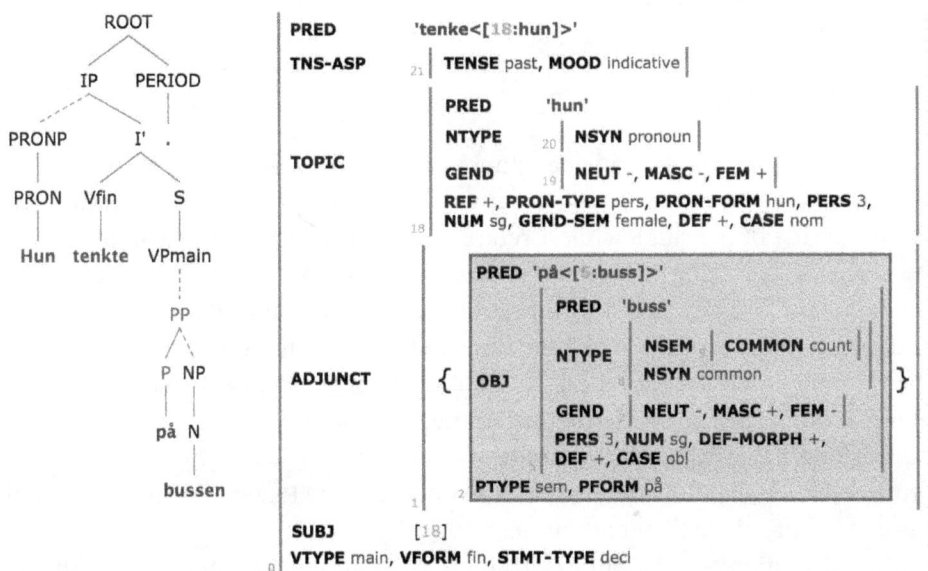

Figure 1: C- and f-structure for *Hun tenkte på bussen*.

This sentence is ambiguous, as shown by the two idiomatic translations. The analysis in Figure 1 concerns the first translation, where the prepositional phrase

---

[3]In this example the morphological structure of the word form *bussen* is indicated since it is relevant for the analysis being discussed. Otherwise, we simplify the glossing by omitting morpheme-by-morpheme analysis and using two English words to render one Norwegian word when necessary.

på bussen 'on the bus' is an adjunct (adverbial). The second reading, where *tenke på* 'think about' is a phrasal verb, will be treated in Section 3.2.

The phrase structure rules and lexicon of an LFG grammar assign the c-structure. NorGram uses a version of X'-syntax that is inspired by Bresnan (2001), with some adjustments which depart from strictly binary branching structures.

The f-structure is projected from the c-structure by the functional description (f-description), which describes correspondences between the two levels. One such correspondence is illustrated in Figure 1 by the highlighting of the PP node and the corresponding partial f-structure. The phrase structure rules that assign this f-structure are given in (2) and (3). The rule daughters are listed vertically after the horizontal arrow, with each node's functional annotations following after a colon.[4]

(2) PP $\rightarrow$ P: $\uparrow=\downarrow$
  NP: $(\uparrow \text{OBJ}) = \downarrow$

(3) NP $\rightarrow$ N: $\uparrow=\downarrow$

The annotations on the rule daughters describe the associated f-structures. In the equations, $\uparrow$ refers to the f-structure of the mother node (the category on the left-hand side of the rule), while $\downarrow$ refers to the f-structure of the daughter node (the category carrying the annotation on the right-hand side of the rule). Thus the equation $\uparrow=\downarrow$ annotated to a rule daughter means that the daughter node and its mother node will project the same f-structure. The equation $(\uparrow \text{OBJ}) = \downarrow$ on the NP node in (2) specifies that the f-structure of the mother node (PP) has an object (OBJ) which is the f-structure of the daughter node (NP). In this way the highlighted f-structure with the index "2" at its lower left corner in Figure 1 is projected from the PP node. Both the PP node and the P node are highlighted in the c-structure since they both project this same f-structure.

The annotations on the phrase structure rules account for only part of the information in the f-structure. Other information comes from the word forms in the terminal nodes of the tree. For instance, the lexical and morphological information for the word *bussen* contributes all the equations in (4). These equations are part of the f-description for the f-structure that is the value of the OBJ attribute (with the index "5") in Figure 1.

---

[4] The examples of rules, lexical entries, and templates in the following are simplified for the purpose of exposition. Neither the format nor the content is exactly the same as in NorGram.

(4) ($\uparrow$ PRED) = 'buss'
     ($\uparrow$ NTYPE NSEM COMMON) = count
     ($\uparrow$ NTYPE NSYN) = common
     ($\uparrow$ GEND NEUT) = −
     ($\uparrow$ GEND MASC) = +
     ($\uparrow$ GEND FEM) = −
     ($\uparrow$ PERS) = 3
     ($\uparrow$ NUM) = sg
     ($\uparrow$ DEF-MORPH) = +
     ($\uparrow$ DEF) = +

The first equation, which assigns the PRED(icate) value 'buss', is specific to this noun, but the others are common to many other words. Some of the equations come from features assigned to the word form *bussen* by the morphological analyzer run prior to parsing; these features are +Noun, +Sg, +Def and +Masc, and they will appear in the string presented to the syntactic parser. Other equations come from the lexical entry for the noun *buss*. Both the features and the noun must have entries in the lexicon; these are shown in (5–9). Each lexical entry specifies a lexical category; SUFF (for suffix) is the category for morphological features.

(5) +Noun SUFF ($\uparrow$ PERS) = 3

(6) +Sg   SUFF ($\uparrow$ NUM) = sg

(7) +Def   SUFF @DEF

(8) +Masc SUFF @MASC

(9) buss   N   @(COUNTNOUN buss)

The equations in the first two entries each contribute one attribute-value pair to the f-structure. Entries (7–9) contain template invocations rather than equations. The @-sign indicates a call to a template, while DEF, MASC and COUNTNOUN are names of templates. A template is an f-description, a collection of equations which it is convenient to refer to by a name rather than listing all the equations. Templates can be used in different places in the grammar and lexicon, and template definitions may refer to other templates.

The definition of the template named DEF is shown in (10). All nouns inflected in the definite form will carry these two equations, so it can be convenient to refer to them together.

Helge Dyvik, Gyri Smørdal Losnegaard & Victoria Rosén

(10)   DEF =
          $(\uparrow$ DEF-MORPH) = +
          $(\uparrow$ DEF) = +

Norwegian has a complicated system of gender agreement because of some nouns that may have either masculine or feminine agreement, and because adjectives and determiners may be unspecified for certain gender distinctions. To account for this, each noun must receive a plus or minus value for each of the three genders. The equations needed for specifying masculine gender are included in the template in (11). These equations do not simply describe attribute-value pairs; they describe paths through the f-structure. The equation $(\uparrow$ GEND MASC) = + states that the f-structure has an attribute GEND which has as its value a subsidiary f-structure which in its turn has an attribute MASC with the value +.

(11)   MASC =
          $(\uparrow$ GEND MASC) = +
          $(\uparrow$ GEND FEM) = −
          $(\uparrow$ GEND NEUT) = −

Like the template MASC, the template COUNTNOUN also describes paths through the f-structure. The NTYPE NSYN features distinguish between common nouns, proper nouns, pronouns, etc. while the NTYPE NSEM COMMON features distinguish between count nouns, mass nouns, etc. All nouns must contribute a PRED feature to the f-structure, but the PRED feature itself will differ from noun to noun. The template in (12) is parameterized; the parameter P will be substituted by the argument supplied in the invocation of the template, for example the word *buss* in (9).

(12)   COUNTNOUN (P) =
          $(\uparrow$ PRED) = P
          $(\uparrow$ NTYPE NSEM COMMON) = count
          $(\uparrow$ NTYPE NSYN) = common

The value of a PRED attribute is a semantic form. A semantic form is always enclosed in single quotation marks, indicating that the value is unique, which means that it cannot be unified even with an identical-looking value of some other attribute. For some words the semantic form includes not only the word itself, but also a syntactic argument list. This is the case for two of the words in *hun tenker på bussen* (in the interpretation being considered in this section). The verb has the semantic form 'tenke⟨[SUBJ]⟩', meaning that the verb is intransitive

76

and subcategorizes only for a subject, and the preposition has the semantic form 'på⟨[OBJ]⟩', indicating that it requires an object.

Verbs can of course subcategorize for several arguments. For example, the verb *slå* 'hit' has the semantic form 'slå⟨[SUBJ,OBJ]⟩' since it requires a subject and an object. The completeness requirement for f-structures stipulates that each of the syntactic functions mentioned in the semantic form of a PRED feature must occur on the same level of f-structure as that PRED. There is also a coherence requirement to the effect that subcategorizable syntactic functions may only occur on the same level of f-structure as a PRED feature if they are mentioned in its semantic form. The argument lists in semantic forms are thus crucial for determining grammaticality. The semantic forms "govern the process of semantic interpretation" (Kaplan & Bresnan 1982: 177).

3 Implementing MWEs

The crucial challenge of representing MWEs is that they defy normal compositional analysis. The LFG solution that is implemented in NorGram is to assign to each MWE a special lexical entry that has its own PRED value and thus its own argument structure. Each MWE has a semantic form with a special predicate name and a list of any syntactic arguments that this predicate requires. This will be shown in detail for the various types of MWEs in the following.

3.1 Fixed expressions

Fixed expressions, such as *ad hoc*, *déjà vu*, and *vice versa*, are those that do not vary with respect to inflection and that do not admit any internal modification. They are also called inflexible expressions or "words with spaces". Fixed expressions are the simplest MWEs to implement; they are entered into the NorGram lexicon as single graphical words containing white space, so they are literally treated as words with spaces.

(13) Hun likte **i bunn og grunn** ikke **New York i det hele tatt**.
     she liked in bottom and ground not New York in the whole taken
     'She basically didn't like New York at all.'

The sentence in (13) contains three such expressions: *i bunn og grunn*, *New York*, and *i det hele tatt*.[5] The c-structure of (13) is shown in Figure 2. The simplified

---

[5] In this and subsequent examples the lexically fixed words making up the MWE are highlighted with boldface.

f-structure is shown in Figure 3; this is the "PREDs only" view of f-structure where feature paths that do not end in PRED values are suppressed. The three expressions belong to different parts of speech: ADVcmt (commitment adverb), PROP (proper noun), and ADVs (sentence adverb). The adverbs have the function ADJUNCT in the f-structure while the proper noun functions as the OBJ. There are numerous fixed expressions in most parts of speech in Norwegian.

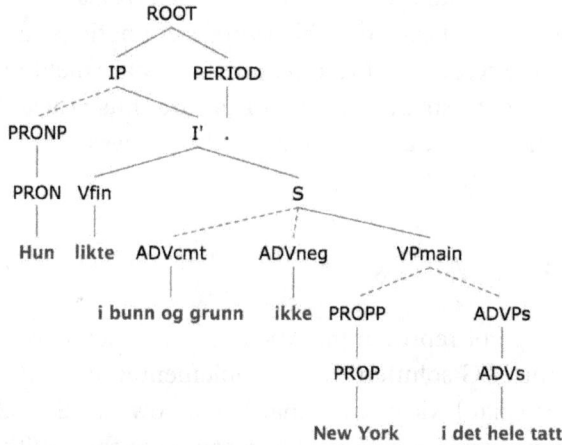

Figure 2: C-structure for example (13)

Figure 3: F-structure for example (13)

3.2 Basic properties of flexible MWEs and method of analysis

Flexible expressions may exhibit a great deal of syntactic variation, but in some respects they are inherently fixed or restricted. One of the characterizing features of MWEs is that they are lexically fixed, meaning that they consist of at least two words that cannot be substituted with near-synonyms or semantically related words without the expression losing its idiomatic meaning. The verbal idiom *komme på kant med* in (14) has four such fixed lexical words.

(14)   Hun var ikke villig   til å **komme på kant med** det gode selskap.
      she was not willing to to come   on edge with the good company

      'She was not willing to fall out with the in-crowd.'

Flexible MWEs are often also morphosyntactically restricted, with constraints on grammatical features, on the modification of component words, and on specifiers such as quantifiers and determiners. For instance, the noun *kant* in (14) can only be in the singular indefinite form, and it does not admit any specifiers or modifiers. The PP *på kant med*, however, does admit modifiers; in (15) the modifier *helt* 'completely' has scope over the entire expression. In NorGram, no distinction is currently made in the representation of internal and (semantically) external modification of MWEs.

(15)   Hun **kom** helt **på kant med** det gode selskap.
      she   came fully on edge with the good society

      'She completely fell out with the in-crowd.'

The mechanisms for representing lexical and morphological restrictions in flexible MWEs are the same as the ones used for regular constructions. As described in Section 2, simplex words are assigned predicate values through equations in the lexical entry, as in the entry for the simplex lexeme *buss* in example (4), which has the predicate assignment equation ($\uparrow$ PRED) = 'buss'. For words that subcategorize for other elements, such as verbs, this is done through the assignment of a predicate-argument structure (or subcategorization frame). For instance, the intransitive verb *klage* 'complain' is assigned a frame through the template call @(V-SUBJ klage) in the lexical entry, invoking the template V-SUBJ. Part of this template is shown in (16).

(16)   V-SUBJ (P) =
            ($\uparrow$ PRED) = 'P$\langle$($\uparrow$ SUBJ)$\rangle$'

The predicate value of the verb is parameterized and listed together with its arguments in the subcategorization frame, which includes everything between quotation marks in (16). When the template is invoked, the lemma form *klage* in the template call replaces the parameter P. The equation on the second line assigns one argument, the subject, to P, yielding the predicate-argument structure 'klage$\langle$($\uparrow$ SUBJ)$\rangle$' as the PRED value for the intransitive reading of this verb.

Lexical fixedness in flexible MWEs is handled through lexical selection in the entry of the subcategorizing word. In addition to its usual intransitive reading, the verb *klage* 'complain' is the syntactic head of the VP idiom *klage sin nød* 'pour out one's troubles', where it subcategorizes for the object noun *nød* 'need'.

(17) Og hun **klaget**   **sin nød** til alle som ville   høre.
      and she complained her need to all   who wanted hear

'And she poured out her troubles to everyone who wanted to listen.'

Lexical entries for VP idioms are listed as alternative subcategorization frames under the entry of the verb. As in the case of simplex verbs, templates assign predicate-argument structures and other relevant features. The word that subcategorizes for the other parts of the MWE lists the predicate values of the selected arguments together with its own predicate value in the template invocation. The template call in (18) shows that the verb *klage* selects the noun *nød*.

(18)   @(VPIDIOM-DEFOBJ klage nød)

(19) $(\uparrow$ PRED$) = $'%FN$\langle(\uparrow$ SUBJ$)\rangle(\uparrow$ OBJ$)$'

The predicate values of the fixed MWE components, i.e. the verb and its selected complements, are merged to form one single idiom predicate which is substituted for the relevant parameter in the predicate-argument structure. In one of the equations in the template, the predicate assignment in (19), the parameter %FN is replaced by the predicate name textsfklage#nød, where we use the symbol "#" to signal idiomatic combinations of this kind. Only the free arguments of verbal MWEs are specified as semantic arguments to the verb. The subcategorization frame 'klage#nød$\langle(\uparrow$ SUBJ$)\rangle(\uparrow$ OBJ$)$' lists the semantic argument, in this case SUBJ, inside the angled brackets, while the selected argument OBJ is placed outside the brackets. The parameter %FN and the construction of predicate names such as klage#nød are accounted for in Section 3.3.1.

Constraints on grammatical features are specified with constraining equations and existential constraints in the entries or templates. A constraining equation is an equation with a "c" attached to the equal sign. This means that the equation does not actually assign the specified value to the attribute in the f-structure; instead it requires that this value has been assigned to the attribute somewhere else. The restriction that the object *sin nød* in (17) must be definite is specified with the equation in (20). The constraint in (21) is an existential constraint which simply provides a path of attributes without assigning a particular value. The interpretation is that this path of attributes must have some value in the f-structure, thus ensuring that there is a possessive.

(20) $(\uparrow$ OBJ DEF$) = $c +.

(21) (↑ OBJ SPEC POSS POSS-TYPE)

(22) ~(↑ OBJ SPEC)

The selection of grammatical words and modifiers is handled in a slightly different way from the selection of syntactic heads. If a determiner is selected or otherwise restricted, this is specified with a constraint requiring that the type or form of the determiner must match the specification. The existential constraint in (21) ensures that a possessive will specify *nød*. If no determiner is possible in an idiom, this is specified with a negative constraint, as in (22).

Lexical constraints on modifiers are represented in the same way as grammatical constraints, using equations. Some nouns do not admit modification at all, such as *kant* in (14). Others may require that the choice of modifier is restricted to a specific predicate or set of predicates, such as *øye* 'eye' in the VP idiom *ha et godt øye til* 'have eyes for' in (23), where the only possible modifier is the adjective *god* 'good'.

(23) Det kan være han **har et godt øye til** deg.
      it   can be   he has a good eye to you
      'He might have eyes for you.'

When a modifier is lexically restricted, a constraint equation is used to specify the possible modifier predicate(s). In the entry for *ha et godt øye til*, the equation in (24) ensures that the modifier (ADJUNCT) of the selected object (the noun *øye*) has the PRED value god.

(24) (↑ OBJ ADJUNCT PRED) = c god

The treatment of lexical restrictions in VP idioms in NorGram thus depends on the function of the component word within the MWE. While syntactic heads are subcategorized for by the verb, dependents are specified using constraint equations.

3.3 Phrasal verbs

Phrasal verbs are MWEs consisting of a verb and an adverb, preposition or other word that together have a meaning that is in some way idiosyncratic. It is common to distinguish between two main classes of phrasal verbs, prepositional verbs and verb-particle constructions. We present these two types in Sections 3.3.1 and 3.3.2, respectively. There are also constructions where both prepositions and particles occur; these are presented in Section 3.3.3.

3.3.1 Prepositional verbs

In Section 2 the sentence in (1) *Hun tenkte på bussen* was shown to have two readings. When the prepositional phrase functions as an adjunct, the analysis shown in Figure 1 obtains. When the preposition is selected by the verb, the verb and the preposition constitute an MWE, as indicated in (25), where these words are boldfaced. The analysis corresponding to this reading is shown in Figure 4.

(25) Hun **tenkte** **på** bussen.
      she   thought on the bus
      'She thought about the bus.'

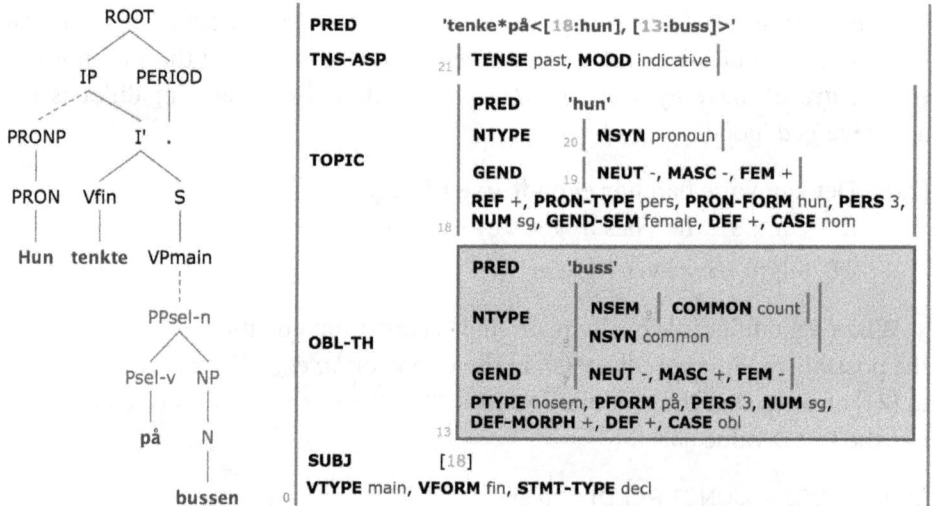

Figure 4: C- and f-structure for example (25)

In the c-structure *på bussen* forms a prepositional phrase PPsel-n, marked as selected by sel-n in the node label. This analysis captures the fact that the selected preposition *på* can only occur before the object, and that the preposition and its complement behave as one constituent with respect to movement, as in the topicalized version *På bussen tenkte hun ofte* 'The bus she was often thinking of'. The preposition does not provide its own predicate in the f-structure, but is analyzed as incorporated in the predicate expressed by the verb to form the predicate name tenke*på. In predicate names the symbol "*" is used to signal such combinations of a lexical predicate with a selected particle or preposition. The complement of the preposition, *bussen*, fills the function OBL-TH – oblique-theta – as an argument of this predicate, i.e., an oblique argument expressing a theta role.

The lexical entry for *tenke* is associated with the relevant frame through an invocation of the template describing this class of constructions. The relevant part of the lexical entry for *tenke* is shown in (26).

(26)   tenke V   { [...]
                  | @(V-SUBJ-POBJ tenke på)
                  | [...] }

The invocation of the template V-SUBJ-POBJ has two parameters, the predicate name for the verb *tenke* and the form of the selected preposition *på*. In (27) part of the template is shown (other parts of this template for handling passive and other modifications are discussed in Section 4).

(27)   V-SUBJ-POBJ (P prp) =
          @(CONCAT P '* prp %FN)
          (↑ PRED) = '%FN⟨(↑ SUBJ)(↑ OBL-TH)⟩'
          (↑ OBL-TH CHECK P-SELFORM) = prp

The template invokes another template CONCAT, which concatenates the predicate name P and the preposition form prp as the value of the variable %FN. In this example the result is the predicate name tenke*på, which is then included in the value of PRED. The last line assigns the value of prp (*på* in the example) as the value of the attribute P-SELFORM under the OBL-TH argument. This feature is checked by the syntactic rule which introduces the selected PP, ensuring that only the preposition selected by the verb is accepted.

3.3.2 Verb-particle constructions

Verb-particle constructions consist of a verb and a selected particle in the form of an adverb or an intransitively used preposition; in NorGram such elements are classified as PRT in the c-structure. The verb and the particle express an idiosyncratic meaning. As in English, verb-particle constructions in Norwegian can have the particle either before or after an object, and obligatorily after if the object is pronominal; cf. Baldwin & Kim (2010: 276). The analysis is illustrated in Figures 5 and 6 for the sentence in (28).

(28)   Han **skrev opp** nummeret.
       he   wrote up   the number
       'He wrote down the number.'

```
                    ROOT
                   /    \
                  IP    PERIOD
                 / \      |
             PRONP  I'    .
               |   / \
             PRON Vfin  S
              |    |    |
             Han skrev VPmain
                       /  \
                     PRTP  NP
                      |    |
                     PRT   N
                      |    |
                     opp nummeret
```

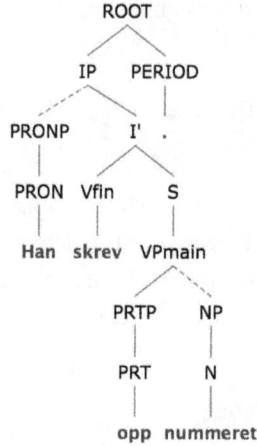

Figure 5: C-structure for example (28)

PRED	'skrive*opp<[13:han], [11:nummer]>'
TNS-ASP	17	TENSE past, **MOOD** indicative

TOPIC:
PRED	'han'
NTYPE	15	NSYN pronoun
GEND	14	NEUT -, MASC +, FEM -
13 REF +, PRON-TYPE pers, PRON-FORM han, PERS 3, NUM sg, GEND-SEM male, DEF +, CASE nom

OBJ:
PRED	'nummer'
NTYPE	NSEM 9 COMMON count	8 NSYN common
GEND	7	NEUT +, MASC -, FEM -
11 PERS 3, NUM sg, DEF-MORPH +, DEF +, CASE obl

SUBJ [13]

0 VTYPE main, VFORM fin, STMT-TYPE decl, PRT-FORM opp

Figure 6: F-structure for example (28)

In the c-structure the particle PRT is a separate constituent which may also occur after the NP under VPmain. In the f-structure the verb and the particle are analyzed as forming one predicate skrive*opp, and the particle also provides a value to the feature PRT-FORM.

As in the case of selected prepositions, the lexical entry for *skrive* is associated with the relevant frame through an invocation of the template describing this class of constructions. Part of the lexical entry for *skrive* is shown in (29).

(29)   skrive V   { [...]
                    | @(V-SUBJ-PRT-OBJ skrive opp)
                    | [...] }

Part of the invoked template V-SUBJ-PRT-OBJ is shown in (30).

(30)   V-SUBJ-PRT-OBJ (P prt) =
            @(CONCAT P '* prt %FN)
            $(\uparrow$ PRED) = '%FN$\langle(\uparrow$ SUBJ)$(\uparrow$ OBJ)$\rangle$'
            $(\uparrow$ CHECK PRT-VERB) = +
            $(\uparrow$ PRT-FORM) = c prt

The CONCAT template functions as in the template (27), yielding the predicate name skrive*opp as the value of PRED. The second last line assigns the value "+" to the path CHECK PRT-VERB, a feature which is checked by the syntactic rule introducing the particle PRT; see the VPmain rule in (43) below. The last line is a constraining equation[6] which checks that the value of the feature PRT-FORM, which is introduced in the sentence by the particle, is the value of prt, i.e. *opp* in the template invocation in (29).

3.3.3 Verb-particle constructions with selected prepositions

The preceding sections have shown how prepositional verbs and verb-particle constructions are analyzed. Phrasal verbs also allow both selected prepositions and particles in the same MWE. An example involving both, in addition to a reflexive object, is provided in the treebank example in (31). The analysis of (31) is shown in Figures 7 and 8.

(31)   Vi   har   et   så   enormt   stort område å **sette oss inn i.**
       we   have a   such enormously large area   to set   us in into

       'We have such an enormously large area to immerse ourselves in.'

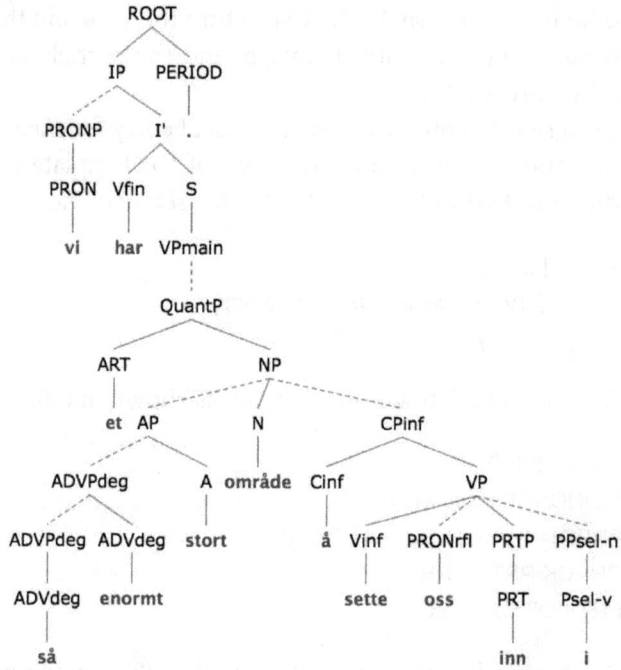

Figure 7: The c-structure of sentence (31)

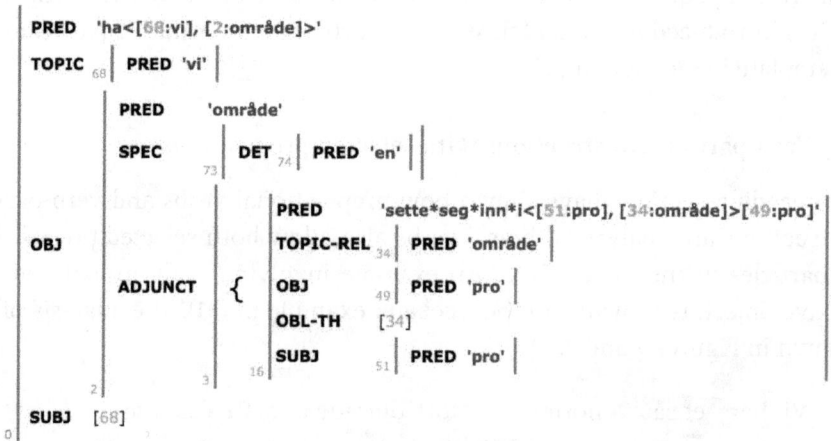

Figure 8: Part of the simplified f-structure of sentence (31)

In this example the MWE *sette oss inn i* occurs in an infinitival relative (CPinf) in an NP with the head *område* 'area'. In the f-structure the infinitival relative occurs as a member of the set of adjuncts to the predicate område, also occurring as the second argument of sette*seg*inn*i as its relativized argument (see Section 4.2 for the analysis of long-distance dependencies like relativization and topicalization). The template invoked by the verb *sette*, V-SUBJ-OBJrefl-PRT-POBJ, provides an analysis along the lines of the templates in (27) and (30).

3.4 Verbal idioms

A VP idiom is a flexible MWE in which at least one predicate-bearing lexeme (such as a noun or an adjective) is selected, with possible restrictions as to number, definiteness or other morphological properties applying. VP idioms are handled by a specific set of templates. For example, an idiom like *holde øye med* 'keep an eye on' is analyzed by means of a lexical template covering idioms consisting of a selected indefinite object plus a selected prepositional phrase. The treebank sentence in (32) is analyzed as shown in Figures 9 and 10.

(32) Samtidig   **holdt** han umerkelig   et skarpt **øye med** jentungen.
      simultaneously kept he unnoticeably a sharp eye with the girl child
      'At the same time he furtively kept a close eye on the girl.'

The analysis of the selected prepositional phrase *med jentungen* is as described in Section 3.3.1 for example (25). The selected lexeme in (32) is *øye*. In the f-structure in Figure 10 the idiomatic meaning is represented by incorporating øye in the predicate name, deriving the predicate name holde#øye*med. The phrase *et skarpt øye* fills the function of OBJ, but is not analyzed as a semantic argument of the sentence predicate, which appears from its position outside the angled brackets ⟨...⟩ surrounding the argument list. This position signals that the constituent is syntactically subcategorized for without being a semantic argument.

The lexical entry for *holde* is associated with the VP idiom through an invocation of the idiom template describing the relevant class of idioms. Part of the lexical entry for *holde* is shown in (33). The template invocation has three parameters, the predicate name for the verb *holde*, the predicate of the selected noun *øye*, and the form of the selected preposition *med*. Part of the template is shown in (34); the full template is discussed in Section 4.3.

---

[6]This concept is explained in connection with example (20) above.

Helge Dyvik, Gyri Smørdal Losnegaard & Victoria Rosén

```
                         ROOT
                        /    \
                      IP      PERIOD
                     /  \       |
                  AP'    I'      .
                   |    /  \
                  AP  Vfin    S
                   |   |    /--\------
                   A  holdt PRONP APsmpl   VPmain
                   |        |     |       /      \
               Samtidig   PRON   A    QuantP    PPsel-n
                           |      |    /  \       /   \
                          han umerkelig ART NP  Psel-v NP
                                         |   /\    |    |
                                        et AP N   med   N
                                           |  |         |
                                           A øye    jentungen
                                           |
                                        skarpt
```

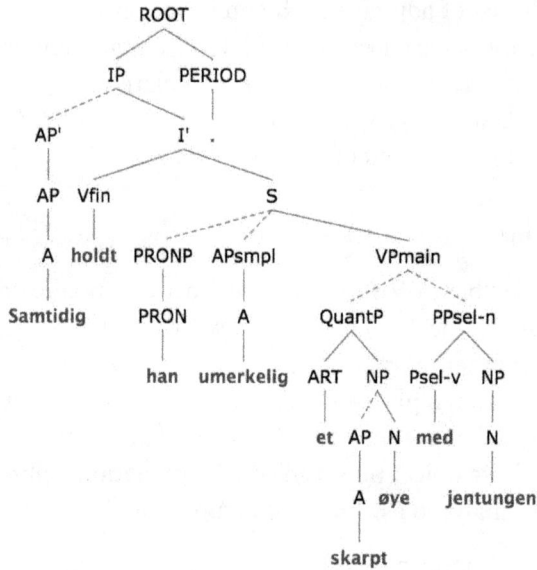

Figure 9: The c-structure of sentence (32)

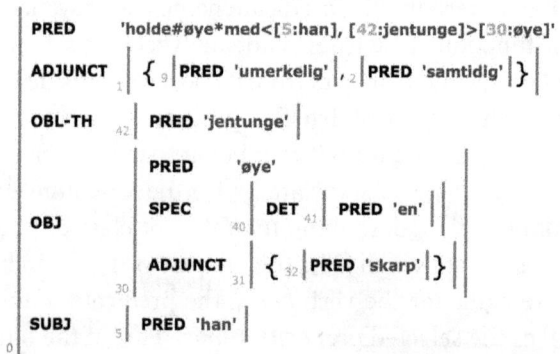

Figure 10: The simplified f-structure of sentence (32)

(33)   holde V   { [...]
                  | @(VPIDIOM-INDEFOBJ-POBJ holde øye med)
                     ($\uparrow$ OBJ NUM) = c sg
                  | [...] }

(34)   VPIDIOM-INDEFOBJ-POBJ (P OP prp) =
           @(CONCAT P '# OP '* prp %FN)
           ($\uparrow$ PRED) = '%FN$\langle$($\uparrow$ SUBJ)($\uparrow$ OBL-TH)$\rangle$($\uparrow$ OBJ)
           ($\uparrow$ OBL-TH CHECK P-SELFORM) = prp
           ($\uparrow$ OBJ PRED FN) = c OP
           ~($\uparrow$ OBJ DEF) = +

In addition to the template call, the lexical entry in (33) also specifies that the selected object should be singular. It is a matter of choice whether such information should be included in the individual lexical entry or give rise to a distinction between more fine-grained templates. In the template definition in (34), OP (object predicate) is the variable for the selected noun predicate and prp for the selected preposition. As in the case of the template in (30), the template invokes the CONCAT template which builds the predicate name. The second last equation requires the object to have the value of OP as its predicate (in this case 'øye'), and the final equation requires the object not to be definite. As for the equation mentioning P-SELFORM, see the explanation of the template in (27).

3.5 Nonverbal flexible expressions

3.5.1 Nouns with selected prepositions

Nouns may also form MWEs by selecting prepositional phrases as their arguments. For example, the noun *ansvar* 'responsibility' may select the preposition *for* 'for', which can take a nominal phrase, an infinitival, or a nominal subclause as complement, as in the treebank examples in (35–37).

(35)   Hadde jeg **ansvar**   **for** gutten?
       had   I   responsibility for the boy
       'Did I have responsibility for the boy?'

(36)   Han fikk **ansvar**   **for** å overta   søket.
       he got responsibility for to take over the search
       'He got the responsibility for taking over the search.'

(37) Jeg kan ikke ta **ansvar**   **for** at det ble   lekket.
     I   can not take responsibility for that it   became leaked
     'I cannot take responsibility for its having been leaked.'

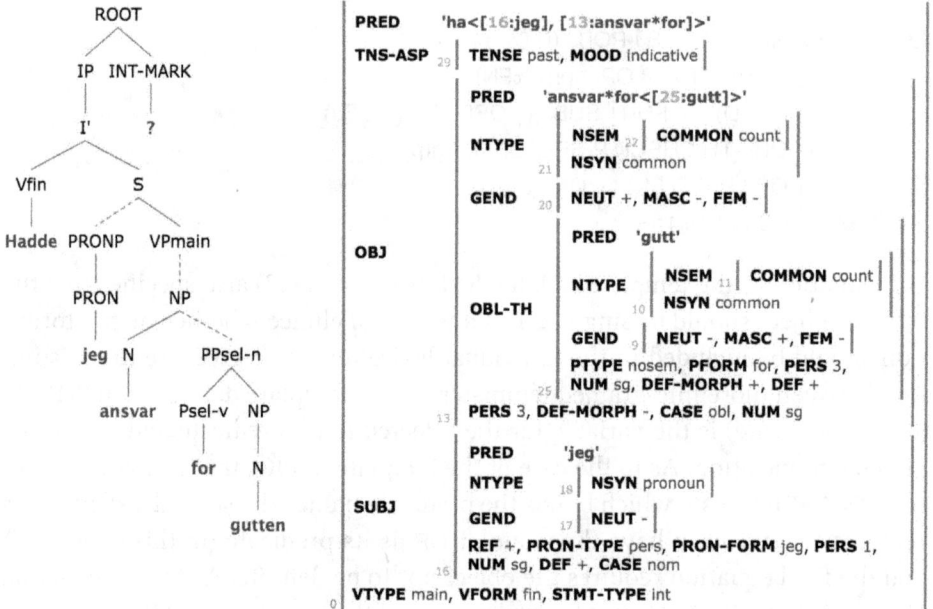

Figure 11: C- and f-structure for the sentence (35)

Example (35) is analyzed as in Figure 11. As in the case of prepositional verbs, the selected preposition does not contribute a PRED of its own, but is analyzed as forming a single predicate ansvar*for with the noun, taking the complement of the preposition as an argument with the function OBL-TH (an oblique argument expressing a theta role). With an infinitival or a clausal complement the syntactic function is COMP. The lexical entry for *ansvar* in (38) invokes three alternative templates for the three possible kinds of complements, in addition to its basic template as a mass noun.

(38)   ansvar N   {   @(MASSNOUN ansvar)
                  | @(N-POBJ ansvar for)
                  | @(N-PINFCOMP ansvar for)
                  | @(N-PCOMP ansvar for) }

3.5.2 Adjectives with selected prepositions

Similarly, adjectives may select prepositional phrases as complements, for instance *flink til* 'clever at', as in the treebank example in (39).

(39) Hva er egentlig du **flink til**?
      what are after all you clever at
      'What are you clever at, after all?'

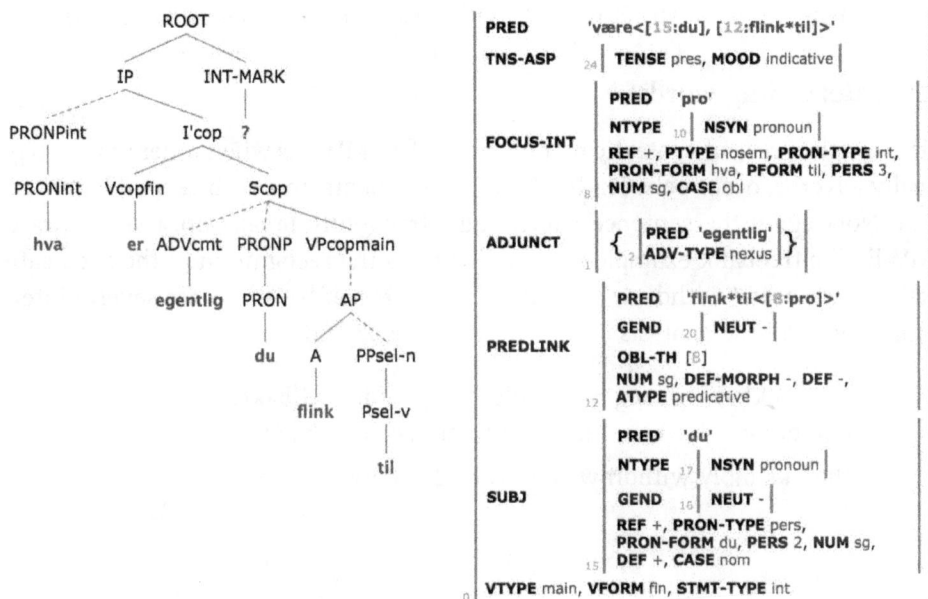

Figure 12: C- and f-structure for the sentence (39)

Example (39) is analyzed as in Figure 12. In this example the complement of the selected preposition has been questioned and occurs in the f-structure as the value of FOCUS-INT, i.e., interrogative focus. The predicative complement (PREDLINK) has the predicate flink*til, taking the prepositional complement as its OBL-TH. The value of OBL-TH is identical with the value of FOCUS-INT, which is indicated by the shared index 8, resulting from the general analysis of *wh*-questions in the grammar.

4 Representing flexibility

Flexible MWEs must be recognizable across different types of syntactic modifications which separate their parts from each other in the sentence. Such modifications include the simple occurrence of other words between the MWE parts, long-distance dependencies like topicalization, relativization and *wh*-question formation, presentative constructions, and various types of passive constructions. When flexible MWEs are treated by means of LFG templates, such modifications are automatically taken care of within the regular grammar. Having both a c-structure and an f-structure representation allows us to capture both the close semantic and functional association between the selecting and the selected words (in the f-structure) and their syntactic independence as different constituents (in the c-structure). We will present the analyses of some cases.

4.1 Intervening words

The simplest case of syntactic modification of an MWE is when other words, typically adverbs, occur between the MWE components. In a verb-second language like Norwegian the sentence subject also frequently breaks up a verb phrase MWE. The treebank example in (40) illustrates the recognition of the predicate trekke*seg*tilbake ('withdraw', literally: 'draw oneself back') across several intervening words. The analysis is shown in Figures 13 and 14.

(40) Da **trekker** jeg **meg** bare stille   og rolig   **tilbake**.
      then draw   I   me   only silently and calmly back

      'Then I simply withdraw silently and calmly.'

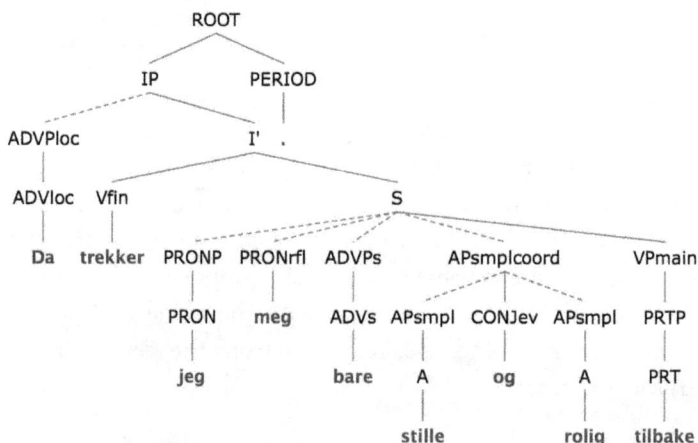

Figure 13: C-structure of sentence (40)

$$
\begin{bmatrix}
\textbf{PRED} & \text{'trekke*seg*tilbake<[84:jeg]>[76:pro]'} \\[4pt]
\textbf{TOPIC} & {}_{14}\begin{bmatrix} \textbf{PRED 'da'} \end{bmatrix} \\[6pt]
\textbf{ADJUNCT} & {}_{1}\Big\{ {}_{15}\big\{ {}_{39}\big[\textbf{PRED 'rolig'}\big], {}_{24}\big[\textbf{PRED 'stille'}\big]\big\}, [14], {}_{2}\big[\textbf{PRED 'bare'}\big]\Big\} \\[6pt]
\textbf{OBJ-BEN} & {}_{76}\begin{bmatrix} \textbf{PRED 'pro'} \end{bmatrix} \\[6pt]
\textbf{SUBJ} & {}_{84}\begin{bmatrix} \textbf{PRED 'jeg'} \end{bmatrix}
\end{bmatrix}_{0}
$$

Figure 14: Simplified f-structure of sentence (40)

The mechanism for achieving this lies in the projection architecture of LFG, in which different constituents in c-structure may project the same f-structure, within which dependencies may be formulated. To illustrate we may consider the relevant fragments of the c-structure rules for I', S and VPmain in (41–43).

(41) I' $\longrightarrow$ Vfin: $\uparrow = \downarrow$
   (S: $\uparrow = \downarrow$)

(42) S $\longrightarrow$ (PRONP: $(\uparrow \text{SUBJ}) = \downarrow$
           @SUBJCASE)
     [...]
     (PRONrfl: { $(\uparrow \text{OBJ-BEN}) = \downarrow$
           | $(\uparrow \text{OBJ}) = \downarrow$ })
     [...]
     (ADVPs+: $\downarrow \in (\uparrow \text{ADJUNCT})$)
     [...]
     (APsmpl: $\downarrow \in (\uparrow \text{ADJUNCT})$)
     [...]
     (VPmain: $\uparrow = \downarrow$)
     [...]

(43) VPmain $\longrightarrow$ [...]
         (PRTP: $\uparrow = \downarrow$
             $(\uparrow \text{CHECK PRT-VERB}) =_c +$)
         [...]

As explained in Section 2, the equation ↑ = ↓ annotated to a rule daughter means that the rule daughter and its mother will project the same f-structure. Thus it can be seen that the Vfin daughter of I' (the verb) and the PRTP daughter of VPmain (the particle) will project the same f-structure.

A particle verb presupposes the presence of the required particle in the sentence, and a particle presupposes the presence of a particle verb. This mutual dependency is captured through two features, one feature PRT-VERB = +, carried by the verb and required by the rule introducing the particle, and, conversely, one feature PRT-FORM, carried by the particle and required by the verb to have the appropriate value. Thus, the constraint equation annotated to PRTP, (↑ CHECK PRT-VERB) = c +, demanding that its f-structure should have a feature PRT-VERB = + (i.e., that the verb should be a particle verb), will be satisfied if the finite verb has contributed such a feature to this common f-structure. A similar constraint equation associated with the verb, ((↑ PRT-FORM) = c prt in (45) below), ensures that the particle has the form required by the verb.

The lexical entry for *trekke* is associated with the relevant frame through an invocation of the template for reflexive verb-particle constructions. Part of the lexical entry for *trekke* is shown in (44). The template has the form shown in (45).

(44)   trekke V   { [...]
                    | @(V-SUBJ-OBJrefl-PRT trekke tilbake)
                    | [...] }

(45)   V-SUBJ-OBJrefl-PRT (P prt) =
            @(CONCAT P '* seg '* prt %FN)
            { (↑ PRED) = '%FN⟨(↑ SUBJ)⟩(↑ OBJ-BEN)'
            | (↑ PRED) = '%FN⟨↑ OBJ)⟩(↑ OBJ-BEN)(↑ SUBJ)'
               (↑ PRESENTATIVE) = +
               (↑ SUBJ PRON-TYPE) = c expl
               ~(↑ OBJ DEF) = + }
            @(REFLEXIVE OBJ-BEN)
            (↑ CHECK PRT-VRB) = +
            (↑ PRT-FORM) = c prt
            ~(↑ PASSIVE) = +

The template CONCAT constructs the predicate name trekke*seg*tilbake as the value of PRED. The reflexive occurring with reflexive verbs is analyzed as OBJ-BEN (indirect object). The reason for this is that there will be a direct object in the alternative presentative construction with an expletive *det* subject, such as

Det trekker seg tilbake store styrker 'There are big forces withdrawing', in which *store styrker* occurs as a syntactic object (OBJ); there can only be one OBJ. The presentative construction is described as the second alternative in the disjunction {...|...} in the template. The reflexive, like the expletive subject, is analyzed as a non-argument, which appears from the fact that it is placed outside the argument list enclosed by ⟨...⟩ in the value of PRED. The features PRT-VRB and PRT-FORM are explained in the discussion of the template in (30).

4.2 Long-distance dependencies

Long-distance dependencies involve syntactic dependencies across an arbitrary number of clause boundaries and comprise topicalization by fronting, relative clauses and *wh*-questions. Such dependencies are handled in the f-structure by means of a special type of equations using regular expressions to specify a set of alternative attribute paths into the f-structure. The term for this mechanism is FUNCTIONAL UNCERTAINTY. The rule in (46) shows a simplified version of the functional uncertainty equation handling the dependency between the topic and some embedded gap further down in the structure.

(46)   IP → XP: (↑ TOPIC) = ↓
                  (↑ {COMP | XCOMP}* {SUBJ | OBJ | OBL-TH}) = ↓
       [...]

The first equation annotated to XP in (46) specifies that the f-structure of the XP daughter (↓) is the value of the attribute TOPIC of the f-structure of the IP mother (↑). The second equation specifies that the daughter f-structure is also the value of one of a set of alternative attribute paths. COMP and XCOMP are the attributes of embedded finite and non-finite clauses. The regular expression {COMP | XCOMP}* describes all possible strings over the elements COMP and XCOMP (with repetitions), and the final disjunction specifies the last attribute of the string, enabling the TOPIC to be identical with an embedded SUBJ, OBJ or OBL-TH. We may illustrate with the treebank example in (47) of a prepositional verb *fortelle om* 'tell about' in a sentence where the OBL-TH, i.e., the selected prepositional phrase, has been topicalized.

(47)   **Om**   dette skal jeg **fortelle** nå.
       about this shall I   tell   now
       'This I will now tell about.'

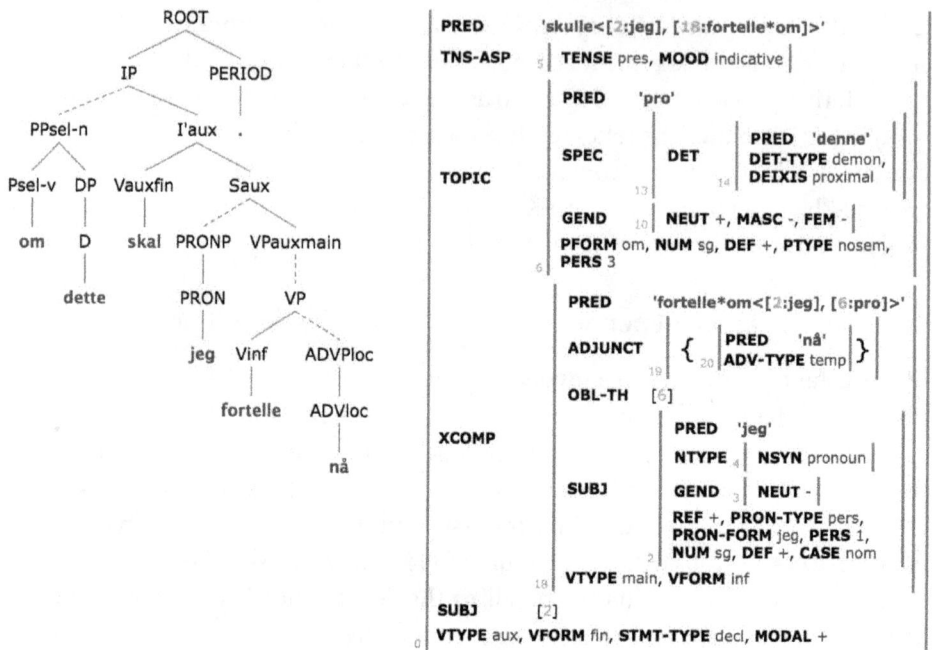

Figure 15: C- and f-structure for example (47)

The analysis of (47) is shown in Figure 15. In the f-structure the value of TOPIC, indexed 6, is also found as the value of OBL-TH in the embedded XCOMP with fortelle*om as predicate. Thus the attribute string from the set specified by the functional uncertainty equation in (46) for this example is (↑ XCOMP OBL-TH).

4.3 Passive alternations

Passive is another source of verbal MWE modifications, changing the syntactic functions of selected constituents. In LFG passive is analyzed as a lexical phenomenon modifying the value of PRED in a lexical entry for a verb, changing the mapping between argument positions and syntactic functions. In NorGram this is handled by passive templates invoked by the verb templates. The full version of the VP idiom template in (34) for idioms like *holde øye med* 'keep an eye on' is shown in (48), where different types of passive alternations are handled.

(48) VPIDIOM-INDEFOBJ-POBJ (P OP prp) =
       @(CONCAT P '# OP '* prp %FN)
       { @(PASS-OBL-TH [(↑ PRED) = '%FN⟨(↑ SUBJ)(↑ OBL-TH)⟩(↑ OBJ)])
       | { (↑ PRED) = '%FN⟨NULL(↑ OBL-TH)⟩(↑ SUBJ)(↑ OBJ)'

96

  | (↑ PRED) = '%FN⟨↑ OBL-AG)(↑ OBL-TH)⟩(↑ SUBJ)(↑ OBJ)' }
  (↑ PASSIVE) = c +
  (↑ PRESENTATIVE-TYPE) = passive
  (↑ SUBJ PRON-TYPE) = c expl }
 (↑ OBL-TH CHECK P-SELFORM) = prp
 (↑ OBJ PRED FN) = c OP
 ~(↑ OBJ DEF) = +

After the second line there follows a disjunction of two alternatives. The first alternative invokes the template PASS-OBL-TH, taking the predicate-argument structure as a parameter. This template allows the active/passive alternation whereby the OBL-TH, i.e., the complement of the selected preposition (see the discussion of example 25), may be the subject in a passive construction, as in the treebank example in (49).

(49) De var derimot   ikke klar over at de ble   **holdt øye**
      they were on the other hand not clear over that they became held eye
      med.
      with
      'On the other hand, they weren't aware that someone was keeping an eye on them.'

The second alternative in the main disjunction describes the impersonal (presentative) passive option with an expletive subject, as in the example in (50).

(50) Det ble   **holdt øye med** dem.
      it   became held eye with them
      'Someone was keeping an eye on them.'

The embedded disjunction of two predicate-argument structures in the fourth and fifth lines of the template describes the possibility of including an OBL-AG, i.e., an oblique agent in a prepositional phrase with *av* 'by'. The remaining equations require the passive form of the verb and expletive type of the subject pronoun.

5 Complementation patterns

Verbal MWEs in Norwegian show considerable variation in terms of subcategorizational properties. Like simple verbs, MWEs can have transitivity shifts, take different types of arguments, and take different combinations of arguments. The verb-particle construction *si opp*, for instance, has both an intransitive reading, as in (51), and a transitive reading, as in (52) and (53). While the shift in transitivity does not significantly affect the semantics of the expression in (52), the shift in (53) leads to a change in meaning.

(51) 150 befal   **sier opp**.
      150 officers say up
      '150 officers resign.'

(52) Hun **sa**   **opp** jobben.
      she said up the job
      'She resigned from her job.'

(53) Man må   **si opp** sjefen   for Statkraft.
      one must say up the boss for Statkraft
      'The head of Statkraft must be fired.'

More precisely, the theme object that is implicit in the intransitive usage in (51) is explicit in (52), while in (53) the object has the semantic role of experiencer instead of theme. The frames V-SUBJ-PRT and V-SUBJ-PRT-OBJ represent the intransitive and the transitive usages of *si opp*. NorGram, being mainly a syntactic framework, has one frame for both transitive readings, leaving semantic roles underspecified.

Most of the verbal MWEs in NorGram are phrasal verbs or VP idioms. Such MWEs have free subjects, so that any argument variation is in the complements.[7] The lexical entries display a wide range of complementation patterns, one type being MWEs where the verb selects all of its complements. Table 2 presents types of VP idioms in NorGram with only selected complements. In idioms where the verb subcategorizes for only one selected complement, the selected element is either a nominal (O), a prepositional ([P + O]) or a predicative (PC) complement. There is also a type of VP idiom with two selected complements (O + PRT).

Most verbal MWEs in NorGram have free complements in addition to their selected complements. In the VP idiom *legge merke til* 'notice', the verb *legge* 'lay' selects the object *merke* 'mark' in the indefinite form and a prepositional complement which is either nominal, as in (54), clausal, as in (55), or an interrogative clausal complement, as in (56), all headed by the selected preposition *til* 'to'.

---

[7]The exception to free subjects in VP idioms is expressions with the expletive subject *det* 'it'. However, this type of argument variation is analyzed as a grammatical rather than a lexical selection of the subject and is thus not considered here.

Table 2: Verbal MWEs with only selected complements

Pattern	Example	Lit. translation	Id. translation
V + O	*slå følge*	'beat company'	'accompany'
	slå leir	'beat camp'	'camp'
	ta feil	'take wrong'	'be wrong'
	ta fyr	'take fire'	'catch fire'
V + [P + O]	*gå i oppløsning*	'go in dissolution'	'dissolve'
	komme for en dag	'come for a day'	'be revealed'
	løfte i flokk	'lift in flock'	'join forces'
	legge på svøm	'lay on swim'	'start swimming'
V + PC	*stå brud*	'stand bride'	'get married'
V + O + PRT	*sette livet til*	'put the life to'	'lose one's life'

(54) Ingen **legger merke til** mannen som står urørlig og venter.
no one lays mark to the man who stands motionless and waits
'No one notices the man who is standing waiting motionlessly.'

(55) Ingen **legger merke til** at mannen står urørlig og venter.
no one lays mark to that the man stands motionless and waits
'No one notices that the man is standing waiting motionlessly.'

(56) Ingen **legger merke til** om mannen står urørlig og venter.
no one lays mark to if the man stands motionless and waits
'No one notices whether the man is standing waiting motionlessly.'

MWEs that subcategorize for different types of complements are represented in the lexicon with one frame for each subcategorization pattern. In the template invocations in (57), POBJ, PCOMP and PCOMPint represent the different types of prepositional complements that occur with *legge merke til* in (54), (55), and (56), respectively.

(57) a. @(VPIDIOM-INDEFOBJ-POBJ legge merke til)

   b. @(VPIDIOM-INDEFOBJ-PCOMP legge merke til)

   c. @(VPIDIOM-INDEFOBJ-PCOMPint legge merke til)

While Table 2 shows different types of selected complements, examples (54–56) illustrate how one MWE may take different types of free complements. In both cases, we see that variation in the complementation is limited for individual MWEs. While *slå følge* 'accompany', *gå i oppløsning* 'dissolve' and the other examples in Table 2 all have fixed complement structures, *legge merke til* 'notice' has three different frames in which only one of the complements varies. To give an impression of the variety of complementation patterns in the lexicon it is thus necessary to turn to the inventory of unique frames, reflected in the number of templates. For instance, NorGram has more than 80 templates for phrasal verbs; these may be grouped into seven main classes according to the types and number of complements (Table 3).

Table 3: Main types of complementation patterns in phrasal verbs in NorGram

Type	Example frame	Example MWE
V + PRT	V-SUBJ-PRT	*stryke med*
V + PRT + 1 complement	V-SUBJ-PRT-XCOMP	*få til*
V + PRT + 2 complements	V-SUBJ-PRT-OBJ-OBJ	*gjøre etter*
V + PPsel	V-SUBJ-POBJ	*advare mot*
V + PPsel + 1 complement	V-SUBJ-OBJ-PACOMP	*erklære for*
V + PPsel + 2 complements	V-SUBJ-OBJ-POBJ-PCOMP	*vedde med på*
V + PRT + PPsel	V-SUBJ-PRT-POBJ	*gå med på*
V + PRT + PPsel + 1 complement	V-SUBJ-PRT-OBJ-POBJ	*venne av med*

Table 3 presents the different types of complementation patterns for verb-particle constructions, prepositional verbs, and verb-particle constructions with selected prepositions. The first column in the table is the pattern type, represented in terms of the main complement(s), which may be a particle (PRT), a selected prepositional phrase (PPsel), or both, and the number of additional complements.[8] Examples of subcategorization frames for each type are given in the second column using template names. The example MWEs, represented in the table with only their fixed components, are instances of the example frames and are discussed in more detail in (58–70).

---

[8]"Main complement" in this context refers to the selected complement which determines the type of the overall construction, such as PRT in verb-particle constructions.

As Table 3 shows, verb-particle constructions in NorGram may either be intransitive, such as *stryke med* 'die' in (58), or have one or two free complements, such as *få noe til* 'accomplish something' in (59) and *gjøre noen noe etter* 'repeat something after someone' in (60).

(58) Og vi fortsetter å banke deg til   du **stryker med**!
      and we continue to beat   you until you stroke with
      'And we will continue to beat you until you're dead!'

(59) Nå **fikk** han **til** å tenke igjen.
      now got he to to think again
      'Now he managed to think again.'

(60) Ikke mange kunne ha   **gjort** ham noe   slikt   **etter**!
      not many could have done him something like that after
      'Not many people could have done what he did!'

The example *få noe til* in (59) is an instantiation of the frame V-SUBJ-PRT-XCOMP, with one free complement in the form of the infinitival complement *å tenke igjen* 'to think again'. There is one other frame for this particular MWE in the lexicon, with a nominal object instead of the infinitival complement (V-SUBJ-PRT-OBJ). Example (61) illustrates this complement structure.

(61) Dette er hva   du **fikk til**.
      this is what you got to
      'This is what you accomplished.'

The lexicon also has a frame for *få til* with two free complements, in the form of an object and an infinitival complement. The difference in the number of complements also yields a difference in meaning, as shown in (62). These should thus be considered different MWEs.

(62) Hvorfor **får** vi ikke dem **til** å bli?
      why   get we not them to to stay
      'Why can't we make them stay?'

The last type of verb-particle construction in Table 3, with two free complements in addition to the particle, is exemplified with the frame V-SUBJ-PRT-OBJ-OBJ. This argument structure, illustrated in (60) for *gjøre noen noe etter*, involves both an indirect object (OBJ-BEN), *ham* 'him', and a direct object (OBJ), *noe slikt* 'something like that' (OBJ-BEN is shortened to OBJ in the name of the template). A second frame of this type, which is slightly more complex with a nominal object and a clausal complement (COMP) as well as an expletive subject, is V-SUBJexpl-PRT-OBJ-COMP. The MWE *det faller noen noe inn* 'something occurs to someone' in (63) is an example of this frame, literally translating into 'it falls someone something in'. Except for the expletive subject and the particle, the frame has the same arguments as V-SUBJ-OBJ-COMP for single verbs such as *forklare* 'explain'. The frame is thus regular in terms of argument structure.

(63) Det **falt** ikke britene **inn** at særlig   mange hadde lyst.
      it fell not the Brits in that particularly many had   desire
      'It did not occur to the Brits that more than a few should want to.'

In contrast to verb-particle constructions which may be intransitive, prepositional verbs will always have a free complement, introduced by the selected preposition. Prepositional verbs can subcategorize for exactly one prepositional phrase, as in *advare mot noe* 'warn against something' in (64), where *mot segregering* 'against segregation' is a PPsel.

(64) Han **advarer mot**   segregering.
      he warns   against segregation
      'He warns against segregation.'

Similar to verb-particle constructions, the prepositional verbs in NorGram can take one or two complements in addition to the selected complement. In (65), *erklære noen for noe* 'declare someone something' has one complement, the free object *marken* 'the mark', in addition to the selected prepositional phrase *for død* 'for dead'.

(65) Der måtte myndighetene **erklære** marken **for** død.
      there had to the government declare the mark for dead
      'There the authorities had to declare the (German) mark dead.'

The relevant frame in (65) is V-SUBJ-OBJ-PACOMP, where PACOMP is the selected prepositional phrase. In this case, the preposition *for* takes the adjectival predicative complement *død* 'dead'. While PPsel is the c-structure category for constituents headed by selected prepositions and may refer to any type of prepositional complement, PACOMP is a syntactic variable that reflects the type of complement.

The final type of prepositional verb in Table 3 is illustrated in (66) with the MWE *vedde noe med noen på noe* 'bet something with someone on something'.

(66) Abrams **veddet** en sigarett **med** Browne **på** at det regnet.
      Abrams bet   a cigarette with Brown on that it rained
      'Abrams bets a cigarette with Brown that it was raining.'

This example is an instance of the frame V-SUBJ-OBJ-POBJ-PCOMP, which has two complements in addition to a PPsel, in this case a free object and a second PPsel. The free object is *en sigarett* 'a cigarette'. In the first PPsel, which corresponds to POBJ in the subcategorization frame, the selected preposition *med* 'with' takes the nominal object *Brown*. In the second PPsel, corresponding to PCOMP, the preposition *på* 'on' takes the clausal complement *at det regnet* 'that it was raining'.

Like prepositional verbs, verb-particle constructions with selected prepositions always subcategorize for at least one free complement. Such constructions can have one complement, as in *gå med på noe* 'go along with something' in (67), which is an instance of the frame V-SUBJ-PRT-POBJ.

(67) I land   som Sverige **gikk** fagbevegelsen **med på** de nye tankene.
      in countries like Sweden went the unions   with on the new thoughts
      'In countries like Sweden the unions went along with the new ideas.'

In (67), the particle is *med* 'with', and the free argument *de nye tankene* 'the new thoughts' is the complement of the selected preposition *på* 'on'. The prepositional complement could, however, also be clausal, as in (68), or infinitival, as in (69). With the infinitival complement, there is a shift in meaning from 'go along with'/'admit' to 'agree'.

(68) Han vil ikke **gå med på** at hun er utpreget   modig.
      he will not go with on that she is exceptionally brave
      'He will not admit that she is exceptionally brave.'

(69) Til Libbys forbauselse hadde Jerry **gått med på** å prøve.
      to Libby's surprise   had   Jerry gone with on to try
      'To Libby's surprise, Jerry had agreed to try.'

Verb-particle constructions with selected prepositions may also have two free complements. This is the case for *venne noen av med noe* 'wean someone off something' in (70). This example, instantiating the frame V-SUBJ-PRT-OBJ-POBJ, has the particle *av* 'off', the free pronominal object *meg* 'me', and the selected prepositional object *med det* 'with that'. Also here, the prepositional complement may vary. The alternative frame is V-SUBJ-PRT-OBJ-PXCOMP, allowing an infinitival prepositional complement, but in this case yielding no difference in meaning.

(70) Mor   klarte   aldri   å **venne**   meg **av med** det.
      mother managed never to accustom me   off with that
      'Mother never managed to wean me off that habit.'

The examples of complementation patterns for phrasal verbs in NorGram show that the subcategorizational properties of MWEs can be the source of variation both at the syntactic and the semantic levels. We have seen that the main types of complementation patterns in Table 3 are shared by a number of subcategorization frames. Table 4 presents some of the frames that are variants of the type V + PPsel + 1 complement in Table 3 (prepositional verbs with one free complement). The frames are divided into groups of MWEs that share the same or similar types of arguments, resulting in five categories of argument patterning for this type.[9] While the current section provides only superficial observations about the types of MWE argument patterns in the NorGram lexicon, it seems that a more systematic study of their subcategorizational properties could provide useful information about MWE types and tokens and perhaps also new insights into the relationship between argument patterns and the semantics of MWEs.

6 Conclusion

In this chapter we have shown how the modularization of NorGram makes it possible to integrate MWEs into the LFG analyses in a way that does justice to the proper division of labor between the lexicon and the grammar. On the one hand, each MWE is entered into the lexicon with the information necessary for its idiomatic meaning. On the other hand, the syntactic treatment uses ordinary syntactic rules to the extent that the flexibility of the individual MWE allows.

Up until now MWEs have been severely underrepresented in lexical resources for Norwegian, as they have been for many other languages. The main strategy for NorGram has been to incorporate them into the lexicon and grammar when they are encountered during the construction of NorGramBank. MWEs have thus been added to NorGram in tandem with the development of the treebank. As a natural consequence of the way in which the MWEs are represented

---

[9]Several frames of this type are not listed here, including frames with expletive subjects and objects and subtypes of clausal complements.

Table 4: Some variants of V + PPsel + 1 complement

Complementation type	Subcategorization frame
Free object and PPsel	V-SUBJ-OBJ-PACOMP
	V-SUBJ-OBJ-POBJACOMP
	V-SUBJ-OBJ-POBJNCOMP
	V-SUBJ-OBJ-POBJ
	V-SUBJ-OBJ-PCOMP
	V-SUBJ-OBJ-PCOMPinf
	V-SUBJ-OBJ-PCOMPint
	V-SUBJ-OBJ-PXCOMP
	V-SUBJ-INDOBJ-POBJ
	V-SUBJexpl-OBJ-POBJ
Reflexive object and PPsel	V-SUBJ-OBJrefl-POBJ
	V-SUBJ-OBJrefl-PCOMP
	V-SUBJ-OBJrefl-PCOMPat
	V-SUBJ-OBJrefl-PCOMPint
	V-SUBJ-OBJrefl-PXCOMP
PPsel and free nominal complement	V-SUBJ-POBJ-COMP
	V-SUBJ-POBJ-XCOMP
	V-SUBJ-POBJ-OBL
	V-SUBJ-POBJ-OBLBEN
Prepositional reflexive object and free nominal complement	V-SUBJ-POBJrefl-OBJ
	V-SUBJ-POBJrefl-COMP
PPsel and PPsel	V-SUBJ-POBJ-PXCOMP
	V-SUBJ-POBJrefl-POBJ

in the grammar and lexicon, it is possible to search for the various MWE types in the treebank. The wealth of information provided by the LFG representations enables searching for many different properties of the MWEs, and the MWEs may be recovered in all the syntactic variations they occur in. As a result, NorGramBank is now an important resource for studying Norwegian MWEs in context.

Acknowledgments

We thank Koenraad De Smedt and two anonymous reviewers for valuable comments and suggestions for improvements. This work was partially financed by the Norwegian Research Council and the University of Bergen through the INESS project.

Abbreviations

=c	symbol in a constraint equation: constrained to be equal to
[P + O]	selected prepositional complement
⟨...⟩	brackets enclosing the list of semantic arguments of a predicate
*	element in the name of the predicate of a lexeme with a selected semantically light element (e.g., a preposition)
#	element in the name of the predicate of a lexeme with a selected semantically heavy element (e.g., a noun, forming an idiom)
%FN	variable over predicate names in a lexical template
→	phrase structure rule expansion
↑	metavariable in an equation, referring to the f-structure of the node immediately dominating the node to which the equation is annotated
↓	metavariable in an equation, referring to the f-structure of the node to which the equation is annotated
~	negation in an equation defining f-structure
INESS	Infrastructure for the exploration of syntax and semantics
LFG	Lexical-Functional Grammar
XLE	the development platform Xerox Linguistic Environment

References

Baldwin, Timothy & Su Nam Kim. 2010. Multiword expressions. In Nitin Indurkhya & Fred J. Damerau (eds.), *Handbook of natural language processing*, Second edition, chap. 12, 267–292. Boca Raton, FL, USA: Chapman & Hall/CRC.

Bresnan, Joan. 2001. *Lexical-functional syntax.* Malden, MA: Blackwell.

Butt, Miriam, Helge Dyvik, Tracy Holloway King, Hiroshi Masuichi & Christian Rohrer. 2002. The parallel grammar project. In John Carroll, Nelleke Oostdijk & Richard Sutcliffe (eds.), *Proceedings of the workshop on Grammar Engineering and Evaluation at the 19th international conference on Computational Linguistics (COLING)*, 1–7. Taipei, Taiwan: Association for Computational Linguistics.

Dalrymple, Mary. 2001. *Lexical functional grammar.* Vol. 34 (Syntax and Semantics). San Diego, CA: Academic Press.

Dalrymple, Mary, Ronald M. Kaplan & Tracy Holloway King. 2004. Linguistic generalizations over descriptions. In Miriam Butt & Tracy H. King (eds.), *Proceedings of the LFG'04 conference*, 200–208. University of Canterbury, Christchurch, New Zealand: CSLI Publications.

Dyvik, Helge. 2000. Nødvendige noder i norsk: Grunntrekk i en leksikalsk-funksjonell beskrivelse av norsk syntaks [Necessary nodes in Norwegian: Basic properties of a lexical-functional description of Norwegian syntax]. In Øivin Andersen, Kjersti Fløttum & Torodd Kinn (eds.), *Menneske, språk og felleskap*, 25–45. Oslo: Novus forlag.

Dyvik, Helge, Paul Meurer, Victoria Rosén, Koenraad De Smedt, Petter Haugereid, Gyri Smørdal Losnegaard, Gunn Inger Lyse & Martha Thunes. 2016. NorGramBank: A 'deep' treebank for Norwegian. In Nicoletta Calzolari, Khalid Choukri, Thierry Declerck, Marko Grobelnik, Bente Maegaard, Joseph Mariani, Asunción Moreno, Jan Odijk & Stelios Piperidis (eds.), *Proceedings of the tenth international conference on Language Resources and Evaluation (LREC 2016)*, 3555–3562. Portorož, Slovenia. http://www.lrec-conf.org/proceedings/lrec2016/summaries/943.html.

Kaplan, Ronald M. & Joan Bresnan. 1982. Lexical-Functional Grammar: A formal system for grammatical representation. In Joan Bresnan (ed.), *The mental representation of grammatical relations*, 173–281. Cambridge, MA: The MIT Press.

Lønning, Jan Tore, Stephan Oepen, Dorothee Beermann, Lars Hellan, John Carroll, Helge Dyvik, Dan Flickinger, Janne Bondi Johannessen, Paul Meurer, Torbjørn Nordgård, Victoria Rosén & Erik Velldal. 2004. LOGON: A Norwegian MT effort. In *Proceedings of the workshop in Recent Advances in Scandinavian Machine Translation.* Uppsala, Sweden.

Losnegaard, Gyri Smørdal, Gunn Inger Lyse, Martha Thunes, Victoria Rosén, Koenraad De Smedt, Helge Dyvik & Paul Meurer. 2012. What we have learned from Sofie: Extending lexical and grammatical coverage in an LFG parsebank. In Jan Hajič, Koenraad De Smedt, Marko Tadić & António Branco (eds.), *META-RESEARCH workshop on advanced treebanking at LREC'2012*, 69–76. Istanbul, Turkey.

Maxwell, John & Ronald M. Kaplan. 1993. The interface between phrasal and functional constraints. *Computational Linguistics* 19(4). 571–589.

Meurer, Paul. 2012. INESS-Search: A search system for LFG (and other) treebanks. In Miriam Butt & Tracy Holloway King (eds.), *Proceedings of the LFG'12 conference* (LFG Online Proceedings), 404–421. Stanford, CA: CSLI Publications.

Nordgård, Torbjørn. 2000. Nordkompleks: A Norwegian computational lexicon. In *COMLEX 2000 workshop on Computational Lexicography and Multimedia Dictionaries*, 89–92. Patras, Greece: University of Patras.

Nunberg, Geoffrey, Ivan Sag & Thomas Wasow. 1994. Idioms. *Language* 70(3). 491–538.

Rosén, Victoria, Koenraad De Smedt, Paul Meurer & Helge Dyvik. 2012. An open infrastructure for advanced treebanking. In Jan Hajič, Koenraad De Smedt, Marko Tadić & António Branco (eds.), *META-RESEARCH workshop on advanced treebanking at LREC'2012*, 22–29. Istanbul, Turkey.

Rosén, Victoria, Paul Meurer & Koenraad De Smedt. 2007. Designing and implementing discriminants for LFG grammars. In Tracy Holloway King & Miriam Butt (eds.), *The proceedings of the LFG'07 conference*, 397–417. Stanford: CSLI Publications.

Rosén, Victoria, Martha Thunes, Petter Haugereid, Gyri Smørdal Losnegaard, Helge Dyvik, Paul Meurer, Gunn Inger Lyse & Koenraad De Smedt. 2016. The enrichment of lexical resources through incremental parsebanking. *Language Resources and Evaluation* 50(2). 291–319.

Sag, Ivan, Timothy Baldwin, Francis Bond, Ann Copestake & Dan Flickinger. 2002. Multiword expressions: A pain in the neck for NLP. In *Proceedings of the 3rd international conference on Computational Linguistics and Intelligent Text Processing* (Lecture Notes in Computer Science 2276), 1–15. Springer.

Chapter 4

Issues in parsing MWEs in an LFG/XLE framework

Stella Markantonatou

Institute for Language and Speech Processing/Athena RIC

Niki Samaridi

Institute for Language and Speech Processing/Athena RIC

Panagiotis Minos

Institute for Language and Speech Processing/Athena RIC

We present an LFG/XLE system coupled with an independent lexicographic environment for encoding and parsing Modern Greek MWEs. The system assigns a flat structure to the fixed sequences of words within MWEs, the so-called "words with spaces" (WWSs) with the help of a preprocessing module that receives the morphologically analysed string from a tagger external to XLE. We describe the overall system and discuss certain implications of the designing choices.

1 Introduction

This paper presents the system for parsing Modern Greek (MG) Multiword Expressions (MWEs) with LFG/XLE grammars that is schematically depicted in Figure 1 and discusses the issues encountered with the LFG/XLE representations. The main idea of the adopted parsing strategy is that the parser treats the sequential fixed parts of the MWEs as a type of "words with spaces" (WWS) (Sag et al. 2002). Our WWSs are fixed sequences of fixed words that may contain one word that declines (for instance, see example 7 in Table 1). The rigid word order is an important criterion of fixedness in the case of MG that has a relatively free word order. Morphological fixedness is also important in a language with rich

Stella Markantonatou, Niki Samaridi & Panagiotis Minos. 2019. Issues in parsing MWEs in an LFG/XLE framework. In Yannick Parmentier & Jakub Waszczuk (eds.), *Representation and parsing of multiword expressions: Current trends*, 109–126. Berlin: Language Science Press. DOI:10.5281/zenodo.2579039

morphology but, exactly for the same reason, the existence of an inflected word within an otherwise rigid structure is not a surprise. The usage of (this type of) WWSs has practical and theoretical implications.

WWSs have been used by Copestake et al. (2002), by Attia (2006) for parsing Arabic MWEs with LFG grammars, by Korkontzelos & Manandhar (2010) for shallow parsing and was recently shown to be beneficial for a transition-based dependency grammar parser of Modern Greek (Apidianaki et al. 2018). We have adopted the WWS approach in an effort to move as much as possible of the parsing burden from the LFG/XLE component to an external MWE recognizer (the "filter" from now on). At the same time, we have tried to allow for natural LFG analyses. The system depicted in Figure 1 consists of:

1. The ILSP FBT Tagger

2. IDION: A lexicographic tool that allows for formal descriptions of the MWEs

3. The filter

4. The XLE/LFG grammars

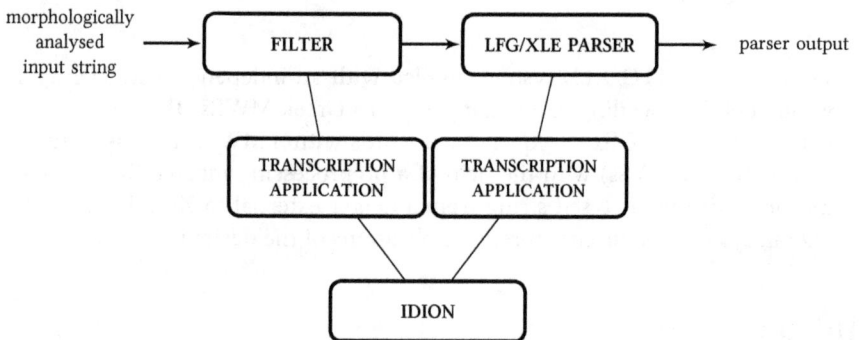

Figure 1: The overall structure of the parsing system

The ILSP FBT Tagger and IDION are independent pieces of NLP software; they are compatible with the "core" parsing system that consists of the filter and the grammars (Samaridi & Markantonatou 2014). In what follows, we describe the parts 1–4 in separate sections in this order. We will use (1) as a working example. (1) is a verb MWE that contains a fixed NP *mavra matia* 'black eyes' and an obligatory sentential complement that is controlled by the MWE subject. The subject is free and fully agrees with the verb of the MWE (MG is a pro-drop language therefore in (1) no explicit subject is present):

(1)   kano   mavra   matia   na do   kapion   / kati
        make.1SG black.ACC.PL eye.ACC.PL to see.1SG.PERF someone   something
        'I have not seen someone/something for a long time.'

2 The LFG analysis adopted: Challenging options

It has already been stated that the main idea of the adopted parsing strategy is that the fixed parts of the MWEs are treated as "words with spaces" (WWSs) (Sag et al. 2002). WWSs are used only if an MWE contains fixed sequences of words; the WWS stands only for the fixed sequence and not for the whole MWE – if the remaining MWE is flexible. The fixed sequences are identified with diagnostics involving word order permutations, the ability to introduce an XP between words and diathesis alternations (if applicable). As an example, in (1) there is the WWS *mavra_matia* 'black eyes'. The sequence *mavra_matia* is morphologically and syntactically fixed, it can be moved to the beginning of a sentence in emphatic structures and it accepts neither a determiner nor modification. The remaining parts of the MWE in (1), with the exception of certain morphological constraints on the subordinated verb, behave like the parts of a compositional structure and are treated as such.

The LFG/XLE lexicon has to recognize the WWSs as words that are assigned some part of speech (PoS) value. However, the selection of the PoS value is not always straightforward with MWEs, all the more when no WWS occurs in the MWE. Examples (2–4) illustrate the issue (the identified WWSs are in square brackets "[]"). We often find nouns functioning as adverbs; in (2) the NP headed by *zachari* 'sugar' is normally questioned with *how much*. Furthermore, the WWS in (2) could be analysed as a syntactic complex, consisting of an "object" clitic and a verb; clitics are used widely in MG. We treat this complex as a fully inflected verb. The WWS in (3) could have been generated with the rule NP → Det N; given that the head is a common noun (*dromous* 'roads') probably the PoS tag "N" is a natural choice for the WWS *tous dromous* 'the roads'. In (4), the WWS is a fixed sequence of fixed words that behaves exactly as the WWS in (3) with respect to word order phenomena (4a,b) and unlike the corresponding compositional copula structures of MG (4c,d). However, there is no phrase structure rule that would generate the WWS *to_psomi_psomaki* 'the bread little-bread' and of course, there is no likely head.

(2)   [tin   pernao] zachari
        her.ACC.FEM pass.1ST sugar.ACC
        'I have an easy time.'

(3) perno [tous dromous]
    take   the   roads.ACC

    'I wander'

(4) a. leo [to psomi   psomaki]
          call the bread.ACC little-bread.ACC

          'to starve'

    b. to psomi psomaki leo   (emphatic)

    c. * to psomi leo psomaki   (emphatic)

    d. * psomaki leo to psomi   (emphatic)

In addition, the identification of the syntactic function of the fixed parts of verb MWEs is not straightforward in LFG. This is so because the governable grammatical functions (GFs) of LFG[1] are defined on the basis of particular semantic and syntactic properties (Dalrymple 2001). Alas it is very often the case that the fixed parts of MG MWEs are not characterized by these particular properties. And still, one cannot avoid using a large choice of grammatical functions to model MG MWE phenomena because the language allows for some word order flexibility within verbal MWEs (4a,b) and often there are control (1) and binding phenomena (5) that have to be accounted for. LFG models these phenomena on the f-structure with the use of syntactic functions. (In (5) the WWS *to ksilo tis chronias tis* 'the beating the.GEN year.GEN hers' can be thought to have a noun head *ksilo* 'beating'; the structure contains a possessive pronoun that is bound by the free subject of the MWE.)

(5) I   Maria   efage [to ksilo   tis chronias tis   / *tou]
    the Maria.FEM ate   the beating the year.GEN hers / *his

    'Maria has been beaten up.'

The OBJ function makes a good example of a GF that does not fit well to the MWE data. The WWS *tous_dromous* 'the roads' in (3) is a fixed simple NP; one would be tempted to assign the OBJ function to it but, on the other hand, the fixed NP never turns up as the subject of a passive form although the verb *perno* 'take' passivises. Furthermore, the WWS in (3) presents an idiosyncratic behavior with clitics; normally it cannot be replaced by a clitic, while this is absolutely possible in a compositional structure; the fixed NP can be replaced only in a very

---

[1] The governable GFs of LFG are: SUBJ, OBJ, OBJ2, POSS, COMP, XCOMP.

restricted context, namely when the same MWE precedes the structure with the clitic (Markantonatou & Samaridi 2018) producing an ironic or emphatic effect. Passivisation is a defining property of the OBJ GF in LFG (Dalrymple 2001) and free replacement by a clitic is definitely a defining property of objects in MG. On the other hand, the WWS in (4) behaves just as the WWS in (3) with respect to passivisation and cliticisation and all the other flexibility diagnostics; evidence mandates that the two WWSs are assigned the same GF and the question is whether they should be assigned the OBJ GF or some other GF. It is possible that the idea that MWEs use exactly the syntax employed in the analysis of compositional structures (Gross 1988a,b; Kay & Sag 2012; Bargmann & Sailer 2018) could be imported in LFG and the classical GFs could be assigned to fixed constituents along with a tree-like structure and constraints on inflection, passivisation, modifiability, cliticisation and linear precedence that do the job (Waszczuk & Savary 2015). The problem with the "compositional structure" approach is that it questions the notion of syntactic functions and the generalizations expressed with them: for instance, the OBJs of MG MWEs will be peculiar in that they hardly passivise and they are not replaced by clitics freely unless they occur in highly constrained contexts.

The system we present here uses the classical LFG GFs. This means that *zachari* 'sugar' in (2) is treated as a noun and the phrasal projection is assigned the OBL(ique) GF; on the same par, the bracketed strings in (3), (4) and (5) are assigned the PoS "No"(un) and project NPs that are assigned the OBJ GF. So far we have not used a set of GFs different from the one established in the literature because linear precedence phenomena in the fixed parts are captured with the use of WWSs and modifiability and cliticisation seem to require a more careful modeling than simply allowing or prohibiting them: cliticisation heavily depends on the context and modifiability seems to be rather restricted in MG. A concrete, corpus-based, analysis of both the phenomena has not been made available yet, to the best of our knowledge. This set-up demands that passivisation is blocked with a feature (and not with the absence of an OBJ GF as it would be the case if some other GF was used in the place of the OBJ GF). Of course, a similar blocking feature would be used in the grammar anyway for several non-passivisable transitive verbs of MG MWEs; this fact definitely emphasizes the problematic situation with the OBJ GF and passivisation. In a nutshell, we have used the OBJ GF not because it served our purposes well but because the in-depth exploration of the alternatives is considered a future challenge.

In the remainder of this document we will present and discuss the parts of the system as they are depicted in Figure 1.

3 ILSP FBT Tagger

The mature ILSP FBT Tagger (Papageorgiou et al. 2000) is an adaptation of the Brill tagger trained on MG text. It uses a PAROLE compatible tagset (Bilgram & Keson 1998) of 584 different tags that capture the morphological particularities of MG. The tagger works on the output of a sentence detection and tokenisation tool and assigns both a lemma and a set of tags corresponding to an exhaustive morphological analysis of each token. Figure 2 shows the output of the ILSP FBT Tagger for (1). We decided to use the ILSP FBT Tagger because the effort to develop an XFST morphological component is a project on its own. In the set-up of Figure 1, the tagger is a black box that allows for no identification of the fixed parts of MWEs at the level of morphological analysis, as it would be possible if, for instance, the XFST/XLE component was used as in Attia (2006). For this reason, the morphologically analysed output of the ILSP tagger that offers information only about tokens, is processed with a filter (Samaridi & Markantonatou 2014) that scans the output of the tagger for strings containing MWEs and feeds a script ("formatter") that transforms the output to a format readable by an LFG/XLE grammar; the filter informs the XLE parser whether an MWE exists, whether it contains any WWSs – if so, the WWSs are marked on the output string that feeds the parser – and whether the input string can receive both a compositional and a MWE interpretation.

4 IDION

The XLE parser receives lexical knowledge on MWEs from IDION[2], an open source lexicographic environment for MWEs that is addressed both to the human user and to NLP applications and encodes, among others, morphosyntactic properties of MWEs in a, as much as possible, theory-neutral formalism. IDION is connected to the parsing system with an application that transcribes the IDION formalism to the XLE formalism (Minos et al. 2016). As opposed to other MWE DBs, such as DUELME (Grégoire 2010), that use a simplified formal language for encoding morphological features, IDION exhaustively describes morphological features with the ILSP-PAROLE compatible tagset that is also used by the ILSP FBT Tagger.

It is important to note that syntactic functions are assigned to phrasal constituents in Modern Greek (and not to parts of a word); therefore, diagnostics for constituent identification are also required along with diagnostics for the

---

[2]http://idion.ilsp.gr/

```
<cesDoc version="0.4">
  <cesHeader version="0.4"/>
    <text>
      <body>
        <p id="p1">
          <s id="s1" casing="lowercase">
            <t id="t1" word="έκανα" tag="VbMnIdPa01SgXxIpAvXx" lemma="κάνω"/>
            <t id="t " word="μαύρα" tag="AjBaNePlAc" lemma="μαύρος"/>
            <t id="t3" word="μάτια" tag="NoCmNePlAc" lemma="μάτι"/>
            <t id="t4" word="να" tag="PtSj" lemma="να"/>
            <t id="t5" word="τον" tag="PnPeMa03SgAcWe" lemma="εγώ"/>
            <t id="t6" word="δω" tag="VbMnIdXx01SgXxPeAvXx"lemma="βλέπω"/>
          </s>
        </p>
      </body>
    </text>
</cesDoc>
```

Figure 2: The output of the ILSP FBT tagger for the verb MWE in (1)

identification of WWSs. In IDION the following diagnostics are used for these purposes (Markantonatou & Samaridi 2018): possible word order permutations, the ability of XPs (modifiers included) to intervene between two words thus possibly indicating the border between two constituents, passivisability, clitic replacement, wh-questioning and causative-inchoative alternations. Grammatical functions are identified with diagnostics that apply to compositional expressions such as morphological marking and wh-questions (in MG subjects are always in the nominative case and objects almost always in the accusative case, verbs agree with their subjects and objects can be replaced by clitics).

The IDION encoding of the MWE structure corresponds to a rather flat tree and does not make use of powerful expressive means, such as inheritance, that in the literature have been combined with tree-based formalisms (Pollard & Sag 1987; Crabbé et al. 2013). The reason for choosing a perhaps redundant but rather simple encoding is that we aim at ensuring IDION's reusability. For this purpose, we try to make sure that we use expressive means that are shared by or can be easily transcribed to many formalisms and that the encoding does not rely on implicit assumptions concerning the overall grammar of the language.[3] To this end, the IDION representation of verbal MWEs defines the following nodes: (i)

---

[3]For instance, in MG possession is expressed with the sequence "DET noun Possessive". In IDION the whole sequence is encoded as fixed rather than encoding only the noun as fixed.

the root category (default) (ii) the phrasal categories shown in (6) that are used to denote free nominal constituents of the MWE (iii) leaf nodes (words). Phrasal categories and words are directly linked to the root category. IDION only indexes the fixed contiguous parts of an MWE (the WWSs of our implementation) and does not assign them a phrasal structure.

(6)   NP-NOM/NP-NOM-anim/NP-NOM-nonanim;
       NP-GEN/NP-GEN-anim/NP-GEN-nonanim;
       NP-ACC/NP-ACC-anim/NP-ACC-nonanim;

The Java-based transcription application provides for the remaining phrasal categories needed for an LFG representation that requires the definition of constituents and typically involves trees deeper than the ones defined in IDION. All in all, IDION only specifies the phrasal categories shown in (6) and it is on the transcription applications to specify the categories that are necessary for any given formalism.

The IDION encoding of the MWE in (1) is given in Figure 3. On the first column it is specified whether the annotated part of the MWE is a phrasal category (phrasal categories are shown in 6) or a word and whether it is optional or not (for instance, the MWE of example (1) that is depicted in Figure 3 has only obligatory parts). Words are encoded as lemmas and only complementisers are encoded as such (in Figure 3, the depicted MWE contains a complementiser). On the second column, the lemmas of the parts of the expression are listed, namely the verb head *kano* 'make', the lemmatized parts of the WWS *mavros mati* 'black eye', the complementizer *na* 'to' that always introduces a sentential complement and the lemma form of the irregular verb head *vlepo* 'see' of the sentential complement. On the third column are encoded the actual form of the WWS and the control facts; in the case depicted in Figure 3, the sentential complement is controlled by the NP-NOM-anim. The fourth column provides the full morphological analysis of the fixed or semi-fixed parts of the MWE, for instance it is specified that the head verb of the controlled sentential complement is always in the active voice and in a form denoting perfect aspect; person and number of the controlled verb are not specified as they are determined by the free subject of the MWE. On the last column the parts of the WWS are indexed.

We developed a Java transcription application that generates XLE entries from the IDION specifications.

The LFG/XLE entries listed below are developed out of the IDION representation of (1) shown in Figure 3. As a first step, the transcription application generates lexical entries for the WWSs that are indexed in the IDION representation of

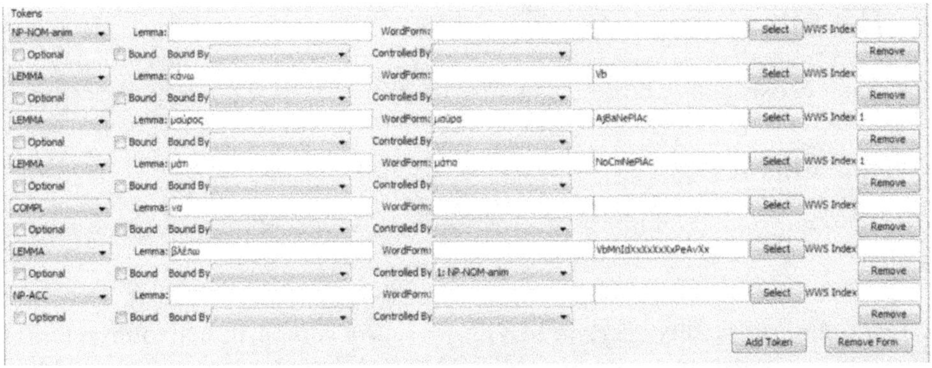

Figure 3: The IDION encoding of the MWE in (1)

the MWE; if one or more WWSs have been indexed in the IDION representation of the MWE, a corresponding number of XLE entries are produced and stored in the XLE lexicon. Morphological information about the entries, here the WWS and the verb head of the controlled sentential complement, is received from the annotation encoded on the fourth column. Next, the application generates the entry for the head verb of the MWE as follows: the NP-NOM-anim slot in the first column shows that the verb selects a free subject NP, the WWS that contains a noun and an adjective both in the accusative case shows that the head verb selects a fixed object and finally, the existence of a COMPL(ementiser) slot in the first column coupled with the control information on the third column shows that the head verb subcategorises for an XCOMP controlled by the subject of the main verb. This information generates the entry of the head verb *kano*. Finally, the head verb of the sentential complement is retrieved from the second column as it immediately follows COMPL. The application knows that the verb *vlepo* is transitive because it has a controlled subject and it is followed by an NP-ACC.

The WWS in MWE (1):   mavra_matia, NoCmPlAc

The verb head of MWE (1):   kano<SUBJ,OBJ,XCOMP>

$\uparrow$ OBJ PRED = mavra matia

$\uparrow$ XCOMP PRED = vlepo<SUBJ,OBJ>

$\uparrow$ XCOMP PRED FINITE = +

$\uparrow$ XCOMP SUBJ= $\uparrow$SUBJ

5 The filter

The filter consists of two parts: the filter lexicon and the filtering part proper.

5.1 The filter lexicon

The filter consults the filter lexicon where each MWE entry is specified for the following:

1. Compositionality: Certain MWEs can take a compositional interpretation. For instance, the free subject verbal MWE in (1) has no compositional interpretation while the semi-fixed MWE in (7) can also take the compositional interpretation 'I grab them.FEM'.

    (7) tis   arpazo
         them.FEM grab.1SG
         'I am beaten up.'

2. The "signifier": the lemma of the substring of an MWE that instructs the filter to look at the appropriate filter lexicon entries. For the MWE in (1), the signifier is the lemma *kano* 'make, do'. If the expression is fixed as in (8) the symbol "~" is used as a signifier. (8) has no translation, it is a kind of swearing (often accompanied with an offensive gesture) meaning that someone has made a serious mistake or is totally idiot:

    (8) pare   pente
         take.2SG.IMP five

3. The lemmatised form of "words with spaces" (WWSs) whether they are independent fixed MWEs as in (8) or substrings of an MWE as in (1). In the case of (8) the lemmatised WWS would be *perno pente* 'take five'. In the case of (1) the fixed part is *mavra matia* 'black eyes' and the corresponding lemmatised form is *mavros mati* 'black eye'.

4. PoS and morphological constraints on the parts of the WWS. For the fixed part of (1) *mavra matia* the constraints would be: *mavros*: adjective, plural, accusative, basic; *mati*: noun, common, plural, accusative.

5.2 The filtering part

The filter proper, implemented in Perl, reads the tagged sentence from an XML file (the output of the tagger) and stores it. Then, it checks whether a signifier exists and,

A1. If no signifier is found, the string is copied as it is on the formatter.

A2. If a signifier is found, the filter lexicon is scanned for some WWS entry. The filter checks whether the morphological constraints on the filter lexicon entries (headword and remaining words) match the lemma and the tags on the input string and:

B1. If they do not match, the input string is copied as it is on the formatter.

B2. If they match, the filter consults the filter lexicon whether the MWE can take a compositional reading and,

C1. if it can, it sends to the formatter the input string and goes to step C2

C2. if it cannot, the part of the string that has been recognized is replaced with the corresponding WWS and morphological constraints and the resulting new string is sent to the formatter.

6 The LFG analysis (implemented with XLE grammars)

The output of the formatter is processed with an LFG grammar of Modern Greek with sub-lexical rules that can parse the output of the tagger. The grammar runs on XLE, a parsing environment dedicated to writing, running and debugging LFG grammars.[4] The trees generated by the sub-lexical rules can be seen in the c-structure of Figure 5.

Modern Greek verbal MWEs are rich in syntactic structure despite any simplifications that might result from the usage of WWSs. In Section 2 we discussed why we have adopted an LFG analysis that applies the classical LFG Grammatical Functions on MWEs despite the obvious problems. Thus, so far we have manipulated the lexicon by introducing the idiomatic lexical entries but we have not manipulated the grammar rules.

---

[4]XLE is the basis for the Parallel Grammar Project, which is developing industrial-strength grammars for English, French, German, Norwegian, Japanese, and Urdu. XLE is written in C and uses Tcl/Tk for the user interface. It currently runs on Solaris Unix, Linux, and Mac OS X.

With the reservations discussed in Section 2 in mind, we proceed to present Table 1 where the various types of parsed MWE structures are listed. In all, simple sentences containing 850 verb MWEs have been parsed. In Table 1 we give the basic form of the MWEs: the reader should keep in mind that MG is a pro-drop language with no infinitives, therefore the 1st person singular present indicative (or the 3rd person present indicative if the verb is an impersonal one) are used as the verb's lemma. Our system parses strings in the Greek alphabet but in Table 1 we have used Latin characters for reasons of readability. We represent WWSs as sequences of words joined with underscores, e.g. *pare_pente* (**1** in Table 1 and example 8). The column headed with "C" indicates whether the MWE receives a compositional interpretation (Y) or not (N). Lastly, the column headed with "FX" shows whether the MWE is flexible (FL), semi-flexible (SF) or fixed (F). We have marked as SF the MWEs that allow for no word order permutations but their head verb declines fully. MWEs that allow for word order permutations and their head verb declines fully are marked as FL.

With the approach described here, the lexicon has to be enriched with verb-like predicates such as *ego_arpazo* (**2** in Table 1) and *piano_gematos* (**9** in Table 1), noun-like predicates such as *mavros_mati* (**10** in Table 1) and adjective-like predicates such as *tapi_ke_psichremos* (**7** in Table 1) and their morphological paradigms. Therefore, the morphological paradigm of the verb *arpazo* has to be duplicated in order to develop the paradigm of *tis_arpazo*. Similarly, (**7** in Table 1) *meno tapi_ke_psichremos* contains a WWS that consists of the cranberry word *tapi*, the conjunction *ke* 'and' and a fully declinable adjective *psichremos* 'cool' that occurs freely in compositional structures. However, the overall amount of new lexical entries is not more than the entries required when MWEs are parsed like compositional structures (that is, without assuming WWSs) because in a "compositional approach" the same number of entries (or more) would be listed as "idiomatic". We have already pointed out that if the presented system is provided with the appropriate lexical entries and their morphological paradigms, it uses the grammar developed for compositional structures to parse sentences containing verb MWEs.

A wide variety of structures is shown in Table 1. **1** is a sentence but functions as an adverb, the MWE in **2** and **3** function as intransitive verbs, **4** and **5** function as transitive verbs with **5** featuring a case of where the subject binds a possessive selected by the fixed object. **6** and **7** are predicative structures that contain a controlled adjectival constituent normally modeled as an XCOMP in LFG. **8**, **9** and **10** are MWEs that contain sentential complements, either free (8) or subject to constraints such as control **9**, **10** and strong selection requirements on the form of the subordinated verb. These structures capture the typology of the 850

Table 1: Types of MG verb MWEs

	MWE	LFG representation	WWS lemma	C	FX
1	perno pente take five :a type of swearing	PRED pare_pente	ADV: perno_pente	Y	F
2	tis arpazo them.CL.ACC grab 'I am beaten up'	PRED ego_arpazo <SUBJ>	V: ego_arpazo	Y	SF
3	tin pernao zachari her.ACC pass sugar.ACC 'I have an easy time'	PRED ego_pernao <SUBJ,OBL> ↑OBL PRED =zachari	V: ego_pernao	N	FL
4	richni touloumia nero pours bags.ACC water.ACC 'It rains cats and dogs'	PRED richno <SUBJ,OBJ> ↑OBJ PRED=touloumia_nero	N: touloumia_nero	N	FL
5	troo to ksilo tis chronias mou eat the beating the year.GEN mine 'I am beaten up'	PRED troo <SUBJ,OBJ> OBJ PRED=o_ksilo_tis_chronias<POSS> ↑OBJ POSS PRED= ego ↑OBJ POSS PERS =↑SUBJ PERS ↑OBJ POSS NUM =↑SUBJ NUM ↑OBJ POSS GEN =↑SUBJ GEN	N: o_ksilo_o_chronia	N	FL
6	meno stili alatos remain stele.ACC salt.GEN 'I am left speechless'	PRED meno <SUBJ,XCOMP> ↑XCOMP PRED=stili_alas<SUBJ> ↑XCOMP SUBJ=↑SUBJ	N: stili_alas	N	FL
7	meno tapi ke psichremos remain tapi and cool 'I lose all my money'	PRED meno <SUBJ,XCOMP> ↑XCOMP PRED=tapi_ke_psichremos <SUBJ> ↑XCOMP SUBJ=↑SUBJ	ADJ: tapi_ke_psichremos	N	FL
8	echi yousto na S has preference to S 'don't tell me that S'	PRED echi_yousto <COMP> ↑COMP COMPL=vα (impersonal)	V: echo_yousto	N	SF
9	richno adia na piaso yemata throw empty to catch full 'I fish out of/from'	PRED richno <SUBJ,OBJ,XCOMP> ↑XCOMP COMPL=na ↑OBJ PRED=adios ↑XCOMP PRED=piano_yematos<SUBJ> ↑XCOMP SUBJ=↑SUBJ ↑XCOMP PERF=+, ¬(↑XCOMP TENSE)	V: piano_yematos	N	FL
10	kano mavra matia na do NP make black eyes to see NP 'I have not met NP for a long time'	PRED kano <SUBJ,OBJ,XCOMP> ↑XCOMP COMPL=na ↑OBJ PRED= mavros_mati ↑XCOMP PRED=vlepo <SUBJ, OBJ> ↑OBJ PRED=ego ↑XCOMP SUBJ=↑SUBJ ↑XCOMP PERF=+, ¬(↑XCOMP TENSE)	N: mavros_mati	N	FL

verb MWEs that we parsed. Below we give selected parse-outs of the material in Table 1. Please notice that all f-structures contain a sentential feature IDIOM that is of semantic nature and conveys the meaning of the MWE. Figure 4 shows the f-structure of (9) that features the verb MWE **5** in Table 1. This MWE contains an OBJ GF headed by a WWS and a possessive anaphor that is analysed as a specifier of the projection of the WWS and is bound by the free subject; as a result the free subject and the anaphor are of the same gender and number.

(9) I   Maria   efage to ksilo   tis chronias tis
      the Maria.3SG.FEM ate   the beating the year   hers.3SG.FEM

      'Maria was beaten up.'

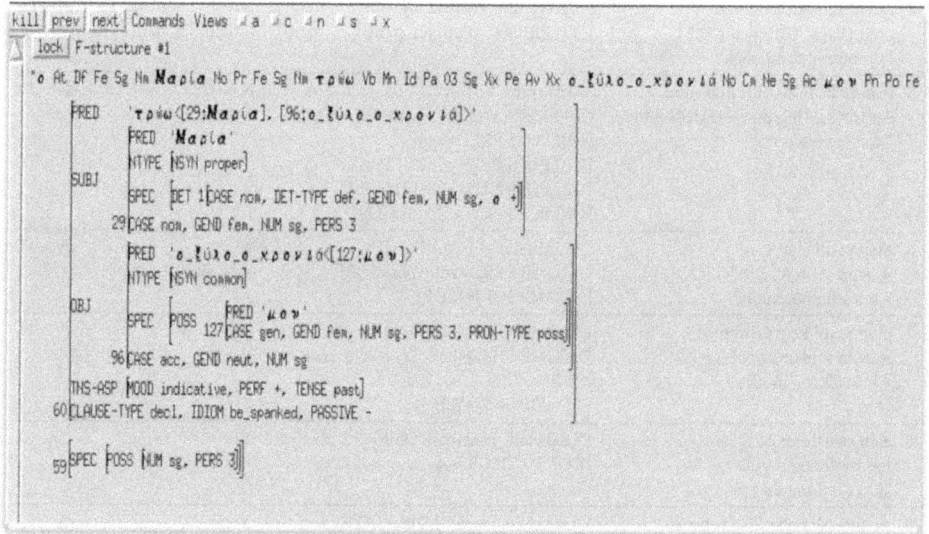

Figure 4: f-structure for *I Maria efage to ksilo tis chronias tis.* 'Maria was beaten up.', example (9), MWE **5** in Table 1

Figure 5 shows the c- and the f-structure of (10) that features an example of use of the verb MWE **10** in Table 1 and of example (1) that contains an OBJ GF headed by a WWS and a controlled sentential complement, an XCOMP in LFG terms. The result of the application of the sub-lexical rules is shown on the c-structure.

(10) Ekana   mavra matia na tin do.
      made.1SG black eyes to her see.1SG

      'I have not seen her for a very long time.'

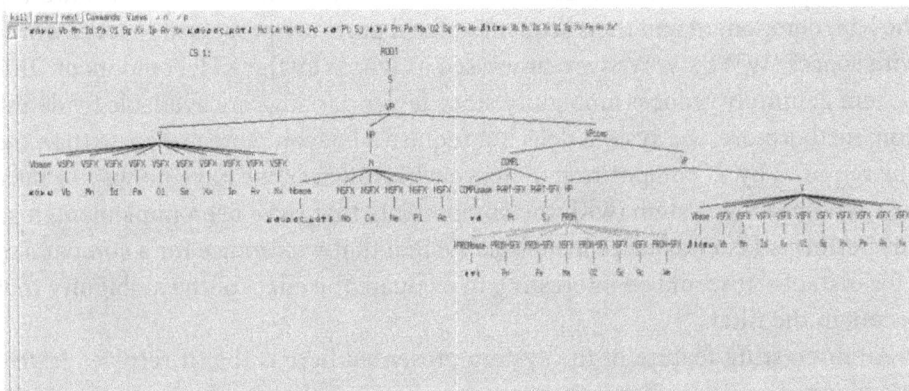

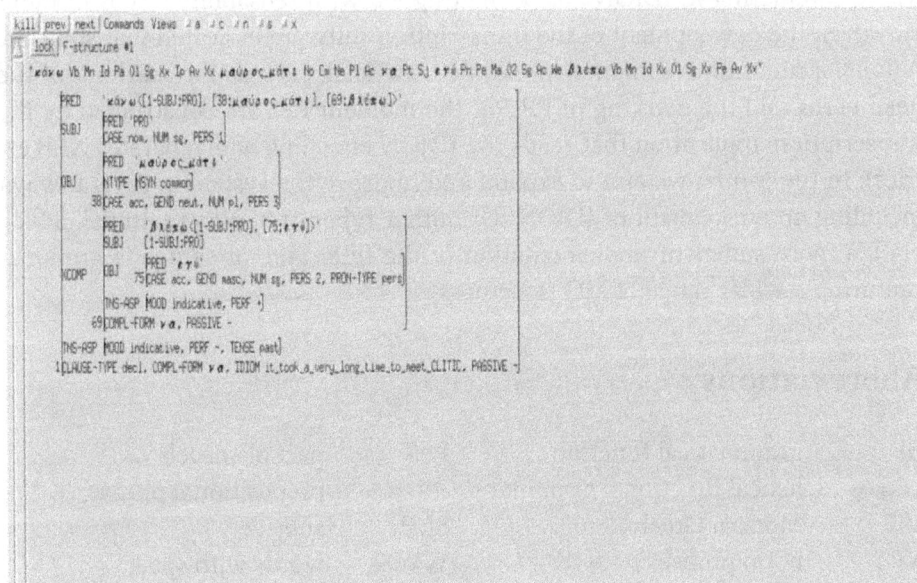

Figure 5: c- and f-structure for *Ekana mavra matia na tin do.* 'I have not seen her for a long time.', example (10), MWE **10** in Table 1

7 Discussion

We have presented a symbolic system for parsing MWEs that uses XLE and LFG grammars as its main components. MWEs are recognized as such before entering the XLE component and their sequential fixed parts are processed to form words with spaces (WWS). WWSs are processed as words by the XLE component. This system definitely reduces ambiguity since fewer parsings are available by definition; furthermore, the system does not require a lexicon more elaborate than the one required by a "compositional" approach. However, we have no way to measure whether the system (with the components that have been implemented so far) performs faster as there is no base system that we can use for a comparison – for instance, it would be interesting to evaluate the effect of the ambiguity that occurs in the filter.

An interesting feature of the system presented here is that it receives lexical knowledge from a lexicographic resource (IDION) that has been developed independently. The embedding of IDION into the LFG/XLE parsing system is a way of evaluating it. IDION has been designed with reusability issues in mind. However, the development of the transcription software indicated that some additional structural information would be beneficial, such as the marking of the head verbs and the marking of PPs (at the moment PPs are constructed by the transcription application that reads the IDION encoding and generates XLE entries). In the future, we aim to expand and improve the system in several ways, including an enrichment of IDION with other types of MWEs (nominal, adverbial), a more sufficient implementation of the filter and, of course, a grammar capturing a wider range of MG structures.

Abbreviations

GF	grammatical function	PoS	part of speech
LFG	lexical functional grammar	PP	prepositional phrase
MG	Modern Greek	SUBJ	subject
NP	noun phrase	WWSs	words with spaces
OBJ	object		

References

Apidianaki, Marianna, Prokopis Prokopidis & Haris Papageorgiou. 2018. Combining cross-lingual and syntactic evidence for Greek multiword expression identification. *Bulletin of Scientific Terminology and Neologisms of the Academy of Athens, Special issue on MWEs in Greek and other languages: From theory to implementation.*

Attia, Mohammed A. 2006. Accommodating multiword expressions in an Arabic LFG grammar. In Tapio Salakoski, Filip Ginter, Tapio Pahikkala & Tampo Pyysalo (eds.), *Advances in natural language processing: 5th international conference, FinTAL, proceedings* (Lecture Notes in Computer Science 4139), 87–98. Berlin & Heidelberg: Springer.

Bargmann, Sascha & Manfred Sailer. 2018. The syntactic flexibility of semantically non-decomposable idioms. In Manfred Sailer & Stella Markantonatou (eds.), *Mutliword expressions: Insights from a multi-lingual perspective*, 1–40. Language Science Press. DOI:10.5281/zenodo.1182587

Bilgram, Thomas & Britt Keson. 1998. The construction of a tagged Danish corpus. In *Proceedings of the 11th Nordic conference of Computational Linguistics (NODALIDA 1998)*, 129–139. Copenhagen, Denmark: Center for Sprogteknologi, University of Copenhagen, Denmark. http://www.aclweb.org/anthology/W98-1614.

Copestake, Ann, Fabre Lambeau, Aline Villavicencio, Francis Bond, Timothy Baldwin, Ivan Sag & Dan Flickinger. 2002. Multiword expressions: Linguistic precision and reusability. In *Proceedings of the third international conference on Language Resources and Evaluation (LREC 2002)*, 1941–1947. Las Palmas, Canary Islands, Spain.

Crabbé, Benoît, Denys Duchier, Claire Gardent, Joseph Le Roux & Yannick Parmentier. 2013. XMG: eXtensible MetaGrammar. *Computational Linguistics* 39(3). 591–629. DOI:10.1162/COLI_a_00144

Dalrymple, Mary. 2001. *Lexical functional grammar.* Vol. 34 (Syntax and Semantics). San Diego, CA: Academic Press.

Grégoire, Nicole. 2010. DuELME: A Dutch electronic lexicon of multiword expressions. *Language Resources and Evaluation* 44(1–2). 23–39.

Gross, Maurice. 1988a. Les limites de la phrase figée. *Langage* 90. 7–23.

Gross, Maurice. 1988b. Sur les phrases figées complexes du français. *Langue française* 77. 47–70.

Kay, Paul & Ivan Sag. 2012. *A lexical theory of phrasal idioms.* Stanford, CA. http://www1.icsi.berkeley.edu/~kay/idiom-pdflatex.11-13-15.pdf.

Korkontzelos, Ioannis & Suresh Manandhar. 2010. Can recognising multiword expressions improve shallow parsing? In *Proc. of the 11th annual conference of the North American chapter of the Association for Computational Linguistics: Human Language Technologies NAACL/HLT 2010*, 636–644. Los Angeles, California.

Markantonatou, Stella & Niki Samaridi. 2018. Revisiting the grammatical function "object" (OBJ and OBJ_θ). In Manfred Sailer & Stella Markantonatou (eds.), *Mutliword expressions: Insights from a multi-lingual perspective*, 187–213. Language Science Press. DOI:10.5281/zenodo.1182599

Minos, Panagiotis, Stella Markantonatou, Georgios Zakis & Elpiniki Margariti. 2016. *Generating LFG/XLE MWE entries from IDION (a theory neutral lexical DB)*. Struga, fYROM. http://typo.uni-konstanz.de/parseme/index.php/2-general/156-selected-posters-struga-7-8-april-2016. 6th PARSEME general meeting.

Papageorgiou, Haris, Prokopis Prokopidis, Voula Giouli & Stelios Piperidis. 2000. A unified POS tagging architecture and its application to Greek. In M. Gavrilidou, G. Carayannis, S. Markantonatou, S. Piperidis & G. Stainhauer (eds.), *Proceedings of the 2nd Language Resources and Evaluation Conference (LREC 2000)*, 1455–1462. Athens, Greece.

Pollard, Carl & Ivan Sag. 1987. *Information-based syntax and semantics* (CSLI Lecture Notes 13). Stanford: CSLI.

Sag, Ivan, Timothy Baldwin, Francis Bond, Ann Copestake & Dan Flickinger. 2002. Multiword expressions: A pain in the neck for NLP. In *Proceedings of the 3rd international conference on Computational Linguistics and Intelligent Text Processing* (Lecture Notes in Computer Science 2276), 1–15. Springer.

Samaridi, Niki & Stella Markantonatou. 2014. Parsing Modern Greek verb MWEs with LFG/XLE grammars. In *10th workshop on Multiword Expressions (MWE 2014), European chapter of the Association for Computational Linguistics 2014*, 33–37. Gothenburg, Sweden.

Waszczuk, Jakub & Agata Savary. 2015. *Modeling syntactic properties of MWEs in LFG*. La Valletta. 4th PARSEME general meeting.

Chapter 5

Multiword expressions in multilingual applications within the Grammatical Framework

Krasimir Angelov

University of Gothenburg

The main focus of Grammatical Framework (GF) is in multilingual applications where the same type of content is produced and analyzed in several languages at once. This is achieved by joining the grammars for all languages with a shared interlingual representation. In designing the interlingua, multiword expressions are an important factor that must be considered. Here, I adopt the broader definition where everything that translates non-compositionally accross languages is considered an expression. In this chapter I present multiword expressions from a cross-lingual perspective in relation to an interlingual grammar.

1 Introduction

Grammatical Framework (GF, Ranta 2011) is a programming language for developing multilingual applications. The typical applications are in natural language generation, dialogue systems, machine translation or in question answering systems where it is feasible to assume a limited language domain. In these scenarios it is possible to design a controlled language which can be completely covered with a formal grammar. On the other hand, these applications are typically highly multilingual. It is not uncommon to have a single grammar which supports simultaneously more than twenty languages. There are a number of challenges in this kind of application.

First of all, in order to scale to a high number of languages, GF is designed to work with an interlingua. Every grammar is divided into an abstract syntax and one or more concrete syntaxes. The abstract syntax is a language-independent

Krasimir Angelov. 2019. Multiword expressions in multilingual applications within the Grammatical Framework. In Yannick Parmentier & Jakub Waszczuk (eds.), *Representation and parsing of multiword expressions: Current trends*, 127–146. Berlin: Language Science Press. DOI:10.5281/zenodo.2579041

interlingual representation of the application domain, while each of the concrete syntaxes renders an abstract syntax tree into a string in the corresponding natural language. In that setting, translation, for instance, is reduced to parsing the input sentence into an abstract tree and then rendering of the same tree into another concrete language.

Furthermore, developing even a small language fragment would normally require several low-level details, such as word order and gender/number agreement, to be reimplemented from scratch for every language and for every application. This would be highly ineffective if it was not aided by the development of the Resource Grammars Library (RGL, Ranta 2009) in GF. RGL is a library of wide coverage grammars for more than thirty languages developed by a community of linguists and computer scientists. By reusing the library, new applications can be built in short time by people who do not even have to be linguistically trained and who may not be experts in the target languages.

Working on the level of the RGL is still too low-level though. The library is trying to hide syntactic differences across languages but this is still not what we ultimately want in an application. What is needed is a model which can abstract over the language-independent semantics of the sentence. Phenomena like constructions and multiword expressions translate non-compositionally across languages, and thus are recurring obstacles that have to be resolved in every application. For that purpose there is a different grammar for each application. Application grammars, for example, are more semantically oriented. On the other hand, resource grammars are syntactic. Another difference between these two grammars is that resource grammars are highly lexicalized, but lexical entries often become semantic functions in application grammars. This is a key design decision which allows us to have an abstract language-independent representation. For example, such a representation lets us hide the language-specific multiword expressions in the modules for the concrete languages, without affecting the abstract syntax.

This strategy has been proven efficient in limited domains, and most of this chapter will be about how language-specific multiword expressions and constructions are represented in GF.

We have recently started to scale up from limited-domain applications to wide coverage parsing and translation. For this to be successful, it is important to have a library of commonly used constructions across different languages. Although this is still a moving target, I will report on the current efforts to build such a library by either reusing existing resources, or by creating those using automatic methods. This also shows that the strategy used for limited domains can scale to an open domain, when there is a wide-coverage resource of raw data that can be ported to the platform.

Please note that moving from lexicalized syntactic grammars to unlexicalized semantic grammars requires, for many languages, syntax to be represented in a discontinuous way. Just to give a simple example, forming questions in English requires that we move or add auxiliary verbs in front of the sentence, while the rest of the verb phrase is left somewhere in the middle. Other languages might not use auxiliaries at all or they might just form questions differently. This means that the verb phrase in English must be modelled as a single phrase with two discontinuous parts. The implications from this for the implementation of the framework will be discussed as well.

2 The basic principles of GF

GF is designed as a multilingual framework from the ground up. A typical application starts by identifying the relevant domain and then describing the desired phrases within that domain in multiple languages. In order to accommodate and link several diverse languages, the framework separates the grammar into two distinct conceptual layers: abstract and concrete syntax.

The ABSTRACT SYNTAX is a logical framework which acts as a language independent interlingua. It defines a collection of types and functions which can be used to build abstract syntax trees. Each abstract tree represents a phrase which is realized by using one of the available CONCRETE SYNTAXES. In this section, I will informally introduce the abstract and the concrete syntax in GF by example. For a more detailed introduction to GF we refer to Ranta (2011).

We start with the lexicon. On an abstract level, the lexicon consists of a simple inventory of word senses. For example, we might have:

```
cat N
fun horse_N : N
```

Here the first line declares that there is a category N, which will denote the type of all nouns. The second line defines a function with no arguments, a.k.a. a constant of type N. These abstract constants serve as cross-lingual lemmas. By convention we use names composed of an English lemma followed by a part of speech tag. When these are not sufficient to disambiguate the meaning of the word, then we can add more elements. For example, we could use WordNet's sense numbers for disambiguation:

```
fun arm_1_N : N          (body part)
fun arm_3_N : N          (weapon)
```

The lexicon starts to get interesting only when we move to the concrete syntax. The concrete syntax for English looks something like:

```
lincat N = Number => Str
lin horse_N = table {Sg => "horse" ; Pl => "horses"}
```

Here the keyword `lincat` introduces the linearization category for nouns, i.e. for the type N, and `lin` introduces the linearization of the function horse_N itself.

In programming language parlance, the abstract category N is like an abstract data type, i.e. a mere name with a hidden implementation, while the linearization category in the concrete syntax is its actual implementation. In GF, unlike in other programming languages, a single type or a single function might have several different implementations – one for every concrete syntax. In this case, the implementation in English says that N is a table or an array of strings (Str) indexed by a Number. The number itself is another data type defined as an enumeration with two possible values – singular (Sg) and plural (Pl):

```
param Number = Sg | Pl
```

The linearization of horse_N, on the other hand, gives the actual values in the table. In English these would be the word forms *horse* and *horses*, and in French *cheval, chevaux*. In French, however, we also need to know the gender of the noun in order to take care of the word agreement in the syntax. Because of that the corresponding definition in the concrete syntax for French is slightly more complicated:

```
lincat N = {s : Number => Str ; g : Gender}
lin horse_N =
          {s = table {Sg => "cheval"; Pl => "chevaux"};
           g = Masc
          }
```

```
param Gender = Masc | Fem
```

Here the linearization category for N is not a simple table of word forms but a record with two fields – s and g. The field s is still an inflection table like in English, but there is also the field g of type Gender with two possible values, Masc and Fem. The linearization for horse_N assigns to the field s the inflection table for French and sets the field g to Masc.

It is also possible to have records which combine together more than one string field. This is used for instance in English where phrasal verbs consist of a main verb and a particle. Those verbs are modelled as records:

```
lincat V2          = {s : VForm => Str; part : Str; prep : Str}
lin swith_off_V2 = {s = table {VInf =>"switch";
                                VPres=>"switches";
                                ...};
                    part = "off"
                    prep = ""}
```

The field part keeps the particle while the s field is the inflection table of the main verb. There is also a third field, prep, which stores the potential preposition for transitive verbs. Since there is no preposition in this case, an empty string is added. In prepositional verbs, however, this field will be non-empty. It is even possible to have verbs with both a particle and a preposition.

It is possible to have multiple string fields in nouns as well. This happens for instance in Chinese where a noun is characterized by its lemma and its classifier. Both are string fields and they could be arbitrarily far apart in the final sentence. For that reason they are stored as two different fields in the record:

```
lincat N = {s : Str; c : Str}
lin horse_N = {s = "ma"; c = "pi"}
```

The structure of the lexicon in all languages is conceptually very similar. There might be more numbers and genders, or there might be grammatical cases, but in general a lexical entry in GF is an inflection table indexed by one or more parameters, and there might be additional fields for features such as gender, word class, classifier, or a particle.

The records shown above are rarely what the GF grammarian actually writes. Instead it is possible to isolate common patterns into reusable operations which allow us to have succinct definitions like:

```
lin horse_N = mkN "horse" ;
lin switch_off_V2 = mkV2 (partV (mkV "switch") "off");
```

Here the smart paradigm (Détrez & Ranta 2012) operations mkN and mkV are responsible for predicting the inflection tables of nouns and verbs from the lemma. When the inflection is not predictable from the lemma alone then it is possible to specify extra arguments, i.e.:

```
lin mouse_N = mkN "mouse" "mice";
```

In this case the second argument of mkN is the irregular plural form of *mouse*. Auxiliary operations like partV and mkV2 are used to set the particle or the transitivity of the verb.

Having set the basics of the lexicon we can move on to the syntax. In the abstract syntax, the syntax is represented as a collection of n-ary functions. For example, adjectival modification requires two functions, AdjCN and UseN:

```
cat AP; CN
fun AdjCN : AP -> CN -> CN
fun UseN : N -> CN
```

This yields to two syntactic categories: adjectival phrases (AP) and common nouns (CN). The simplest common noun consists of just a single noun (N) and is produced by the function UseN. The function AdjCN lets us to modify the noun with one or more adjectival phrases. How exactly the adjectival phrases are attached is language specific.

In English, there is no gender and the adjective is always before the noun. The linearizations for AdjCN and UseN are simply:

```
lincat AP = Str
lincat CN = Number => Str

lin UseN n = n
lin AdjCN ap cn = table {Sg => ap ++ cn ! Sg;
                         Pl => ap ++ cn ! Pl}
```

Note that when building common noun phrases it is still not known whether the phrase should be used in singular or in plural. It will remain unknown until a determiner is fixed and a complete noun phrase built. For that purpose, the linearization category for CN is an inflection table indexed by number just like for the N category. Since the linearizations for CN and N are the same, the linearization rule for UseN is just the identity function. Since I have defined the linearization for adjectives to be a plain string, the linearization for AdjCN simply concatenates the adjective phrase in front of the common noun. Here the (++) operator indicates concatenation of token sequences, and the exclamation mark (!) is used to fetch the element from the table that corresponds to a given parameter.

Note that the two elements in the table of the last example are identical except that they select different numbers. There is a handy shorthand notation for this case:

```
lin AdjCN ap cn = \\n => ap ++ cn ! n
```

Here the operator (\\) creates a table whose index is the variable n. After the double arrow (=>) is the value itself, which is defined by using the variable n. When I substitute n with Sg and Pl I get the same values as in the previous example.

In French, the adjectival modification requires gender and number agreement. In addition, the adjective is sometimes put before and sometimes after the noun. This means that we need a more complex linearization type for AP:

```
lincat AP = {s : Gender => Number => Str;
             isPrefix : Bool}
```

This type consists of an inflection table for the adjective and a Boolean parameter which determines whether the adjective should be placed before or after the noun. The linearization rule for AdjCN now is:

```
lincat CN = {s : Number => Str; g : Gender}
lin AdjCN ap cn = {
  s = \\n => let
                aps = ap.s ! cn.g ! n;
                cns = cn.s ! n
             in case ap.isPrefix of {
                    True  => aps ++ cns;
                    False => cns ++ aps
                }
  g = cn.g
  }
```

Here, in the let expression I first compute the right forms of the adjective and of the basic common noun. After that, I concatenate them in the right order depending on the parameter isPrefix. Note that cn.g is used in two different places. First it gives the right gender to use for the adjective, and second it is used to propagate the gender from the smaller common noun which is an argument of AdjCN to the bigger phrase. The rest of the syntax is built in a similar fashion by adding more and more syntactic combinators.

This section had the goal to demonstrate the essential features of GF and how these make it possible to hide language-specific details. In the abstract syntax I merely say that there are adjectives and nouns and that those can be combined together. How exactly this happens is determined by the concrete syntax. In this way, the abstract syntax can stay language-independent while all language-specific features can still be handled. It could be rightfully argued that the level of abstractness as it is presented so far is still not sufficiently high. For example, I still assume that all languages have adjectives and nouns, which might be questioned for some languages. It did, however, work for the 30+ languages that are already supported in the framework. The most important problem that I will address in the next section, however, is that what is an adjective, noun, or verb in one language might not belong to the same part of speech in another language. This is a source of non-compositional constructions and multiword expressions that need to be handled on a different level in the framework.

3 Constructions and multiword expressions in GF

I shall divide expressions in two non-overlapping classes since they are handled differently in GF. The first class are expressions that have meaning only as a whole and that cannot be understood by interpreting their parts compositionally. Examples for those are *by and large, after all, long time no see, instead of, because of*, etc. Such expressions are composed of smaller units which have in general their own semantic and syntactic uses, but inside the expressions they are just tokens constituting a larger unit. MWEs cannot be parsed by using meaningful grammatical rules. For instance, in order to parse *instead of* compositionally, a syntactic rule could be added, which combines an adverb and a preposition to form another preposition:

```
fun foo : Adv -> Prep -> Prep
```

A rule like this would have no other use but to cover controversial syntactic sequences which do not have any compositional meaning anyway. This makes even less sense in a multilingual setting, since the internal structure of those expressions in English does not persist in other languages. In Swedish, for instance, *because of* translates as *på grund av*, and in Bulgarian, *instead of* translates as *vmesto*. In both cases the translation is another prepositional expression, but its internal composition is very different. The solution is very simple: to ignore the bogus internal composition of those expressions and to add them as multiword units in the lexicon:

```
fun instead_of_Prep, because_of_Prep : Prep
lin instead_of_Prep = mkPrep "instead of"
lin because_of_Prep = mkPrep "because of"
```

The implication of this choice is that the parser in GF (Angelov 2011) has to work, not on the level of words, but on a different, more semantic level. In the case of multiword expressions, this semantic level is a cross-words level, and, in agglutinative languages, it is often a sub-word level (Angelov 2015). This complication means, for instance, that unlike in most other statistical parsers, GF parsing is not done on top of a part of speech tagged input. Instead, the parser performs both parsing and tagging, where a single tag might span several tokens or conversely only a part of a token.

A subclass of non-compositional expressions is the class of phrasal and prepositional verbs. Examples of those were shown in the previous section. The complication in this case is that they are not only composed of multiple words but the words are not even consecutive. Unlike in frameworks based on context-free grammars, in GF this is a trivial matter. Discontinuous expressions are modelled by simply using more than one string fields inside a record. On a low-level both tables and records in GF are modelled as tuples of strings which reduces the formalism to a Parallel Multiple Context-Free Grammar (PMCFG, Seki et al. 1991) which is beyond context-free grammars. When an expression is embedded in a sentence, then the syntactic rules know where to put each of the constituents. The assumption, however, is that all lexical units of the same type have the same types of discontinuities. For instance, the linearization type for all two-argument verbs in English is:

```
lincat V2 = {s : VForm => Str; part : Str; prep : Str}
```

However, only some verbs have particles and only some others have prepositions. In a monolingual grammar it is possible to split the category into a category for simple verbs and a category for phrasal/prepositional verbs but this does not scale across languages. Phrasal verbs in English, for example, are often translated to simple verbs in Slavic languages, where the information from the particle is encoded as a prefix attached to the root. Conversely, simple verbs in English might become prepositional verbs in other languages or vice versa.

The second class of expressions is those that have both a compositional and a non-compositional meaning. It is often the case that the second is the most frequent meaning but the former cannot be excluded either. Since GF is a multilingual framework, the most natural way of identifying multiword expressions is cross-lingual. If an expression has a non-compositional meaning then it is quite likely that it will be expressed in a very different way in another language. This is a very empirical criterion which makes it easier to detect multiword expressions, but on the other hand, it fuses multiword expressions with constructions. Basically anything with a non-compositional abstract syntax across languages is considered a multiword expression. This kind of expressions is obviously a problem in an interlingua-based system.

The solution is to identify and factorize expressions. Figure 1 shows the abstract syntax trees for the sentences *My name is John* in English and the equivalent *Ich heiße John* in German. The translation is non-compositional because English has no equivalent for the German verb *heißen*. In a transfer-based translation system, I would have to explicitly manipulate the trees to get the one from the other. In an interlingual system I can factorize.

We add in the abstract syntax a new function which takes as input all fragments from the individual trees that stay invariable. In each of the concrete syntaxes we define that the function produces the corresponding language specific trees where the invariable subtrees are just plugged in the right places. In the particular case we would get:

Abstract:

```
fun have_name_Cl  : NP -> PN -> Cl
```

English:

```
lin have_name_Cl p n = PredVP (DetCN (PossNP p) (UseN name_N))
                              (UseComp (CompNP (UsePN n)))
```

German:

```
lin have_name_Cl p n = PredVP p (CompV2 (mkV "heissen") (UsePN n))
```

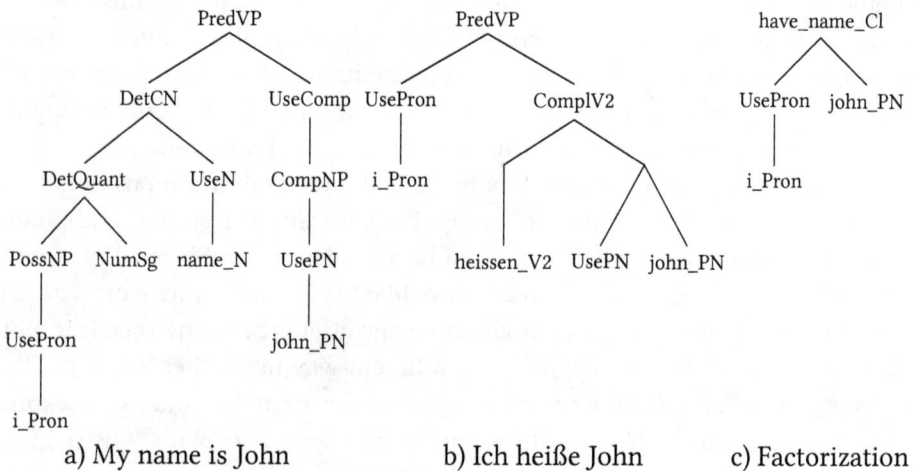

a) My name is John   b) Ich heiße John   c) Factorization

Figure 1: An example for non-compositional abstract syntax

The new function takes as arguments the subject (NP) and the proper name (PN) and produces a clause (Cl). In the German example the subject is actually the pronoun *ich* with an abstract syntax UsePron i_Pron. In English, on the other hand, the syntactic subject is *my name* but we are only interested in varying *my* so the argument UsePron i_Pron is wrapped with PossNP which in English generates a possessive determiner from an NP, i.e. from *I* we get *my*. The determiner is then applied to the noun *name*. The result is of category clause which is the same as a sentence except that it has variable tense and word order. This makes it possible to reuse it for building relative clauses, questions and sentences. We can also inflect it in tense and polarity. This means that it is enough to factorize the construction only once and then it automatically becomes available in all possible forms. Once we have the new abstract function then we can use a language-independent tree as shown on Figure 1c.

Note that in the linearization rules, unlike in the lexicon and in the syntax of the grammar, tables and records were not used. Instead we are free to reuse the already existing syntactic functions that are available in the grammar. In the previous section, how to define functions, such as AdjCN and UseN, was introduced. These functions can be used not only for parsing/generating sentences but also inside the definitions of new functions. This is exactly what is done here and thus, a lot of low-level details can be avoided.

For lexical units we can either reuse existing lexical definitions like name_N or define locally new ones like mkV "heissen". This is handy since nouns like name_N are more common across languages and thus we would probably want them in the general lexicon anyway. On the other hand, verbs equivalent to *heißen* can be found in only some languages.

The previous example can be explained as a construction which differs across languages because of a lexical gap, i.e. the missing *heißen* verb in English. However, exactly the same solution can be also used for pure idioms. For example, a prototypical multiword expression like *kick the bucket* in English can be defined as a lexical verb phrase:

```
fun kick_the_bucket_VP : VP
lin kick_the_bucket_VP = ComplSlash (SlashV2a kick_V2)
                                    (DetCN (DetQuant DefArt NumSg)
                                           (UseN bucket_N))
```

A translation to another language could be realized either as a single verb equivalent to *die* or as another idiom. In either case the translation should still function as a verb phrase. Note that the verb phrase above is not just a complicated way to encode the string *kick the bucket*. When the expression in the example is evaluated it is reduced to a complex data structure which, among other things, contains all inflection forms of *kick* as well as all auxiliary verbs that must be used for forming the different tenses in English.

The common feature between the last two examples is that in both cases we have to move from lexical categories such as noun and verb to a higher-level syntactic categories. For example instead of assuming the existence of a specific verb we just assume that there is a specific verb phrase or a sentence that conveys the same meaning. Similarly instead of nouns we use noun phrases and instead of adjectives – adjective phrases. Basically we move upwards in the hierarchy of syntactic categories until we reach a level where the differences across languages are entirely contained within the selected category.

If the multiword expression contains variable parts then they become arguments of the abstract syntax function. The order in which the arguments are listed in the type of the function is completely irrelevant since in the concrete syntax we are free to use the arguments in an arbitrary order regardless of the order in which they are declared. It is just by convention that we usually choose to use the order in which they are used in English. Note, however, that this freedom does not come for free. For instance, most statistical PMCFG parsers assume that the arguments to a function are used in the order in which they are defined. This assumption is always satisfiable if the grammar is monolingual but in a multilingual setting there is simply no natural order. Moreover, the grammar in a typical statistical parser is learned from corpora and is generally not intended to be interpreted, so any argument order is just as good. In contrast the typical GF grammar is developed by a grammarian who might have his/her own aesthetic preferences.

Using functions with arguments is just one of the ways to make a multiword expression variable. Sometimes general modifiers are admitted in the middle of an expression. Typical examples are light verb constructions such as *I am back* which also admit modifications like *I am **already** back*. It is not difficult to model the verb phrase copula+back:

```
lin am_back_VP = UseComp (CompAdv back_Adv)
```

What is not visible here, however, is that the computed verb phrase is discontinuous. The two important parts are an inflection table with all forms of the copula and a second field which contains the argument of the copula, i.e. the adverb *back*. Now if we modify the new lexical verb phrase:

```
AdVVP already_AdV am_back_VP
```

then the Resource Grammar automatically knows that the adverb *already* should be inserted between the copula and the argument. The insertion is possible only because of the discontinuity of the verb phrase. Note also that the same adverbial modification in another language may not require discontinuity. For example the equivalent in Bulgarian for *I am back* consists of a single verb and then the adverb is placed before the verb. None of this, however, is visible in the abstract syntax.

In general the ability of the framework to deal with discontinuous phrases is heavily exploited in the resource grammar. It is one of the most powerful features that allows us to hide language specific details and it helps in the implementation of some constructions.

4 Libraries of constructions in GF

Constructions and multiword expressions are really abundant in any natural language, and it is part of our mission to collect and organize GF resources for as many languages as possible. The main realization of that mission, so far, is the RGL. In the recent years we have also started to collect general lexical resources. Ultimately we would like to have a Resource Lexicons Library with a multilingual translation lexicon for many languages. Even that is not the end and we should also consider collecting libraries of constructions. There were two pilot projects in that direction: Gruzitis et al. (2015) and Enache et al. (2014).

In Gruzitis et al. (2015) the goal is to formalize the Swedish Constructicon (Lyngfelt et al. 2012). The original constructicon is a semi-formal database which covers common constructions in Swedish relevant for second language learners. There is also an ongoing work to link the resource with the Berkeley Constructicon for English (Bäckström et al. 2014). The focus, however, is in language learning rather than parsing or translation. As such it was not the primary goal to organize the constructicon as a formal grammar usable for automatic processing. Instead each entry in the resource combines an informal textual description with a syntactic pattern written in a semi-formal style. The syntactic patterns were parsed and converted to GF rules which extend the Swedish Resource Grammar.

The original constructicon contains 374 entries of which the project focused on the 105 constructions for verb phrases. Due to inconsistencies in the original resource in the first round only 43 out of the 105 constructions were successfully converted. After several iterations of manual inspection and correction, the number of successful constructions increased to 93. The remaining cases were consistently annotated but are corner cases that are currently not supported by the conversion algorithm. The necessary corrections and inconsistencies were sent back to the developers of the constructicon and are fixed by now. The experiment, however, clearly showed the advantage of using a formal system that can guard against accidental errors that are imminent in a free text format.

At the end each of the constructions was converted to one or more GF functions which in total resulted in 127 abstract functions. For 98 out of these 127 abstract functions, the corresponding concrete syntax was also successfully constructed automatically. A logical continuation of the project would be to also convert the aligned entries from the Berkeley Constructicon and later to add other languages.

Enache et al. (2014) started from a much lower level and tried to find candidates for multiword expressions from the Wikitravel phrase collection in English, German, French and Swedish. The general idea is that, given a pair of parallel sentences, the algorithm extracts all possible abstract syntax trees for each sentence and if there is no common abstract tree for both sentences, then the pair must contain a non-compositional expression. The candidates are then manually examined and the new constructions are added in a library of constructions. The majority of constructions found in this way span over larger syntactic structures and are thus above the level of a simple lexicon. For example out of 171 candidates 142 expressions were syntactic. They can be roughly classified as: greetings, weather reports, time expressions, money, units of measurement and spatial deixis. The remaining 29 expressions are lexical. For example *locker* in English translates as *låsbart skåp* ('lockable closet') in Swedish.

Another experiment in Enache et al. (2014) is to learn a lexicon of compound nouns between English and German. The method uses automatic word alignment in a parallel corpus. The candidates for compounds are pairs of phrases where: the English side must be parsable as a noun phrase with the GF grammar, the German side must consist of a single word, and finally the overall probability for the pair must be above a fixed threshold level. The compound nouns extracted in this way were added to the lexicon of a statistical machine translation system and the evaluation showed a noticeable improvement in the BLEU score.

5 Application grammars

The discussions so far were on the level of the Resource Grammars. The typical GF applications, however, never use the resource grammars directly. Instead they are used as libraries to build application grammars. The main difference is that while the abstract syntax of a resource grammar describes some kind of abstracted syntactic level, the application grammar describes an abstracted domain semantics. Another way to see the difference is to think about the abstract syntax of the application grammar as an ontological language for describing the application domain. The abstract syntax of the resource grammar, on the other hand, is an ontology which describes the syntactic constructions that someone would expect to find in a natural language.

While in the resource grammar we work with categories like noun phrase and verb phrase, in the application grammar we switch to semantic categories like person, agent, food, drink, etc. The abstract syntax functions, on the other hand, are semantic predicates which take, for instance, an agent and a drink and produce a statement like:

someone(person) *drinks something*(drink)

The main role of these new semantic categories is to provide sortal restrictions on the types of nouns that can be used for the different arguments of the predicates. Otherwise the predicates are implemented in a fashion that is very similar to the one for multiword expressions presented in Section 3. In particular most of the predicates are de-lexicalized which gives us more freedom to keep the abstract syntax language-independent while hiding all differences in the concrete syntax.

The sortal restrictions might be relevant for general multiword expressions as well. For example part of the annotations in the Swedish Constructicon are about semantic roles such as Actor, Theme, Result, etc. Those were ignored while converting the resource to GF, but it is possible that some of these constructions are valid only when the constraints are satisfied.

There are several advantages in working with application grammars. First, they are typically much smaller than the resource grammars, which also makes them computationally much more efficient. Second, since the application grammars cover only a specific domain, they can guarantee translation with publishing quality. However, when the resource grammars are used directly in translation then the quality is much worse. Most of the problems can be attributed to multiword expressions which are simply not covered by the vanilla resources. Having a comprehensive grammar of multiword expressions should improve the quality a lot, but since building a general and comprehensive resource is very expensive, we currently do it on application by application basis.

The main disadvantage of the application grammars is that they lack robustness. They can analyse input conforming to the grammar but fail completely if there is even a minor violation. For that reason they are mostly used for controlled languages (Angelov & Ranta 2010) where the users must use authoring tools that help them to stay within the scope of the grammar. A screenshot of one of those tools (Ranta et al. 2010) is shown on Figure 2. With this interface the users are not allowed to enter free text but instead they compose a sentence by choosing words from a list of options. The sentence is built incrementally and at each step the list contains only words that are permitted as a possible next word in the sentence.

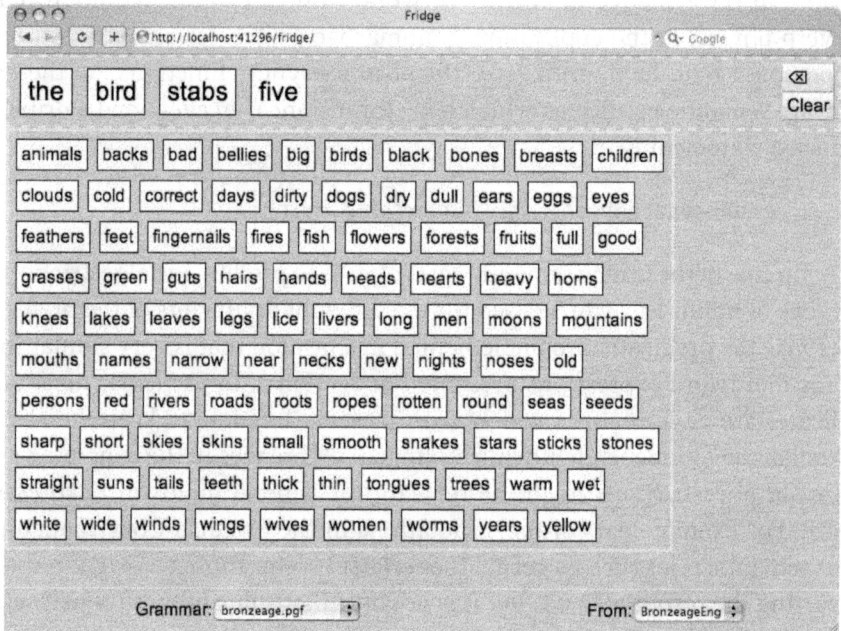

Figure 2: An authoring interface for writing Controlled Languages

The controlled language authoring is useful only when the grammar is restrictive. If the same interface is used with the resource grammar, then since there are very little restrictions, almost every word can appear almost everywhere. The analysis of a strange combination of words, however, could be equally strange. The other disadvantage of that interface is that it is not possible to get an overview of all constructions that are available in the grammar. In a sense, that interface gives us the ant's point of view which sees each word one by one. What we sometimes want is the bird's view which sees the grammar from the top.

One such interface was developed in Hedström et al. (2016). With that interface the user is first presented with a list of all possible constructions. When a particular construction is chosen then he/she is guided to a customization interface like the one on Figure 3. There the user sees an example of the construction rendered in two languages. Below the example, there is a list of options that can be used

to customize the construction. On the figure, the example is the construction is
have_name_Cl from Section 3 rendered in Swedish and Bulgarian. The possible
customizations are to turn the construction from a statement to a question or to
change the subject, i.e. *Who are we talking about?.*

Figure 3: A browsing interface for an application grammar

This particular interface is not restricted to controlled languages. It can be
configured to work with any grammar where the configuration describes which
phrases should be included in the browser. For example, if it is coupled with the
resource grammar, then it is not necessary to make the whole of the grammar
visible. Instead the browser can only include phrases that are relevant for a particular purpose. For example, the interface is currently used in an offline mobile
translation application (Angelov et al. 2014) which can translate free text. The
browsing interface, however, does not expose the entire grammar, and instead
it only covers common tourist phrases for which we can guarantee publishing
quality.

6 Wide coverage grammars

The resource grammars and the application grammars are the two main types of
grammars that we usually deal with in GF. Just in the last few years, however,
we have started scaling up the framework to an open domain. The milestone
that made that possible is the numerous improvements in the compiler and the
interpreter for bigger grammars, and in particular the improvements in the GF
parser (Angelov 2011).

Krasimir Angelov

There are two challenges that we have to deal with in the open domain. The first is robustness and the second disambiguation. We get the robustness by using a wide coverage grammar which basically consists of the resource grammar plus a large lexicon. On top of that we added minor extensions that deal with ungrammatical input. The disambiguation relies on a statistical ranking trained on the Penn Treebank (Angelov 2011).

As we mentioned earlier, translation via the vanilla resource grammar is far from perfect. We compensate, however, by plugging a high-quality application grammar for a particular domain. By combining the two we get decent quality as long as we stay close to the target domain. For example, Ranta et al. (2015) reports BLEU scores above 70% for technical descriptions of places and objects related to accessibility by disabled people. Translations outside of the domain are still possible thanks to the resource grammar.

Again, one of the major roles of the application module in the wide-coverage translator is to provide proper translations for non-compositional expressions. We expect that scaling further the quality of the generic translator will also critically depend on the availability of a wide-coverage resource of constructions.

7 Conclusion

In general we have no doubt that GF can cope with multiword expressions. Almost every application grammar in GF must deal with some of them. Moreover, we often have to deal with constructions across languages. The key enabling device to allow variability in the constructions is the fact that the framework allows for discontinuities. The interesting challenge that we see, however, is how to collect a good inventory of constructions. Our current case by case solution does not scale well for open-domain applications.

References

Angelov, Krasimir. 2011. *The mechanics of the Grammatical Framework*. Chalmers University of Technology dissertation.
Angelov, Krasimir. 2015. Orthography engineering in Grammatical Framework. In *Proceedings of the Grammar Engineering Across Frameworks (GEAF) workshop, 53rd annual meeting of the ACL and 7th IJCNLP*, 33–40. Beijing, China.

Angelov, Krasimir, Björn Bringert & Aarne Ranta. 2014. Speech-enabled hybrid multilingual translation for mobile devices. In *Proceedings of the demonstrations at the 14th conference of the European chapter of the Association for Computational Linguistics*, 41–44. Gothenburg, Sweden: Association for Computational Linguistics. http://aclweb.org/anthology/E14-2011.

Angelov, Krasimir & Aarne Ranta. 2010. Implementing controlled languages in GF. In *Proceedings of the workshop on Controlled Natural Language* (CNL'09), 82–101. Marettimo Island, Italy: Springer-Verlag.

Bäckström, Linnéa, Benjamin Lyngfelt & Emma Sköldberg. 2014. Towards interlingual constructicography: On correspondence between constructicon resources for English and Swedish. *Constructions and Frames* 6. 9–33.

Détrez, Grégoire & Aarne Ranta. 2012. Smart paradigms and the predictability and complexity of inflectional morphology. In *Proceedings of the 13th conference of the European chapter of the Association for Computational Linguistics (EACL 2012)*, 645–653. Avignon, France: Association for Computational Linguistics. http://aclweb.org/anthology/E12-1066.

Enache, Ramona, Inari Listenmaa & Prasanth Kolachina. 2014. Handling noncompositionality in multilingual CNLs. In *Controlled Natural Language . CNL 2014* (Lecture Notes in Computer Science 8625), 147–154. Cham: Springer.

Gruzitis, Normunds, Dana Dannells, Benjamin Lyngfelt & Aarne Ranta. 2015. Formalising the Swedish constructicon in Grammatical Framework. In *Proceedings of the Grammar Engineering Across Frameworks (GEAF) 2015 workshop*, 49–56. Beijing, China: Association for Computational Linguistics. http://aclweb.org/anthology/W15-3307.

Hedström, Björn, Matilda Horppu & David Michaëlsson. 2016. *Parlira: An interactive phrasebook for Android devices.* Tech. rep. Chalmers University of Technology.

Lyngfelt, Benjamin, Lars Borin, Markus Forsberg, Julia Prentice, Rudolf Rydstedt, Emma Sköldberg & Sofia Tingsell. 2012. Adding a constructicon to the Swedish resource network of Språkbanken. In Jeremy Jancsary (ed.), *Proceedings of KONVENS 2012*, 452–461. ÖGAI. LexSem 2012 workshop.

Ranta, Aarne. 2009. The GF Resource Grammar Library. *Linguistic Issues in Language Technology*.

Ranta, Aarne. 2011. *Grammatical Framework: Programming with multilingual grammars.* Stanford: CSLI Publications.

Ranta, Aarne, Krasimir Angelov & Thomas Hallgren. 2010. Tools for multilingual grammar-based translation on the web. In *Proceedings of the 48th annual meeting of the Association for Computational Linguistics (ACL 2010) system demonstrations*, 66–71. Uppsala, Sweden.

Ranta, Aarne, Christina Unger & Daniel Vidal Hussey. 2015. Grammar engineering for a customer: A case study with five languages. In *Proceedings of the Grammar Engineering Across Frameworks (GEAF) 2015 workshop*, 1–8. Beijing, China: Association for Computational Linguistics. http://aclweb.org/anthology/W15-3301.

Seki, Hiroyuki, Takashi Matsumura, Mamoru Fujii & Tadao Kasami. 1991. On multiple context-free grammars. *Theoretical Computer Science* 88(2). 191–229.

Chapter 6

Statistical MWE-aware parsing

Mathieu Constant
ATILF UMR 7118, Université de Lorraine/CNRS

Gülşen Eryiğit
Istanbul Technical University

Carlos Ramisch
Aix-Marseille Université

Mike Rosner
University of Malta

Gerold Schneider
University of Konstanz and University of Zurich

This chapter aims at presenting different strategies that have been designed to incorporate multiword expression (MWE) identification in the process of syntactic parsing using statistical approaches. We discuss MWE representation in treebanks, pipeline and joint orchestrations, the integration of external lexicons and the evaluation of MWE-aware parsers, concluding with our suggestions for future research.

1 Introduction

Supervised STATISTICAL PARSING is nowadays an important and challenging field of natural language processing (NLP). It consists in predicting the most probable syntactic structure of a new sentence, given a statistical model that has been trained on a TREEBANK, that is, a syntactically annotated corpus. Since the seminal works of Nivre & Nilsson (2004) for dependency parsing and Arun & Keller

Mathieu Constant, Gülşen Eryiğit, Carlos Ramisch, Mike Rosner & Gerold Schneider. 2019. Statistical MWE-aware parsing. In Yannick Parmentier & Jakub Waszczuk (eds.), *Representation and parsing of multiword expressions: Current trends*, 147–182. Berlin: Language Science Press. DOI:10.5281/zenodo.2579043

(2005) for constituency parsing, a new research line has emerged: incorporating the analysis of multiword expressions (MWEs) in such parsers. The main objective of this chapter is to present different approaches that have been developed and evaluated for statistical MWE-aware parsing systems.

The design of MWE-aware parsers must address the following questions: How are MWEs represented in combination with syntactic trees? When is MWE identification performed with respect to parsing? What algorithms and machine learning techniques are to be used for the two tasks? How can external lexical resources be integrated to improve MWE coverage? How are systems evaluated?

Answering the question about MWE REPRESENTATION is fundamental as it enables the definition of a system's output. Hence, it influences the design of datasets used for training and testing, including treebanks, as shown in Section 3.

The ORCHESTRATION issue is also crucial in order to position MWE identification with respect to parsing: should it be performed before, during, or after it? The answer is not straightforward as it might depend on the type of MWE (Eryiğit et al. 2011). Orchestration also implies determining how the two components interact. For instance, in pipeline strategies (before or after) discussed in Section 4, should the intermediate input/output be computed using MWE concatenation strategies or MWE substitution ones? Joint strategies (during) discussed in Section 5 alongside n-best strategies, might involve different methods like adapting a grammatical formalism for constituency parsing (Green et al. 2013) or concatenating arc labels in dependency parsing (Vincze et al. 2013).

Concerning ALGORITHMS and machine learning, most techniques use workaround approaches by adapting the MWE-aware representation to existing representations directly exploitable by off-the-shelf tools (Nasr et al. 2015). Nonetheless, new parsing algorithms have been recently proposed that include specific handling of MWEs, notably when using joint strategies (Nivre 2014).

The integration of EXOGENOUS LEXICAL KNOWLEDGE in the system, discussed in Section 6, is non-trivial but potentially helpful. Indeed, supervised systems are trained on datasets of limited size. Therefore, one drawback of such systems is the limited coverage in terms of MWEs. One possible solution consists in integrating knowledge coming from large-scale MWE lexicons, either manually built and/or validated (Candito & Constant 2014) or automatically acquired (Schneider 2012).

The last issue concerns EVALUATION: what is the impact of MWE identification on syntactic parsing and vice-versa? What types of measure are adequate to quantify this impact? We try to answer these questions in Section 7.

The outline of this chapter is as follows. First, we briefly explain some basic concepts and terms in statistical parsing in Section 2. Then, each section addresses the questions above. We conclude in Section 8 by providing a summary of the current research in statistical MWE-aware parsing and presenting pointers that, in our opinion, may lead to significant advances in the field in the future.

2 Statistical parsing

Parsing, also referred as syntactic analysis, is the process of assigning a syntactic structure to a given input sentence. The analysis is aimed at producing a valid syntactic tree conforming to a hand-written or automatically induced language grammar. With the emergence of manually annotated datasets (i.e. treebanks) and machine learning techniques, statistical parsing (Collins 1996; Charniak 2000) has become the dominant approach in the parsing literature.

Statistical parsing aims at selecting the most probable parse tree from the set of all possible parse trees for a given sentence. These data-driven parsing models may be basically grouped under generative or discriminative approaches. GENERATIVE parsing models generally rely on a grammatical formalism whereas DISCRIMINATIVE ones are usually performed without any underlying grammar. There exist also joint approaches where a discriminative model is used to rerank the top *n* candidates of a generative parser.

Constituency and dependency formalisms are the two most common parsing formalisms used in statistical parsing. Figure 1 and Figure 4 each provide constituency and dependency parse tree samples for the sentence *The prime minister made a few good decisions.*

In the CONSTITUENCY FORMALISM, a sentence is regarded as being composed of phrases and parsing is the task of determining the underlying phrase structure. For example, a statistical generative constituency parser aims to assign probabilities to a parse tree by combining the probabilities of each of its sub-phrases. In the DEPENDENCY FORMALISM, parsing is defined as correctly determining the dependency relations between words of an input sentence. More precisely, the aim of dependency parsing is to correctly determine the dependent-head relationships between words and also the type of these relationships such as subject, object, predicate. Dependency parsing is nowadays strikingly more popular than constituency parsing and attracts the attention of an ever-growing community in NLP. Furthermore, most existing MWE-aware parsers are developed in the dependency framework. Therefore, in this chapter, we focus mainly on different orchestration scenarios applied for different statistical dependency parsing approaches.

The two commonly used approaches for statistical dependency parsing in the literature are transition-based (Yamada & Matsumoto 2003; Nivre et al. 2007) and graph-based (Eisner 1996; McDonald et al. 2006; Nakagawa 2007). TRANSITION-BASED approaches treat the dependency parsing task as the determination of parsing actions (such as push/pop operations in a shift-reduce parser) by the use of a machine learning classifier. GRAPH-BASED approaches treat parsing as finding the most likely path within a graph, such as the highest-scoring directed spanning tree in a complete graph. Most MWE-aware parsing strategies are adaptations of standard parsers experimenting with various models of orchestration concerning the scheduling of MWE identification with respect to syntactic analysis.

MWEs pose *challenges* for all areas of NLP, and statistical parsing is not an exception. An MWE may be *ambiguous* among accidental co-occurrence, literal, and idiomatic uses. The possible surface forms of an MWE *vary*, especially due to morphological variations which may become radical in morphologically rich languages. MWE components do not have to appear in consecutive locations within a sentence and it is hard to correctly identify a *discontinuous* MWE by ignoring the intervening words. The syntactic *non-compositionality* of MWEs may result in irregular parse trees. The ambiguous, discontinuous, non-compositional and variable nature of MWEs needs to be carefully handled during parsing in order to produce a valid syntactic structure. Additionally, annotated datasets (treebanks) are crucial resources for the training of data-driven statistical parsers. The *scarcity and limited size* of MWE-annotated treebanks is a great challenge faced by MWE-aware parsing.

3 MWE representations in treebanks

The choice of an appropriate MWE representation is crucial, with strong consequences on the format of treebanks. Representational choices that have affected existing treebanks in this way range from words-with-spaces – e.g., the French treebank (Candito & Crabbé 2009) – to the use of special MWE syntactic relations – e.g., the Universal Dependencies project (Nivre et al. 2016). Some treebanks may not even contain MWE representations at all, while others may have sophisticated multi-layer representations (Bejček et al. 2012).

The number and variety of available MWE-aware treebanks is growing (Rosén et al. 2015). They do not necessarily cover the same kinds of MWEs. They often belong to the constituency or the dependency frameworks, but some can also be compatible with different types of grammatical formalisms, like lexical functional grammar (Dyvik et al. 2016). To narrow down the scope of this section, we focus on MWE representations in relation to treebanks *that are useful to or that have been used in statistical MWE-aware parsing.*

```
                            S
                ┌───────────┴───────────┐
               NP                       VP
            ┌───┴───┐              ┌─────┴─────┐
            D       N              V           NP
            │       │              │      ┌────┼────┐
                                          D    A    N
                                          │    │    │
           the  prime_minister  made   a_few good decisions
```

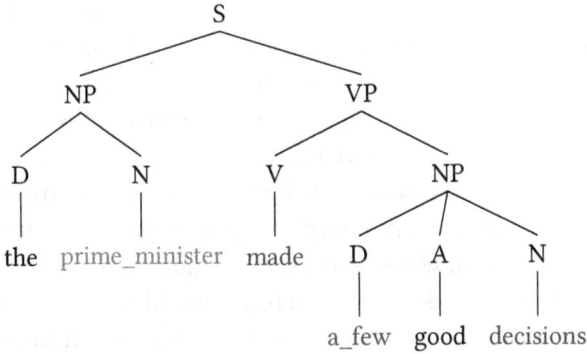

Figure 1: Constituency MWE-aware tree with words-with-spaces representation

3.1 No representation at all

The simplest and most obvious MWE representation is not to consider MWEs at all, only considering separate word tokens. While such a treatment is simplistic, it also has a number of advantages. First and foremost, it is easy to operationalize: no distinction is necessary between single words in combination and MWEs. MWEs include a variety of phenomena: compound nouns, technical terms, multiword entities, light-verb constructions, phrasal verbs, idioms, and proverbs. In general they are partly non-compositional, but due to this characteristic they also border on or overlap with collocations, which are an inherently gradient phenomenon. Not representing MWEs can thus be seen as a tacit assumption that all forms of MWEs are gradient.

Statistical parsers were conceived to improve parsing performance by modeling lexical interactions (Gross 1984; Sinclair 1991; Collins 1999). As MWEs are a subclass of collocations, the statistical attraction between the participating words is typically very strong and errors are therefore much rarer. Statistical parsers generally perform better on relations that are semantically expected (as e.g., in selectional preferences), so performance on verb complements for example is much higher than on verb adjuncts.

3.2 Words-with-spaces representation

A simple representation consists in considering MWEs as single nodes of the syntactic tree (Sag et al. 2002), such as in the strategy adopted in the LFG/XLE parser described by Angelov (2019 [this volume]). This "words-with-spaces" representation implies that MWEs have an atomic interpretation. In the constituency framework, the MWE forms are leafs. Their parent nodes correspond to their parts-of-speech (POS) category, as shown in Figure 1. For instance, *prime minister* has a noun parent node and *a few* has a determiner parent node. A concrete example where MWEs are represented this way is the first version of the French treebank distributed for parsing (Candito & Crabbé 2009). In the dependency framework, the MWE node has the same linguistic attributes as a single word token: POS tag, lemma and morphological features. For instance, *hot dogs* would be a noun in plural, whose lemma is *hot dog*. Such representations imply that MWEs have been pre-identified and represented as word-with-space tokens before parsing. Moreover, they have several drawbacks in terms of linguistic expressiveness. First, discontinuous MWEs like the light-verb construction *make decisions* in Figure 1 cannot be represented this way. Then, the semantic processing of semi-compositional MWEs might be problematic as the internal syntactic structure is impossible to retrieve.

3.3 Chunking representations

Another way of representing MWEs uses CHUNKING. Chunks are a polysemous concept, but its two meanings are related. On the one hand, chunks are seen as psycholinguistic units that are partly or fully lexicalized, that is, stored as one entity in the mental lexicon (Miller 1956; Pawley & Syder 1983; Tomasello 1998; Wray 2008). On the other hand, they are the concrete output of applying finite-state technology to obtain base-NPs and verb groups deterministically. While the psycholinguistic and the computational concepts are related, the latter has the drawback that chunks need to be continuous.

Black et al. (1991) pointed out that dependency grammars are particularly suited to model chunks and parse between heads of chunks. In fact, chunks are close to Tesnière's original conception of nucleus, which is typically not a single word (Tesnière 1959). Some dependency parsers following this scheme exist, for example Schneider (2008). Nivre (2014) has proposed a transition-based parser that performs MWE merging as it syntactically parses a sentence. This operation can be seen as MWE chunking.

A standard way of representing chunks in tagging systems is the IOB annotation scheme (Ramshaw & Marcus 1995).[1] Such representations have been successfully adapted to named entity recognition (Tjong Kim Sang 2002) and MWE identification (Vincze et al. 2011; Constant et al. 2012). For MWEs, there are variants covering continuous MWEs (Blunsom & Baldwin 2006) and gappy

---

[1]Tokens are tagged as "B" for *begin*, "I" for *inside* and "O" for *outside* a chunk.

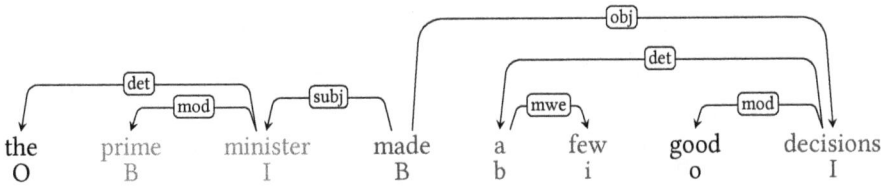

Figure 2: Chunking-based representation with IOB tags (Schneider et al. 2014)

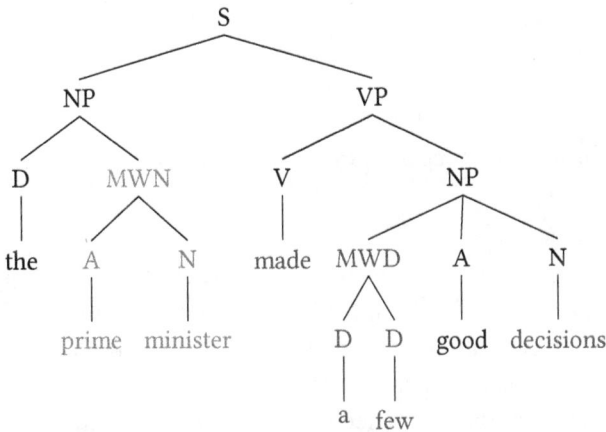

Figure 3: Flat constituency subtree representation (Green et al. 2011)

ones (Schneider et al. 2014). For instance, Schneider et al. (2014) use a 6-tag set (with additional lowercased tags in order to emphasize nested MWE structures) to represent MWEs enabling 1-level nesting, as shown in Figure 2. Such representations can be used in treebanks for training pipeline MWE-aware systems (Section 4) and joint MWE-aware parsers (Section 5).

3.4 Subtree representations

Another way of representing MWEs is to annotate them as SUBTREES made of several nodes of the syntactic tree. Many treebanks using such representations can be found in Rosén et al. (2015). Several types of subtree MWE representations were proposed in treebanks, according to the language, MWE type and syntactic formalism.

For processing purposes, words-with-spaces representations have often been automatically converted into flat subtrees. In the constituency framework, an

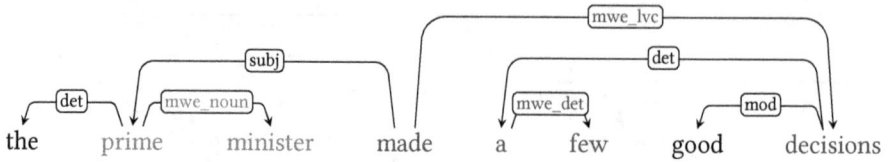

Figure 4: Flat head-initial dependency subtree representation

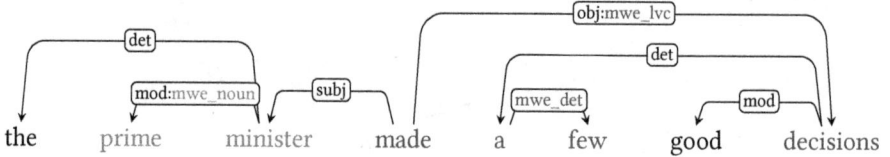

Figure 5: Structured dependency subtree representation with extended labels

MWE is considered as a special constituent with a given POS tag. MWE components are leaves of the MWE subtree, as shown in Figure 3.[2] There exist different variants for constituency treebanks (Głowińska & Przepiórkowski 2010). This representation has been used by Arun & Keller (2005) and Green et al. (2011), especially for compounds. In the dependency framework, flat subtrees can be either head-initial, that is, the root of the subtree is the first token (Nivre et al. 2004; Seddah et al. 2013), or head-final, with the root being the last token of the MWE (Eryiğit et al. 2011). All other MWE component tokens depend on this arbitrarily defined head, as shown in Figure 4. This representation is used, for example, in the Universal Dependencies treebanks (Nivre et al. 2016).

Flat subtree representations have a disadvantage: the internal syntactic structure of MWEs, required for semi-fixed MWEs in particular, is lost, like for words-with-spaces representation. To retain the internal syntactic structure as well as the MWE status, some authors propose representing an MWE with its syntactic subtree, where arc labels are extended with MWE tags, as shown in Figure 5. This kind of representation has been used, for instance, for annotating light-verb constructions (Vincze et al. 2013) and continuous MWEs (Candito & Constant 2014).

Candito & Constant (2014) adopt a hybrid representation scheme to distinguish regular from irregular MWEs. Regular MWEs have a regular syntactic

---

[2]MWE-related symbols MWN and MWD respectively stand for *multiword noun* and *determiner*.

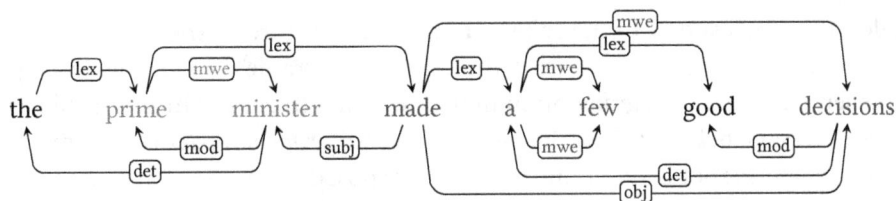

Figure 6: Representation on two distinct layers (Constant et al. 2016)

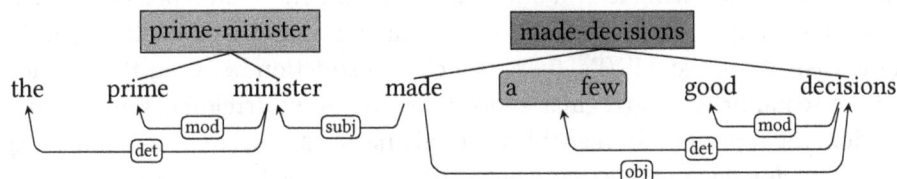

Figure 7: Representation on factorized lexical and syntactic layers (Constant & Nivre 2016)

structure[3] whereas they display semantic irregularity. They are represented with structured MWE subtrees, as in Figure 5. Irregular MWEs display an irregular syntactic structure (e.g., *by and large* is the coordination of a preposition and an adjective) and therefore cannot be analysed syntactically in a compositional way. They are represented with flat subtrees, as in Figure 4.

3.5 Multilayer representations

One of the most interesting MWE representations combined with (deep) syntactic analysis is the one used in the Prague Dependency Treebank (Bejček et al. 2012). It combines three different analysis layers in the form of trees: morphological (*m*-layer), syntactic (*a*-layer) and "semantic" ones (*t*-layer). Nodes of one layer can be linked to nodes of another layer to model the interleaving of the different types of analysis. MWEs are represented on the t-layer and are associated with MWE entries of a lexicon. To our knowledge, there is unfortunately no statistical parser outputting such combined structures.

Though less linguistically expressive, other multilayer representations have been proposed on top of a combined lexical and syntactic parser. The proposal of Constant et al. (2016) is to have two distinct layers for representing lexical and syntactic analysis in the form of dependency trees. The two layers share the same

---

[3]The distinction between irregular and regular MWEs is arbitrary, being defined by a manually-built set of POS patterns.

nodes, that correspond to the tokens, as shown in Figure 6. The syntactic layer represents the syntactic structure in the dependency framework. The lexical layer represents the lexical segmentation in the form of a tree. Arcs in MWE subtrees have a special label "mwe". For instance, the MWE *prime minister* corresponds to a subtree whose root is *prime* and which is composed of an "mwe" arc from *prime* to *minister*. In order to form a unique tree for the lexical layer, lexical units are sequentially related via arcs labeled "lex". For instance, the MWE *prime minister* is linked to the following lexical unit *made decisions*. This dual representation has several advantages. First, syntactic and lexical analyses are explicitly separated. In the case of regular MWEs, there is a clear distinction between the syntactic and the semantic status (regular syntactic structure vs. irregular semantics). In addition, the representation enables not only nested MWEs to be annotated (e.g., *a few* in *made a few good decisions*) but also fully overlapping expressions (e.g., the noun compound *rain check* inside the light verb construction *to take a rain check*). On the down side, irregular MWEs are duplicated on the two layers because there is no possible compositional syntactic analysis (e.g., *a few*). Additionally, arcs linking lexical units could be made implicit, as they can straightforwardly be computed from their positions in the sequence.

Constant & Nivre (2016) correct the main drawbacks of the previous two-layer representation by making it more compact and more factorized. The representation is still composed of two layers, but the lexical layer is a forest of constituent-like trees representing complex lexical units like MWEs, as shown in Figure 7. Here, the discontinuous MWE *made decisions* is represented by a tree whose root corresponds to a new lexical node having linguistic attributes like any token: a form (*made decisions*), a lemma (*make decision*), a POS tag (verb) and morphological features (past tense). It is straightforward to elegantly represent embedded and fully overlapping MWEs, as lexical units are trees. Irregular MWEs like *a few* and simple words are called SYNTACTIC NODES. The syntactic layer is a dependency tree over such nodes. Therefore, irregular MWE nodes and simple word nodes are shared by the two layers. For example, there is a "det" arc from *decisions* to *a few*, as it is compositionally modified by the complex determiner. This representation is not without some limitations: the lexical layer cannot represent an MWE that strictly requires a graph (and not a tree). For instance, it is impossible to represent the coordinated MWEs *had shower* and *had bath* in the sentence *John had$_{1,2}$ a shower$_1$ then a bath$_2$*.

4 Pipeline approaches

A minimal processing pipeline consists of a collection of two processes arranged in a chain so that the output of the first process is the input of the other. Thus, a processing pipeline for statistical MWE parsing involves two processes, one to identify the MWEs in the input sentence, and another for parsing the sentence into one or more structures that include the MWEs. The question that we address in this section concerns the order in which these two processes are arranged, and there are clearly two possibilities referred to as preprocessing (Section 4.1), and postprocessing (Section 4.2).

4.1 Preprocessing approaches

Preprocessing means that the MWE identification task takes place before parsing. For the parser to benefit from this, a decision must be made about how to represent MWEs in the input. As discussed earlier, there are different approaches, the most important of which employ concatenation (Section 4.1.1), or substitution (Section 4.1.2) operations, as discussed in the following sections.

4.1.1 Concatenation approach

A widely used pipeline approach to statistical MWE-aware parsing is to have a RETOKENIZATION phase before parsing. It consists in first pre-identifying MWEs, then concatenating their components in one single token, and finally applying a syntactic parser trained on a treebank where MWEs have a words-with-spaces representation (Section 3.2). Note that this approach is limited to continuous MWEs.

For example, given the input token sequence *The prime minister made a few good decisions*, the MWEs *prime minister* and *a few* are first pre-identified. Each of them is then merged by concatenating its components into a single token. The sequence is retokenized as *The prime_minister made a_few good decisions* and is then parsed. This approach has the advantage of reducing the token-count of the sentence and hence reducing the search space of the parser. However, it may not be realistic to recognize some types of MWEs without access to morpho-syntactic information.

Seminal studies on gold MWE identification performed before either constituency parsing (Arun & Keller 2005) or dependency parsing (Nivre et al. 2004; Eryiğit et al. 2011) showed that it may have a great impact on parsing accuracy. Other studies confirmed that more realistic MWE pre-identification actually helps parsing. Korkontzelos & Manandhar (2010) evaluated MWE pre-identification using Wordnet 3.0 for lexicon lookup before shallow parsing. The set of MWEs was limited to two-word continuous compound nominals, proper names, and adjective-noun constructions. The authors showed that the approach improves shallow parsing accuracy. For instance, without MWE pre-identification, *he threw the fire wheel up into the air* is erroneously parsed as: *(he) (threw) (the fire) (wheel up) (into) (the air)*, whereas with MWE pre-identification the result is: *(he) (threw) (the fire_wheel) (up) (into) (the air)*. Cafferkey et al. (2007) carried out similar experiments with a probabilistic constituency parser. MWEs were automatically identified by applying a named entity recognizer and list of prepositional MWEs. A slight but statistically significant improvement was observed. We should note that in the above studies, MWE identification itself was not evaluated.

The SPMRL shared task (Seddah et al. 2013) had a special track dedicated to MWE-aware parsing in French. The provided treebank included continuous MWE annotations represented as flat subtrees (Figure 4). All but one competing team did not develop special treatments for MWEs. The winning team was the only one to have a preprocessing stage to identify MWEs using a tagger based on linear conditional random fields (Constant, Candito, et al. 2013). The tagger model also incorporated features based on an MWE lexicon (Section 6.3).

4.1.2 Substitution approach

Another approach is to use substitution: whenever an MWE from the lexicon matches, it is replaced by its head word. Such approach is employed by Weeds et al. (2007) for technical terms (Section 6.2), and by Schneider (2008) on all chunks. In a typical substitution approach, for example, the term *natural language processing* would be replaced by *processing* before parsing.

The advantage of keeping the lexical head is that resources taking lexical relations into account, such as bi-lexical disambiguation (Collins 1999), can use the lexical information. Thus, potential sparsity problems are reduced in comparison to the concatenation approach. For example, the prepositional phrase attachment ambiguity in *We help users with natural language processing* can be resolved properly, even if *natural language processing* is unseen in the training data. As long as *processing* exists in the training corpus, the ambiguity can be solved because the combination *help-with-processing* is more likely than *user-with-processing*.

The potential drawbacks of this approach are that, on the one hand, strings may be ambiguous, and on the other hand non-compositionality may affect the results. Ambiguous strings are illustrated below: while the first sentence of each example is an MWE, the second is accidental cooccurrence. The last example involves light verbs, for which Tu & Roth (2011) use token-wise disambiguation, as ambiguity is relatively frequent.

(1)   a. I saw her, and *by the way* she went there on foot.
      b. I recognized her *by the way* she walks.

(2)   a. In *natural language processing*, humans are also challenged.
      b. In *natural language processing* can be difficult.

(3)   a. The politician *took* a strong *position* on the issue.
      b. The soldier *took* a vanguard *position* on the mountain top.

Non-compositionality may lead to situations in which the head is semantically so different that attachment preferences are also affected.

(4)   a. I saw the road with the *torch light*.
      b. I saw the road with the *traffic light*.

If the MWE *traffic light* is reduced to *light*, the chances are that the prepositional phrase is erroneously attached to the verb, as *see-with-light* is likely. If *traffic light* is treated as an MWE, bi-lexical disambiguation can only profit if very large annotated resources exist. Unless a backoff method to treat MWE components is included, the increased data sparseness may easily lead to worse results.

4.2 Postprocessing approach

In this section, we present approaches where parsing precedes MWE processing. We make a distinction between MWE identification and discovery. We define IDENTIFICATION as the process of recognizing MWEs in context, that is, as tokens inside running text. On the other hand, DISCOVERY aims at creating a lexicon of MWE types from the corpus. This lexicon can later be used to guide MWE identification and parsing. In this section, we describe approaches for identification after parsing (Section 4.2.1) and for discovery after parsing (Section 4.2.2), focusing on works in which the result of discovery was later employed for identification.

4.2.1 Post-parsing MWE identification

Identifying MWEs after syntactic parsing is a natural approach to MWE-aware parsing as an MWE generally constitutes a syntactic constituent. In the dependency framework, there is usually a path continuously linking the MWE components in the syntactic tree. As a consequence, pre-parsing is particularly relevant for detecting discontinuous MWEs, that is, MWEs that include alien elements, by employing adapted lexicon lookup methods. In Figure 7, the MWE *made decisions* is discontinuous. As there is an object arc from *made* to *decisions*, the two words are *syntactically* adjacent. A matching procedure taking the syntactic structure into account can therefore be beneficial for MWE identification. Furthermore, MWEs can have different syntactic variants. For instance, *a **decision** was **made** by John* is the passive voice variant of *John made a decision*. The detection of such syntactic variants obviously benefits from the result of syntactic parsing.

Fazly et al. (2009) identify verb-noun expressions in a parsed text based on a list of 60 candidate expressions. First, they identify candidate occurrences of the expressions using rules based on syntactic annotations and lexical values. Then, they discriminate MWEs from literal expressions using different methods. One is based on the assumption that a verbal MWE expression has *fewer syntactic variants* than its literal counterparts, giving rise to the heuristic that canonical forms are idiomatic (e.g., *pull one's weight*) and non-canonical variants are literal (e.g., *pull a weight, pull the weights*). Another method compared the distributional contexts of co-occurring verb-object pairs to two sets of gold-standard contexts: one for idiomatic readings and another one for literal readings.

Nagy T. & Vincze (2014) compare the use of parsers and of a syntax-based pipeline approach to identify verb particle constructions in English. English off-the-shelf parsers usually have a specific syntactic arc label to identify occurrences of verb-particle constructions. Nonetheless, such parsers tend to get good precision but low recall, as they do not use dedicated features for this task. The pipeline method developed in this paper uses a standard parser to identify a first set of candidates. This set is subsequently enlarged using other syntactic relations. A classifier is then applied in order to decide whether they are verb-particle constructions or not. They show a significant gain in terms of recall and F-score with respect to standard parsers on the Wiki50 corpus (Vincze et al. 2011).

4.2.2 Post-parsing MWE discovery

This section discusses the discovery of new MWEs after parsing. This is particularly useful for the creation of resources that can be used for MWE-aware parsing (Section 6). For instance, such lexicon of newly discovered MWEs can be subsequently used for MWE pre-identification at the next cycle of processing. Seretan (2011) has shown that discovery based on parsed corpora provides considerably cleaner results than those relying on shallow analysis (e.g., POS-tagged corpora). Foufi et al. (2019 [this volume]) discuss the integration of resources built with the help of MWE discovery into a language-independent symbolic parser.

Since the literature in MWE discovery is huge, we focus on two studies that represent a sample of this type of approach. Lehmann & Schneider (2011) and Ronan & Schneider (2015) used automatically parsed data for discovering MWEs of different types, including idiomatic verb + prepositional phrase (PP) combinations and light-verb constructions in English. These cases involved the use of different collocation extraction scores.

For discovering Verb-PP idioms the O/E score was used, combined with filters including T-score and Yule's K (which estimates the degree of non-modifiability of a candidate). Table 1 reproduces the results of discovery, sorting the candidates by descending O/E score. Among the top-ranked candidates, many are genuine idioms (e.g., *to kill two birds with one stone*).

Table 1: Top-ranked verb-object + preposition-noun tuples, using the the O/E score (Lehmann & Schneider 2011)

verb	object	prep	desc. noun	T-score	O/E
send	*shiver*	*down*	*spine*	5.74456	2.21477×10^8
tap	*esc*	*for*	*escape*	6.40312	2.1134×10^8
separate	*shield*	*from*	*plate*	6.78233	2.33384×10^7
refer	*gentleman*	*to*	*reply*	8.24621	7.8143×10^6
obtain	*property*	*by*	*deception*	5.2915	7.60043×10^6
ask	*secretary*	*for*	*affairs*	6.40312	5.01529×10^6
kill	*bird*	*with*	*stone*	5.38516	3.37917×10^6
add	*insult*	*to*	*injury*	6.08276	2.21769×10^6
throw	*caution*	*to*	*wind*	5.09902	2.03157×10^6
refer	*friend*	*to*	*reply*	7.54983	1.36298×10^6
report	*loss*	*on*	*turnover*	7.14142	1.34742×10^6

For discovering light-verb constructions, the t-score was used together with a number of filters including WordNet and NomBank lookup (Ronan & Schneider 2015). An example of analysis is shown in Figure 8, showing a precision and recall plot by candidate list length. The vertical axis shows precision and recall, respectively, the horizontal axis (which is logarithmic) gives the cutoff in the ranked list of candidates to be included in the evaluation. For the cutoff at 20, the reported candidates for *give*+object, precision is 100%, while recall is 10%. At rank 2560, about 88% of all instances in the gold standard were found.

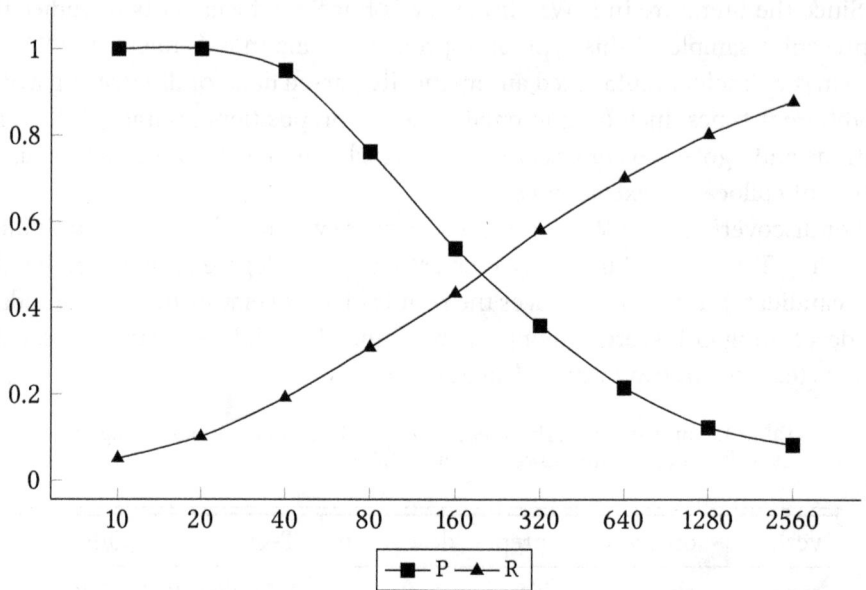

Figure 8: Precision vs. recall curve of the light verb *give* in the British National Corpus, using t-score (Ronan & Schneider 2015)

5 Joint approaches

Joint approaches perform parsing and MWE identification simultaneously. Since syntactic and lexical-semantic information are complementary, both processes can help each other if performed together. In such systems, MWE lexical-semantic segmentation is often seen as a by-product of syntactic analysis, or vice-versa.

Some MWEs require quite sophisticated syntactic information to be recognized, such as subcategorization frames and phrase structure. Joint approaches favor delaying the decision as to whether a given combination is an MWE to the parser, where this information is available. In other words, the system has access to the right information at the right moment.

Parser evaluation scores are often reported on standard test sets, where MWEs have been manually pre-identified (gold). Jointly performing MWE identification and parsing is more realistic than parsing pre-annotated test sets, where MWEs are often represented as words with spaces (Figure 1). Indeed, when moving from standard test sets to real texts, gold MWE identification is not necessarily available. It may be hard to use a pipeline approach (Section 4) if the target MWEs are ambiguous or discontinuous.

On the downside, parsers that perform both syntactic analysis and MWE identification simultaneously are harder to design. First, ambiguity is increased, often by a larger number of labels and/or parsing decisions that are possible at a given moment. It is crucial, for such systems, to have coherent MWE annotations in treebanks, datasets that are large enough, and features that generalize well.

We classify such approaches according to the degree of "MWE-awareness" of the parser. In shallow approaches, the parser generates n-best solutions without putting any particular emphasis on MWEs, then uses MWE information for reranking (Section 5.1). The majority of joint approaches add MWE information to training and test treebanks, and then use off-the-shelf parsers enriched with dedicated MWE features (Section 5.2). We also present fully MWE-aware parsers that take them into account in the parsing algorithm itself (Section 5.3).

5.1 n-best and reranking approaches

One possible orchestration solution is to consider MWE identification as a reto-kenization problem, as described in Section 4.1.1. In n-best approaches, however, the text is first segmented into tokens in a non-deterministic way, considering *several possible segmentations*. Usually, the output of such non-deterministic to-kenizer is a lattice containing all possible segmentation paths for a sentence (Sagot & Boullier 2005). This representation is particularly suited for ambiguous irregular constructions, that could be considered as MWEs or as accidental co-occurrence, depending on the context. The parser then must take this ambiguous segmentation and uses simple parsing models to disambiguate the input and generate a parse tree (Nasr et al. 2011).

An n-best MWE identifier is used by Constant, Le Roux & Sigogne (2013), producing a lattice of possible segmentations. Then, a PCFG-LA parser is used to disambiguate the possible readings. The authors test two variants. First, they consider that MWEs in the lattice are single nodes (words with spaces). Thus, different segmentation possibilities in the lattice are represented by paths with different lengths. Second, they consider that MWE components are individual nodes tagged using an IOB scheme, like in Figure 2. The latter obtains better performance because all possible paths in the lattice have the same length, resulting in more accurate parsing scores.

Conversely, the parser can use the same kind of approach and also generate n-best parsing trees. A reranker can then use MWE-aware features, among others, to choose the highest scoring tree. Constant et al. (2012), for instance, use a deterministic tokenizer but output n-best MWE-aware syntactic trees using the Berkeley constituency parser. Then, they use a discriminative reranker to choose the correct parse tree that includes MWE features.

These are considered joint approaches because, even though MWE segmentation and parsing are independent processes, one needs to be aware of the format of the input/output of the other. For example, the parser has to be able to process lattices as input, provided by the non-deterministic MWE identifier.

5.2 Treebank modification approaches

In Section 3, we discussed several ways to represent MWEs in treebanks. Standard statistical parsers trained on such treebanks will be inherently aware of MWEs, provided that they can handle the particular MWE representation in that treebank. For example, if MWEs are represented as subtrees (Figure 5), then there is no need to explicitly handle MWEs (Nivre et al. 2016). This subsection covers MWE-aware parsing studies in which the learning and parsing algorithms *remain unchanged* with respect to their standard version.

Approaches discussed in this section face several challenges. First, most of the time MWEs are either *absent* from treebanks, or the available representation requires *adaptations* in order to be usable by the parser. Second, parsers learned from MWE-annotated treebanks often require *extra features* to take MWEs into account properly. Third, these features may suffer from data *sparseness*, as individual MWEs may not occur often enough in limited-size treebanks.[4]

In this subsection, we present approaches that tackle the challenges posed by MWEs by:

- adding or modifying the MWE representation in the treebanks, and/or

- adding MWE-dedicated features to the parsing model.

The last challenge, related to data sparseness and domain adaptation, is tackled by integrating external resources in the parser, as discussed in Section 6.

In constituency parsing, several parsers, MWE representations and feature sets have been tested, especially on continuous MWEs in the French treebank. Constant, Le Roux & Sigogne (2013) experiment with two implementations of a PCFG-LA parser, using a representation similar to the one of Green et al. (2011) and a variant similar to IOB encoding.

When MWE annotation is absent, a reasonably straightforward solution is to automatically project an MWE lexicon on the treebank before training the parser. For instance, Kato et al. (2016) project a lexicon of compound function words (e.g., *a number of*) onto the English Ontonotes constituency treebank. Syntactic trees

---

[4]Some MWE categories may never occur (e.g., colloquial idioms) because many existing treebanks cover a single register (e.g., newspapers).

are modified to take MWEs into account. Constituents are then automatically transformed into dependencies and a standard first-order graph-based parser is learned. While the training data is modified, no MWE features are added to the model.

Early experiments on MWE-aware dependency parsing compared two representation variants: MWEs as subtrees or as words with spaces (Nivre & Nilsson 2004). The results indicated that the subtree representation (joint approach) is worse than parsing MWEs as words with spaces (pipeline approach). However, these results were obtained assuming gold MWE segmentation.

Vincze et al. (2013) were among the first to use a dependency parser to perform realistic MWE identification. They focus on light-verb constructions (LVCs) in Hungarian. They first perform an automatic matching of two annotation layers in the Szeged treebank: syntactic dependencies and LVCs. As a result, the dependency link between a light verb and a predicative noun (e.g., OBJ) is suffixed with a LVC tag, whereas regular verb-argument links remain unchanged, like in Figure 5. An off-the-shelf parser is used to predict the syntactic structure of sentences, including LVC links. Given that Hungarian is a relatively free word-order language, LVCs often involve long-distance dependencies. When compared with a classifier baseline, the parser performs slightly worse on continuous LVC instances (F1 = 81% vs. 82.8%) but considerably better on discontinuous LVCs (F1 = 64% vs. 60%).

Treebanks containing MWEs as words with spaces pose problems when converted into subtrees. When splitting an MWE, one needs to manually or semi-automatically assign POS tags, lemmas and morphological features to the individual MWE components. Additionally, the internal syntactic structure must be inferred. Since it is difficult to automate this task, the internal syntactic structure of decomposed MWEs is often underspecified using flat head-initial subtrees (Seddah et al. 2013), head-initial (Nivre et al. 2016) or head-final chained subtrees (Eryiğit et al. 2011), as detailed in Section 3.4. Eryiğit et al. (2011) compare parsing and MWE identification accuracy on different treebank representations for different MWE types. Their original treebank includes MWEs as words with spaces, which are semi-automatically transformed into subtrees. Contrary to previous conclusions (Nivre & Nilsson 2004), results indicate that subtrees may be a more suitable solution for some MWE types, specially when looking at MWE-aware parsing evaluation metrics (Section 7). In this study, the words-with-spaces representation is shown to have a harming effect on the types where it increases lexical sparsity, such as in Turkish light-verb constructions.

Candito & Constant (2014) explore several orchestrations for combining syntactic parsing and continuous MWE identification in French, distinguishing syntactically regular from irregular multiword constructions. In particular, they experimented with an off-the-shelf graph-based parser that was learned from an MWE-aware treebank where the subtrees representing regular and irregular expressions have their usual labels suffixed by the POS of the MWE, as shown in Figure 5. They showed on-par results with different pipeline variants.

Nasr et al. (2015) focus on ambiguous compound grammatical words in French of the form ADV+*que* and *de*+DET. While these represent a limited scope, such constructions are pervasive and hard to identify without access to syntactic information, because its component words can co-occur by chance. For instance, the two sentences below have the same sequences of POS and similar lexical units, but the first one contains an MWE whereas the second one does not:

(5) Je chante *bien que* je sois triste.
    I   sing   well that I   am   sad

    'I sing even though I am sad'

(6) Je pense *bien que* je suis triste.
    I   think   well that I   am   sad

    'Indeed, I think that I am sad.'

In order to deal with these constructions, the training treebank is modified similarly to Candito & Constant (2014), splitting MWEs originally represented as words with spaces into two tokens linked by a special dependency. For example, since *bien que* functions as a conjunction, the conjunction *que* becomes the head, modified by the adverb *bien*. Using a standard graph-based dependency parser, the authors evaluate the identification of the target MWEs on a dedicated dataset. As described in Section 6.3, the use of subcategorization frame information for verbs, coming from an external lexicon, improves the results.

5.3 MWE-aware parsing models

The models discussed up to now have the advantage of being simple and fast to deploy. Provided that the training treebank contains MWEs in a suitable representation (which can be manually or automatically converted), the parsing algorithm itself does not need to be changed to accommodate MWEs. These approaches achieve reasonably good results, specially if compared to MWE systems based on purely sequential models. However, they often use language-specific or treebank-specific workarounds and are not always generalizable. Therefore, some recent contributions focus on designing parsing models that are truly awa-re of MWEs in the model, with promising results.

In the framework of constituency parsing, Green et al. (2011) propose and eval-uate an MWE-aware parser based on tree substitution grammars (TSGs). This work was latter extended, comparing the TSG with a PCFG model enriched with a factorized lexicon (Green et al. 2013). The authors apply these models to MWE-rich treebanks for French and Arabic, showing gains for both parsing and MWE identification. The authors state that TSGs are more powerful than PCFGs, be-ing able to store lexicalized tree fragments. They are therefore more suitable for idiomatic MWEs, whose particular syntactic analysis requires larger contexts to be predicted.

Along the same lines, Le Roux et al. (2014) design a joint parsing and MWE identification model based on dual decomposition. In this work, however, a spe-cialized sequence model performs lexical segmentation of MWEs. The MWE iden-tification module uses conditional random fields, while the parsing module uses a PCFG-LA also including MWE identification, using the approach of Green et al. (2013). Both models are combined using penalty vectors that are updated in an iterative way. In other words, until reaching consensus on MWE identification, the MWE identifier and parser analyse the input sentence. If the systems do not agree, they are penalized in proportion to the difference between the given so-lution and the average solution. This model reaches impressive performance on the French treebank, reaching an MWE identification F-score of up to 82.4% on the test set.

Constant & Nivre (2016) propose a new dependency parsing system that jointly performs syntactic analysis and lexical segmentation (including MWE identifica-tion). The authors design and evaluate a transition-based parser using two syn-chronized stacks: one for syntactic parsing and another for lexical segmentation. The synchronization of both stacks is guaranteed by a unique PUSH transition which pushes the first element of the buffer on both stacks. The parser mod-els MWE-dedicated transitions MERGE_N and MERGE_F, which respectively create new merged lexical nodes for regular MWEs and lexico-syntactic nodes for fixed MWEs. An additional COMPLETE transition marks that a given lexical node has been fully parsed (while being potentially implicit). This approach obtains re-sults that compare with or exceed state-of-the-art performance on French and English MWE-rich treebanks. Finally, the authors show that lexical information can guide parsing, leading to slightly better syntactic trees. The converse assump-tion does not seem to hold, though, as adding syntactic information to a purely lexical parser tends to slightly degrade its performance.

6 Integration of lexical resources

Lexical resources are large-scale repositories of information typically about simple words, more rarely about MWEs. They can play different roles with respect to statistical MWE-aware parsing, and in this section we discuss three of them. We show how lexical information can help in general to resolve parsing ambiguities (Section 6.1). Then, we focus on the availability of lexical information within pipeline approaches (Section 6.2). Finally, we shift the emphasis to the effect of lexical resources on MWE identification rather than on parsing itself (Section 6.3).

6.1 General integration of lexical resources in statistical parsers

Statistical parsers have several drawbacks due to the limited size of available gold standard treebanks used for training. Many words in the datasets are infrequent, which makes it very difficult to learn relevant (lexical) regularities. In addition, when parsing an unseen text, some words are simply absent from the training dataset, which negatively impacts parsing accuracy. Experiments with different solutions have been undertaken within the parsing community, notably by incorporating external resources mostly (but not only) learned automatically from large raw corpora.

The use of word clusters is one method to deal with the lexical sparsity issue. Clusters (e.g., Brown clusters), consist of groups of words occurring in the same context. Replacing words by clusters or using clusters as features has each been shown to improve parsing accuracy (Koo et al. 2008; Candito & Seddah 2010). Pairs of words that co-occur frequently in large corpora tend to be related syntactically. The provision of information about such lexical affinities to the parser has been shown to usefully support syntactic attachment decisions. Lexical affinities might be integrated using either soft constraints (Bansal & Klein 2011; Mirroshandel et al. 2012) or hard ones (Mirroshandel & Nasr 2016). The deep learning revolution has opened new perspectives to help handle lexical sparsity, as words are represented as continuous space vectors (i.e., word embeddings) learned from large corpora. Words having similar syntactic behaviors have vectors that are geometrically close to each other (Durrett & Klein 2015; Dyer et al. 2015).

The use of external lexicons has also turned out to be of great interest, notably for dependency parsing. For instance, Candito et al. (2010) successfully use the MElt tagger (Denis & Sagot 2012), thereby incorporating features based on a large-scale morphological lexicon. The integration of hard constraints based on syntactic lexicons was also shown to have a positive impact (Mirroshandel et al. 2013).

6.2 MWE resources help parsing

We now give examples of MWE lexical resource integration using a pipeline approach (Section 4) in which MWEs are replaced by their syntactic heads. We do so on two levels: general NP chunking and technical terms.

On the chunking level, replacing chunks with their head words reduces parsing complexity considerably. According to experiments carried out by Prins (2005), parsing performance also increases slightly. However, experiments on technical terms have not confirmed this hypothesis. In other words, replacing chunks with their heads does not necessarily lead to improved results in other settings.

Weeds et al. (2007) used a substitution approach (Section 4.1.2) for term identification in the domain of biomedical research, where gene and protein names in particular are often MWEs. Because taggers, unless they are trained on the domain, perform very poorly, they report better results when replacing technical terms with their head, using a large lexicon of domain terms.[5]

A comparable example is the situation in which a sentence such as ... *he did not see the traffic_N light_V* is POS-tagged incorrectly (*light_V* instead of *light_N*). Here, a pipeline substitution approach relying on an MWE lexicon can clearly improve results. This improvement is passed on to the subsequent parsing step. When domain-adapted taggers are available, though, the advantages of the substitution approach tend to disappear. The performance of adapted taggers is often comparable or slightly higher than that of the substitution approach, as tagging accuracy of technical terms increases. In short, sometimes it is better to adapt statistical models (in this case, a domain-adapted tagger) rather than using lexical resources (in this case, an MWE gazetteer of the domain).

Schneider (2014) conducted an experiment using LT-TTT2, an off-the-shelf rule-based named entity recognizer (Grover 2008) on the standard evaluation suite GREVAL (Carroll et al. 2003) with the same approach of replacing multiword named entities by the head of the MWE. The performance of the substitution approach was slightly worse than when leaving the MWE unchanged. Also this experiment did confirm that statistically motivated resources are usually better than purely lexical resources.

6.3 Lexical resources help MWE-aware parsing

Having discussed the effect of lexical resources on parsing accuracy, we now turn to two different ways to use them as a source of features for dependency parsers, to help MWE identification as well as parsing accuracy.

[5]Such a lexicon is often referred to as "gazetteer".

The first is to use MWE lexicons to alleviate the low coverage of MWEs in the training dataset. The idea is to perform an MWE pre-segmentation of the input text by lexicon lookup. The pre-segmentation, encoded in an IOB-like format, is then used as source of features during MWE-aware parsing, either in the parser itself for joint approaches (Candito & Constant 2014), or in the MWE tagger applied before parsing in pipeline approaches (Constant et al. 2012; Constant, Candito, et al. 2013).

One advantage of using soft constraints like features is their ability to handle ambiguous MWEs. Let us take the sequence *up to*, which can be either a complex preposition (*no more than*) or an accidental co-occurrence (*look up to the sky*). A naive segmentation will systematically consider it to be an MWE, independently of the context. However, a better decision can be made taking the context (i.e., the set of other features) into account. Using a joint approach on the French treebank, Candito & Constant (2014) managed to gain around 4 points in terms of tagged MWE identification F-score using such lexicon-based features: F1 = 74.5 (with) vs. F1 = 70.7 (without). We should recall, however, that their approach is limited to continuous MWEs.

A second method proposed by Nasr et al. (2015) is to incorporate subcategorization frame information, derived from a syntactic lexicon, as features in a joint parser. This was used to improve the resolution of ambiguities between grammatical compound MWEs and accidental co-occurrences. An example is the French sequence *bien que* which is either a multiword conjunction ('although') or an adverb ('well') followed by a relative conjunction ('that'), as exemplified in Section 5.2. This ambiguity may be resolved using information about the verb in the syntactic neighborhood. The authors included specific features indicating whether a given verb accepts a given complement: *manger* ('to eat') –QUE –DE, *penser* ('to think') +QUE –DE, *boire* ('to drink') –QUE –DE, *parler* ('to speak') –QUE +DE. In particular, they show for French that there is a 1-point gain in F-score, 85.24 (without) vs. 86.41 (with), for MWEs of the form ADV+*que* (ADV+*that*). The effect is spectacular for compounds of the form *de*+DET, that display a 15-point gain: 75.00 (without) vs. 84.67 (with).

7 Evaluation

Evaluating a syntactic parser generally consists in comparing the output to reference (gold-standard) parses from a manually labeled treebank. In the case of constituency parsing, a constituent is treated as correct if there exists a constituent in the gold standard parse with the same labels, starting and ending points. These parsers are traditionally evaluated through precision, recall and F-score (Black et al. 1991; Sekine & Collins 1997).

In standard dependency parsing with single-head constraint[6], the number of dependencies produced by a parser is equal to the number of total dependencies in the gold-standard parse tree. Common metrics to evaluate these parsers include the percentage of tokens with correct head, called UNLABELLED ATTACHMENT SCORE (UAS), and the percentage of tokens with correct head *and* dependency label, called LABELED ATTACHMENT SCORE (LAS) (Buchholz & Marsi 2006; Nilsson et al. 2007).

The evaluation of MWE-aware parsers and the evaluation of whether or not MWE pre-identification helps improving the parsing quality should be carefully carried out. As stated in previous sections, in most works where MWE identification is realized before parsing, the MWEs are merged into single tokens. As a result, the common metrics for parsing evaluation given above become problematic for measuring the impact of MWE identification on parsing performance (Eryiğit et al. 2011). For example, in dependency parsing, the concatenation of MWEs into single units decrements the total number of evaluated dependencies. It is thus possible to obtain different scores without actually changing the quality of the parser, but simply the representation of the results. Instead of UAS and LAS metrics, the attachment scores on the surrounding structures, namely UAS_{surr} and LAS_{surr} (i.e., the accuracy on the dependency relations excluding the ones between MWE elements) are more appropriate for extrinsic evaluation of the impact of MWE identification on parsing. Similar considerations apply to constituency parsing.

Figure 9 provides two example sequences for the phenomena discussed above; one containing a continuous MWE (on the left side) and another one containing a non-continuous MWE (on the right side). The dependency trees in this figure provide the gold standard unlabeled dependency relations for both examples. Correctly predicted dependencies are presented with check marks (✓) over the relations, whereas the wrongly predicted dependencies are presented with a cross mark (✗). The continuous MWE of the left side sequence consists of three tokens (w_4, w_5 and w_6). In other words, the two dependency relations of the overall sequence belong to the relations between MWE elements. The non-continuous MWE of the right side sequence consists of two tokens (w_3 and w_6).

The first examples of each column (A and E) show the success of a dependency parser without any prior MWE identification process. In the remaining settings, an MWE identifier is run over the given sequence before parsing. Both

---

[6]Each dependent node has at most one head in the produced dependency tree.

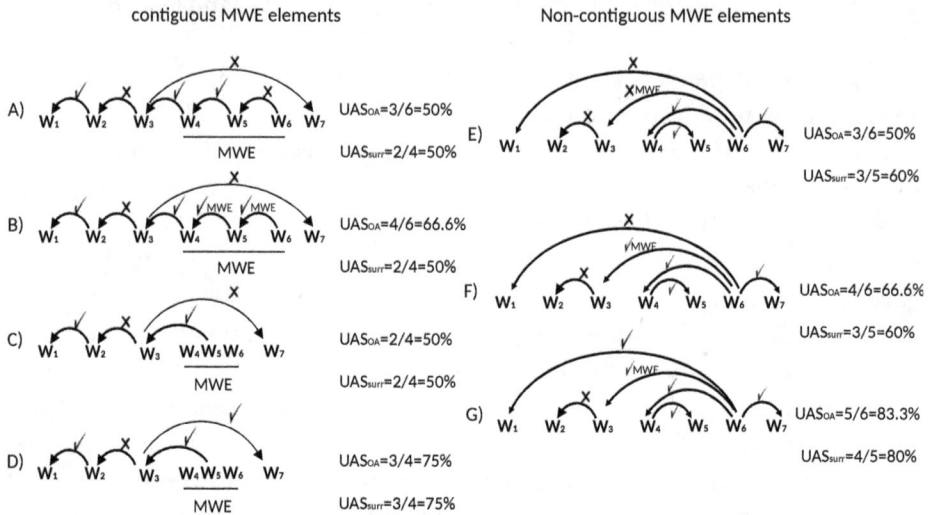

Figure 9: Extrinsic evaluation examples of the impact of MWE identification on dependency parsing performances

the overall unlabeled accuracy UAS_{OA} and the accuracy of the surrounding structures UAS_{surr} are provided next to the trees. Examples (B), (C) and (D) show the correctly detected relations by applying an MWE identifier prior to the syntactic parsing. In (C) and (D), the detected MWE is combined into a single unit $(w_4 w_5 w_6)$ whereas in (B), the detected MWE is represented as a subtree.

In (A), (B) and (C), although the parser success does not change on detecting the syntactic dependencies, UAS_{OA} is affected by the total number of evaluated dependencies, whereas UAS_{surr} remains stable, as expected. In (D), MWE identification helps the parser to detect one more dependency relation, which is reflected in UAS_{surr}. Similarly, in (F), the pre-identification of "w_3 - w_6" MWE has no impact on the parser's performance. Although this can be directly observed by UAS_{surr} (60%), UAS_{OA} mistakenly gives the impression of an improvement in parsing performance (50% $\Rightarrow$ 66.6%). This is because in this setting (second column of Figure 9) UAS_{OA} evaluates the performance of MWE pre-identification and dependency parsing as a whole. In (G), the parser performs better after MWE identification, which is again reflected in the surrounding structure evaluation.

Although UAS_{surr} and LAS_{surr} are valuable scores for measuring the impact of identifying different MWE types on parsing performance, they are troublesome with automatic MWE identification, when gold-standard MWE segmentation is not available. Then, erroneous MWE identification would degrade parsing scores

on the surrounding dependencies. An alternative solution is to detach the con-
catenated MWE components (if any) into a dependency or constituency subtree
(Candito & Constant 2014; Eryiğit et al. 2011). This way, the standard evaluation
scores UAS and LAS are still applicable in all different orchestration scenarios,
for both continuous and non-continuous MWEs, successfully assessing the performance of joint syntactic parsing and MWE identification as a whole.

8 Conclusions

In this chapter, we elaborated upon several approaches for combining MWE processing with statistical parsing to yield statistical MWE-aware parsing. These approaches depend on different parameters such as MWE representation, orchestration and external resource integration. First of all, the selected MWE representation combined with syntactic analysis have a strong impact on the system
implementation, since the more elaborated and hence more linguistically expressive the representation is, the more complex the computational system has to be.
Representations vary from simple words with spaces to multilayer structures.
The timing of MWE identification with respect to syntactic parsing, namely orchestration, is a crucial feature that needs to be carefully taken into account when
designing a statistical MWE-aware parser, as the best choice partly depends on
MWE type under consideration. MWE identification may be performed before,
after, or during parsing. The first two were discussed under the rubric "pipeline"
approaches in Section 4; the third, under "joint" approaches, in Section 5. Last,
we showed that the use of external resources is another important feature that
is required to handle the sparsity problem, not only to support syntactic attachment decisions, but also MWE identification.

Although it is difficult to draw hard and fast conclusions, it seems that further
investigation of dedicated MWE-aware parsing models is called for. Such models
can benefit from joint modeling of closely related tasks, with information from
one layer helping to disambiguate the other. Joint approaches seem to offer a
very promising line of research, as has been shown for other NLP tasks: e.g.,
joint POS tagging and parsing (Bohnet et al. 2013), joint syntactic and semantic
parsing (Henderson et al. 2013). Such approaches are now becoming prominent
in NLP alongside the deep learning revolution. In fact, most joint approaches to
statistical MWE-aware parsing are not truly joint, as they consist of workaround
solutions. We saw how many studies investigated the use of off-the-shelf parsers
by modifying training data, thus making the datasets MWE-aware. Truly joint
systems are rarer, requiring the use of specific grammatical formalisms for con-

stituency parsing or the development of new dependency parsing mechanisms dedicated to MWE identification.

As a consequence, there is much ground for future work. However, special emphasis should be given to the development of MWE-rich treebanks. Not only are these resources lacking for many languages, but also the representation and covered MWE types vary considerably among different resources. We believe that the development of new MWE-aware parsing models and resources would enable satisfactory solutions for this hard problem. Such solutions could then be further integrated into downstream applications, taking a significant step towards semantic processing of MWEs, and thus of a key element of language itself.

Acknowledgements

This work was supported by the PARSEME action (COST IC1207). It was also partially funded by the French National Research Agency (ANR) through the PARSEME-FR project (ANR-14-CERA-0001) and by a TUBITAK 1001 grant (no: 112E276).

References

Angelov, Krasimir. 2019. Multiword expressions in multilingual applications within the Grammatical Framework. In Yannick Parmentier & Jakub Waszczuk (eds.), *Representation and parsing of multiword expressions: Current trends*, 127–146. Berlin: Language Science Press. DOI:10.5281/zenodo.2579041

Arun, Abhishek & Frank Keller. 2005. Lexicalization in crosslinguistic probabilistic parsing: The case of French. In *Proceedings of the 43rd annual meeting of the Association for Computational Linguistics (ACL'05)*, 306–313. Ann Arbor, Michigan: Association for Computational Linguistics. http://aclweb.org/anthology/P05-1038.

Bansal, Mohit & Dan Klein. 2011. Web-scale features for full-scale parsing. In *Proceedings of the 49th annual meeting of the Association for Computational Linguistics: Human Language Technologies (ACL-HLT'11)*, 693–702. Portland, Oregon. http://www.aclweb.org/anthology/P11-1070.

Bejček, Eduard, Jarmila Panevová, Jan Popelka, Pavel Straňák, Magda Ševčíková, Jan Štěpánek & Zdeněk Žabokrtský. 2012. Prague Dependency Treebank 2.5 – A revisited version of PDT 2.0. In *Proc. of COLING 2012*, 231–246. Bombay, India.

Black, E., S. Abney, S. Flickenger, C. Gdaniec, C. Grishman, P. Harrison, D. Hindle, R. Ingria, F. Jelinek, J. Klavans, M. Liberman, M. Marcus, S. Roukos, B. Santorini & T. Strzalkowski. 1991. Procedure for quantitatively comparing the syntactic coverage of English grammars. In *Proceedings of the workshop on Speech and Natural Language*, 306–311. Pacific Grove, California: Association for Computational Linguistics. DOI:10.3115/112405.112467

Blunsom, Phil & Timothy Baldwin. 2006. Multilingual deep lexical acquisition for HPSGs via supertagging. In *Proceedings of the 2006 conference on Empirical Methods in Natural Language Processing (EMNLP 2006)*, 164–171. Sydney.

Bohnet, Bernd, Joakim Nivre, Igor Boguslavsky, Richard Farkas, Filip Ginter & Jan Hajic. 2013. Joint morphological and syntactic analysis for richly inflected languages. *Transactions of the Association for Computational Linguistics (TACL)* 1. 415–428.

Buchholz, Sabine & Erwin Marsi. 2006. CoNLL-X shared task on multilingual dependency parsing. In *Proceedings of the tenth conference on Computational Natural Language Learning (CoNLL-X 2006)*, 149–164. New York, NY.

Cafferkey, Conor, Deirdre Hogan & Josef van Genabith. 2007. Multi-word units in treebank-based probabilistic parsing and generation. In *Proceedings of the international conference on Recent Advances in Natural Language Processing (RANLP 2007)*. Borovets, Bulgaria.

Candito, Marie & Mathieu Constant. 2014. Strategies for contiguous multiword expression analysis and dependency parsing. In *Proceedings of the 52nd annual meeting of the Association for Computational Linguistics (volume 1: long papers)*, 743–753. Baltimore, Maryland: Association for Computational Linguistics. http://aclweb.org/anthology/P14-1070.

Candito, Marie & Benoît Crabbé. 2009. Improving generative statistical parsing with semi-supervised word clustering. In *Proc. of the 11th International Conference on Parsing Technologies (IWPT'09)*, 138–141. Paris, France: Association for Computational Linguistics. http://www.aclweb.org/anthology/W09-3821.

Candito, Marie, Joakim Nivre, Pascal Denis & Enrique Henestroza Anguiano. 2010. Benchmarking of statistical dependency parsers for French. In *Proceedings of COLING 2010, 23rd international conference on Computational Linguistics , posters volume*, 108–116. Beijing, China.

Candito, Marie & Djamé Seddah. 2010. Parsing word clusters. In *Proceedings of the NAACL HLT 2010 first workshop on Statistical Parsing of Morphologically-Rich Languages*, 76–84. Los Angeles, California.

Carroll, John, Guido Minnen & Edward Briscoe. 2003. Parser evaluation:Using a grammatical relation annotation scheme. In Anne Abeillé (ed.), *Treebanks: Building and using parsed corpora*, 299–316. Dordrecht: Kluwer.

Charniak, Eugene. 2000. A maximum-entropy-inspired parser. In *Proceedings of the 1st North American chapter of the Association for Computational Linguistics conference*, 132–139. Seattle, Washington.

Collins, Michael. 1996. A new statistical parser based on bigram lexical dependencies. In *Proceedings of the 34th annual meeting of the Association for Computational Linguistics (ACL 1996)*, 184–191. Santa Cruz, California.

Collins, Michael. 1999. *Head-driven statistical models for natural language parsing*. Philadelphia, PA: University of Pennsylvania Ph.D. thesis.

Constant, Mathieu, Marie Candito & Djamé Seddah. 2013. The LIGM-Alpage architecture for the SPMRL 2013 shared task: Multiword expression analysis and dependency parsing. In *Proceedings of the fourth workshop on Statistical Parsing of Morphologically-Rich Languages*, 46–52. Seattle, Washington, USA: Association for Computational Linguistics. http://aclweb.org/anthology/W13-4905.

Constant, Mathieu, Joseph Le Roux & Anthony Sigogne. 2013. Combining compound recognition and PCFG-LA parsing with word lattices and conditional random fields. *ACM Transaction on Speech and Language Processing (TSLP), Special Issue on MWEs* 10(3).

Constant, Mathieu, Joseph Le Roux & Nadi Tomeh. 2016. Deep lexical segmentation and syntactic parsing in the easy-first dependency framework. In *Proceedings of the 15th annual conference of the North American chapter of the Association for Computational Linguistics: Human Language Technologies (NAACL HLT 2016)*, 1095–1101. San Diego, California.

Constant, Mathieu & Joakim Nivre. 2016. A transition-based system for joint lexical and syntactic analysis. In *Proceedings of the 54th annual meeting of the Association for Computational Linguistics*, vol. 1: *Long papers*, 161–171. Berlin, Germany: Association for Computational Linguistics. http://www.aclweb.org/anthology/P16-1016.

Constant, Mathieu, Anthony Sigogne & Patrick Watrin. 2012. Discriminative strategies to integrate multiword expression recognition and parsing. In *Proceedings of the 50th annual meeting of the Association for Computational Linguistics: Long papers*, vol. 1 (ACL '12), 204–212. Jeju Island, Korea: Association for Computational Linguistics. http://dl.acm.org/citation.cfm?id=2390524.2390554.

Denis, Pascal & Benoît Sagot. 2012. Coupling an annotated corpus and a lexicon for state-of-the-art POS tagging. *Language Resources and Evaluation* 46(4). 721–736. DOI:10.1007/s10579-012-9193-0

Durrett, Greg & Dan Klein. 2015. Neural CRF parsing. In *Proceedings of the 53rd annual meeting of the Association for Computational Linguistics and the 7th*

International Joint Conference on Natural Language Processing, vol. 1: Long Papers, 302–312. Beijing.

Dyer, Chris, Miguel Ballesteros, Wang Ling, Austin Matthews & Noah A. Smith. 2015. Transition-based dependency parsing with stack long short-term memory. In *Proc. of ACL 2015*, 334–343. Beijing.

Dyvik, Helge, Paul Meurer, Victoria Rosén, Koenraad De Smedt, Petter Haugereid, Gyri Smørdal Losnegaard, Gunn Inger Lyse & Martha Thunes. 2016. NorGramBank: A 'deep' treebank for Norwegian. In Nicoletta Calzolari, Khalid Choukri, Thierry Declerck, Marko Grobelnik, Bente Maegaard, Joseph Mariani, Asunción Moreno, Jan Odijk & Stelios Piperidis (eds.), *Proceedings of the tenth international conference on Language Resources and Evaluation (LREC 2016)*, 3555–3562. Portorož, Slovenia. http://www.lrec-conf.org/proceedings/lrec2016/summaries/943.html.

Eisner, Jason M. 1996. Three new probabilistic models for dependency parsing: An exploration. In *Proceedings of the 16th conference on Computational Linguistics (ACL 1996)*, 340–345. Santa Cruz, California.

Eryiğit, Gülşen, Tugay İlbay & Ozan Arkan Can. 2011. Multiword expressions in statistical dependency parsing. In *Proceedings of the second workshop on Statistical Parsing of Morphologically Rich Languages*, 45–55. Dublin, Ireland.

Fazly, Afsaneh, Paul Cook & Suzanne Stevenson. 2009. Unsupervised type and token identification of idiomatic expressions. *Computational Linguistics* 35(1). 61–103.

Foufi, Vasiliki, Luka Nerima & Eric Wehrli. 2019. Multilingual parsing and MWE detection. In Yannick Parmentier & Jakub Waszczuk (eds.), *Representation and parsing of multiword expressions: Current trends*, 217–237. Berlin: Language Science Press. DOI:10.5281/zenodo.2579047

Głowińska, Katarzyna & Adam Przepiórkowski. 2010. The design of syntactic annotation levels in the National Corpus of Polish. In *Proc. of the seventh international conference on Language Resources and Evaluation (LREC 2010)*. Valletta, Malta.

Green, Spence, Marie-Catherine de Marneffe, John Bauer & Christopher D. Manning. 2011. Multiword expression identification with tree substitution grammars: A parsing tour de force with French. In *Proc. of EMNLP 2011*, 725–735. Edinburgh.

Green, Spence, Marie-Catherine de Marneffe & Christopher D. Manning. 2013. Parsing models for identifying multiword expressions. *Computational Linguistics* 39(1). 195–227.

Gross, Maurice. 1984. Lexicon-grammar and the syntactic analysis of French. In *Proceedings of the 10th international conference on Computational Linguistics and 22nd annual meeting of the Association for Computational Linguistics*, 275–282. Stanford, California, USA: Association for Computational Linguistics.

Grover, Claire. 2008. *LT-TTT2: Example pipelines documentation*. Tech. rep. Edinburgh Language Technology Group.

Henderson, James, Paola Merlo, Ivan Titov & Gabriele Musillo. 2013. Multilingual joint parsing of syntactic and semantic dependencies with a latent variable model. *Computational Linguistics* 39(4). 949–998.

Kato, Akihiko, Hiroyuki Shindo & Yuji Matsumoto. 2016. Construction of an English dependency corpus incorporating compound function words. In *Proceedings of the tenth international conference on Language Resources and Evaluation (LREC 2016)*. Portorož, Slovenia: European Language Resources Association (ELRA).

Koo, Terry, Xavier Carreras & Michael Collins. 2008. Simple semi-supervised dependency parsing. In *Proceedings of ACL-08: HLT*, 595–603. Columbus, Ohio.

Korkontzelos, Ioannis & Suresh Manandhar. 2010. Can recognising multiword expressions improve shallow parsing? In *Proc. of the 11th annual conference of the North American chapter of the Association for Computational Linguistics: Human Language Technologies NAACL/HLT 2010*, 636–644. Los Angeles, California.

Le Roux, Joseph, Antoine Rozenknop & Mathieu Constant. 2014. Syntactic parsing and compound recognition via dual decomposition: Application to French. In *Proc. of COLING 2014*. Dublin, Ireland.

Lehmann, Hans Martin & Gerold Schneider. 2011. A large-scale investigation of verb-attached prepositional phrases. In S. Hoffmann, P. Rayson & G. Leech (eds.), *Studies in variation, contacts and change in English, volume 6: Methodological and historical dimensions of corpus linguistics*. Helsinki: Varieng.

McDonald, Ryan, Kevin Lerman & Fernando Pereira. 2006. Multilingual dependency analysis with a two-stage discriminative parser. In *Proceedings of the tenth conference on Computational Natural Language Learning (CoNLL-X)*, 216–220. New York City: Association for Computational Linguistics. http://www.aclweb.org/anthology/W/W06/W06-2932.

Miller, George Armitage. 1956. The magical number seven, plus or minus two: Some limits on our capacity for processing information. *Psychological Review* 63. 81–97.

Mirroshandel, Seyed Abolghasem & Alexis Nasr. 2016. Integrating selectional constraints and subcategorization frames in a dependency parser. *Computational Linguistics* 42(1). 55–90.

Mirroshandel, Seyed Abolghasem, Alexis Nasr & Joseph Le Roux. 2012. Semi-supervised dependency parsing using lexical affinities. In *Proceedings of the 50th annual meeting of the Association for Computational Linguistics (volume 1: long papers)*, 777–785. Jeju Island, Korea: Association for Computational Linguistics. http://aclweb.org/anthology/P12-1082.

Mirroshandel, Seyed Abolghasem, Alexis Nasr & Benoît Sagot. 2013. Enforcing subcategorization constraints in a parser using sub-parses recombining. In *Proceedings of the 2013 conference of the North American chapter of the Association for Computational Linguistics: Human Language Technologies*, 239–247. Atlanta, Georgia: Association for Computational Linguistics.

Nagy T., István & Veronika Vincze. 2014. VPCTagger: Detecting verb-particle constructions with syntax-based methods. In *Proceedings of the EACL 2014 workshop on MWEs*, 17–25. Gothenburg.

Nakagawa, Tetsuji. 2007. Multilingual dependency parsing using global features. In *Proceedings of the CoNLL shared task session of EMNLP-CoNLL 2007*, 952–956. Prague, Czech Republic: Association for Computational Linguistics. http://www.aclweb.org/anthology/D07-1100.

Nasr, Alexis, Frederic Bechet, Jean-Francois Rey, Benoit Favre & Joseph Le Roux. 2011. MACAON: An NLP tool suite for processing word lattices. In *Proceedings of ACL 2011 demonstrations*. Portland, Oregon.

Nasr, Alexis, Carlos Ramisch, José Deulofeu & André Valli. 2015. Joint dependency parsing and multiword expression tokenisation. In *53rd annual meeting of the Association for Computational Linguistics*, 1116–1126. Beijing, China.

Nilsson, Jens, Sebastian Riedel & Deniz Yuret. 2007. The CoNLL 2007 shared task on dependency parsing. In *Proceedings of EMNLP/CoNLL 2007 CoNLL shared tasks session*, 915–932.

Nivre, Joakim. 2014. *Transition-based parsing with multiword expressions.* Athens.

Nivre, Joakim, Marie-Catherine de Marneffe, Filip Ginter, Yoav Goldberg, Jan Hajič, Christopher D. Manning, Ryan McDonald, Slav Petrov, Sampo Pyysalo, Natalia Silveira, Reut Tsarfaty & Dan Zeman. 2016. Universal dependencies v1: A multilingual treebank collection. In *Proceedings of the 10th international conference on Language Resources and Evaluation (LREC 2016)*. Portorož, Slovenia.

Nivre, Joakim, Johan Hall & Jens Nilsson. 2004. Memory-based dependency parsing. In *Proceedings of CoNLL 2004*, 49–56. Boston, Massachusetts.

Nivre, Joakim, Johan Hall, Jens Nilsson, Atanas Chanev, Gülsen Eryigit, Sandra Kübler, Svetoslav Marinov & Erwin Marsi. 2007. MaltParser: A language-independent system for data-driven dependency parsing. *Natural Language Engineering* 13(02). 95–135.

Nivre, Joakim & Jens Nilsson. 2004. Multiword units in syntactic parsing. *Proceedings of Methodologies and Evaluation of Multiword Units in Real-World Applications (MEMURA)*.

Pawley, Andrew & Frances Hodgetts Syder. 1983. Two puzzles for linguistic theory : Native-like selection and native-like fluency. In J. C. Richards & R. W. Schmidt (eds.), *Language and communication*, 191–226. London: Longman.

Prins, Robbert. 2005. *Finite-state pre-processing for natural language analysis*. Behavioral & Cognitive Neurosciences (BCN) research school, University of Groningen dissertation.

Ramshaw, Lance A. & Mitchell P. Marcus. 1995. Text chunking using transformation-based learning. In *Proceedings of the 3rd ACL workshop on Very Large Corpora*, 82–94.

Ronan, Patricia & Gerold Schneider. 2015. Determining light verb constructions in contemporary British and Irish English. *International Journal of Corpus Linguistics* 20(3). 326–354.

Rosén, Victoria, Gyri Smørdal Losnegaard, Koenraad De Smedt, Eduard Bejček, Agata Savary, Adam Przepiórkowski, Petya Osenova & Verginica Barbu Mititelu. 2015. A survey of multiword expressions in treebanks. In *Proc. of 14th international workshop on Treebanks and Linguistic Theories (TLT 2015)*, 179–193. Warsaw, Poland.

Sag, Ivan, Timothy Baldwin, Francis Bond, Ann Copestake & Dan Flickinger. 2002. Multiword expressions: A pain in the neck for NLP. In *Proceedings of the 3rd international conference on Computational Linguistics and Intelligent Text Processing* (Lecture Notes in Computer Science 2276), 1–15. Springer.

Sagot, Benoît & Pierre Boullier. 2005. From raw corpus to word lattices: Robust pre-parsing processing with SxPipe. *Archives of Control Sciences* 15(4). 653–662.

Schneider, Gerold. 2008. *Hybrid long-distance functional dependency parsing*. Institute of Computational Linguistics, University of Zurich Doctoral Thesis.

Schneider, Gerold. 2012. Using semantic resources to improve a syntactic dependency parser. In *Proceedings of Semantic Relations II workshop (SEM-II) at LREC 2012*, 67–76. Istanbul, Turkey.

Schneider, Gerold. 2014. Improving PP attachment in a hybrid dependency parser using semantic, distributional, and lexical resources. In *Second PARSEME meeting*. Athens, Greece.

Schneider, Nathan, Spencer Onuffer, Nora Kazour, Emily Danchik, Michael T. Mordowanec, Henrietta Conrad & Noah A. Smith. 2014. Comprehensive annotation of multiword expressions in a social web corpus. In *Proceedings of* the ninth international conference on Language Resources and Evaluation (LREC 2014), 456–461. Reykyavik.

Seddah, Djamé, Reut Tsarfaty, Sandra Kübler, Marie Candito, Jinho Choi, Richárd Farkas, Jennifer Foster, Iakes Goenaga, Koldo Gojenola, Yoav Goldberg, Spence Green, Nizar Habash, Marco Kuhlmann, Wolfgang Maier, Joakim Nivre, Adam Przepiorkowski, Ryan Roth, Wolfgang Seeker, Yannick Versley, Veronika Vincze, Marcin Woliński, Alina Wróblewska & Eric Villemonte de la Clérgerie. 2013. Overview of the SPMRL 2013 shared task: A cross-framework evaluation of parsing morphologically rich languages. In *Proceedings of the fourth international workshop on Statistical Parsing of Morphologically-Rich Languages (SPRML IV)*. Seattle, WA.

Sekine, Satoshi & Michael Collins. 1997. *EVALB bracket scoring program*. http://www.%20cs.%20nyu.%20edu/cs/projects/proteus/evalb.

Seretan, Violeta. 2011. *Syntax-based collocation extraction* (Text, Speech and Language Technology 44). Dordrecht: Springer.

Sinclair, John. 1991. *Corpus, concordance, collocation*. Oxford: Oxford University Press.

Tesnière, Lucien. 1959. *Eléments de syntaxe structurale*. Klincksieck.

Tjong Kim Sang, Erik F. 2002. Introduction to the CoNLL-2002 shared task: Language-independent named entity recognition. In *Proceedings of the 6th conference on Natural Language Learning (CoNLL) – volume 20*, 1–4. Taipei, Taiwan.

Tomasello, Michael. 1998. Cognitive linguistics. In W. Bechtel & G. Graham (eds.), *A companion to cognitive science*. Basil Blackwell.

Tu, Yuancheng & Dan Roth. 2011. Learning English light verb constructions: Contextual or statistical. In *Proceedings of the ACL 2011 workshop on MWEs*, 31–39. Portland, OR.

Vincze, Veronika, István Nagy T. & Gábor Berend. 2011. Multiword expressions and named entities in the Wiki50 corpus. In *Proceedings of the international conference Recent Advances in Natural Language Processing 2011*, 289–295. Hissar, Bulgaria: Association for Computational Linguistics.

Vincze, Veronika, János Zsibrita & István Nagy T. 2013. Dependency parsing for identifying Hungarian light verb constructions. In *Proceedings of the sixth International Joint Conference on Natural Language Processing (IJCNLP)*, 207–215. Nagoya, Japan: Asian Federation of Natural Language Processing. http://aclweb.org/anthology/I13-1024.

Weeds, Julie, James Dowdall, Gerold Schneider, Bill Keller & David Weir. 2007. Using distributional similarity to organise biomedical terminology. In Fidelia

Ibekwe-SanJuan, Anne Condamines & M. Teresa Cabré Castellví (eds.), *Application-driven terminology engineering*. Amsterdam/Philadelphia: Benjamins.

Wray, Alison. 2008. *Formulaic language: Pushing the boundaries*. Oxford University Press.

Yamada, Hiroyasu & Yuji Matsumoto. 2003. Statistical dependency analysis with support vector machines. In *Proceedings of the International Workshop on Parsing Technologies (IWPT)*, vol. 3, 195–206. Nancy, France.

Chapter 7

Investigating the effect of automatic MWE recognition on CCG parsing

Miryam de Lhoneux
Uppsala University

Omri Abend
Hebrew University of Jerusalem

Mark Steedman
University of Edinburgh

We investigate the use of automatic Multiword Expressions (MWEs) recognition in parsing with Combinatory Categorial Grammar. We transform the representation of MWEs in CCGbank by collapsing them to one token. Our model significantly outperforms the baseline on the transformed gold standard showing the benefit of having this information at training time. It also performs significantly better on the transformed gold standard when the transformation is done before parsing as opposed to after parsing which shows that it can help the parser at prediction time. We conclude that despite the limited settings (our transformation algorithm is only able to deal with MWEs that do not cross constituent boundaries), our method can lead to improvements. We obtain different results with MWE recognisers that detect different types of MWE and therefore emphasize the need to experiment with different recognisers to find out which ones this method is best suited to.

1 Introduction

1.1 Motivation

Multiword Expressions (henceforth MWE(s)) are increasingly receiving attention in NLP. They represent a wide variety of phenomena with different properties but are generally agreed to be a group of multiple lexemes which have some

Miryam de Lhoneux, Omri Abend & Mark Steedman. 2019. Investigating the effect of automatic MWE recognition on CCG parsing. In Yannick Parmentier & Jakub Waszczuk (eds.), *Representation and parsing of multiword expressions: Current trends*, 183–215. Berlin: Language Science Press. DOI:10.5281/zenodo.2579045

level of idiomaticity or irregularity (Sag et al. 2002). They represent varied phenomena but, due to this irregularity, they are all generally considered a problem for NLP tasks and they are often a problem for syntactic parsing.

Recent research is showing that information about MWEs can help the syntactic parsing task (Nivre & Nilsson 2004; Korkontzelos & Manandhar 2010) and inversely, information about syntactic analysis helps MWE identification (Green et al. 2013; Weller & Heid 2010; Martens & Vandeghinste 2010). Working on either of the tasks by using information from the other has thus proven to be a useful thing to do and adding MWE information to the syntactic parsing task has proven useful in that it has helped increase parsing accuracy. Work on adding MWE information to syntactic parsing so far has been restricted to certain types of MWEs (multiword nouns, numerical expressions and compound function words in Nivre & Nilsson (2004), compound nominals, proper names and adjective-noun constructions in Korkontzelos & Manandhar (2010)) and hence leaves room for improvement.

Combinatory Categorial Grammar (henceforth CCG) is a strongly lexicalized formalism that is increasingly being used for parsing in NLP applications because of its computational and linguistic properties and because CCG parsers perform relatively well on the Penn Treebank (PTB). To give just a few examples, CCG is used in Machine Translation (e.g. Birch et al. 2007), sentence realization (e.g White 2006), semantic parsing and language acquisition (e.g. Krishnamurthy & Mitchell 2012), open-domain question answering and entailment (e.g. Lewis & Steedman 2013).

For these reasons, CCG parsing is an ideal framework to carry on the work on the interaction between syntactic parsing and MWEs and because CCG is a lexicalized formalism and thus encodes a lot of information in the lexicon, it would be useful to work on it by providing it with information about MWEs.

1.2 Aims

No work so far has tried to use MWE information to improve CCG parsing which is what we intend to do in this work. Different approaches to using MWE information for improving syntactic parsing have been conducted so far with different syntactic models. We conduct one of them which will be argued to be far from ideal but a necessary first step useful to build a sound baseline. The approach we pursue consists in altering training and test data, i.e. transforming the representation of MWEs so that they form one lexical item in them (and hence retokenize the sentence). We experiment with different MWE recognition methods so as to find out if the approach works better with certain types of MWEs than with others.

The two research questions we therefore try to answer are first whether or not we can improve CCG parsing with MWEs and second whether or not applying the same transformation approach to different types of MWEs can lead to different results.

1.3 Overview of the chapter

We give an overview of the background literature to further support our motivations and elaborate on the research questions in Section 2. We then explain and motivate the methodology we propose to use in order to answer the research questions in Section 3. We present our experiments and results in Section 4. We conclude from our study and propose avenues of research in Section 5.

2 Background

2.1 Multiword expressions

MWEs is an umbrella term that has been used to characterize a wide variety of phenomena. The most commonly acknowledged definition of this term since Sag et al. (2002) is that it is a group of multiple lexemes which have some level of idiomaticity or irregularity. The multiple lexemes in a MWE are called MWE units in the remainder of this chapter for convenience. This idiomaticity may be lexico-syntactic such as in the unusual coordination of a preposition and an adjective in *by and large*. It may be semantic such as in the idiom *kick the bucket* in which the meaning of the whole is not dividable into the meaning of the parts. It may be pragmatic such as in *good morning* which has a meaning attached to the situation in which it is said. Finally, it may be statistical such as the collocation *strong coffee* in which both units occur more frequently than expected.

Different MWE types present different properties. They vary in flexibility: words may appear between the units of a flexible collocation (*strong home-made coffee*, for example) but not between the units of a lexically fixed figurative expression such as *it's raining cats and dogs*. They also vary in compositionality: *Strong coffee* is fully compositional whereas *kick the bucket* is not and *spill the beans* is semantically decomposable, i.e. the meaning of the whole is not predictable from the meaning of the parts but can be decomposed into its parts: if *spill* is interpreted as *reveal* and *the beans* as *the secret* (Nunberg et al. 1994). Despite these varied properties they are all generally agreed to be hard to deal with in NLP applications (Sag et al. 2002) and the importance of dealing with them properly has been increasing over the past decade. As described at length in Kim's (2008) thesis, "dealing with" MWEs consists in developing systems and models for various kinds of tasks. For syntactic analysis, it is important to identify them in text and extract them to a dictionary. For semantic understanding, it is important to measure their compositionality, classify and interpret them.

2.2 Combinatory Categorial Grammar

2.2.1 Presentation

Combinatory Categorial Grammar (Steedman 2000) is a strongly lexicalized grammar formalism which is currently gaining popularity in the NLP community.

CCG was built with the intent of being linguistically aware as well as computationally tractable partly as a reaction to transformationalist ideas which were predominant in formal grammars at the time. It differs from the latter mainly in having one component including syntactic and semantic information instead of having separate modules for each in the grammar. Similarly, instead of having a large amount of rules and a lexicon as is the case in traditional grammars, it has a small set of universal rules and a lexicon which encodes most syntactic information. For the sentence *John buys shares*, a traditional grammar has information in the lexicon: that *John* is an NP, that *buys* is a verb, that *shares* is an NP, and in the grammar: that a V and an NP form a VP and that an NP and a VP form a sentence S, as in Figure 1. By contrast, for the same sentence, CCG has information in its lexicon that *John* is an NP, that *shares* is an NP and that *buys* first takes an NP to its right then an NP to its left to form a sentence S, as in Figure 2.

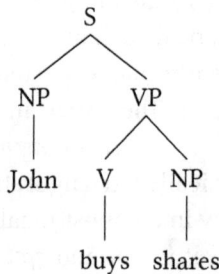

Figure 1: PTB-style tree

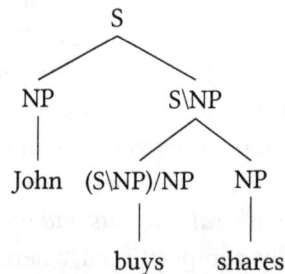

Figure 2: CCG tree

Without going into too much detail about how this works, lexical categories work either as functor or as argument and a set of combinatory rules allow them to combine. For example, the category (S\NP)/NP works as a functor that takes an NP to the right (indicated by the forward slash followed by an NP). The category of *buys* therefore can combine with the category of *shares* to result in the category S\NP which in turns takes an NP argument to the left (indicated by the backslash followed by an NP), which it finds in the category of *John* to form a sentence S.

This grammar architecture allows CCG to deal elegantly with long-range dependencies. Instead of adding a level of representation in the form of a trace as in Figure 3, the grammar has universal rules which allow the combination of lexical items, as shown in Figure 4. This has computational advantages and linguistic plausibility: linguistics is increasingly adopting a view of grammar where syntax and the lexicon are two modules that are not completely separate in the grammar but instead interact with each other. It is a tenet of the recently emerging framework of Construction Grammar (Hoffmann & Trousdale 2013). These linguistic and computational properties have made it a widely used framework across NLP research.

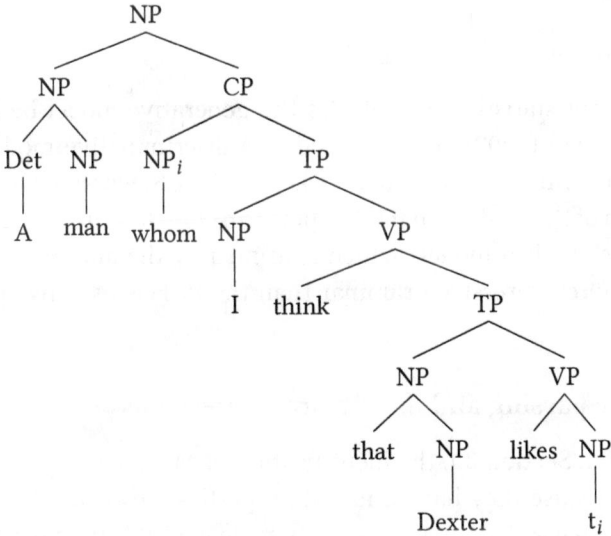

Figure 3: PTB-style tree

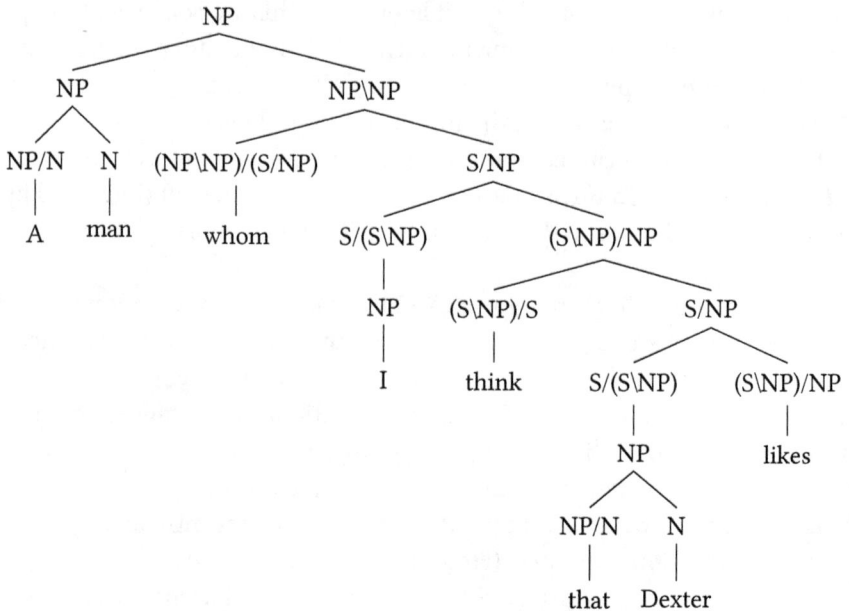

Figure 4: CCG tree

2.2.2 CCG parsing

The first efficient statistical model was the generative model built by Hocken-maier & Steedman (2002) and extended to a discriminative model by Clark & Curran (2007). Both use CCGbank (Hockenmaier & Steedman 2007), a CCG converted version of the PTB. Both models perform close to state-of-the-art although with simpler statistical models which is argued by the authors to be the result of having a more expressive grammar than the PCFGs used by state-of-the-art parsers.

2.3 Syntactic parsing and multiword expressions

As mentioned in Section 2.1, the identification of MWEs is important for syntactic analysis. Because they have unusual properties, however, their analysis can be quite problematic. The question of how to deal with MWEs for syntactic parsing has been raised by many researchers. It has been approached in different ways. Researchers working with precision grammars such as HPSG for example have accommodated the lexical entries for MWEs in the lexicon so that MWEs are not a problem for parsing. Researchers on data-induced grammars have accommodated the testing and/or training data before parsing. Recent research has proposed to both change the lexicon and the parsing algorithm. A last recent approach is to learn MWE representations and dependency trees jointly. We briefly describe each of these approaches in turn. We describe the second approach in more details than the other two because this is the one we use in this work for reasons explained in Section 3.1.

2.3.1 Transforming the lexicon

Different types of lexical entries have been proposed for MWEs in the grammar. A lot of research proposes to simply analyse all MWEs as "words-with-spaces", i.e. group the MWE units together in the syntactic analysis. This analysis has been argued against by many. Sag et al. (2002) have suggested sophisticated ways of representing the different MWE types in a grammar, which have been partly implemented within the framework of the precision grammar HPSG, as described by Copestake et al. (2002). Zhang et al. (2006) established that MWEs are a tremendous source of parse failures when parsing with a precision grammar such as HPSG and henceforth proposed a way of using this information to identify new MWEs and enrich a lexicon: they suggested using parse failures to predict the existence of a MWE.

2.3.2 Transforming the data

Since the seminal work of Nivre & Nilsson (2004), research has shown that treating MWEs as one token or a "word-with-spaces" in test and/or in training data before parsing and/or training leads to an improvement in parsing accuracy. Nivre & Nilsson (2004) have shown that to be true for deterministic dependency parsing and Korkontzelos & Manandhar (2010) have shown that to be true for shallow parsing.

The approaches adopted in these two papers are quite different and we describe each in turn.

2.3.2.1 Transforming training and test data

Nivre & Nilsson (2004) created two versions of a treebank, one in which MWEs are annotated as if compositional and one in which they are joined as one lexical item. They show that training a parser on the second version of the treebank leads to a better parsing accuracy. They use a corpus with manual MWE annotation to create both versions of the treebank and hence simulate "perfect" MWE recognition. MWE annotation, however, only consists in a few MWE types so it is not comprehensive. They report improvement in parsing accuracy of the MWEs themselves but also of their surrounding syntactic structure. They opened the gate for improving syntactic parsing with MWE information but left many questions unanswered. For example, the question of whether or not their results port to other syntactic parsing models, whether or not the full potential they obtained with "perfect" recognition of MWEs can be obtained with an automatic recogniser and whether or not this potential can be increased when recognising other types of MWEs. Some of these questions have been partially addressed since then. Constant et al. (2012) have shown that with an automatic recogniser, the parsing accuracy improvement is not as dramatic as predicted by Nivre & Nilsson (2004). Eryiğit et al. (2011) found out that in the case of a morphologically rich language (e.g., Turkish), the approach works with some types of MWEs but not with others.

2.3.2.2 Transforming test data

Korkontzelos & Manandhar (2010) reported similar parsing accuracy improvements for shallow parsing, showing that Nivre & Nilsson (2004)'s results do seem to port to at least one other parsing model. Their technique is, however, quite different. They created a corpus containing a large number of pre-selected MWEs (randomly chosen from WordNet) and converted it to a version in which the MWE units are collapsed to one lexical item. They POS-tag the two versions of the corpus before parsing each. They subsequently analyse the differences in output. In order to do so, they randomly select a sample of output from both parsed corpora and build a taxonomy of changes they observe from one to the other. For each class in the taxonomy, they determine whether the change in output led to increased accuracy, decreased accuracy or did not change the accuracy. They automatically classify the rest of the output data and observe an overall increase in accuracy. Their work not only confirms the results obtained from previous work but also provides an insightful qualitative analysis of changes obtained with their method. They believe the improvement in accuracy is partly due to the fact that the parsing model backs off to POS-tags for rare and unseen words. When MWE units are collapsed to one token, that token is not known by the parser but it still gets assigned a sensible POS-tag because the POS-tagger uses contextual information.

2.3.3 Transforming the lexicon and the parsing algorithm

A lot of work has shown that although MWE information improves syntactic parsing, the reverse is also true: syntactic analysis improves MWE identification.

Green et al. (2013) successfully tuned a parser for MWE identification, Weller & Heid (2010) and Martens & Vandeghinste (2010) showed that using parsed corpora for MWE identification is beneficial. These findings led Seretan (2013) to propose that neither accommodating the grammar with MWE information, nor recognising MWEs in raw text as a help to parsing are appropriate ways of dealing with the issue of MWEs in syntactic parsing because neither approach takes advantage of the fact that MWE information and syntactic analysis are mutually informative. She proposes instead to have a MWE lexicon and to deal with potential MWEs during parsing.

2.3.4 Joint learning of MWE identification and parsing

Based on the same observation that the tasks of MWE identification and parsing can inform each other, Constant & Nivre (2016) propose to learn both jointly. They use corpora that both have dependency and MWE annotations and modify the parsing algorithm so as to learn both representations jointly. They show that this approach is effective.

2.3.5 Advantages and caveats of the different approaches

All of these researchers have shown the importance of MWEs for syntactic parsing but all of the approaches presented have caveats. Research on HPSG seems to have found the most sophisticated methods of dealing with MWEs but parsing with precision grammars is known to be much less robust (Zhang & Kordoni 2008) than parsing with data-induced grammars which make it a suboptimal solution for practical parsing. Learning MWE representations and syntactic parsing jointly is probably the most promising approach but it requires a lot of manual work since it requires a corpus that is annotated both with MWEs and dependency trees. As far as other solutions are concerned, they are often very much limited by the type of MWEs that have been dealt with. All other solutions presented as a matter of fact concentrate on a few types of MWEs. However, as argued by Kim (2008), because of the different but interrelated properties of MWEs, it is neither appropriate to try and generalize from MWEs and find a single representation which works for all types, nor is it appropriate to deal with each MWE type at a time. An approach for improving syntactic parsing on all MWE types is still lacking and previous approaches leave the question of whether the results can be reproduced with different types of MWEs unanswered.

2.4 Research questions and objectives

In Section 2.3, it was said that MWE identification information improves syntactic parsing although current approaches to doing so leave room for improvement. Trying to improve syntactic parsing with MWE information therefore looks like a promising avenue of research. In Section 2.2, arguments for working with CCG parsing were put forward.

Very little attention has, however, been given to MWEs in CCG parsing. Constable & Curran (2009) modified CCGbank to have a better representation of verb-particle constructions but did not report any parsing accuracy improvement. No work has tried to establish whether CCG parsing accuracy could be improved by adding information about MWEs which is what we intend to do in this work. Our aim is twofold: we want to find out whether or not MWE information can improve CCG parsing and we wish to find out if using methods that have been used for a restricted set of types of MWEs can be extended to different types of MWEs.

3 Methodology

3.1 Approach

As explained in the last section, in this work we concentrate on an approach that consists in transforming the representation of MWEs in treebanks. In Section 2.3.2, two different versions of this kind of approach have been described. In the first, manual annotation is used to create two versions of the treebank. This left questions unanswered, two of which being whether or not the approach can work with automatic recognition and whether or not the approach can work with different types of MWEs. In this work, we conduct the type of approach described by Nivre & Nilsson (2004) using an automatic recogniser to answer the first of these questions in the context of CCG parsing. We also experiment with the recogniser by using different versions of it to answer the second of these two questions. This approach is especially interesting in that, as has been shown in Schneider et al. (2014) who attempted a comprehensive annotation of MWEs in a corpus, even manual annotation of MWEs is a difficult task and experimenting with different MWE recognisers could lead to interesting results.

Our approach therefore involves transforming both training and test data. Transforming the training data can help the parsing model learn more sensible representations of language. For example in the tree for *part of speech*, *of speech* is considered a modifier of *part* as in Figure 5 which does not make much sense. Instead, grouping the three lexical items as in Figure 6 gives a better representation of this group of words.

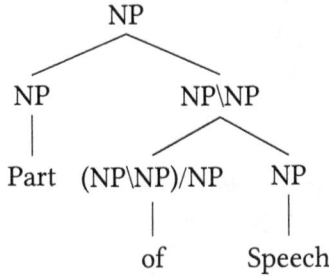

```
                        NP
               ╱────────────╲
           NP                NP\NP
            |           ╱──────────╲
          Part    (NP\NP)/NP        NP
                       |             |
                       of         Speech
```

Figure 5: Traditional tree for *Part of Speech*

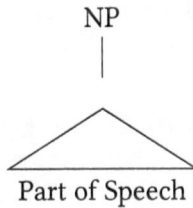

```
              NP
               |
        ╱──────────────╲
       ╱────────────────╲
          Part of Speech
```

Figure 6: Tree for *Part of Speech* where tokens are grouped

Transforming the test data by for example collapsing the three lexical items *part, of* and *speech* to one token *part+of+speech* can help the parser make sensible decisions locally by telling it to consider the three words as one. For example, if this token is followed by a coordinator, the parser knows that coordinating one of the units is not a possibility. In the sentence *it gives part+of+speech and lemma information,* the parser cannot coordinate *speech* with *lemma* which would be a possibility otherwise. Transforming MWEs in training and test data leads to two different effects of adding MWE information to the syntactic parsing pipeline and it is best if we can differentiate both in the experiments. We call the first type of effect *training effect* and the second *parsing effect*. We repeat the definition of these two effects below.

Training effect: the parser learns more sensible representations of MWEs and its units.

Parsing effect: the parser is helped locally in its decision by considering the MWE units as one unit.

3.2 Parsing model

As mentioned in Section 2.2, both generative and discriminative models exist for parsing with CCG. There are different generative models with different properties. We chose to use StatOpenCCG, developed by Christodoulopoulos (2008) and recently further expanded by Deoskar et al. (2014) because of its ease of use, flexibility and fast training. The expansion of the parser by Deoskar et al. (2014) is particularly well suited to our purposes: it was extended so that it works better on unknown lexical items. Joining lexical items to one token will increase the sparsity of the data and being able to deal with unknown data is therefore a concern for our approach. More particularly, the model proposed by Christodoulopoulos (2008) and Deoskar et al. (2014) is based on one of Hockenmaier (2003)'s models called LexCat which conditions probabilities on lexical categories. Deoskar et al. (2014) make use of this LexCat model instead of the fully lexicalized model which conditions it on words precisely so that the parser is better equipped to deal with unseen lexical items. They introduce a smoothed lexicon to deal with these. They POS-tag the test data in a pre-processing stage and use POS-information to determine the lexical categories of words by using probabilities of lexical categories that appear with each POS-tag of unseen word in the seen data. Because, as mentioned in Section 2.3.2.2, Korkontzelos & Manandhar (2010) have shown that POS-tags assigned automatically to MWEs were useful when parsing, the LexCat model therefore looks ideal for our purposes. We follow Deoskar et al. (2014) in using the C&C tools (Curran et al. 2007) to POS-tag our test data so as to have a model that is comparable with theirs.

3.3 Extending the parsing model with MWE information

As explained in Section 3.1, the objective is first to recognise MWEs in the unlabeled version of CCGbank and then to collapse MWEs to one lexical item in the annotated version of the treebank and in the unlabeled test data. The MWE recognition part is described in Section 3.3.1 and the CCGbank conversion is described in Section 3.3.2.

3.3.1 Recognising MWEs

For MWE recognition, we use a tool developed by Finlayson & Kulkarni (2011). It can be used to build an index of MWEs with information about their probability. It can also be used with a default index which contains all the MWEs and inflections extracted from Wordnet 3.0 and Semcor 1.6 and statistics for each MWE. There are three different tools of interest to us. Simple detectors detect MWEs in text. There is a detector to find proper nouns, one to find all types of MWEs that are in the index, one that finds MWEs that contain only stop words, etc. These simple detectors can also be combined to form a complex detector. There are filters which filter the results of detectors. One for example only accepts MWEs that are continuous, one throws out MWEs which have a score under a certain threshold, one only keeps MWEs under a certain length. The last tool we need is called a RESOLVER and it resolves conflicts when lexical items are assigned to more than one MWE. Conflicts can be resolved in different ways: one resolver picks the leftmost MWE. For example, let us say we have an input sentence that includes *new york life insurance*. If the MWE index contains *new york life* and *life insurance*, the resolver will return *new york life* but will not consider *insurance* as part of a MWE. Another resolver picks the longest matching MWE. For example, let us say we have an input sentence which contains *new york stock exchange*. If the MWE index contains *stock exchange, new york* but also *new york stock exchange*, the longest matching resolver will return *new york stock exchange* as a match.

Let us take the following sentence as an example of input for a resolver:

(1)   Mr. Spoon said the plan is not an attempt to shore up a decline in ad pages in the first nine months of 1989; Newsweek's ad pages totaled 1,620, a drop of 3.2 % from last year, according to Publishers Information Bureau.

The resolver returns a list of its MWEs from left to right. In the case of our example (1), the output for example looks like this:

(2)   mr._spoon, shore_up, according_to, publishers_information_bureau

The presented protocol can work with any type of MWE recogniser, provided that it is filtered to output only continuous MWEs and resolved so that any word can only appear in one MWE. This library therefore serves our purposes perfectly since it leaves quite a lot of room for experiments. Experiments are described in Section 4.

3.3.2 Transforming the treebank

The algorithm collapses the MWE units to one node when they form a constituent in the tree. The label of the node is the label of that constituent. For example, given the MWE *publishers_information_bureau* and the subtree in Figure 7, the algorithm returns the subtree in Figure 8.

```
                      N
              _____/_____
          N/N                    N
           |              _____/_____
       Publishers      N/N              N                    N
                        |                |                    |
                   Information      Bureau       publishers_information_bureau
```

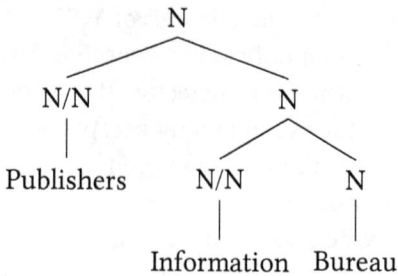

Figure 7: Original subtree   Figure 8: Transformed subtree

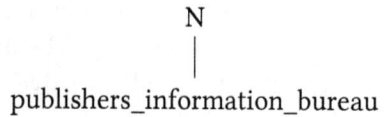

The algorithm discards MWEs if they do not form a constituent in the tree. An example of tree in which MWE units (e.g., *according to*) are not siblings in the tree is given in Figure 9. The ideal way in which it should be transformed is given in Figure 10 but attempting to find an algorithm which would work for all non-sibling cases is beyond the scope of this work. We tried our algorithm with a good recogniser, collected statistics and found that 79.5% of the cases (42,309/53,208) were siblings in the tree which we considered a good basis for experimentation. Note, however, that modifying those non-sibling MWEs would make bigger changes to the tree as it would not only remove the lexical categories of MWE units but it would additionally remove the parent category of the MWE units involved and create a new category for the whole MWE. As we will see in Section 4, dealing only with sibling MWEs leads to slight improvements, we hypothesize that an improved algorithm that can deal with non-sibling MWEs can lead to more substantial improvements.

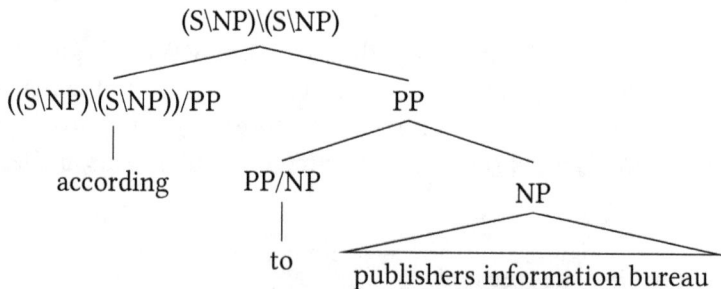

```
                         (S\NP)\(S\NP)
                 _____/_____
        ((S\NP)\(S\NP))/PP              PP
               |                 _____/_____
          according          PP/NP             NP
                               |          _____/\_____
                              to      publishers information bureau
```

Figure 9: Tree with MWE units that are not siblings

Because, as explained in Section 3.5, we evaluate our method on dependency trees (which can be read off CCG trees), we also need to modify the gold standard dependency trees. Transforming dependency trees involves merging nodes

$$(S\backslash NP)\backslash(S\backslash NP)$$

(S\NP)\(S\NP)/NP   NP

according_to   publishers information bureau

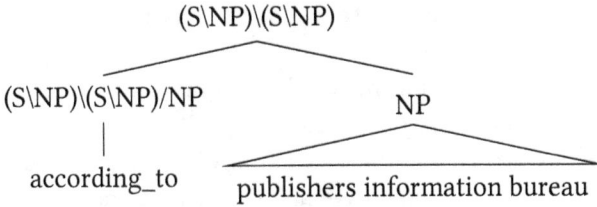

Figure 10: Ideal MWE non-sibling transformation

in the graph and changing edges according to the new nodes. When the nodes are merged, edges from the original dependency graph fall into three different categories. Let us take the dependency graph in Figure 11 as an example in which *Mr. Vinken* is a MWE. There are edges between two units of a MWE such as the one between *Mr.* and *Vinken*. We call these INTERNAL EDGES for convenience. Our algorithm removes them as shown in Figure 12. There are edges between a MWE unit and another word in the sentence such as the edge between *Vinken* and *is*. We call this type of edge a MEDIATING EDGE. In the transformed graph, the whole MWE becomes the node of that incoming or outgoing edge. The edge between *is* and *chairman* does not connect any MWE and does not need changing. We call it EXTERNAL EDGE.

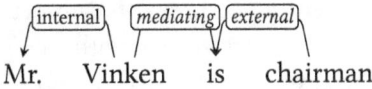

| internal | mediating | external |
| Mr. | Vinken | is | chairman |

| mediating | external |
| Mr._Vinken | is | chairman |

Figure 11: Dependency graph   Figure 12: Transformed dependency graph

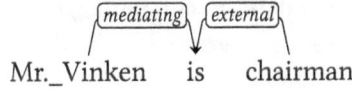

The downside of this algorithm is that it can create cyclic dependencies between lexical items, i.e. two nodes are connected by two edges going in the opposite direction. We tested the algorithm on the CCGbank and found that in practice this is not a major issue: only 7 cyclic dependencies were created in the ~48,000 sentences.

3.4 Training and parsing

We follow the tradition and use sections 01–22 of CCGbank for training, section 00 for development and section 23 for testing.

Using the same parameters as in Deoskar et al. (2014) to train and parse the test data, we obtain around 87% of correct lexical categories, which is similar to the result they report. This model serves as our baseline and we henceforth call it *model$_A$*.

For each experiment, we run the MWE recogniser on an unlabeled version of the CCGbank[1]. We then apply our cascaded algorithms described in the previous section to every sentence from the CCGbank. We train the model and parse the test file. We call the transformed treebank CCGbank$_B$ and the model trained on it *model$_B$*.

3.5 Evaluation

The traditional parsing accuracy metric PARSEVAL has been argued (for example by Clark & Hockenmaier (2002)) to be too harsh on CCG derivation trees because they are always binary, as opposed to PTB-style trees which can have flat constructions with more than one branching node. This binary nature of CCG trees make them prone to having more errors. Consequently evaluation of dependencies has generally been preferred for CCG parsing. As further argued by Clark & Hockenmaier (2002), it also makes sense to use dependencies to evaluate CCG parsing since one of the advantages of CCG over other formalisms is precisely its treatment of long-range dependencies.

In order to evaluate our models, we can thus extract dependencies from the parsed files and compare them with the gold standard. Because we changed the gold standard as compared to *model$_A$* (as defined in the previous subsection), however, the results obtained from comparing our parsed files with our gold standard are not directly comparable with the results obtained when applying the same evaluation scheme to *model$_A$*. Therefore, we cannot directly compare *model$_A$* with our *model$_B$*s (as defined in the previous subsection) which is essential in answering our research questions. Instead, we have to transform the data of one of the models so as to compare each of the models with the same gold standard. Because we assume that we have created a sensible gold standard with our transformation algorithm, we mainly use gold standard$_B$ for evaluation.

As mentioned in Section 3.1, transforming training and test data can lead to two different effects which can lead to an improved parsing accuracy, i.e. training (the parser learns useful information during training) and parsing effects (the trained parser is helped in its decisions by MWE information) which we would like to differentiate. This can be achieved by conducting different experiments with our existing models. We can assess training effect by testing whether or not *model$_B$* can outperform *model$_A$* when evaluated on the same gold standard.

---

[1]We created an unlabeled version of CCGbank from the tree leaves to make sure the data is compatible with the trees we work with when transforming trees.

We can assess parsing effect by testing whether or not $model_A$ can outperform itself when given transformed test data. We discuss these evaluation schemes in Section 3.5.1.

If there is training and/or parsing effect, we can assume that automatic recognition of MWEs can be used to improve syntactic parsing. We can verify this by testing whether or not we can use information from $model_B$ to outperform $model_A$ on gold standard$_A$. We use a second evaluation scheme where we combine information from output from $model_A$ and output from $model_B$ (henceforth called MODEL COMBINATION) to test this which we discuss in Section 3.5.2.

As mentioned in Section 2.4, we not only want to know whether or not information about MWEs can help CCG parsing but we are also interested in finding out whether or not different types of MWEs impact parsing accuracy in different ways. As will be explained in Section 4, we created different versions of CCGbank$_B$ and different versions of $model_B$ with these. Because we created different gold standard for each of these models, they cannot directly be compared. Instead, comparing how different $model_B$s can improve $model_A$ is possible by comparing their combination with it against gold standard$_A$. Again then we can use model combination and combine information from output from $model_A$ with information from output from $model_B$. We compare this combined model output against gold standard$_A$ and compare the results when combining $model_A$ with different versions of $model_B$. We discuss how this can be achieved in Section 3.5.3.

3.5.1 Assessing training and parsing effects

Modifying the output from $model_A$ so that it is comparable with the gold standard from $model_B$ is straightforward: we just need to apply the transformation algorithms to the output from $model_A$ with the MWEs found in the test data. We can also test $model_A$ on data transformed before parsing.

3.5.1.1 Parsing effect

Testing whether there is a parsing effect can be done by testing whether or not $model_A$ can perform better on test data transformed before parsing than on test data transformed after parsing. We conduct this evaluation. There is a caveat in this evaluation, however: we are using information from the gold standard in the test data, i.e. we know which MWEs are siblings in the test data. This introduces an artefact which makes the results somewhat difficult to interpret: the transforming before parsing method has sibling information which the transforming after parsing method does not. There can be parsing and sibling effects and the two cannot be decoupled. A way to circumvent this problem is to transform MWEs regardless of their sibling status (i.e. treat all detected MWEs as if they were siblings) and compare the model when we transform before parsing with the model when we transform after parsing. Transforming all MWEs in unlabeled test data is straightforward. As mentioned in Section 3.3.2, we do not have an algorithm to transform MWEs that are not siblings in trees so we cannot transform the output parse trees. However, since we are working only with dependencies for evaluation, it is possible to transform all MWEs in all the dependencies of the sentence. The problem with this evaluation is that the output cannot perform well on gold standard$_B$ because it is not tokenized in the same way and we treat dependencies wrongly tokenized as errors. However, both transforming before and transforming after parsing suffer from the same problem and the comparison between the two is fair.

3.5.1.2 Training effect

Testing whether there is a training effect consists in comparing the results of *model$_A$* on transformed data with the results of *model$_B$* on transformed data. In this evaluation, the caveat that we are using information from the gold standard in the test data can also be considered problematic because *model$_B$* is trained on data with information about siblings. This information is unseen by *model$_A$*. We therefore test both models on data where only siblings are transformed (called GOLD TEST for convenience) and on data where all MWEs are transformed (called FULLY TRANSFORMED TEST for convenience). Again, the problem with this evaluation is that the output cannot perform well on gold standard$_B$ because it is not tokenized in the same way. Again, however, both models suffer from the same problem and the comparison between the two is fair.

3.5.2 Verifying whether or not automatic recognition of MWEs can improve CCG parsing on the original gold standard

Results which will be discussed in Section 4 seem to indicate that there is both a training and a parsing effect and that *model$_B$* performs better than *model$_A$* on some dependencies. Our findings support the claim that automatic recognition of MWEs can improve CCG parsing. These results, however, led us to want to verify whether or not *model$_B$* can improve the score on the standard evaluation benchmark, i.e. on gold standard A. This involves "detransforming" the output from *model$_B$* and splitting MWEs back into their units. However, by transforming the data, we have lost information about some dependencies in the sentence.

We have no *internal edges* (edges between MWE units of the same MWE) and when there is a *mediating edge* (edges between MWE units of any MWE and other words in the sentence) we do not know which MWE unit of the MWE should the incoming or outgoing node of that edge. In Figure 12 reproduced in Figure 13 for convenience, we do not know whether the label between *is* and *mr._- vinken* should come from *mr* or *vinken*. For this reason, we propose to combine information obtained from parsing the test data with our transformed model *model$_B$* with information obtained from parsing the test data with the original model *model$_A$*. We therefore take some dependencies from output$_A$ and some from output$_B$.

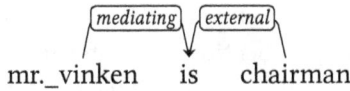

$$\text{mediating} \quad \text{external}$$

mr._vinken   is   chairman

Figure 13: Transformed dependency graph

External edges can be taken from output$_B$. *Internal edges* do not exist in output$_B$. Hence we propose to take them from output$_A$. For *mediating edges*, there are different possibilities. We can take them from output$_A$ and therefore only test whether or not *model$_B$* performs better than *model$_A$* on *external edges*. We call this combination method *medFromA*. If we want to test *model$_B$* on *mediating edges*, we can take *mediating edges* from output$_B$. For this to work, the model combining algorithm needs to choose one node as the incoming or outgoing node of that edge: in our example, it should either be *Mr.* or *Vinken*. We use two additional combination methods. We use one in which the rightmost node is chosen as incoming or outgoing node for *mediating edges* from output$_B$ which we call the *rightmostMed* scheme. We also use one in which the leftmost node is chosen which we call the *leftmostMed* scheme. In order for the model combining algorithm to work, we need to recover information about MWEs and their units and hence to know for each dependency if we are dealing with an *internal, external* or *mediating edge*. This can easily be done because MWE and their units are annotated in the unlabeled data.[2]

When these models are combined in these three different ways, we have a new combined model that we can compare with *model$_A$* on gold standard$_A$. In this case, using "gold test" data is again problematic. As a matter of fact, if we use output$_B$ as obtained after parsing "gold test" data, we are using information obtained during the conversion of the gold standard and we are using a parsing

---

[2] Our MWE recogniser joins MWE units of a MWE by a "+" symbol.

pipeline which is not fully automatic. In order to make sure that we can outperform *model$_A$* in a fully automatic way, we can use parses of *model$_B$* tested on the "fully transformed test" data set as described in Section 3.5.1, and combine them in the same three ways as described above.

3.5.3 Testing whether or not different MWE types impact the results differently

As mentioned before, we use different MWE recognisers to create different versions of CCGbank$_B$ and hence different versions of *model$_B$*. Because we created a different gold standard for each, results from different models are not directly comparable. We can, however, convert output parses using the model combination algorithm described in Section 3.5.1 and test each model against gold standard$_A$. In this way, different versions of *model$_B$* can be compared.

3.6 Summary of the experimental setup

Figures 14 and 15 summarize our experimental setup.

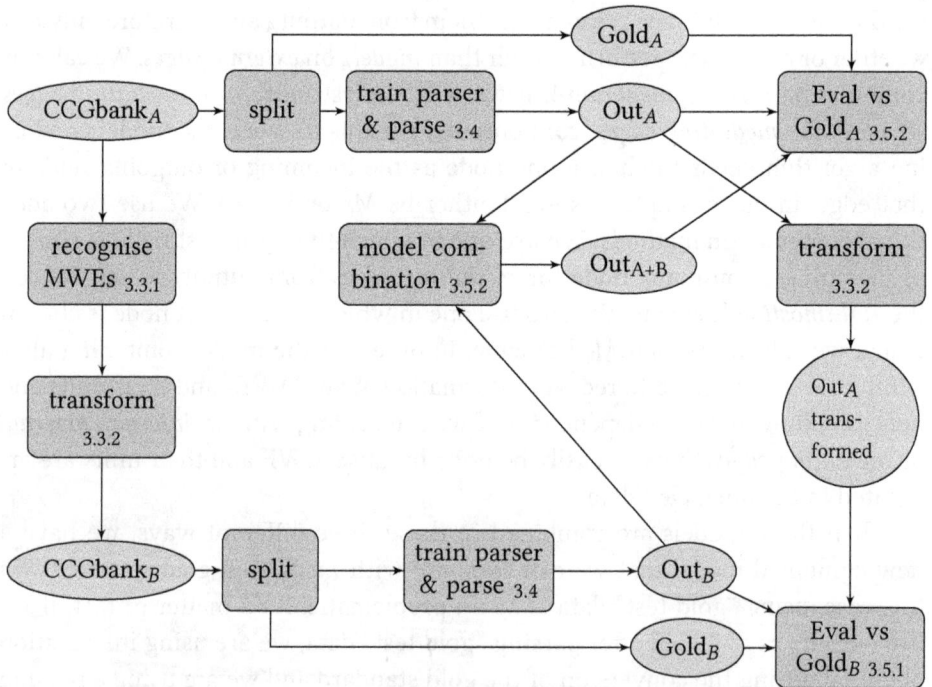

Figure 14: Pipeline of an experiment on one version of one application of MWE recognition to the parsing pipeline with all the evaluation schemes that can be applied to it. The transforming before parsing of *model$_A$* (see Section 3.5.1) is omitted for clarity and given in Figure 15.

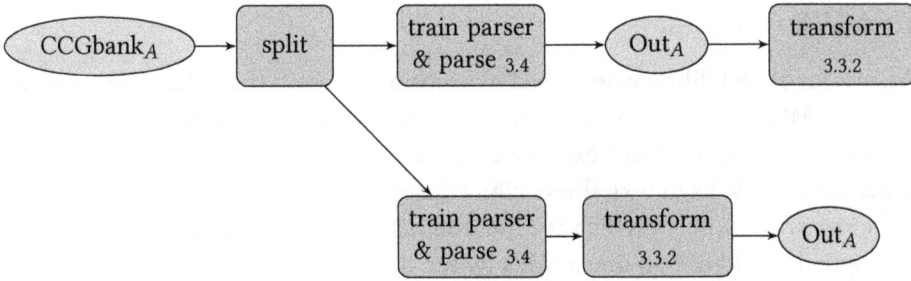

Figure 15: Pipeline of the "transforming before parsing" against the "transforming after parsing experiment."

In Section 2, we motivated our study and identified two research questions: whether or not information about MWEs can improve CCG parsing and whether or not different types of MWEs can influence parsing accuracy in different ways. In this Section, we proposed a methodology for testing this. We refined the first research questions: what we want to find out is whether or not automatic recognition of MWEs can improve CCG parsing. Additionally, we separated it into two further research questions: whether we can observe a parsing effect (the parser is helped in its decisions by transformed data) and/or whether we can observe a training effect (the parser learns something useful). We proposed to use different MWE recognisers to answer the second question. When defining an algorithm for transforming the treebank, however, we could not find a straightforward algorithm to transform MWEs that are not siblings in the tree and decided to settle for an algorithm that only transforms siblings. This led to further complications in the evaluation schemes because it makes it harder to give a fair evaluation of our models. We found ways to circumvent the problems: we proposed different evaluation schemes together with cross-validations. We now turn to the results of our experiments.

4 Results

In this section, we look at each of the research questions in turn. To assess statistical significance of our best results, we use a one-tailed randomized shuffling test with 10,000 iterations. We use the software created by Padó (2006) (slightly modified in order to make it a one-tailed test instead of a two-tailed one) for our tests.

4.1 MWE recognition

We use the jMWE library described in Section 3.3.1 with the default index which contains MWEs from Wordnet 3.0 and Semcor 1.6. We use the library's three different tools which were explained in that section. Those tools are detectors which detect MWEs in text, filters which filter through the results of one or more detectors and resolvers which resolve conflicts between MWEs when one word is assigned to more than one MWEs by the detector.

We use the following tools:

- Detectors:

    - Proper Nouns: detects proper nouns, like *wall street*.

    - Stop words: detects MWEs that only contain stop words, like *instead of*.

    - Exhaustive: finds all MWEs that are in the index.

- Filters:

    - MoreFreqAsMWE: only keeps MWEs if its units appear more often together than apart in the corpora in which they were collected.

    - ConstrainLength: only keeps MWEs that have 2 units.

- Resolvers:

    - Longest: always picks the longest matching MWEs.

    - Leftmost: picks the MWE that starts earliest in the sentence.

We build 5 different MWE recognisers with different combinations of these tools. This means that the study is by no means exhaustive. Information about our recognisers and statistics about the MWEs they detect are summarized in Table 1. The numbers in column "ID" denote the recognisers used in the remainder of this section. Similarly, each $model_B$ is denoted by the recogniser which was used to train it as indicated by this number.

4.2 Can we improve CCG parsing accuracy with automatic MWE recognition?

As explained in Section 3.5, we use different evaluation schemes to answer this question. First we evaluate $model_B$ and $model_A$ against gold standard$_B$ and determine whether there is training and/or parsing effects. Then we verify whether

Table 1: Description (detector, filter and resolver) of MWE recognisers used and statistics of MWEs collected with them in the treebank

ID	detector	filter	resolver	MWE #	Sibling #	Sibling %
1	Exhaustive	MoreFreqAsMWE	Longest	53,208	42,309	79.51
2	Exhaustive	MoreFreqAsMWE	Leftmost	51,543	21,532	41.85
3	Proper Nouns	no filter	Longest	32,583	28,068	86.14
4	Exhaustive	ConstrainLength	Leftmost	49,587	19,984	40.30
5	Stop words	no filter	Longest	13,623	286	2.09

we can use *model_B* to improve over *model_A* on gold standard_A by using model combination with *model_A* and *model_B*. We deal with each of these in turn. We test all evaluation schemes on all of our versions of *model_B*. Results fluctuate according to the recognisers as discussed in Section 4.3. We give general remarks about results and report our best results in this Section.

4.2.1 Can representing MWEs as one token introduce a training effect?

In order to find out whether or not training data on an MWE-informed corpus can lead to an improved accuracy, i.e. leads to training effect, we compare the output of *model_B* against the output of *model_A* tested on the "gold test" data. 3 out of our 5 *model_B*s outperform *model_A* on unlabeled_B, although generally by a slight margin. The best results are obtained by model_{B3} and are given in Table 2. Model_B significantly outperforms *model_A* by 0.24% (p = 0.006) which supports the hypothesis that there is indeed a training effect.

Table 2: Precision (P), recall (R), and F_1-measure of unlabelled dependencies against gold standard B with recogniser 3

model	test data	P	R	F_1
A	gold test	84.53	84.76	84.64
B3	gold test	84.48	85.28	84.88

Because using gold test data gives *model_B* an unfair advantage, we also test these models on the "fully transformed test" data. In this case 3 of our 5 *model_B*s outperform *model_A* again although by an even slighter margin. The biggest difference in results is obtained with model_{B1} and results are given in Table 3. Although the margin is smaller, *model_B* still significantly outperforms *model_A* by 0.15% (p = 0.047) which shows that there is a training effect.

Table 3: Precision (P), recall (R), and F_1-measure of unlabelled dependencies against gold standard B with recogniser 1

model	test data	P	R	F_1
A	fully transformed test	73.15	72.38	72.77
B1	fully transformed test	73.08	72.74	72.92

4.2.2 Can representing MWEs as one token introduce a parsing effect?

In order to test whether there can be a parsing effect, we compare the output of $model_A$ when data are transformed before parsing with $model_A$ when data are transformed after parsing. In this case $model_B$ always outperforms $model_A$. Our best results are shown in Table 4 in which $model_B$ highly significantly outperforms $model_A$ ($p < 0.0001$).

Table 4: Precision (P), recall (R), and F_1-measure of unlabelled dependencies against gold standard B with recogniser 1 when transforming before parsing uses gold sibling information and only siblings are transformed after parsing

model	transformed	P	R	F_1
A	before parsing	83.88	84.24	84.06
A	after parsing	78.92	79.41	79.17

The problem with these results is that "transforming before parsing" method has gold standard information about siblings which the "transforming after parsing" method does not. In order to cross-validate our result, we transform all MWEs both before and after parsing and compare the results. In this case, $model_A$ when data are transformed before parsing outperforms $model_A$ when data are transformed after parsing only in one of the 5 cases which undermines a little the previous argument about the parsing effects showing that there can also be undesirable effects to transforming test data. It could, however, be partly due to the fact that we transformed non-siblings, which may have triggered errors during parsing. In any case, our best results still show a significant improvement with the "transforming before parsing" method over the "transforming after parsing" method. These results are obtained when using recogniser$_3$ and are given in Table 5. Model$_A$ transformed before parsing significantly outperforms $model_A$

transformed after parsing by 0.20% ($p = 0.008$). This indicates that there can be a parsing effect.

Table 5: Precision (P), recall (R), and F_1-measure of unlabelled dependencies against gold standard B with recogniser 3 when all MWEs are considered siblings

model	transformed	P	R	F_1
A	before parsing	79.83	79.54	79.69
A	after parsing	79.38	79.60	79.49

4.2.3 Can we improve the parsing model on the original gold standard?

We now verify if we can also outperform the baseline on the untransformed gold standard. This means testing whether or not $model_B$ improves over $model_A$ on *external edges* and/or on *mediating edges*. We test this by combining dependency edges obtained from $model_A$ and $model_B$. We combine these edges with 3 different methods. *Internal* edges are always taken from $model_A$ and *external edges* are always taken from $model_B$. *Mediating edges* are taken from A in the *medFromA* evaluation and from B in the 2 other cases. In the *rightmostMed* evaluation, the rightmost MWE unit is always chosen as incoming or outgoing node and in the *leftmostMed* evaluation, it is the leftmost MWE unit that is always taken as incoming or outgoing node. Our best results are given in Table 6 in which $model_B$ only outperforms $model_A$ in the *medFromA* case by 0.13% which is not significant ($p > 0.05$). This seems to show that $model_B$ may perform better than $model_A$ on *external edges* but as far as *mediating edges* are concerned, the picture is unclear. If we take the *mediating edge* from B, it seems clearly better to choose the rightmost MWE unit as incoming or outgoing node (which is not surprising since compound nouns are almost always right-headed) but doing so does not seem to be a big help in parsing accuracy. $Model_B$ might perform better than $model_A$ on *mediating edges* if we had a better mechanism to recover the head word but with our simple method we cannot say whether or not this is the case.

In this result, $model_B$ is again helped in the parsing decisions by being told which MWEs are siblings. In order to test whether we can improve on $model_A$ in a fully automatic manner, we test $model_B$ on the "fully transformed test" data which is a version of the test data obtained automatically, i.e. by transforming all MWEs in the text instead of only the siblings. All MWEs are then parsed as a unit. When we combine the models, we have more MWEs than we should

Table 6: Precision (P), recall (R), and F_1-measure of unlabelled dependencies against gold standard A using recogniser 3

model	combination type	P	R	F_1
A		**85.27**	85.02	85.15
A+B3	medFromA	84.89	**85.68**	**85.28**
A+B3	rightmostMed	84.84	85.46	85.15
A+B3	leftmostMed	81.43	82.02	81.72

have and consequently, more edges are considered to be *mediating* and *internal* edges and less edges are considered to be *external* edges. Hence, we are led to choose edges from *model$_A$* where *model$_A$* is not expected to perform better than *model$_B$*. When combining both models with the *medFromA* method, however, we still outperform *model$_A$* by 0.04% when using recogniser$_3$ showing that *model$_B$* may have learnt something useful although there is no significant evidence for it at this point.

4.3 Does using different MWE recognisers impact parsing accuracy differently?

As explained in Section 3.5.3, the last experiment we conduct is to test our model using different recognisers, combine the output using the model combination algorithm explained in Section 3.5.1 and compare it to gold standard$_A$. This provides a way to compare different versions of our *model$_B$*.

As can be seen in Table 7, different MWE recognition methods seem to make a difference in results. There is a significant difference between our best model (based on recogniser$_3$) and our worst model (based on recogniser$_2$) of 0.26 ($p = 0.01$). Some recognisers lead to decreases in parsing accuracy while others lead to increases. It appears from the table that using a leftmost resolver (a resolver that always chooses the leftmost MWE when there is a conflict) has a bad impact on parsing accuracy. Looking at the different models, it is interesting to note that there is a much lower percentage of MWEs that are siblings in the tree and hence a much lower amount of changes made in the treebank. It is interesting to note that the best model is based on a detector that only detects proper nouns. This seems to show that they are the best candidates for being treated as words-with-spaces. This is not surprising because they are not flexible and never get inflected. For other types of MWE, an analysis as word-with-spaces might not be the most appropriate, as argued by many researchers (Sag et al. 2002) to give just one example, see Section 2).

Table 7: F_1-measure of unlabelled dependencies against gold standard A using different recognisers from the $model_A$ combining method

model	detector type	resolver type	F_1
A			85.15
B1	exhaustive	longest	85.18
B2	exhaustive	leftmost	85.02
B3	Proper Nouns	longest	**85.28**
B4	Length 2	leftmost	85.07
B5	Stop words	longest	85.19

4.4 Summary of our findings

We summarise our findings in Table 8.

Table 8: Summary of our findings

question	answer	tables concerned
Can there be a parsing effect?	yes	Table 2 and 3
Can there be a training effect?	yes	Table 4 and 5
Can we improve parsing on the untransformed gold standard?	not significantly	Table 6
Do different types of MWEs impact the results differently?	yes	Table 7

Table 2 and 3 are respectively upper and lower bounds on the training effect that can be obtained with our method with these recognisers. Similarly, Table 4 and 5 are respectively upper and lower bounds on the parsing effect that can be obtained. Given that the lower bounds are still significantly above the baselines in both cases, we can conclude that there can be both a training and a parsing effect, and that we can improve CCG parsing with information about MWEs.

5 Conclusion

5.1 Contributions

Our main contributions in this work are:

- Improvements on CCG parsing with automatic MWE recognition
- Significant results despite limited settings
- An algorithm to automatically transform MWEs in a treebank
- Techniques for distinguishing training from parsing effects
- Empirical support that there is both training and parsing effects
- Interesting differences in results when using different recognisers

The task we have been trying to improve in this work is the task of syntactic parsing. Adding MWE information to CCG parsing was singled out as a useful direction because it has proven useful in the past with other parsing frameworks and because it seemed an interesting approach to attempt within the framework of a lexicalized grammar. We built on previous work which had shown the benefits of giving information about MWEs to a syntactic parser. It had been shown to work for deterministic dependency parsing, shallow parsing and deterministic constituency parsing but not for statistical constituency parsing. We implemented an existing pipeline which consists in transforming the representation of MWEs in training and test data by collapsing its units to one token and adapted it to our purposes. We gave further evidence supporting these studies and showed that statistical constituency parsing with a lexicalized grammar too can benefit from MWE information. Our study provided further empirical support to the hypothesis that MWE information can improve syntactic parsing by showing that we can improve CCG parsing with information about MWEs.

MWE identification was also identified as a notoriously difficult task although important for many applications because MWEs violate usual compositional rules and can be the source of many errors if not handled properly. We have shown that using an existing automatic recogniser as a source of MWE information was useful which had so far been left a bit unclear in the literature.

Our results have shown small but significant improvements over previous models which is very encouraging given the restricted settings we have worked with. We have as a matter of fact hypothesized that the results were very much limited by the methodology used and have suggested ways of improving the current approach. Our biggest contributions, however, are not in the results we obtained but in the techniques we proposed. The study has proposed novel techniques to improve on previous pipelines. We have proposed an algorithm to automatically transform MWEs in a treebank which can be used with other formalisms although this algorithm is limited to transforming MWEs which form a constituent in the tree. More importantly, we have proposed ways of experimenting with our models in a way that we can distinguish parsing (the parser is helped in its decisions by transformed data) from training effects (the parser learns something useful) in the evaluation and have shown evidence for both. In addition, we have proposed to experiment with different MWE recognisers and study the impact of different MWE recognition methods on parsing accuracy. This is especially interesting in that it is never quite clear in the literature what counts as an MWE. Experimenting with recognisers that detect different types of MWEs can help find out what types of MWEs this method is most suitable for. Our results in this work have shown that collapsing MWE units to one token is most useful for MWEs that are made of proper nouns. It makes intuitive sense that treating them as words with spaces is appropriate since they are not flexible and do not get inflected.

5.2 Future work

We propose the following for future work:

- Extending the transformation algorithm to the non-sibling case
- Testing more MWE recognition methods
- Conducting error analysis

A lot more interesting research can still be done on the interaction between MWE identification and syntactic parsing. Theoretical research has emphasized the need to give different syntactic representations for different types of MWEs but a lot of empirical work is still needed if we want to automatically assign sensible syntactic representations to MWEs. Extending our transformation algorithm to the non-sibling case would allow conducting more extensive experiments. We also believe that testing more recognition methods could lead to interesting discussions where we could find out more about what type of MWE is dealt best with by what method. This could also help discover interesting properties of MWEs. Conducting error analysis could also lead to further insight into why the method is sometimes successful, sometimes less successful.

In the meantime, we believe to have offered new perspectives in the study of the integration between syntactic parsing and MWE identification especially in relation to CCG parsing. We have given encouraging results on a difficult task and suggested ways of improving them. We have given further evidence that the integration of MWE identification with syntactic parsing is a promising and exciting research direction.

References

Birch, Alexandra, Miles Osborne & Philipp Koehn. 2007. CCG supertags in factored statistical machine translation. In *Proceedings of the second workshop on Statistical Machine Translation*, 9–16.

Christodoulopoulos, Christos. 2008. *Creating a natural logic inference system with Combinatory Categorial Grammar*. University of Edinburgh MA thesis.

Clark, Stephen & James Curran. 2007. Wide-coverage efficient statistical parsing with CCG and log-linear models. *Computational Linguistics* 4(33). 493–552.

Clark, Stephen & Julia Hockenmaier. 2002. Evaluating a wide-coverage CCG parser. In *Proceedings of the LREC 2002 beyond PARSEVAL workshop*, 60–66.

Constable, James & James Curran. 2009. Integrating verb-particle constructions into CCG parsing. In *Proceedings of the Australasian Language Technology Association workshop 2009*, 114–118. Sydney, Australia. http://aclweb.org/anthology/U09-1017.

Constant, Mathieu & Joakim Nivre. 2016. A transition-based system for joint lexical and syntactic analysis. In *Proceedings of the 54th annual meeting of the Association for Computational Linguistics*, vol. 1: *Long papers*, 161–171. Berlin, Germany: Association for Computational Linguistics. http://www.aclweb.org/anthology/P16-1016.

Constant, Mathieu, Anthony Sigogne & Patrick Watrin. 2012. Discriminative strategies to integrate multiword expression recognition and parsing. In *Proceedings of the 50th annual meeting of the Association for Computational Linguistics: Long papers*, vol. 1 (ACL '12), 204–212. Jeju Island, Korea: Association for Computational Linguistics. http://dl.acm.org/citation.cfm?id=2390524.2390554.

Copestake, Ann, Fabre Lambeau, Aline Villavicencio, Francis Bond, Timothy Baldwin, Ivan Sag & Dan Flickinger. 2002. Multiword expressions: Linguistic precision and reusability. In *Proceedings of the third international conference on Language Resources and Evaluation (LREC 2002)*, 1941–1947. Las Palmas, Canary Islands, Spain.

Curran, James, Stephen Clark & Johan Bos. 2007. Linguistically motivated large-scale NLP with C&C and Boxer. In *Proceedings of the 45th annual meeting of the Association for Computational Linguistics, companion volume, proceedings of the demo and poster sessions*, 33–36. Prague, Czech Republic: Association for Computational Linguistics.

Deoskar, Tejaswini, Christos Christodoulopoulos, Alexandra Birch & Mark Steedman. 2014. Generalizing a strongly lexicalized parser using unlabeled data. In Gosse Bouma & Yannick Parmentier (eds.), *Proceedings of the 14th conference of the European chapter of the Association for Computational Linguistics (EACL'2014)*, 126–134. Gothenburg.

Eryiğit, Gülşen, Tugay İlbay & Ozan Arkan Can. 2011. Multiword expressions in statistical dependency parsing. In *Proceedings of the second workshop on Statistical Parsing of Morphologically Rich Languages*, 45–55. Dublin, Ireland.

Finlayson, Mark Alan & Nidhi Kulkarni. 2011. Detecting multi-word expressions improves word sense disambiguation. In *Proceedings of the workshop on Multiword Expressions: From parsing and generation to the real world* (MWE '11), 20–24. Stroudsburg, PA, USA: Association for Computational Linguistics.

Green, Spence, Marie-Catherine de Marneffe & Christopher D. Manning. 2013. Parsing models for identifying multiword expressions. *Computational Linguistics* 39(1). 195–227.

Hockenmaier, Julia. 2003. *Data and models for statistical parsing with Combinatory Categorial Grammar*. University of Edinburgh dissertation.

Hockenmaier, Julia & Mark Steedman. 2002. Generative models for statistical parsing with Combinatory Categorial Grammar. In *Proceedings of the 40th annual meeting on Association for Computational Linguistics* (ACL '02), 335–342. Stroudsburg, PA, USA: Association for Computational Linguistics.

Hockenmaier, Julia & Mark Steedman. 2007. CCGbank: A corpus of CCG derivations and dependency structures extracted from the Penn Treebank. *Computational Linguistics* 33(3). 355–396.

Hoffmann, Thomas & Graeme Trousdale. 2013. Construction Grammar: Introduction. In Thomas Hoffmann & Graeme Trousdale (eds.), *The Oxford handbook of Construction Grammar* (Oxford Handbooks in Linguistics), 1–14. Oxford University Press.

Kim, Su Nam. 2008. *Statistical modeling of multiword expressions*. University of Melbourne dissertation.

Korkontzelos, Ioannis & Suresh Manandhar. 2010. Can recognising multiword expressions improve shallow parsing? In *Proc. of the 11th annual conference of the North American chapter of the Association for Computational Linguistics:*

Human Language Technologies NAACL/HLT 2010, 636–644. Los Angeles, California.

Krishnamurthy, Jayant & Tom M Mitchell. 2012. Weakly supervised training of semantic parsers. In *Proceedings of the 2012 joint conference on Empirical Methods in Natural Language Processing and Computational Natural Language Learning (EMNLP/CoNLL)*, 754–765.

Lewis, Mike & Mark Steedman. 2013. Combining distributional and logical semantics. *Transactions of the Association for Computational Linguistics* 1. 179–192.

Martens, Scott & Vincent Vandeghinste. 2010. An efficient, generic approach to extracting multi-word expressions from dependency trees. In *Proceedings of the workshop on Multiword Expressions: From theory to applications (MWE 2010)*, 84–87. Beijing, China: Association for Computational Linguistics.

Nivre, Joakim & Jens Nilsson. 2004. Multiword units in syntactic parsing. In *Workshop on Methodologies and Evaluation of Multiword Units in Real-World Applications*, 39–46.

Nunberg, Geoffrey, Ivan Sag & Thomas Wasow. 1994. Idioms. *Language* 70(3). 491–538.

Padó, Sebastian. 2006. *User's guide to* sigf: *Significance testing by approximate randomisation.*

Sag, Ivan, Timothy Baldwin, Francis Bond, Ann Copestake & Dan Flickinger. 2002. Multiword expressions: A pain in the neck for NLP. In *Proceedings of the 3rd international conference on Computational Linguistics and Intelligent Text Processing* (Lecture Notes in Computer Science 2276), 1–15. Springer.

Schneider, Nathan, Spencer Onuffer, Nora Kazour, Emily Danchik, Michael T. Mordowanec, Henrietta Conrad & Noah A. Smith. 2014. Comprehensive annotation of multiword expressions in a social web corpus. In *Proceedings of the ninth international conference on Language Resources and Evaluation (LREC 2014)*, 456–461. Reykyavik.

Seretan, Violeta. 2013. On collocations and their interaction with parsing and translation. *Informatics* 1(1). 11–31.

Steedman, Mark. 2000. *The syntactic process.* Cambridge, MA, USA: MIT Press.

Weller, Marion & Ulrich Heid. 2010. Extraction of German multiword expressions from parsed corpora using context features. In Nicoletta Calzolari, Khalid Choukri, Bente Maegaard, Joseph Mariani, Jan Odijk, Stelios Piperidis, Mike Rosner & Daniel Tapias (eds.), *Proceedings of LREC 2010*, 3195–3201. Valletta: European Language Resources Association.

White, Michael. 2006. Efficient realization of coordinate structures in Combinatory Categorial Grammar. *Research on Language and Computation* 4(1). 39–75.

Zhang, Yi & Valia Kordoni. 2008. Robust parsing with a large HPSG grammar. In *Proceedings of the sixth international Language Resources and Evaluation conference (LREC'08)*, 1888–1893. Marrakech, Morroco.

Zhang, Yi, Valia Kordoni, Aline Villavicencio & Marco Idiart. 2006. Automated multiword expression prediction for grammar engineering. In *Proceedings of the workshop on Multiword Expressions: Identifying and Exploiting Underlying Properties* (MWE '06), 36–44. Stroudsburg, PA, USA: Association for Computational Linguistics.

Chapter 8

Multilingual parsing and MWE detection

Vasiliki Foufi
University of Geneva

Luka Nerima
University of Geneva

Eric Wehrli
University of Geneva

Identifying multiword expressions (MWEs) in a sentence in order to ensure their proper processing in subsequent applications, like machine translation, and performing the syntactic analysis of the sentence are interrelated processes. In our approach, priority is given to parsing alternatives involving collocations, and hence collocational information helps the parser through the maze of alternatives, with the aim to lead to substantial improvements in the performance of both tasks (collocation identification and parsing), and in that of a subsequent task (machine translation).

1 Introduction

Multiword expressions (MWEs) are lexical units consisting of more than one word (in the intuitive sense of *word*). There are several types of MWEs, including idioms (*a frog in the throat, break a leg*), fixed phrases (*per se, by and large, rock'n roll*), noun compounds (*traffic lights, cable car*), phrasal verbs (*look up, take off*), etc. While easily mastered by native speakers, their detection and/or their interpretation pose a major challenge for computational systems, due in part to their flexible and heterogeneous nature.

Vasiliki Foufi, Luka Nerima & Eric Wehrli. 2019. Multilingual parsing and MWE detection. In Yannick Parmentier & Jakub Waszczuk (eds.), *Representation and parsing of multiword expressions: Current trends*, 217–237. Berlin: Language Science Press.
DOI:10.5281/zenodo.2579047

In our research, MWEs are categorized in five subclasses: compounds, discontinuous words, named entities, collocations and idioms. While the first three are expressions of lexical categories (N, V, Adj, etc.) and can therefore be listed along with simple words, collocations and idioms are expressions of phrasal categories (NPs, VPs, etc.). The identification of compounds and named entities can be achieved during the lexical analysis, but the identification of discontinuous words (e.g., particle verbs or phrasal verbs), collocations and idioms requires grammatical data and should be viewed as part of the parsing process.

In this chapter, we will primarily focus on collocations, roughly defined as arbitrary and conventional associations of two words (not counting grammatical words) in a particular grammatical configuration (adjective-noun, noun-noun, verb-object, etc.). Throughout this chapter, we will refer to words belonging to such associations as CONTENT WORDS. We will argue that the identification of collocations and parsing are interrelated processes – in the sense that one cannot precede the other – and we will show how this has been achieved in the Fips multilingual parser (Wehrli 2007; Wehrli & Nerima 2015).

Section 2 will give a brief review of MWEs and previous work. Section 3 will describe how Fips handles MWEs and the way they are represented in our lexical database. Section 4 will be concerned with the treatment of collocation types which present a fair amount of syntactic flexibility (e.g. verb-object). For instance, verbal collocations may undergo syntactic processes such as passivization, relativization, interrogation and even pronominalization, which can leave the collocation constituents far away from each other and/or reverse their canonical order. Section 5 will present the collocation extraction process, which will be evaluated in Section 6. Finally we will conclude in Section 7.

2 Multiword expressions: A brief review of related work

The standard approach in dealing with MWEs in parsing is to apply a "words-with-spaces" preprocessing step, which marks the MWEs in the input sentence as units which will later be integrated as single blocks in the parse tree built during analysis (Brun 1998; Zhang & Kordoni 2006). This method is not really adequate for processing collocations. Unlike other expressions that are fixed or semi-fixed, several collocation types do not allow a "words-with-spaces" treatment because they have a high morphosyntactic flexibility. On the other hand, Alegria et al. (2004) and Villavicencio et al. (2007) adopted a compositional approach to the encoding of MWEs, able to capture more morphosyntactically flexible MWEs. Alegria et al. (2004) showed that by using a MWE processor in the preprocessing stage, a significant improvement in the POS tagging precision is obtained. Villav-icencio et al. (2007) found that the addition of 21 new MWEs to the lexicon led to a significant increase in the grammar coverage (from 7.1% to 22.7%), without altering the grammar accuracy. However, as argued by many researchers (e.g., Heid 1994; Seretan 2011), collocation identification is best performed on the basis of parsed material. This is due to the fact that collocations are co-occurrences of lexical items in a specific syntactic configuration. For that reason, we have chosen the identification of collocations as soon as possible during parsing. Finkel & Manning (2009) have built a joint model of parsing and named entity recognition, based on a discriminative feature-based constituency parser. They tested their model on the OntoNotes annotated corpus[1] and they achieved a remarkably good performance on both parsing and recognition of named entities. Green et al. (2013) have developed two structured prediction models with the aim to identify arbitrary-length, contiguous MWEs in Arabic and French. The first is based on context-free grammars and the second uses tree substitution grammars, a formalism that can store larger syntactic fragments. They claim that these techniques can be applied to any language for which a syntactic treebank, a MWE list, and a morphological analyzer exist. Nasr et al. (2015) have developed a joint parsing and MWE identification model for the detection and representation of ambiguous complex function words. Constant & Nivre (2016) developed a transition-based parser which combines two factorized substructures: a standard tree representing the syntactic dependencies between the lexical elements of a sentence and a forest of lexical trees including MWEs identified in the sentence.

3 The Fips parser

Fips is a multilingual parser, available for several languages, i.e. French, English, German, Italian, Spanish, Modern Greek, Romanian and Portuguese. It relies on generative grammar concepts and is basically made up of a generic parsing module which can be refined in order to suit the specific needs of a particular language. Fips is a constituent parser that functions as follows: it scans an input string from left to right, without any backtracking. The parsing algorithm, iteratively, performs the following three steps:

- get the next lexical item and project the relevant phrasal category (X → XP);

- merge XP with the structure in its left context (the structure already built);

---

[1]http://www.gabormelli.com/RKB/OntoNotes_Corpus, last accessed 26 February 2019.

- (syntactically) interpret XP, triggering procedures
  - to build predicate-argument structures
  - to create chains linking preposed elements to their trace
  - to find the antecedent of (3rd person) personal pronouns
  - to identify collocations.

The parsing procedure is a one-pass (no pre-processing, no post-processing) scan of the input text, using rules to build up constituent structures and (syntactic) interpretation procedures to determine the dependency relations between constituents (grammatical functions, etc.), including cases of long-distance dependencies. One of the key components of the parser is its lexicon, which contains detailed morphosyntactic and semantic information, selectional properties, valency information, and syntactico-semantic features that are likely to influence the syntactic analysis.

3.1 The Fips lexicon

The lexicon was built manually and contains fine-grained information required by the parser. It is organized as a relational database with four main tables:

words, representing all morphological forms (spellings) of the words of a language, grouped into inflectional paradigms;

lexemes, describing more abstract lexical forms which correspond to the syntactic and semantic readings of a word (a lexeme corresponds roughly to a standard dictionary entry);

collocations, which describe multiword expressions combining two lexical items, not counting function words;

variants, which list all the alternatives written forms for a word, e.g. the written forms of British English vs American English, the spellings introduced by a spelling reform, presence of both literary and modern forms in Greek, etc.

3.2 Representation of MWEs in the lexicon

In the introduction we mentioned that in our research, MWEs are categorized in five subclasses, i.e. compounds, discontinuous words, named entities, collocations and idioms. We will now describe how they are represented in the lexical database.

Compounds and named entities are represented by the same structure as simple words. An entry describes the syntactic and (some) semantic properties of the word: lexical category (POS), type (e.g., common noun, auxiliary verb), subtype, selectional features, argument structure, semantic features, thematic roles, etc. Each entry is associated with the inflectional paradigm of the word, that is all the inflected forms of the word along with the morphological features (number, gender, person, case, etc.). The possible spaces or hyphens of the compounds are processed at the lexical analyzer level in order to distinguish those that are separators from those belonging to the compound.

Discontinuous words, such as particle verbs or phrasal verbs, are represented in the same way as simple words as well, except that the orthographic string contains the bare verb only, the particle being represented separately in a specific field. The benefit of such an approach is that the phrasal verb inherits the inflectional paradigm of the basic verb. For agglutination, a lexical analyzer will detect and separate the particle from the basic verb.

Collocations are defined as associations of two lexical units (not counting function words) in a specific syntactic relation (for instance adjective-noun, verb-object, etc.). A lexical unit can be a word or a collocation. The definition is therefore recursive and enables to encode collocations that have more than two words (Nerima et al. 2010). For instance, the French collocation *tomber en panne d'essence* ('to run out of gas') is composed of the word *tomber* (lit. 'fall') and the collocation *panne d'essence* (lit. 'failure of gas'). Similarly, the English collocation *guaranteed minimum wage* is composed of the word *guaranteed* and the collocation *minimum wage*.

In addition to the two lexical units, a collocation entry encodes the following information: the citation form, the collocation type (i.e., the syntactic relation between its two components), the preposition (if any) and a set of syntactic frozenness constraints.

Some examples of entries are given in (1), (2) and (3).

(1) *ein Schlaglicht werfen* (DE) 'to highlight'
      type : verb-direct object
      lexeme #1 : *Schlaglicht* 'spotlight', noun-noun collocation
      lexeme #2: *werfen* 'throw', _ NP PP verb
      preposition : Ø
      features : {}

(2) *κινητό τηλέφωνο* (kinitó tiléfono) (MG) 'mobile phone'
      type : adjective-noun
      lexeme #1 : *κινητό* (kinitó) 'mobile', adjective

lexeme #2 : *τηλέφωνο* (tiléfono) 'phone', noun
preposition : ∅
features : {}

(3) *banc de poissons* (FR) 'shoal of fish'
type : noun-prep-noun
lexeme #1 : *banc* 'bench', noun
lexeme #2 : *poisson* 'fish', noun
preposition : *de* 'of'
features : {determiner-less complement, plural complement}

For the time being, we represent idioms as collocations with more restriction features (cannot passivize, no modifiers, etc.). They are, therefore, stored in the same database table. Reducing idioms to collocations with specific features though convenient and appropriate for large classes of idioms is nevertheless not general enough. In particular, it does not allow for the representation of idioms with fixed phrases, such as *to get a foot in the door*.

3.3 Fips and collocations

3.3.1 Collocation identification mechanism

The collocation identification mechanism is integrated in the parser. In the present version of Fips, collocations, if present in the lexicon, are identified in the input sentence during the analysis of that sentence, rather than at the end. In this way, priority is given to parsing alternatives involving collocations, and collocational information helps the parser through the maze of alternatives. To fulfill the goal of interconnecting the parsing procedure and the identification of collocations, we have incorporated the collocation identification mechanism within the constituent attachment procedure (see Section 3.3.2). The Fips parser, like many grammar-based parsers, uses left attachment and right attachment rules to build respectively left subconstituents and right subconstituents. The grammar used for the computational modelling comprises rules and procedures. Attachment rules describe the conditions under which constituents can combine, while procedures compute properties such as long-distance dependencies, agreement, control properties, argument-structure building, and so on.

3.3.2 Treatment of collocations

The identification of compounds and named entities can be achieved during the lexical analysis, but the identification of discontinuous words, collocations and idioms requires grammatical data and are, therefore, part of the parsing process. The identification of a collocation occurs when the second lexical unit of the collocation is attached, either by means of a left attachment rule (e.g., adjective-noun, noun-noun) or by means of a right-attachment rule (e.g., noun-adjective, noun-prep-noun, verb-object), as shown in example (4).

(4)   Paul took up a new challenge.
      [$_{TP}$ [$_{DP}$ Paul][$_{VP}$ took up [$_{DP}$ a [$_{NP}$ [$_{AP}$ new] challenge]]]]

When the parser reads the noun *challenge* and attaches it (along with the prenominal adjective) as complement of the incomplete [$_{DP}$ a] direct object of the verb *take up*, the identification procedure considers iteratively all the governing nodes of the attached noun and checks whether the association of the lexical head of the governing node and the attached element constitutes an entry in the collocation database. The process stops at the first governing node of a major category (noun, verb or adjective). In our example, going up from *challenge*, the process stops at the verb *take up*. Since *take up - challenge* is an entry in the collocation database and its type (verb-object) corresponds to the syntactic configuration, the identification process succeeds.

In several cases the two constituents of a collocation can be very far apart, or do not appear in the expected order. We will turn to such examples in Section 4. To handle them, the identification procedure sketched above must be slightly modified so that not only the attachment of a lexical item triggers the identification process, but also the attachment of the trace of a preposed lexical item. In such a case, the search will consider the antecedent of the trace. This shows, again, that the main advantage provided by a syntactic parser in such a task is its ability to identify collocations even when complex grammatical processes disturb the canonical order of constituents.

4 Detection of collocations in free word-order languages

Just as other types of MWEs, collocations are problematic for NLP because they have to be recognized and treated as a whole, rather than compositionally (Sag et al. 2002). On the other hand, there is no systematic restriction on lexical forms which constitute a collocation, on the order of items in a collocation, or on the number of words that may intervene between these items especially in free word-order languages. In such languages, the direct object of a verbal collocation can be found either before or after the verb, with or without intervening material. This is illustrated in the following examples with the Greek verb-object collocation *κάνω έκκληση* (káno éklisi) 'to make an appeal'. In (5a), the direct object follows the verb, while in (5b), it precedes the verb, with several intervening words between them:

(5) a. Ο Υπουργός Παιδείας *έκανε έκκληση* στους διοικητικούς
        O Ipurgós   Pedías   *ékane éklisi*   stus   diikitikús
        υπαλλήλους να σταματήσουν την απεργία.
        ipalílus   ná stamatísun   tín aperyía
        'The Minister of Education *made an appeal* to the administrative staff to stop the strike.'

    b. *Έκκληση* στους διοικητικούς υπαλλήλους να σταματήσουν την
        Éklisi   stus   diikitikús   ipalílus   ná stamatísun   tín
        απεργία *έκανε* ο Υπουργός Παιδείας.
        aperyía *ékane* o Ipurgós   Pedías
        '*An appeal* to the administrative staff to stop the strike *made* the Minister of Education.'

4.1 Nominal collocations

Modifiers can often be attached within a nominal collocation, separating the two terms. For example, between the constituents of a nominal collocation in the form of adjective-noun, other lexemes may interfere. Table 1 shows a part of the analysis of a sentence where the possessive determiner *του* (tu) 'his' occurs between the adjective *παρθενικό* (parthenikó) 'maiden' and the noun *ταξίδι* (taxídi) 'voyage' of the collocation *παρθενικό ταξίδι* (parthenikó taxídi) 'maiden voyage'. Note that, for the POS tagset, we opted for the universal tagset (Petrov et al. 2012).

Table 1: Identification of the nominal collocation *παρθενικό ταξίδι* (parthenikó taxídi) 'maiden voyage'

word	tag	position	collocation
To (to) 'the'	DET	1	
παρθενικό (parthenikó) 'maiden'	ADJ	4	
του (tu) 'his'	PRON	14	
ταξίδι (taxídi) 'voyage'	NOUN	18	*παρθενικό ταξίδι* 'maiden voyage'

4.2 Verbal collocations

Verb-object collocations may undergo syntactic processes such as passivization, relativization, interrogation and even pronominalization, which can leave the collocation constituents far away from each other and/or reverse their canonical order.

4.2.1 Passive

In passive constructions, the direct object is promoted to the subject position leaving an empty constituent in the direct object position. The detection of a verb-object collocation in a passive sentence is thus triggered by the insertion of the empty constituent in direct object position. The collocation identification procedure checks whether the antecedent of the (empty) direct object and the verb constitute a verb-object collocation. In example (6), the noun απόφαση (apófasi) 'decision' of the collocation παίρνω απόφαση (pérno apófasi) 'to make a decision' precedes the verb and is in the nominal case, the usual case for subjects.

(6) Η απόφαση πάρθηκε.
     I apófasi párthike.
     'The decision was made.'

4.2.2 Pronominalization

Another transformation that can affect some collocation types is pronominalization. In such cases, it is important to identify the antecedent of the pronoun which can be found either in the same sentence or in the context. Example (7) illustrates a phrase where the pronoun *it* refers to the noun *money*. Since the pronoun is the subject of the passive form *would be well spent*, it is interpreted as the direct object of the verb and therefore stands for an occurrence of the collocation *to spend money*.

(7) ... though where the money would come from, and how to ensure that *it* would be well *spent*, is unclear.

In example (8) and Table 2, both the verb να αναλάβουν (na analávun) 'to take' of the verb-object collocation αναλαμβάνω ευθύνη (analamváno efthíni) 'to take responsibility' and the pronominalized object τις (tis) 'them' are found in another sentence.

(8) Ας αναλογιστούν τις ευθύνες τους. Να τις αναλάβουν.
     As analogistún   tis efthínes tus. Na tis analávun.
     'Let them consider their responsibilities. Should they take them.'

Table 2: Identification of a verbal collocation

word	tag	position	collocation
Ας (as) 'Let them'	PRT	1	
αναλογιστούν (analogistún) 'consider'	VERB	4	
τις (tis) 'the'	DET	17	
ευθύνες (efthínes) 'responsibilities'	NOUN	21	
τους (tus) 'their'	PRON	21	
.	PUNC	33	
Να (Na) 'Should'	CONJ	35	
τις (tis) 'them'	PRON	35	
αναλάβουν (analávun) 'take'	VERB	42	*αναλαμβάνω την ευθύνη* 'take responsibility'
.	PUNC	51	

Example (9) and Table 3 concern French and show again two sentences. Each one of them contains a collocation with the noun *record*: *établir un record* 'to set up a record' in the first one, and *battre un record* 'to break a record' in the second one, where the noun is pronominalized in the form of a clitic pronoun (*le* 'it').

(9) Ce *record* a   été *établi* l'été dernier. Paul espère *le battre* bientôt.
     This record has been set up last summer. Paul hopes *it break* soon.
     'This record was set up last summer. Paul hopes to break it soon.'

The parser detects collocations in which the nominal element has been pron-ominalized thanks to the anaphora resolution component incorporated in Fips (Wehrli & Nerima 2013).

4.2.3 Wh-constructions

Our parser can also cope with long-distance dependencies, such as the ones found in wh-questions.[2] In sentence (10) and Table 4, the direct object constituent

---

[2]wh-words are interrogative (or relative) words such as *who, what, which*, etc. For a general discussion of wh-constructions, see (Chomsky 1977).

Table 3: Identification of verbal collocations, one with pronominalized object

word	tag	position	collocation
Ce	DET	1	
record	NOUN	4	
a	VERB	11	
été	VERB	13	
établi	VERB	17	établir un record
l'	DET	24	
été	NOUN	26	été dernier
dernier	ADJ	30	
.	PUNC	37	
Paul	NOUN	1	
espère	VERB	6	
le	PRON	13	
battre	VERB	16	battre un record
bientôt	ADV	23	
.	PUNC	30	

occurs at the beginning of the sentence. Again, assuming a generative grammar analysis, we consider that such pre-posed constituents are connected to so-called canonical positions. The fronted element being a direct object, the canonical position is a post-verbal DP position immediately dominated by the VP node. The parser establishes such a link and returns the structure from (10), where [DP e]$_i$ stands for the empty category (the "trace") of the preposed constituent Ποιο ρεκόρ (Pxó rekór) 'Which record'.

(10) Ποιο ρεκόρ θέλει να σπάσει ο Μελισσανίδης? [CP [DP Ποιο ρεκόρ]$_i$] [TP
Pxó rekór théli na spási o Melisanídis
θέλει] [CP να] [TP σπάσει] [VP [DP e]$_i$] [DP ο Μελισσανίδης]
'Which record does Melissanidis want to break?'

In such cases, the collocation identification process is triggered by the insertion of an empty constituent in the direct object position of the verb. Since the empty constituent is connected to the pre-posed constituent, such examples can be easily treated as a minor variant of the standard case described in Section 3.3.1. All so-called wh-constructions are treated in a similar fashion, that is relative clause and topicalization.

Table 4: Identification of verbal collocation in a wh-question

word	tag	position	collocation
Ποιο (Pio) 'Which'	DET	1	
ρεκόρ (rekór) 'record'	NOUN	6	
θέλει (théli) 'wants'	VERB	12	
να (na) 'to'	CONJ	18	
σπάσει (spási) 'break'	VERB	21	*σπάζω το ρεκόρ* 'break the record'
o (o) 'the'	DET	28	
Μελισσανίδης (Melisanídis) 'Melisanidis'	NOUN	30	

4.2.4 *Tough*-movement constructions

In such constructions, the matrix subject is construed as the direct object of the infinitival verb governed by a *tough* adjective. Following Chomsky's (1977) analysis of such constructions, the parser will hypothesize an abstract wh-operator in the specifier position of the infinitival clause, which is linked to the matrix subject. Like all wh-constituents, the abstract operator will itself be connected to an empty constituent later on in the analysis, giving rise to a chain connecting the subject of the main clause and the direct object position of the infinitival clause. The structure as computed by the parser is given in (11), with the chain marked by the index *i*.

(11) $[_{TP} [_{DP} \text{this record}]_i \text{ seems}[_{AP} \text{difficult}[_{TP} [_{DP} \text{ e}]_i \text{ to}[_{VP} \text{break}[_{DP} \text{ e}]_i]]]]$

4.3 Complex collocations

As observed by Heid (1994), among others, collocations can involve more than two content words. Such complex expressions can be described recursively as collocations of collocations. Our identification procedure has been extended to handle such cases. For example, the Greek noun-noun collocation *απεργία πείνας* (aperyía pínas) 'hunger strike', which combines with the verb *κάνω* (káno) 'to do', yields the larger verb-object collocation *κάνω απεργία πείνας* (káno aperyía pínas) 'to go on hunger strike', where the object is itself a noun-noun collocation. Given the strict left-to-right processing order assumed by the parser, the system will first identify the collocation *κάνω απεργία* (káno aperyía) 'to go on strike' when attaching the word *απεργία* (aperyía) 'strike'. Then, reading the last word, *πείνας* (pínas) 'hunger' (here in genitive case), the parser will identify the collocation απεργία πείνας (aperyía pínas) 'hunger strike'. The search succeeds with the verb κάνω (káno) 'to do', and the collocation κάνω απεργία πείνας (káno aperyía pínas) 'to go on hunger strike' is identified.

Moreover, the Greek lexical database comprises nominal collocations formed by a simple noun and a collocation or by two collocations. For example, δύναμη πολιτικής προστασίας (dínami politikís prostasías) 'civil protection force' is formed by a simple noun, δύναμη (dínami) 'force', and a nominal collocation in genitive case, πολιτικής προστασίας (politikís prostasías) 'of civil protection'. The collocation πυρηνικός σταθμός παραγωγής ενέργειας (pirinikós stathmós paragoyís enéryias) 'nuclear power station' is formed by the collocations πυρηνικός σταθμός (pirinikós stathmós) 'nuclear station' and παραγωγής ενέργειας (paragoyís enéryias) 'of energy production'.

5 Collocation extraction

As already mentioned, the parser can only identify collocations that are part of its lexical database. Therefore, it is crucial to have as good a coverage of collocations as possible in the database. To help the linguist/lexicographer in the time-consuming task of inserting collocations, we have designed a collocation extraction tool (Seretan 2011), dubbed FipsCo. Applied to a corpus, FipsCo parses all the sentences, extracting all the pairs of lexical items which co-occur in predefined grammatical configurations (adjective-noun, noun-noun, subject-verb, verb-object, etc.). All those pairs are considered as potential collocations.

Once the corpus has been completely parsed, a statistical filter is used to rank the potential collocations according to their degree of association. By default, we use the log-likelihood ratio measure (LLR), since it was shown to be particularly suited to language data (Dunning 1993). In our extractor, the items of each candidate expression represent base word forms (lemmas) and they are considered in the canonical order implied by the given syntactic configuration (e.g., for a verb-object candidate, the object is postverbal in subject-verb-object (SVO) languages like Greek). Even if the candidate occurs in corpus in different morphosyntactic realizations, its various occurrences are successfully identified as instances of the same type thanks to the syntactic analysis performed by the parser.

Figure 1 displays a list of verb-object collocations extracted from an English corpus taken from the magazine *The Economist*. On the left, candidate collocations are listed and at the same time they are shown in their context.

Our system recognizes a large range of collocation types (more than 30 types), including several nominal and verbal ones. The most frequent types are:

- Adjective-noun, e.g. *nuclear war*;

- Noun-noun, e.g. *flower shop*;

- Noun-preposition-noun, e.g. *casco di banane* ('bunch of bananas');

- Verb-object where the object is a bare noun, e.g. *take part*;

- Verb-preposition-noun, e.g. *bring to light*;

- Verb-adverb, e.g. *put together.*

Once filtered and ordered by means of standard association measures, the candidate collocations are manually validated and added to the lexical database. The current content of the database for six European languages is shown in Table 5.

6 Evaluation and results

The Fips parser performs well compared to other "deep" linguistic parsers (Delphin,[3] ParGram,[4] etc.) in terms of speed. Parsing time depends on two main factors: (i) the type and complexity of the corpus, and (ii) the selected beam size (maximum number of alternatives allowed). By default, Fips runs with a beam size of 40 alternatives, which gives it a speed ranging from 150 to 250 tokens (word, punctuation) per second. At that pace, parsing a one million word corpus takes approximately 2–3 hours. We are going to present the experiments that were performed for Modern Greek and English in order to evaluate the performance of our parser.

6.1 Modern Greek

The evaluation measures the performance of our parser to identify collocations that are lexicalized (i.e. collocations that are present in the lexical database). We also measure the impact of the collocation knowledge on the performance of the parser (in percentage of complete analyses). To achieve the evaluation, we took a small newspaper corpus of about 20,000 words and we manually identified

---

[3]International consortium developing HPSG grammars and other tools, cf. http://www.delph-in.net/wiki/index.php/Home.

[4]ParGram is an international consortium for the development of LFG-based grammars, see http://pargram.b.uib.no.

Concordance

Display Collocations

Collocations   (3890)   Source: D:\Corpus\English\The Economist\Espresso\2015\2015-12-09.odc

kill people
raise interest rate
reach deal
cut cost
claim responsibility
take place
mark anniversary
release video
raise rate
hold election
deny wrongdoing
report result
publish figure
pass bill
call election
win majority
carry out raid
make money
open fire
shoot people
extend bailout
kill soldier
provide information
reject application

Recording choices: Indonesian politics

Today Indonesians engage in one of their favourite pastimes: voting. For the first time, all 269 local elections will be held simultaneously. But most political attention will be on a tribunal in Jakarta where Setya Novanto, speaker of the House of Representatives, is fighting for his career, amid swirling allegations of rampant rent-seeking and corruption in Indonesia's resource sector. Last week the tribunal heard a recording, purportedly made by the local boss of Freeport, a mining giant, in which Mr Novanto and Muhammad Riza Chalid, an oil-and-gas tycoon, appeared to demand a 20% stake in its Indonesian subsidiary—11% for Joko "Jokowi" Widodo, the country's president, and 9% for the vice-president, Jusuf Kalla—in exchange for help in extending its operating contracts. Jokowi and Mr Kalla say their names were falsely invoked; Mr Chalid denies wrongdoing; Mr Novanto says he was "joking", and insists the recording is illegal.

Breaking down: Volkswagen's woes

Crt: 3 of 5   << < > >>   Open source file

Order: ● score   Details
        ○ frequency   Type: Verb - Object   Score: 52.65   Rank: 10
        ○ alphabetical Status: Collocation in lexic.

Options …

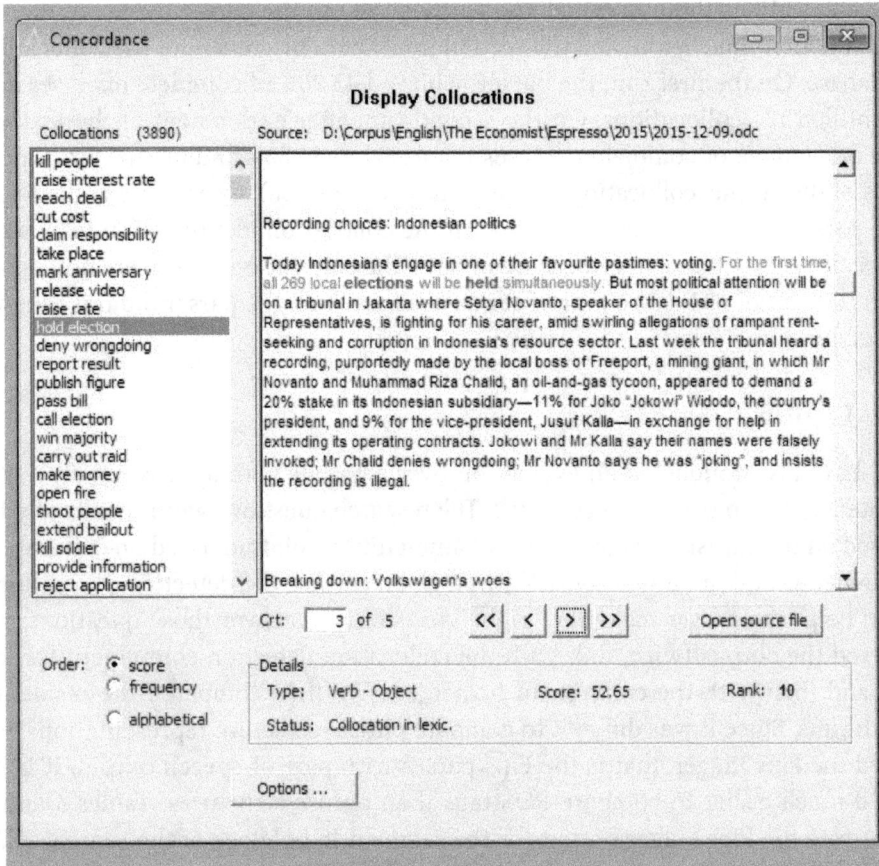

Figure 1: Extraction of verb-object collocations

Table 5: Number and types of collocations in the Fips lexical database

collocation type	English	French	German	Italian	Spanish	Greek
Adjective-noun	3,049	5,935	490	1,325	1,621	20,131
Noun-noun	5,671	454	2,476	131	66	471
Noun-prep-noun	555	7,846	22	1,246	988	11
Verb-object	850	1,560	197	250	1,098	382
Others	932	2,963	330	209	592	126
Total	11,057	18,758	3,515	3,161	4,365	21,122

638 collocations (both nominal and verbal). We ran the parser twice on the corpus: the first time before and the second time after enrichment of the collocation database. On the first run, the parser achieved 43.26% of complete analyses and identified 124 collocations. On the second run, after enrichment of the lexicon, the percentage of complete analyses increased to 44.33% and nearly three quarters of the corpus collocations were identified (482/638). Over this small corpus, the parser achieved a 100% precision in the collocation identification task, with a recall of 75.54% and an F-measure of 86%. The collocations that were not identified (156 out of 638) were part of sentences for which the parser did not achieve a complete analysis.

6.2 English

We have also conducted an evaluation over a corpus with approximately 6,000 sentences taken from *The Economist*. The research questions were specifically focused on the statistical significance of ambiguity resolution based on collocation knowledge and on how frequently, in a given corpus, the detection of a collocation helps the parser make the "right" decision. To answer those questions, we parsed the corpus twice, first with the collocation detection component turned on and then with the component turned off. We then compared the results of both runs. Since it was difficult to compare phrase-structure representations, we used the Fips tagger, that is the Fips parser with part-of-speech output. It is indeed much easier to compare POS-tags than phrase-structures. Tables 6 and 7 illustrate the Fips tagger output for the segment in boldface of the sentence *The researchers estimated **the total worldwide labour costs** for the iPad at $33, of which China's share was just $8.*

Table 6 gives the results obtained with the collocation detection component turned on, and Table 7 the results obtained with the component turned off.

Table 6: Parser output *with* collocation knowledge

word	tag	position	collocation
the	DET	27	
total	ADJ	31	
worldwide	ADJ	37	
labour	NOUN	47	
costs	NOUN	54	*labour costs*

Table 7: Parser output *without* collocation knowledge

word	tag	position	collocation
the	DET	27	
total	ADJ	31	
worldwide	ADJ	37	
labour	NOUN	47	
costs	**VERB**	54	

The sentence segment *the total worldwide labour costs* is displayed in both tables with the words in the first column, the part-of-speech tag in the second column and the position – expressed as position of the first character of each word starting from the beginning of the sentence – in the third column. As we can see, the word *costs* is taken as a noun in the first analysis, as a verb in the second. The (correct) choice of a nominal reading in the first analysis is due to the detection of the collocation *labour costs*. In the second run, given the absence of collocational knowledge, the parser opts for the verbal reading. Both output files could easily be manually compared using a specific user interface as illustrated in the screenshot in Figure 2, where POS differences are displayed in red.

Table 8: POS-tagging with and without collocation knowledge

	with collocations	without collocations
complete analyses	73.41%	72.95%
POS-tag differences	727	-
better tags	382	106
number of collocations	1668	-

A summary of the results of the evaluation is given in Table 8. The first line shows the number of complete analyses. Collocational knowledge increases the number of complete analysis by approximately 0.5%, or about 30 sentences for our corpus of 6,000 sentences. 727 tags are different between the two runs. Of those, excluding differences which do not really matter (some words can be analyzed either as predicative adjectives or as adverbs without much semantic differences, etc.), in 382 cases the tags were better in the first run (with collocational knowledge), and 106 cases better in the second run (without collocational

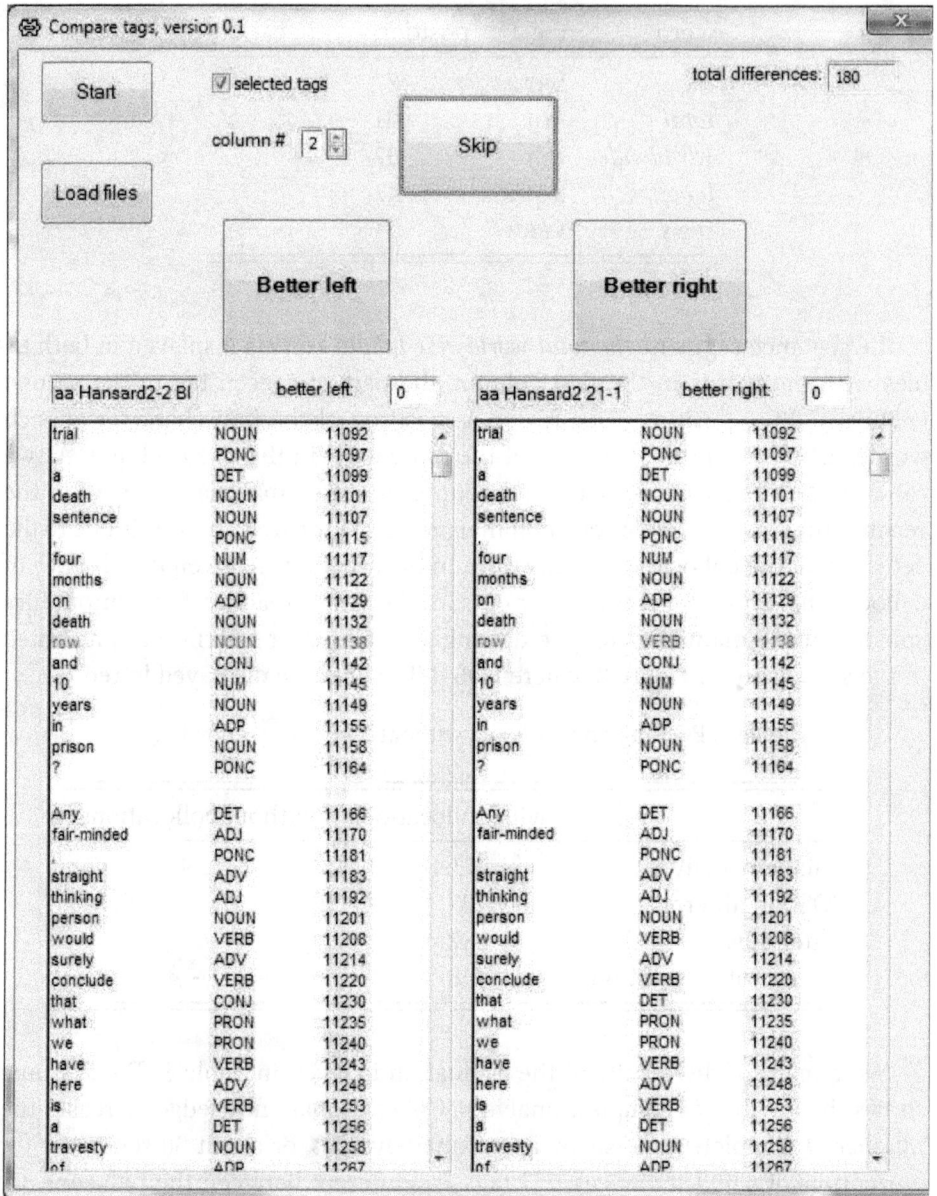

Figure 2: The evaluation user interface

knowledge). In other words, collocational knowledge helped the parser make the better decision four times more than it penalized it. Notice finally that 1,668 collocations were detected in the corpus (more than one in four sentences), which clearly stresses the high frequency of this phenomenon in natural language.

7 Conclusion

In this chapter, we have argued in favour of a treatment of collocations, and by extension of all MWEs, fully integrated in the parsing process. The argument is rather simple. On the one hand, we have shown that the identification of collocations must be based on analyzed data, and therefore cannot be performed before parsing. On the other hand, we have also shown that collocation identification can help the parser, for instance to solve lexical as well as syntactic ambiguities, provided that the identification is done before the end of parsing. The solution to this apparent paradox – collocation identification cannot be done before and cannot be done after parsing – is clear: collocation identification must be part of the parsing process and must be performed as early as possible, that is at the time the parser attaches the second constituent of the collocation, or inserts the trace of that constituent.

Abbreviations

Tagset from Petrov et al. (2012).

ADJ	adjective	NUM	numeral
ADP	adposition	PRON	pronoun
ADV	adverb	PRT	particle
CONJ	coordinating conjunction	PUNC	punctuation
DET	determiner	VERB	verb
NOUN	noun	X	other

References

Alegria, Iñaki, Olatz Ansa, Xabier Artola, Nerea Ezeiza, Koldo Gojenola & Ruben Urizar. 2004. Representation and treatment of multiword expressions in Basque. In Takaaki Tanaka, Aline Villavicencio, Francis Bond & Anna Korhonen (eds.), *Second ACL workshop on multiword expressions: Integrating processing*, 48–55. Barcelona, Spain: Association for Computational Linguistics.

Brun, Caroline. 1998. Terminology finite-state preprocessing for computational LFG. In *COLING 1998 volume 1: The 17th international conference on Computational Linguistics*, 196–200. Montreal, QC.

Chomsky, Noam. 1977. On Wh-movement. In P.W. Culicover, T. Wasw & A. Akmajian (eds.), *Formal syntax*. San Francisco, London: Academic Press.

Constant, Mathieu & Joakim Nivre. 2016. A transition-based system for joint lexical and syntactic analysis. In *Proceedings of the 54th annual meeting of the Association for Computational Linguistics*, vol. 1: *Long papers*, 161–171. Berlin, Germany: Association for Computational Linguistics. http://www.aclweb.org/anthology/P16-1016.

Dunning, Ted. 1993. Accurate methods for the statistics of surprise and coincidence. *Computational Linguistics* 19(1). 61–74. http://dl.acm.org/citation.cfm?id=972450.972454.

Finkel, Jenny Rose & Christopher D. Manning. 2009. Joint parsing and named entity recognition. In *Proceedings of Human Language Technologies: The 2009 annual conference of the North American chapter of the Association for Computational Linguistics*, 326–334. Boulder, Colorado: Association for Computational Linguistics. http://www.aclweb.org/anthology/N/N09/N09-1037.

Green, Spence, Marie-Catherine de Marneffe & Christopher D. Manning. 2013. Parsing models for identifying multiword expressions. *Computational Linguistics* 39(1). 195–227.

Heid, Ulrich. 1994. On ways words work together: Topics in lexical combinatorics. In Willy Martin et al. (ed.), *Proceedings of the VIth Euralex international congress (EURALEX'94)*, 226–257. Amsterdam. Eingeladener Hauptvortrag.

Nasr, Alexis, Carlos Ramisch, José Deulofeu & André Valli. 2015. Joint dependency parsing and multiword expression tokenisation. In *53rd annual meeting of the Association for Computational Linguistics*, 1116–1126. Beijing, China.

Nerima, Luka, Eric Wehrli & Violeta Seretan. 2010. A recursive treatment of collocations. In *Proceedings of the seventh international conference on Language Resources and Evaluation (lrec'10)*, 634–638. Valletta, Malta.

Petrov, Slav, Dipanjan Das & Ryan McDonald. 2012. A universal part-of-speech tagset. In Nicoletta Calzolari, Khalid Choukri, Thierry Declerck, Mehmet Uğur Doğan, Bente Maegaard, Joseph Mariani, Asuncion Moreno, Jan Odijk & Stelios Piperidis (eds.), *Proceedings of the eighth international Language Resources and Evaluation Conference, LREC 2012*, 2089–2096. Istanbul, Turkey. http://www.lrec-conf.org/proceedings/lrec2012/summaries/274.html.

Sag, Ivan, Timothy Baldwin, Francis Bond, Ann Copestake & Dan Flickinger. 2002. Multiword expressions: A pain in the neck for NLP. In *Proceedings of the*

3rd international conference on Computational Linguistics and Intelligent Text Processing (Lecture Notes in Computer Science 2276), 1–15. Springer.

Seretan, Violeta. 2011. *Syntax-based collocation extraction* (Text, Speech and Language Technology 44). Dordrecht: Springer.

Villavicencio, Aline, Valia Kordoni, Yi Zhang, Marco Idiart & Carlos Ramisch. 2007. Validation and evaluation of automatically acquired multiword expressions for grammar engineering. In *Proceedings of the 2007 joint conference on Empirical Methods in Natural Language Processing and Computational Natural Language Learning (emnlp-conll)*, 1034–1043. Prague, Czech Republic: Association for Computational Linguistics. http://www.aclweb.org/anthology/D/D07/D07-1110.

Wehrli, Eric. 2007. Fips: A "deep" linguistic multilingual parser. In *Proceedings of the ACL 2007 workshop on Deep Linguistic Processing*, 120–127. Prague, Czech Republic: Association for Computational Linguistics. http://www.aclweb.org/anthology/W/W07/W07-1216.

Wehrli, Eric & Luka Nerima. 2013. Anaphora resolution, collocations and translation. In J. Monti, R. Mitkov, G. Corpas Pastor & V. Seretan (eds.), *Proceedings of the workshop on Multiword Units in Machine Translation and Translation Technology (MUMTT'2013)*. Nice.

Wehrli, Eric & Luka Nerima. 2015. The Fips multilingual parser. In N. Gala, R. Rapp & G. Bel-Enquix (eds.), *Language production cognition, and the lexicon, Festschrift in honour of Michael Zock*, 473–489. Springer.

Zhang, Yi & Valia Kordoni. 2006. Automated deep lexical acquisition for robust open texts processing. In *Proceedings of the 5th internation conference on Language Resource and Evaluation (LREC-2006)*, 275–280. Genoa, Italy.

Chapter 9

Extracting and aligning multiword expressions from parallel corpora

Nasredine Semmar

CEA LIST, Vision and Content Engineering Laboratory

Christophe Servan

University of Grenoble Alpes – Grenoble Informatics Laboratory
SYSTRAN

Meriama Laib

CEA LIST, Vision and Content Engineering Laboratory

Dhouha Bouamor

Actimos, Groupe Accord

Morgane Marchand

eXenSa

Bilingual lexicons of multiword expressions play a vital role in several natural language processing applications such as machine translation and cross-language information retrieval because they often characterize domain-specific vocabularies. Word alignment approaches are generally used to construct bilingual lexicons automatically from parallel corpora. We present in this chapter three approaches to align multiword expressions from parallel corpora. We evaluate the bilingual lexicons produced by these approaches using two methods: a manual evaluation of the alignment quality and an evaluation of the impact of this alignment on the translation quality of the phrase-based statistical machine translation system Moses. We experimentally show that the integration of the bilingual lexicons of multiword expressions in the translation model improves the performance of Moses.

Nasredine Semmar, Christophe Servan, Meriama Laib, Dhouha Bouamor & Morgane Marchand. 2019. Extracting and aligning multiword expressions from parallel corpora. In Yannick Parmentier & Jakub Waszczuk (eds.), *Representation and parsing of multiword expressions: Current trends*, 239–268. Berlin: Language Science Press. DOI:10.5281/zenodo.3264764

1 Introduction

A MultiWord Expression (MWE) is a combination of words for which syntactic or semantic properties of the whole expression cannot be obtained from its parts (Sag et al. 2002). Such units could be collocations, compound words, named entities, etc. They constitute an important part of the lexicon of any natural language (Jackendoff 1997). Bilingual lexicons of MWEs play a vital role in several Natural Language Processing (NLP) applications such as Machine Translation (MT) and Cross-Language Information Retrieval (CLIR) because they generally characterize domain-specific vocabularies. The manual construction of these lexicons is often costly and time consuming. Word alignment approaches are generally used to automatically construct bilingual lexicons from parallel or comparable corpora. Several word alignment approaches have been explored (Daille et al. 1994; Blank 2000; Barbu 2004) and many automatic word alignment tools are available, such as GIZA++ (Och & Ney 2000). However, most of these tools are efficient only to align single words (Fraser & Marcu 2007).

The chapter is organized as follows. We survey in Section 2 previous works addressing the tasks of extracting and aligning MWEs from parallel corpora. We define in Section 3 the notion of MultiWord Expression and describe different types of MWEs with examples. In Section 4, we introduce three approaches to build bilingual lexicons of MWEs from sentence aligned parallel corpora. The experimental results are reported and discussed in Section 5. Finally, we present in Section 6 the conclusion and future work.

2 Related work

There are mainly two strategies to extract bilingual MWEs from parallel corpora. The first strategy consists to acquire translations of phrases from parallel corpora in one step. Phrases are not necessarily MWEs, they can be contiguous sequences of a few words that encapsulate enough context to be translatable (DeNero & Klein 2008). The second strategy firstly, identifies monolingual MWE candidates and then applies alignment approaches to find bilingual correspondences (Daille et al. 1994; Blank 2000; Gaussier & Yvon 2011; Barbu 2004).

In the second strategy, MWEs extraction can be processed by using symbolic methods based on morpho-syntactic patterns, or, through statistical approaches, which use automatic measures to rank MWE candidates. Finally, MWEs extraction can be done by using hybrid approaches, which combine the two first strategies.

Dagan & Church (1994) proposed to use syntactic analysis to extract terminology. MWEs are extracted by grouping linguistically related terms. In the same way, Okita et al. (2010) proposed to link across two languages MWEs according to their syntactic and lexical information. Tufiş & Ion (2007) and Seretan & Wehrli (2007) introduce a linguistic approach in which they claim that MWEs keep in most cases the same morpho-syntactic structure in the source and target languages.

Statistical approaches also have proven to be useful in collecting bilingual MWEs from parallel corpora. Kupiec (1993) introduced the use of machine learning algorithms such as the Expectation Maximization (EM) to extract MWEs. Similarly, Vintar & Fišer (2008) proposed to extract bilingual MWEs by translating MWEs from a well known language (English) to a low resource language (Slovene) by using machine translation. They have shown that their translation-based approach performs better than using linguistic approaches. But they did not combine these two kind of approaches. The combination of such approaches enables to extract finer MWEs (Daille 2001). In this way Wu & Chang (2003) and later Boulaknadel et al. (2008), proposed to use syntactic and statistical analysis to extract bilingual MWEs from a parallel corpus. The main aspect of their approach is a monolingual parsing to extract MWEs combined with statistical detection in each language, then, they confront candidates from each side to find bilingual MWEs.

Other approaches proposed to use machine translation to translate MWEs candidates found with a syntactic analysis (Seretan & Wehrli 2007). Again, the first step is done on each language independently and then, a second step aims to match candidates across languages.

3 Multiword expressions

3.1 Definition

In NLP, a multiword expression refers to a non-compositional sequence of words whose exact and unambiguous meaning, connotation and syntactic properties cannot be derived from the meaning or connotation of its components (Choueka 1988; Sag et al. 2002). MWEs are frequently used in written texts and constitute a significant part of the language lexicon.

Jackendoff (1997) considers that the frequency of their use is equivalent to that of single words. Although MWEs are easily computed, stored and used by humans, their identification is a major issue for different type of NLP applications, namely for syntactic analysis (Nivre & Nilsson 2004; Constant et al. 2011), automatic summarization (Hogan et al. 2007), information extraction (Vechtomova 2005) and especially for machine translation and cross-language information retrieval (Carpuat & Diab 2010; Ren et al. 2009).

3.2 Multiword expressions typology

In the literature, MWEs are presented under different names or classifications such as idioms, lexicalized phrases or collocations and several authors (Ramisch et al. 2013) give a list of examples instead of giving an exact description of them. According to Calzolari et al. (2002), MWEs are "different but related phenomena" and "At the level of greatest generality, all of these phenomena can be described as a sequence of words that acts as a single unit at some level of linguistic analysis".

Sag et al. (2002) classify them into two main categories: lexicalized phrases and institutionalized phrases (Figure 1). Lexicalized phrases "have at least partially idiosyncratic syntax or semantics, or contain "words" which do not occur in isolation". Institutionalized phrases are "semantically and syntactically compositional, but statistically idiosyncratic".

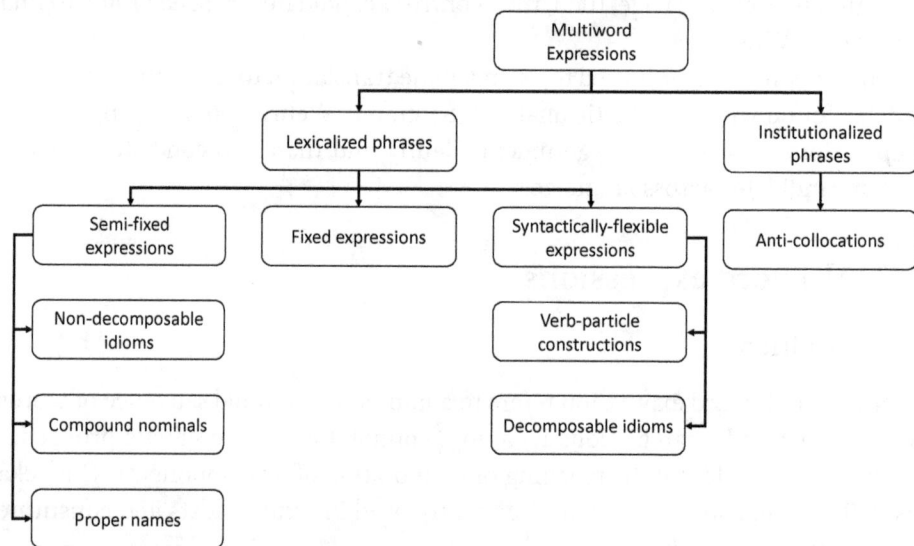

Figure 1: Typology of multiword expressions by Sag et al. (2002)

3.2.1 Lexicalized phrases

In a decreasing order of lexical rigidity, these MWEs are broken down into three classes: fixed expressions, semi-fixed expressions and syntactically-flexible expressions.

3.2.1.1 Fixed expressions

Fixed expressions are non-compositional sequences of words. They are syntactically and morphologically rigid and undergo neither internal modification nor morphological and syntactical variations (e.g. *nest of vipers* in English or *pomme de terre* in French). To determine whether or not a sequence of words is a fixed expression, we can use linguistic criteria such as using synonyms or adding words between its components (cf. *nest of many black vipers* in English or *pomme de jolie terre lointaine* in French). Fixed expressions can be considered as single entries in the dictionary.

3.2.1.2 Semi-fixed expressions

A semi-fixed expression is a non-compositional sequence of words whose components do not contribute to its figurative meaning. Semi-fixed expressions should respect a strict word order and some of them undergo limited lexical and morphological variability such as inflection and some variation in the reflexive form. According to their characteristics, they can be broken down into three basic categories: non-decomposable idioms, proper names and some compound nominals (Sag et al. 2002).

Non-decomposable idioms do not undergo syntax variability but their components accept lexical changes such as pronominal reflexivity form (e.g. *wet himself*, *wet themselves*), verbal inflection (*kick the bucket, kicked the bucket*) or passivization (e.g. *briser le silence* or *le silence est brisé* in French). Proper names "are syntactically highly idiosyncratic" (Sag et al. 2002). They can be complex with two or three proper names as components, including person, places and organization names.

Compound nominals are syntactically unalterable and undergo number inflection (e.g. *car park(s)* in English or *pomme(s) de terre* in French).

3.2.1.3 Syntactically-flexible expressions

Unlike semi-fixed expressions, syntactically-flexible expressions undergo a wide degree of syntactic variation such as passivation (e.g., *The cat was let out of the bag*) and allow external elements to intervene between their components (e.g., *slow the car down*). This type of expressions includes verb-particle constructions, decomposable idioms. Particle verbs constructions are made up of a verb whose meaning is modified by one or more particles. They can be either semantically idiosyncratic such as *brush up on* or compositional such as *take after, look out, go back* and *run over*. Decomposable idioms tend to be syntactically flexible to some degree that is unpredictable (Riehemann 2001). Semantically, they behave as if their components were linked parts contributing independently to the figurative interpretation of the expression as a whole.

3.2.2 Institutionalized phrases

Institutionalized phrases are semantically and syntactically fully compositional, but statistically idiosyncratic (Sag et al. 2002). They occur in a high frequency and their idiosyncrasy is statistical rather than linguistic. They generally allow one available meaning. Institutionalized phrases often refer to "collocations" (Barz 1996; Riehemann 2001; Burger 2010), described as sequences of words that statistically have a high probability to appear together whether they are contiguous or not (e.g., *make love* or *make a difference*).

4 Construction of bilingual lexicons of MWEs from parallel corpora

In this section, we describe three approaches to build bilingual lexicons of MWEs from a sentence aligned parallel corpus. The first two approaches are composed of two steps. The first step identifies MWEs present in the parallel corpus, and the second step establishes correspondence relations between the MWEs of the source text and their translations in the target text. The third approach performs the terminology extraction and alignment tasks in one step.

4.1 Statistical approach for MWEs alignment

The statistical approach for MWEs alignment consists first in identifying the relevant word groups through the use of *n*-gram statistics in both the source and target languages. Then for each source MWE extracted we compile a list of candidate translations through the use of two distance metrics. The list of candidates is then pruned through the use of heuristics like the length of each MWE, and a translation is "found" if it satisfies confidence threshold on the distance metric and the heuristics.

The alignment process has the following four steps (Semmar et al. 2010):

1. Monolingual extraction of MWEs: The role of this step consists to identify all the *n*-grams (up to 6-grams) that may represent a MWE. This is done through frequency analysis and heuristic scoring. This step outputs two lists of terms, which we will refer to as SC (MWE in the Source Language) and TC (MWE in the Target Language).

2. Frequency distance calculation: This step calculates for all source MWEs in SC the distance to each of the target MWEs in TC. The main idea of this metric is that if two MWEs are translations of each other then they must appear together in the corpus segments, and only together. Their frequency distance is then calculated as follows:

(1)
$$FD(s, t) = \frac{|f(s) - f(t)|}{\max(f(s), f(t))}$$

Where $f(s)$ is the frequency of the source MWE and $f(t)$ is the frequency of the target MWE under consideration.

We observe that if t is the translation of s, $f(s) = f(t)$ then we have distance equal to 0. Also, if two MWEs always occur together but one is much more frequent than the other, the distance could have a value other than 0 and they would not be considered translations of each other. Here we chose to apply a threshold of 0.25 as the maximum allowable distance. This threshold is calculated empirically and can be tuned to achieve better precision.

3. Co-occurrence distance (CD): The previous step only considers frequencies so it may be possible for two completely unrelated MWEs to achieve a low distance score. To refine extraction results, we also check for a co-occurrence score as follows:

(2)
$$CD(X, Y) = \frac{\sqrt{\sum(X_i - Y_i)^2}}{N}$$

Where, X_i is the number of occurrences of s in the ith segment of the SL, Y_i is the number of occurrences of t in the ith segment of the TL and N is the number of segments.

This check allows the rejection of the MWEs that fortuitously have similar frequency. Since they would not appear in the same segments, the terms $X_i - Y_i$ would increase. The candidate list can be ordered through CD.

4. Pruning MWEs candidates: After obtaining an ordered list of target MWEs candidates, we remove:

    - The candidates which have a length different from the source MWE;
    - The candidates which have been previously aligned with another source MWE and where the co-occurrence score was better.

Because of the statistical nature of this approach, it performs much better for MWEs that occur often in the corpus. Table 1 illustrates some MWEs and their translations extracted from the bi-sentence *Approval of the Minutes of the previous sitting/Approbation du procès-verbal de la séance précédente*. It should be noted that before applying the MWEs alignment approach, we lemmatize the parallel corpus. This lemmatization is achieved using the CEA LIST Multilingual Analyzer LIMA (Besançon et al. 2010).

Table 1: Some examples of aligned MWEs with the statistical approach

English MWE	French MWE
minute	*procès-verbal*
approval of the minute	*approbation du procès-verbal*
previous sitting	*séance précédent*

4.2 Hybrid approach for MWEs alignment based on morpho-syntactic patterns

The hybrid approach for MWEs alignment is composed of the following two steps (Bouamor et al. 2012a,c,b):

1. MWEs identification: The method used to extract MWEs is based on a symbolic approach relying on morpho-syntactic patterns.

2. MWEs alignment: After extracting MWE candidates, context vectors from the parallel corpus are separately built and similarity scores between one MWE and all target MWEs are computed.

4.2.1 MWEs extraction

The method to extract monolingual MWEs from a parallel corpus is based on a symbolic approach relying on morpho-syntactic patterns. It handles both frequent and infrequent expressions and do not use any lexicon. This method involves a full morpho-syntactic analysis of source and target texts. The analysis is done using the CEA LIST Multilingual Analysis platform LIMA (Besançon et al. 2010), which produces Part-of-Speech (POS) tags and lemmas associated to each word. Since most MWEs consist of noun, adjectives and prepositions, we adopted a linguistic filter. It consists in keeping only n-gram (n from 2 to 4) units, which match with a list of a hand created morpho-syntactic patterns. Such process is used to keep only specific strings and filter out undesirable ones such as candidates composed mainly of stop words (*of a, is a, that was*). The algorithm operates on lemmas instead of surface forms which can draw on richer statistics and overcome the data sparseness problems.

In Table 2, we give an example of MWEs produced for each pattern. There exists extraction patterns (or configurations) for which no MWE has been generated (i.e., Noun-Adj). To this list are added some prepositional idiomatic expressions (*in particular, in the light of, as regards*, etc.) and named entities (*Middle East, South Africa, United States of America*, etc.) recognized by the morpho-syntactic analyzer LIMA. Then, we scored all extracted MWEs with their total frequency of occurrence in the corpus. To avoid an over-generation of MWEs and remove irrelevant candidates from the process, a redundancy cleaning approach is introduced. In this approach, if a MWE is nested in another, and they both have the same frequency, we discard the smaller one. Otherwise we keep both of them. We consider also the case in which a MWE appears in a high number of terms and discard all longer ones.

Our approach does not use any additional correlations statistics such as Mutual Information or Log Likelihood Ratio. It finds translations for all extracted MWEs (both frequent and infrequent ones).

Table 2: Example of morpho-syntactic patterns used to detect MWEs in each language independently

pattern	English MWE	French MWE
Adj-Noun	*plenary meeting*	*libre circulation*
Noun-Noun	*member state*	*état membre*
Noun-Prep-Noun	*point of view*	*point de vue*
Noun-Prep-Adj-Noun	*court of first instance*	*court de première instance*

4.2.2 MWEs alignment

MWEs alignment aims to find for each MWE in a source language its adequate translation in the target one. This task used to be handled through an external linguistic resource such as bilingual lexicons or single words alignment tools. Our approach for MWEs alignment is resource-independent and uses a parallel corpus and a list of input MWEs candidates to translate. It associates a specific representation to each expression (source and target).

We associate to each MWE an N sized vector, where N is the number of sentences in the corpus, indicating whether it appears or not in each sentence of the corpus. Our algorithm is based on the Vector Space Model (Salton et al. 1975). This vector space representation will serve, eventually, as a basis to establish a translation relation between each pair of MWEs.

To extract translation pairs of MWEs, we propose an iterative alignment algorithm operating as follows:

1. Find the most frequent MWE *exp* in each source sentence;

2. Extract all target translation candidates, appearing in all parallel sentences to those containing *exp*;

3. Compute a confidence value V_{Conf} for each translation relation between *exp* and all target translation candidates;

4. Consider that the target MWE maximizing V_{Conf} is the best translation;

5. Discard the translation pair from the process and go back to 1.

To compute the confidence value V_{Conf}, we adopted the *Jaccard* Index. This measure is based on the number I_{st} of sentences shared by each target and a source MWE. I_{st} is normalized by the sum of the number of sentences where the source and target MWEs appear independently of each other (respectively V_s and V_t) decreased by I_{st}.

$$(3) \qquad Jaccard = \frac{I_{st}}{V_s + V_t - I_{st}}$$

We illustrate in Table 3, a sample of aligned MWEs by means of the algorithm described above. When we observe MWE pairs, we noticed that our method has two advantages. On the one hand, it allows the translation of MWEs aligned in most previous work (Dagan & Church 1994; Ren et al. 2009) using single words alignment tools to establish word-to-word alignment relations. The approach can capture the semantic equivalence between expressions such as *insulaire en développement* and *small island developing* in a different way. On the other hand, the approach enables the alignment of idioms such as *à nouveau* ('once more').

Table 3: Some examples of aligned MWEs with the hybrid approach based on morpho-syntactic patterns

English MWE	French MWE
european parliament	*parlement européen*
military coup	*coup d'état*
in favour of	*en faveur de*
no smoking area	*zone non fumeur*
small island developing	*insulaire en développement*
good faith	*de bonne foi*
competition policy	*politique de concurrence*
process of consultation	*processus de consultation*
railway sector	*chemin de fer*
with regard to	*en ce qui concerne*
once more	*à nouveau*
cut in forestation	*coupe forestière*

4.3 Hybrid approach for MWEs alignment based on linear programming

This section describes a hybrid approach combining linguistic and statistical information which performs terminology extraction and alignment of MWEs from parallel texts in one step (Marchand & Semmar 2011).

Most of works on MWEs alignment are divided in two tasks: a monolingual step in which candidate terms are extracted and a bilingual step in which these terms are aligned with their translations (Gaussier & Yvon 2011). Word alignment techniques are generally used to achieve the bilingual step. These approaches in multiple steps have the disadvantage to potentially propagate errors.

The main idea of the hybrid approach for MWEs alignment based on linear programming is to consider the global task of selection and alignment as an optimization problem. The challenge when we deal with alignment of MWEs is the exponential complexity of such a task. The possible number of fragments in a sentence improves exponentially according to the number of the words of the sentence. Several works impose some constraints on the number of fragments of a MWE. In our approach, the only restriction we made on MWEs is contiguity. The advantage to assume the continuity is to enable a linearized formulation of the optimization problem to solve. We use an integer linear programming approach inspired by the work described in DeNero & Klein (2008) to quickly find an approximated optimal solution.

4.3.1 Linear programming model

A sentence pair consists of two word sequences: e and f. e_{ij} is the MWE from between-word positions i to j of e. f_{kl} is the same for f. A link is an aligned pair of MWEs, denoted (e_{ij}, f_{kl}). Each e_{ij} is allowed to be linked with several f_{kl} and each f_{kl} with several e_{ij}. An alignment a of the sentence pair (e, f) is a segmentation of the two sentences in MWEs with the set of links between these MWEs. We use a real-valued function $\phi : \{e_{ij}\} \times \{f_{kl}\} \rightarrow R$ to score links. The score of an alignment is then the product of all the links inside it:

$$(4) \qquad \phi(a) = \prod_{(e_{ij}, f_{kl}) \in a} \phi(e_{ij}, f_{kl})$$

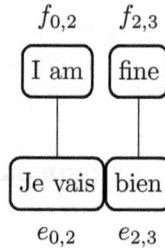

Figure 2: Example of alignment

In the example shown in Figure 2, the score of the alignment is computed as follows:

$$(5) \qquad \phi(a) = \phi(e_{0,2}, f_{0,2}) \times \phi(e_{2,3}, f_{2,3})$$

Formally this function has no constraints other than that of being real. In practice, we choose a function that gives an idea about the relevance to align such fragments. The higher the score, the higher the relevance of alignment is important. Therefore, we look for the alignment (segmentation + links) that maximizes the score described above.

First, we introduce binary variables $A_{i,j,k,l}$ denoting whether $(e_{ij}, f_{kl}) \in a$. Furthermore, we introduce binary indicators $E_{i,j}$ and $F_{k,l}$ that denote whether some $(e_{ij}, \cdot)$ or $(\cdot, f_{kl})$ appears in a, respectively. Finally, we will use $W_{i,j,k,l} = \log \phi(e_{ij}, f_{kl})$ to transform the product into a sum. When optimized[1], the integer program yields the optimal alignment:

---

[1] We used the open source solver GLPK (GNU Linear Programming Kit), available at http://www.gnu.org/s/glpk/.

$$(6) \begin{cases} \max \sum_{i,j,k,l} W_{i,j,k,l} A_{i,j,k,l} \\[2mm] \forall x : 1 \le x \le |e| \qquad \sum_{i,j:i<x\le j} E_{i,j} = 1 \qquad (1) \\[2mm] \forall y : 1 \le y \le |f| \qquad \sum_{k,l:k<y\le l} F_{k,l} = 1 \qquad (2) \\[2mm] \forall i,j \qquad \sum_{k,l} A_{i,j,k,l} \ge E_{i,j} \qquad (3) \\[2mm] \forall k,l \qquad \sum_{i,j} A_{i,j,k,l} \ge F_{k,l} \qquad (4) \\[2mm] \forall i,j,k,l \qquad 2 \cdot A_{i,j,k,l} \le E_{i,j} + F_{k,l} \qquad (5) \end{cases}$$

With the following constraints:

$$(7) \quad \begin{cases} 0 \le i < |e|, \quad 0 < j \le |e|, \quad i < j \\ 0 \le k < |f|, \quad 0 < l \le |f|, \quad k < l \end{cases}$$

Constraints (1) and (2) indicate that a word is inside exactly one phrase. Constraint (3) ensures that each phrase in the selected partition of e appears in at least one link (and likewise constraint (4) for f). Finally, constraint (5) ensures that if a link exists between e_{ij} and f_{kl} (i.e. $A_{i,j,k,l} = 1$) then e_{ij} and f_{kl} are in the selected partitions of e and f.

In that way, our approach differs from the one proposed in DeNero & Klein (2008). Their work focuses on bijective alignments while we consider surjective alignments. We have also modified constraints (3) and (4) and added constraint (5) to allow a phrase to be aligned with several other phrases. We have chosen this formalism because phrases are not necessarily composed of contiguous words.

This integer program can work with any real-valued scoring function.

4.3.2 Co-occurrence based metric

We use a corpus aligned sentence-by-sentence to compute co-occurrence distance. For each MWE, we consider the presence or absence in each sentence. Then the score between two MWEs e_{ij} and f_{kl} is calculated as follows:

$$(8) \quad \phi_c(e_{ij}, f_{kl}) = \frac{\sum_{s' \in S} N_{s'}(e_{ij}) \times N_{s'}(f_{kl})}{\sum_{s \in S} N_s(e_{ij}) + N_s(f_{kl}) - N_s(e_{ij}) \times N_s(f_{kl})}$$

Where $N_s(e_{ij})$ is 1 if the phrase e_{ij} of the first language is present in the sentence s of the corpus S and 0 otherwise. $N_s(f_{kl})$ is similar for the other language.

This score calculates the number of common presence of both phrases divided by the number of total presence of either phrase. Note that if none of e_{ij} or f_{kl} appears in the whole corpus, the score is set to 0. Indeed, if two MWEs appear exactly in the same bi-sentences, they are probably translation of each other and the score will be 1. The example in Table 4 illustrates this score.

Table 4: Example of ambiguous translation of MWEs

Je mange un *avocat*	–	I'm eating an *avocado*
L'*avocat* prend la parole	–	The *lawyer* takes the floor

In this small corpus, $N_1(avocat) = 1$, $N_1(avocado) = 1$, $N_2(avocat) = 1$ and $N_2(avocado) = 0$. Thus, the co-occurence score for the bi-gram *avocat*/*avocado* has the value:

$$(9) \qquad \phi_c(avocado, avocat) = \frac{(1 \times 1) + (1 \times 0)}{(1 + 1 - 1 \times 1) + (1 + 0 - 1 \times 0)} = \frac{1}{2}$$

We observed after aligning some sentences that when both sentence structures are similar, the aligner performs well as shown in Figure 3. The segmentation is word to word or MWE to MWE depending on what is more frequent in the corpus. Moreover, the surjective formulation of the problem allows us to begin to detect expressions in two parts. We can see that *rôle* is linked to both *role* and *play* (Figure 3, Alignment 3).

This would have been impossible with the bijective formulation of DeNero & Klein (2008). This result is encouraging but not yet sufficient. Actually this expression is partially recognized because it includes two plain words. Expressions with postponed prepositions would not be recovered this way because the prepositions are too common to be statistically relevant. If the structure is different we have more difficulties (as shown in Figure 4). Some sentences are also difficult to align because they are not perfect translation: *They*/*la population* or adverbs like *also* or *very* which are not translated.

We also observe that, for common words, the distribution of apparition is meaningless: *to* is linked with *de* and *a*. We should use a measure of information as suggested in Gao (1998). In addition, the program is powerless if it finds an unknown word or if a word co-occurs with no other word of the translated sentence. In that case, all links containing this word will obtain the score of 0 as

(1)

The	timing of	this	U-turn	seems		highly		suspect
Le	moment de	ce	revirement	semble	particulièrement	suspect

(2)

Can we — continue — to turn a blind eye

Pouvons-nous — continuer — à fermer les yeux

(3)

What — role — will — the — Indonesian — armed forces — play

Quel — sera — le — rôle — des — forces armées — indonésiennes

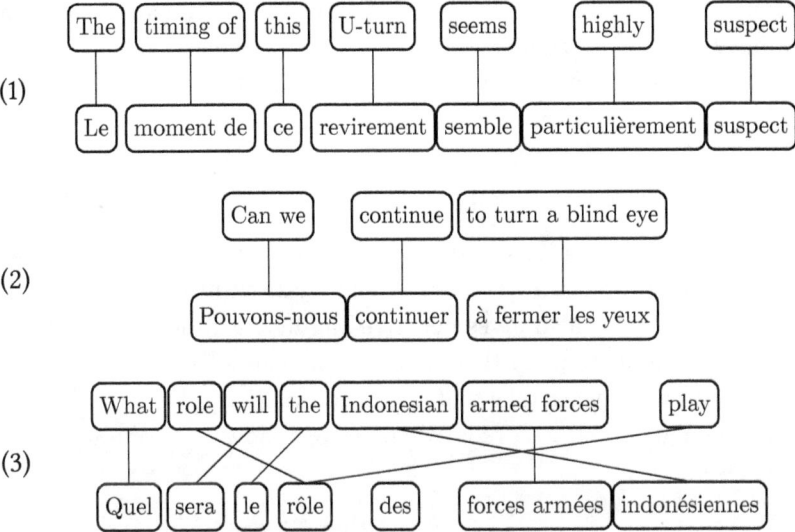

Figure 3: Good alignments with co-occurrence based metric

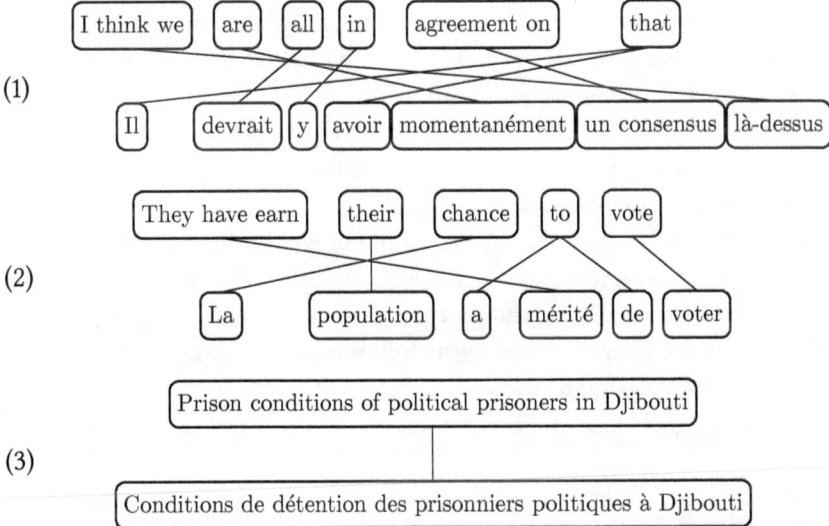

(1)

I think we — are — all — in — agreement on — that

Il — devrait — y — avoir — momentanément — un consensus — là-dessus

(2)

They have earn — their — chance — to — vote

La — population — a — mérité — de — voter

(3)

Prison conditions of political prisoners in Djibouti

Conditions de détention des prisonniers politiques à Djibouti

Figure 4: Bad alignments with co-occurrence based metric

they never occur. And as we use a multiplicative metric, the global score of the alignment will be 0 whatever the other links of the alignment. Unknown links should have a small, non-null score to allow the discovery of new links. More-over, we can use an external resource such as a bilingual lexicon of single words which can improve the alignment of phrases.

4.3.3 Bilingual dictionary based metric

The bilingual dictionary gives us several word-to-word alignments. We want to comply with these alignments as often as possible as we infer that they are mostly correct. The dictionary also gives negative alignment information. Of course if two words are not aligned by the dictionary we cannot take for sure that they should not. But we have to take that into account.

The bilingual dictionary score is calculated as follows:

$$(10) \qquad \phi_c(e_{ij}, f_{kl}) = \frac{a \times R_1 + b \times R_0}{a \times R_1 + b \times R_0 + c \times N_1 + d \times N_0}$$

R_1 is the number of respected links, R_0 is the number of respected non-links, N_1 is the number of non-respected links, and N_0 is the number of non-respected non-links.

The coefficients a, b, c and d can be adapted to balance the relative influence of the four terms. We analyzed a small corpus that allowed us to empirically choose the use of the following values: $a = b = c = 1$ and $d = 0.5$. The score is calculated for each part of the bi-phrase and then the two of them are multiplied. We have to take into account R_0 and N_0 because otherwise the whole bi-sentence would be the optimal segmentation.

As we can see, this metric has a double effect. First, it gives a high score if bi-phrases respect dictionary word to word alignment. And second, due to R_0, it sets a threshold score for unknown couples. Both effects can have a positive role in alignment task as we will see in the following examples. The dictionary-based metric is not intended to be used separately. It is mixed with co-occurrence score. We used an English-French bilingual dictionary containing 243,539 entries with doubles.[2]

In Figure 5, we observe some degradation of alignments. For these sentences, the threshold for unknown couples is too high relatively to the statistical score.

---

[2] http://catalog.elra.info/product_info.php?products_id=666.

(1a)

| What | role | will | the | Indonesian | armed forces | | play |

| Quel | sera | le | rôle | des | forces armées | indonésiennes |

(1b)

| What role will | the | | Indonesian armed forces play |

| Quel sera | le | rôle des forces armées indonésiennes |

(2a)

| My final point | concerns | Nicaragua |

| Mon dernier point | porte sur le | Nicaragua |

(2b)

| My | final point concerns | Nicaragua |

| Mon dernier point | porte sur le | Nicaragua |

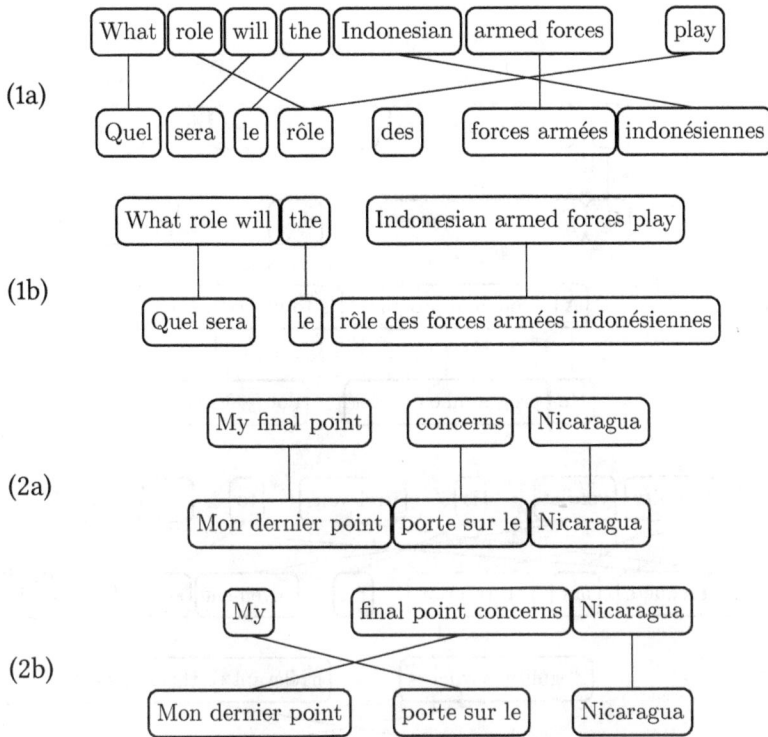

Figure 5: Degradation of alignments – (a) Alignments without the bilingual dictionary and (b) Alignments with the bilingual dictionary

So we lose the benefit of the co-occurrence metric. This problem should be partially solved by scaling the two metrics. However we have already observed some improvements, as presented in Figure 6. In the first example, the bilingual dictionary gives the alignments: *be/être, decided/décidé* and *there/y*. So the program manages to reconstruct the whole expression *is to be decided on there/doit y être décidé*. Moreover the links *concrete/concret* and *programme/programme* are strengthened. The second example is difficult to align due to the difference of structure. The alignment with dictionary is not perfect but is far more better. In this case the dictionary only gives links *verdict/jugement* and *request/requête* which were already aligned. However they are strengthened and others links are weakened. That is why we can observe an improvement.

Finally in the last example, the dictionary gives no links because the words are not lemmatized. The good result is here exclusively due to the threshold effect. The programme is allowed to consider links with no co-occurrence as long as others links have a good co-occurrence score.

(1a)

A | concrete program | is to be decided | on | there

Un | programme concret | doit | y | être décidé

(1b)

A | concrete program | is to be decided on there

Un | programme concret | doit y être décidé

(2a)

A | guilty | verdict | is | irrelevant | to | this | request

La | requête | fait | abstraction | du | jugement | sur | la | culpabilité

(2b)

A guilty verdict is | irrelevant to this request

La requête fait abstraction | du jugement sur la culpabilité

(3a)

Prison conditions of political prisoners in Djibouti

Conditions de détention des prisonniers politiques à Djibouti

(3b)

Prison conditions of | political prisoners | in Djibouti

Conditions de détention des | prisonniers politiques | à Djibouti

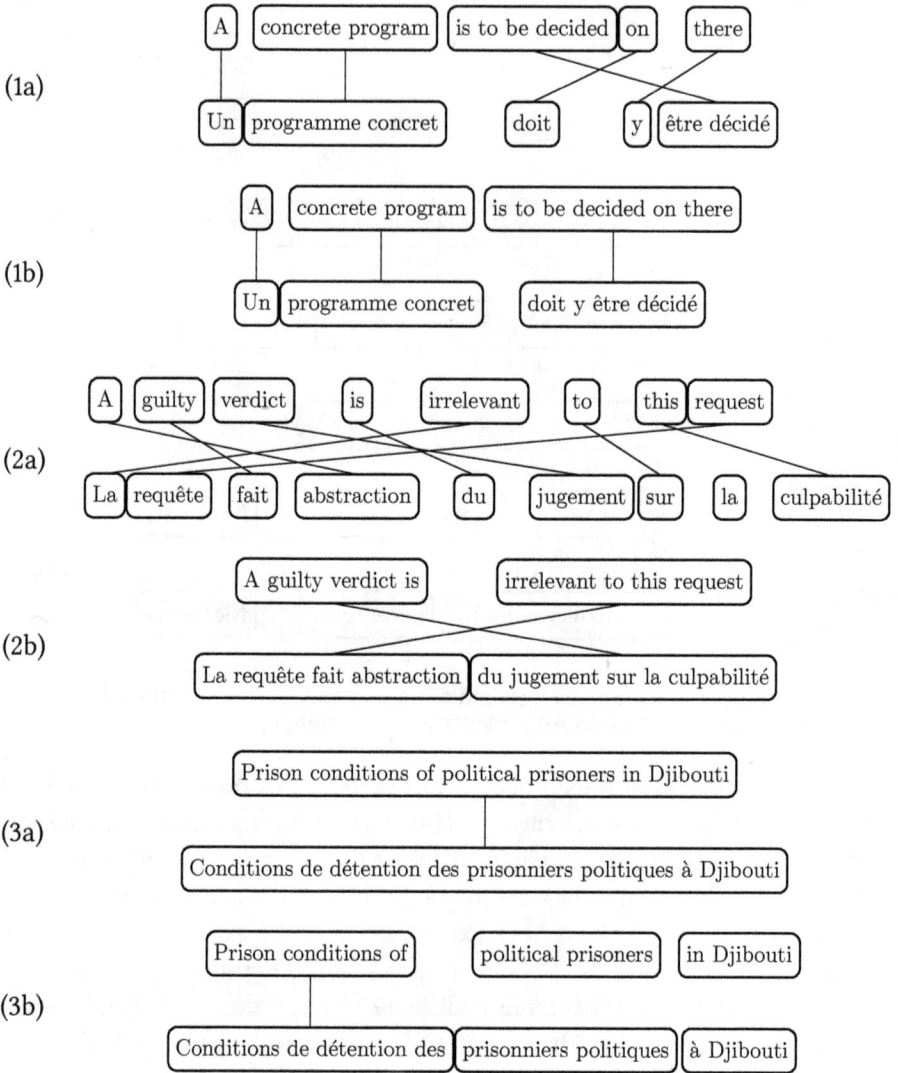

Figure 6: Amelioration of alignments – (a) Alignments without the bilingual dictionary and (b) Alignments with the bilingual dictionary

5 Experimental results

The quality of alignment of MWEs and the impact of using MWEs on machine translation have been evaluated, firstly, manually, by comparing the results of the three MWEs aligners with a reference alignment; and secondly automatically by using the results of the three MWEs aligners to build the translation model of the state-of-the-art statistical machine translation system Moses (Koehn et al. 2007).

5.1 Manual evaluation

The three approaches for MWEs alignment and the baseline Giza++ (Och & Ney 2000) have been evaluated using the following evaluation metrics. Given an alignment A, and a gold standard alignment (reference alignment) G, each such alignment set eventually consisting of two sets (A_s, A_p), and (G_s, G_p) where "s" and "p" correspond respectively to "sure" and "probable" alignments. The following measures are defined (where T is the alignment type, and can be set to either S or P). Each word aligner was evaluated in terms of Precision (P_T), Recall (R_T) and F-Measure (F_T).

(11)
$$P_T = \frac{A_T \cap G_T}{A_T}; \ R_T = \frac{A_T \cap G_T}{G_T}; \ F_T = \frac{2 \times P_T \times R_T}{P_T + R_T}$$

The corpus used to evaluate the performance of the English-French MWE aligners is composed of a set of 1992 parallel sentences extracted from Europarl (European Parliament Proceedings). This parallel corpus is composed of 46265 English words and 49332 French words and has been used to build manually the reference alignment by the Yawat tool (Germann 2008).

Table 5 summarizes the results of the three approaches for English–French MWEs alignments and the baseline (Giza++) in terms of precision, recall and F-measure.

The first observation is that, the hybrid approach based on morpho-syntactic patterns performs better than all the other methods. It clearly appears that the morpho-syntactic patterns used to extract the MWEs present in source and target texts has had a significant impact on the precision of the alignment. On the other hand, the statistical approach has the lower recall but it is better than the recall of the baseline (Giza++). And as a second observation, adding information coming from a bilingual lexicon to the co-occurrence metric used in the hybrid approach based on linear programming, certainly has improved the precision but the recall has dropped.

Table 5: Performance of the different English–French MWE aligners

MWE aligner	precision	recall	f-measure
Baseline (Giza++)	0.83	0.37	0.51
Statistical	0.81	0.39	0.52
Hybrid using morpho-syntactic patterns	0.87	0.55	0.67
Hybrid using co-occurrence	0.61	0.63	0.61
Hybrid using co-occurrence + lexicon	0.85	0.54	0.66

5.2 Alignment evaluation through a translation task

The unavailability of a reference alignment of a significant size for MWEs does not allow us to achieve a large evaluation and to compare our approaches with the state-of-the-art work. That's why we decided to study the impact of MWEs on the quality of translation by integrating the results of our word aligners in the training corpus used to extract the translation model of the phrase based statistical machine translation system Moses. We use the factored translation model (Koehn & Hoang 2007) as our baseline system. It is an extension of the phrase based models which are limited to the mappings of phrases without any explicit use of linguistic information. The factored model enables the use of additional markup at the word level (Figure 7).

Our model operates on lemmas instead of surface forms, in which the translation process is broken up into a sequence of mapping steps that either:

- Translate source lemmas into target's ones.

- Generate surface forms given the lemma.

The features used in the baseline system include: (1) four translation probability features, (2) two language models, (3) one generation model and (4) word penalty.

The goal of these experiments is to study in what respect MWEs are useful to improve the performance of Moses. In Moses, phrase tables are the main knowledge source for the machine translation decoder. The decoder consults these tables to figure out how to translate an input sentence into the target language. These tables are built automatically using the open source word alignment tool Giza++ (Och & Ney 2000). However, Giza++ could produce errors in particular when it aligns multiword expressions (Fraser & Marcu 2007). In order to integrate into Moses the bilingual lexicon which is extracted automatically by the MWE alignment approaches, we propose the following three methods:

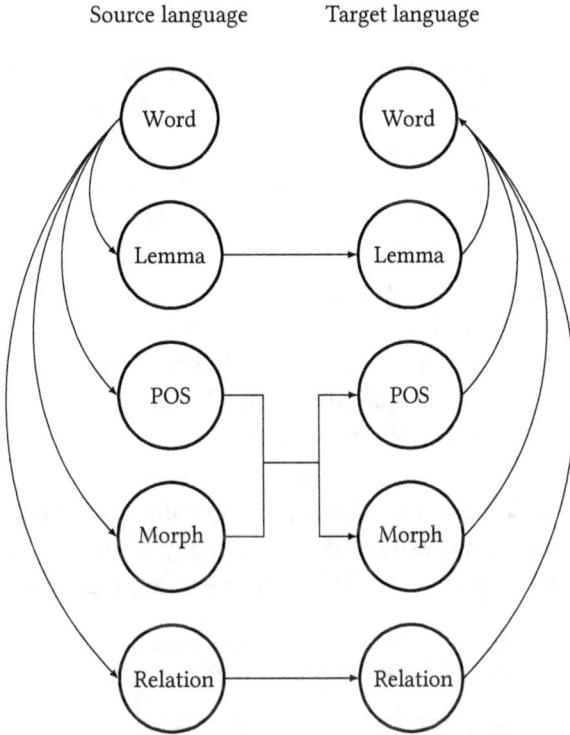

Figure 7: Factored model used in the SMT baseline system

CORPUS: In this method, we add the extracted bilingual lexicon as a parallel corpus and retrain the translation model. By increasing the occurrences of the MWEs and their translations, we expect a modification of alignment and probability estimation.

TABLE: This method consists in adding the extracted bilingual lexicon into Moses's phrase table. We use a smoothed probability estimator to construct a translation probability for each MWE of the bilingual lexicon. This estimator is based on the similarity measure provided by each word alignment approach.

FEATURE: In this method, we extend the "TABLE" method by adding a new feature indicating whether a MWE comes from the bilingual lexicon or not (1 or 0 is introduced for each entry of the phrase table).

5.2.1 Data and experimental setup

In order to study the impact of the bilingual lexicon of MWEs on the performance of Moses, we conducted our experiments on two English-French parallel corpora (Table 6): Europarl (European Parliament Proceedings) and Emea (European Medicines Agency Documents). These corpora were extracted from the open parallel corpus OPUS (Tiedemann 2012). For each MWE alignment approach, we achieved three runs and two test experiments for each run: In-Domain and Out-Of-Domain. For this, we randomly extracted 500 parallel sentences from Europarl as an In-Domain corpus and 500 pairs of sentences from Emea as Out-Of-Domain corpus. The domain vocabulary is represented in the case of our baseline (Moses) respectively by the specialized parallel corpus Emea which is added to the training data (Europarl). Afterwards, we extracted bilingual MWEs from the training corpus and applied the three methods described above. For the three integration methods (CORPUS, TABLE, FEATURE), the domain vocabulary is identified by a bilingual lexicon which is extracted automatically from the specialized parallel corpus Emea using the different MWEs alignment approaches.

Table 6: Europarl and Emea corpora details used to train language and translation models of Moses (K refers to 10^3)

Run n°.	Training (# sentences)	Tuning (# sentences)
1	150K+10K (Europarl+Emea)	2K+0.5K (Europarl+Emea)
2	150K+20K (Europarl+Emea)	2K+0.5K (Europarl+Emea)
3	150K+30K (Europarl+Emea)	2K+0.5K (Europarl+Emea)

5.2.2 Results and discussion

The performance of the SMT system Moses is evaluated using the BLEU score (Papineni et al. 2002) on the two test sets for the three runs described in the previous section. Note that we consider one reference per sentence. The obtained results are reported in Tables 7, 8, 9 and 10.

As shown in Tables 6, 7, 8 and 9, for In-Domain texts, Moses achieve a relatively high BLEU score and the scores of Moses when using the results of the hybrid approach based on morpho-syntactic patterns are better in all the runs. The best improvement is achieved using the "FEATURE" method. The "CORPUS" method (when compared to the baseline system) comes next with a slightly higher BLEU score with an improvement for In-Domain sentences and Out-Of-Domain texts.

Table 7: BLEU scores of Moses when using the results of the statistical approach

Run n°.	In-Domain (Europarl)				Out-Of-Domain (Emea)			
	Baseline	CORPUS	TABLE	FEATURE	Baseline	CORPUS	TABLE	FEATURE
1	32.62	32.41	32.36	32.55	22.96	22.82	22.75	22.91
2	33.81	33.76	33.71	33.79	23.30	23.09	23.04	23.27
3	34.25	34.23	34.21	34.24	24.55	24.49	24.45	24.52

Table 8: BLEU scores of Moses when using the results of the hybrid approach based on morpho-syntactic patterns

Run n°.	In-Domain (Europarl)				Out-Of-Domain (Emea)			
	Baseline	CORPUS	TABLE	FEATURE	Baseline	CORPUS	TABLE	FEATURE
1	32.62	32.82	32.15	32.88	22.96	23.45	23.11	23.69
2	33.81	34.05	33.48	34.09	23.30	24.09	23.76	24.18
3	34.25	34.64	34.11	34.67	24.55	25.43	25.05	25.48

Table 9: BLEU scores of Moses when using the results of the hybrid approach based on linear programming

Run n°.	In-Domain (Europarl)				Out-Of-Domain (Emea)			
	Baseline	CORPUS	TABLE	FEATURE	Baseline	CORPUS	TABLE	FEATURE
1	32.62	32.69	32.64	32.72	22.96	23.03	22.97	23.06
2	33.81	33.88	33.85	33.91	23.30	23.37	23.34	23.40
3	34.25	34.30	34.27	34.33	24.55	24.59	24.56	24.62

Table 10: BLEU scores of Moses when using the results of the hybrid approach based on linear programming and using a bilingual dictionary

Run n°.	In-Domain (Europarl)				Out-Of-Domain (Emea)			
	Baseline	CORPUS	TABLE	FEATURE	Baseline	CORPUS	TABLE	FEATURE
1	32.62	32.71	32.68	32.73	22.96	23.06	22.97	23.07
2	33.81	33.89	33.87	33.92	23.30	23.39	23.32	23.39
3	34.25	34.32	34.29	34.32	24.55	24.62	24.56	24.63

In order to show the impact of the domain vocabulary (represented by the bilingual MWEs extracted with the aligner based on the hybrid approach with morpho-syntactic patterns), on the translation quality of Moses, we manually analyzed an example of translations drawn from the Out-Of-Domain test corpus (Table 11).

Table 11: Translations produced by Moses for an Out-Of-Domain sentence

Input sentence	in the 12 week acute phase of three clinical trials of duloxetine in patients with diabetic neuropathic pain, small but statistically significant increases in fasting blood glucose were observed in duloxetine-treated patients.
Reference translation	lors de la phase aiguë de 12 semaines de trois essais cliniques étudiant la duloxétine chez les patients souffrant de douleur neuropathique diabétique, des augmentations faibles, mais statistiquement significatives de la glycémie à jeun ont été observées chez les patients sous duloxétine.
Moses translation with the "CORPUS" integration method	dans le 12 semaines de la phase aiguë trois études cliniques de duloxetine chez les patients avec douleur neuropathique diabétique, petites mais statistiquement significatif augmentations de répréhensible glycémie artérielle a été observée chez les patients traités duloxetine.
Moses translation with the "TABLE" integration method	dans le 12 semaine de la phase aiguë de trois essais cliniques de duloxetine dans les patients avec douleur neuropathique diabétique, petites mais statistiquement augmentations considérables dans le sang répréhensible glucose ont été constatées dans les patients duloxetine traités.
Moses translation with the "FEATURE" integration method	dans le 12 semaines de la phase aiguë de trois essais cliniques chez les patients avec douleur neuropathique diabétique, petites mais des augmentations statistiquement significatives de la glycémie à jeun ont été observées chez les patients traités duloxétine.

After analyzing the translations of this example, it is clear that in some cases, it is just impossible to perform a word-to-word alignment between two MWEs that are translation of each other. For example, the "FEATURE" method proposes the compound word *glycémie à jeun* as a translation for the expression *fasting blood glucose* which is correct, but, "CORPUS" and "TABLE" methods propose respectively the translations *répréhensible glycémie artérielle* and *sang répréhensible glucose* which are completely wrong. However, all the integration methods translate correctly the multiword expressions *diabetic neuropathic pain/douleur neuropathique diabétique* and *acute phase/phase aiguë*. The multiword expression *clinical trials/essais cliniques* is translated correctly by "TABLE" and "FEATURE" methods. Likewise, the translation provided by the "CORPUS" method for this expression is also correct *clinical trials/études cliniques* but it is different from the translation of the reference. It seems that the probabilities of the alignments proposed by Giza++ for these multiword expressions were very high and helped Moses decoder to choose these alignments. On the other hand, as we can see, all the translations have many spelling and grammatical errors, and in particular, the translations of some multiword expressions ('statistically significant increases'/*statistiquement significatif augmentations*, 'statistically significant increases'/*statistiquement augmentations considérables*) produced by the "CORPUS" and "TABLE" methods are very approximate. This result can be explained by the fact that, on the one hand, statistical machine translation toolkits like Moses have not been designed with grammatical error correction in mind, and on the other hand, Giza++ could produce errors in particular when it aligns multiword expressions (Fraser & Marcu 2007). For the multiword expression *duloxetine-treated patients*, the methods "FEATURE" and "CORPUS" provide a same translation which is more or less correct (*patients traités duloxetine*). However, the method "TABLE" provides a translation in a poor grammar (*patients duloxetine traités*).

Finally on this point, we can observe that the major issues of Moses concern errors produced by Giza++ when aligning multiword expressions (translation model), and incorrect spelling and poor grammar generated by the decoder (language model). To handle the first issue, we proposed to take into account the specialized bilingual lexicon extracted with the MWEs aligner into Moses's phrase table and we added a new feature indicating whether a word comes from this lexicon or not ("FEATURE" method). However, for spelling and grammar errors, Moses has no specific treatment.

6 Conclusion and future work

We have described, in this chapter, three approaches aiming to extract and align MWEs in English-French parallel corpora. We have also presented an experimental evaluation of the impact of integrating the results of these MWEs alignment approaches on the performance of the statistical machine translation system Moses. We have more specifically shown that, on the one hand, the hybrid approach based on morpho-syntactic patterns performs better than the other approaches and the "FEATURE" integration method achieves the best improvement, and on the other hand, using MWEs as additional parallel sentences to train the translation model of Moses improves its BLEU score.

This study offers several open issues for future work. First, we should explore machine learning approaches to extend the morphosyntactic patterns to take into account other forms of MWEs. The second perspective is to explore the integration of bilingual MWEs into other machine translation models such as rule-based translation ones. We also expect to explore the use of LSTM (Long Short-Term Memory) recurrent neural network language models for rescoring the *n*-best translations produced by Moses in order to reduce grammar errors.

References

Barbu, Ana Maria. 2004. Simple linguistic methods for improving a word alignment algorithm. In *Proceedings of the 7th international conference on the Statistical Analysis of Textual Data (JADT 2004)*, 88–98. Louvain-la-Neuve, Belgium.

Barz, Irmhild. 1996. Komposition und Kollokation. In Clemens Knobloch & Burkhard Schaeder (eds.), *Nomination – fachsprachlich und gemeinsprachlich*, 127–146. Springer.

Besançon, R., G. De Chalendar, O. Ferret, F. Gara, M. Laib, O. Mesnard & N. Semmar. 2010. LIMA: A multilingual framework of linguistic analysis and linguistic resources development and evaluation. In *Proceedings of the seventh international conference on Language Resources and Evaluation (LREC 2010)*, 3697–3704.

Blank, Ingeborg. 2000. Terminology extraction from parallel technical texts. In *Parallel text processing*, 237–252. Springer.

Bouamor, Dhouha, Nasredine Semmar & Pierre Zweigenbaum. 2012a. A study in using English-Arabic multiword expressions for statistical machine translation. In *Proceedings of the fourth international conference on Arabic Language Processing (CITALA-2012)*, 71–76. Rabat, Morocco.

Bouamor, Dhouha, Nasredine Semmar & Pierre Zweigenbaum. 2012b. Automatic construction of a multiword expressions bilingual lexicon: A statistical machine translation evaluation perspective. In *Proceedings of the 3rd workshop on Cognitive Aspects of the Lexicon (CogALex-III)*, 95–108. Mumbai, India.

Bouamor, Dhouha, Nasredine Semmar & Pierre Zweigenbaum. 2012c. Identifying bilingual multi-word expressions for statistical machine translation. In *Proceedings of the eigth international conference on Language Resources and Evaluation (LREC 2012)*, 674–679. Istanbul, Turkey.

Boulaknadel, Siham, Béatrice Daille & Driss Aboutajdine. 2008. A multiterm extraction program for Arabic language. In *Proceedings of the international conference on Language Resources and Evaluation (LREC 2008)*, 1485–1488. Marrakech, Morocco.

Burger, H. 2010. Phraseologie: Eine Einführung am Beispiel des Deutschen [Phraseology: An introduction for German]. *Grundlagen der Germanistik* 36(4).

Calzolari, Nicoletta, Alessandro Lenci, Francesca Bertagna & Antonio Zampolli. 2002. Broadening the scope of the EAGLES/ISLE lexical standardization initiative. In *COLING '02: proceedings of the 3rd workshop on Asian Language Resources and International Standardization*, 1–8. Morristown, NJ, USA: Association for Computational Linguistics.

Carpuat, Marine & Mona Diab. 2010. Task-based evaluation of multiword expressions: A pilot study in statistical machine translation. In *Human Language Technologies: the 2010 annual conference of the North American chapter of the Association for Computational Linguistics (NAACL/HLT 2010)*, 242–245.

Choueka, Yaacov. 1988. Looking for needles in a haystack or locating interesting collocational expressions in large textual databases. In *Proceedings of the 2nd international conference on Computer-Assisted Information Retrieval (recherche d'information assistée par ordinateur) - RIAO'88*, 609–624. Cambridge, MA, USA.

Constant, Mathieu, Isabelle Tellier, Denys Duchier, Yoann Dupont, Anthony Sigogne & Sylvie Billot. 2011. Intégrer des connaissances linguistiques dans un CRF: application à l'apprentissage d'un segmenteur-étiqueteur du français. In *Taln*, vol. 1, 321.

Dagan, Ido & Ken Church. 1994. Termight: Identifying and translating technical terminology. In *Proceedings of the fourth conference on Applied Natural Language Processing (ANLP'94)*, 34–40.

Daille, Béatrice. 2001. Extraction de collocation à partir de textes. In *Actes de la 8ème conférence sur le Traitement Automatique des Langues Naturelles (TALN)*, 3–8. Tours, France: Association pour le Traitement Automatique des Langues.

Daille, Béatrice, Eric Gaussier & Jean-Marc Langé. 1994. Towards automatic extraction of monolingual and bilingual terminology. In *Proceedings of the 15th international conference on Computational linguistics (COLING 1994)*, 515–521.

DeNero, John & Dan Klein. 2008. The complexity of phrase alignment problems. In *Proceedings of the 46th annual meeting of the Association for Computational Linguistics on Human Language Technologies: Short papers*, 25–28.

Fraser, Alexander & Daniel Marcu. 2007. Measuring word alignment quality for statistical machine translation. *Computational Linguistics* 33(3). 293–303.

Gao, Zhao-Ming. 1998. Automatic acquisition of a high-precision translation lexicon from parallel Chinese-English corpora. *Language* 248. 254.

Gaussier, Éric & François Yvon. 2011. *Modèles statistiques pour l'accès à l'information textuelle*. Lavoisier.

Germann, Ulrich. 2008. Yawat: Yet another word alignment tool. In *Proceedings of the ACL-08: HLT demo session*, 20–23. Columbus, Ohio, USA: Association for Computational Linguistics. https://www.aclweb.org/anthology/P08-4006.

Hogan, Deirdre, Conor Cafferkey, Aoife Cahill & Josef Van Genabith. 2007. Exploiting multi-word units in history-based probabilistic generation. In *Proceedings of the joint conference on Empirical Methods in Natural Language Processing (EMNLP) and Computational Natural Language Learning (CoNLL)*, 267–276. Prague, Czech Republic.

Jackendoff, Ray. 1997. *The architecture of the language faculty*. Cambridge, MA, USA: MIT Press.

Koehn, Philipp & Hieu Hoang. 2007. Factored translation models. In *Proceedings of the 2007 joint conference on Empirical Methods in Natural Language Processing and Computational Natural Language Learning (EMNLP-CoNLL)*, 868–876.

Koehn, Philipp, Hieu Hoang, Alexandra Birch, Chris Callison-Burch, Marcello Federico, Nicola Bertoldi, Brooke Cowan, Wade Shen, Christine Moran, Richard Zens, Chris Dyer, Ondrej Bojar, Alexandra Constantin & Eva Herbst. 2007. Moses: Open source toolkit for statistical machine translation. In *Proceedings of the 45th annual meeting of the ACL on interactive poster and demonstration sessions*, 177–180. Prague, Czech Republic.

Kupiec, Julian. 1993. An algorithm for finding noun phrase correspondences in bilingual corpora. In *Proceedings of the 31st annual meeting on Association for Computational Linguistics*, 17–22.

Marchand, Morgane & Nasredine Semmar. 2011. A hybrid multi-word terms alignment approach using word co-occurrence with a bilingual lexicon. In *Proceedings of the fifth Language and Technology Conference: Human language technologies as a challenge for computer science and linguistics*, 430–434. Poznań, Poland.

Nivre, Joakim & Jens Nilsson. 2004. Multiword units in syntactic parsing. In *Workshop on Methodologies and Evaluation of Multiword Units in Real-World Applications*, 39–46.

Och, F. J. & H. Ney. 2000. Improved statistical alignment models. In *Proceedings of the 38th annual meeting on Association for Computational Linguistics (acl 2000)*, 440–447.

Okita, Tsuyoshi, Alfredo Maldonado Guerra, Yvette Graham & Andy Way. 2010. Multi-word expression-sensitive word alignment. In *4th international workshop on Cross Lingual Information Access at COLING 2010*, 26–34. Beijing, China.

Papineni, Kishore, Salim Roukos, Todd Ward & Wei-Jing Zhu. 2002. BLEU: A method for automatic evaluation of machine translation. In *Proceedings of the 40th annual meeting on Association for Computational Linguistics (ACL 2002)*, 311–318.

Ramisch, Carlos, Aline Villavicencio & Valia Kordoni. 2013. Introduction to the special issue on multiword expressions: From theory to practice and use. *ACM Transactions on Speech and Language Processing (TSLP)* 10(2). 3.

Ren, Z., Y. Lü, J. Cao, Q. Liu & Y. Huang. 2009. Improving statistical machine translation using domain bilingual multiword expressions. In *Proceedings of the workshop on Multiword Expressions: Identification, Interpretation, Disambiguation and Applications*, 47–54.

Riehemann, Susanne. 2001. *A constructional approach to idioms and word formation*. Stanford University dissertation.

Sag, Ivan, Timothy Baldwin, Francis Bond, Ann Copestake & Dan Flickinger. 2002. Multiword expressions: A pain in the neck for NLP. In *Proceedings of the 3rd international conference on Computational Linguistics and Intelligent Text Processing* (Lecture Notes in Computer Science 2276), 1–15. Springer.

Salton, G., A. Wong & C. S. Yang. 1975. A vector space model for automatic indexing. *Communications of the ACM* 18(11). 613–620.

Semmar, Nasredine, Christophe Servan, Gaël De Chalendar, Benoît Le Ny & Jean-Jacques Bouzaglou. 2010. A hybrid word alignment approach to improve translation lexicons with compound words and idiomatic expressions. In *Proceedings of the 32nd Translating and the Computer conference (ASLIB 2010)*. London, UK.

Seretan, Violeta & Eric Wehrli. 2007. Collocation translation based on sentence alignment and parsing. In *Actes de la 14ème conférence sur le Traitement Automatique des Langues Naturelles (TALN 2007)*, 401–410. Toulouse, France.

Tiedemann, Jörg. 2012. Parallel data, tools and interfaces in OPUS. In *Proceedings of the eighth international conference on Language Resources and Evaluation (LREC-2012)*, 2214–2218. Istanbul, Turkey.

Tufiş, Dan & Radu Ion. 2007. Parallel corpora, alignment technologies and further prospects in multilingual resources and technology infrastructure. In *Proceedings of the 4th international conference on Speech and Dialogue Systems*, 183–195.

Vechtomova, Olga. 2005. The role of multi-word units in interactive information retrieval. In *European conference on Information Retrieval*, 403–420.

Vintar, Špela & Darja Fišer. 2008. Harvesting multi-word expressions from parallel corpora. In *Proceedings of the 6th edition of the Language Resources and Evaluation conference (LREC 2008)*, 1091–1096.

Wu, Chien-Cheng & Jason S Chang. 2003. Bilingual collocation extraction based on syntactic and statistical analyses. In *Proceedings of Research on Computational Linguistics conference XV (ROCLING'2003)*, 33–55. Hsinchu, Taiwan: The Association for Computational Linguistics & Chinese Language Processing (ACLCLP). http://aclweb.org/anthology/O03-1003.

Chapter 10

Cross-lingual linking of multi-word entities and language-dependent learning of multi-word entity patterns

Guillaume Jacquet

European Commission, Joint Research Centre, Ispra, Italy

Maud Ehrmann

Swiss Federal Institute of Technology in Lausanne (EPFL) – Digital Humanities Laboratory

Jakub Piskorski

European Commission, Joint Research Centre, Ispra, Italy

Hristo Tanev

European Commission, Joint Research Centre, Ispra, Italy

Ralf Steinberger

European Commission, Joint Research Centre, Ispra, Italy

We address large-scale multilingual multi-word entity (MWEntity) recognition and variant matching. Firstly, we recognise MWEntities in 22 different languages, identify monolingual variant spellings and link equivalent groups of variants across all languages. We then use the previously recognised MWEntities to learn new recognition rules based on distributional patterns. Not requiring any linguistic tools, the method is suitable for our highly multilingual environment. When adding the new rules to the original rule-based NER system, F1 performance for Spanish increases from 42.4% to 50% (18% increase) and for English from 43.4% to 44.5% (2.5% increase). Besides aiming at turning free text into semi-structured data for search and for machine-processing purposes, we use the system to link related news over time and across languages, as well as to detect trends.

Guillaume Jacquet, Maud Ehrmann, Jakub Piskorski, Hristo Tanev & Ralf Steinberger. 2019. Cross-lingual linking of multi-word entities and language-dependent learning of multi-word entity patterns. In Yannick Parmentier & Jakub Waszczuk (eds.), *Representation and parsing of multiword expressions: Current trends*, 269–297. Berlin: Language Science Press.   DOI:10.5281/zenodo.2579049

G. Jacquet, M. Ehrmann, J. Piskorski, H. Tanev & R. Steinberger

1 Introduction

Named Entities (NEs) such as persons, organisations, locations and events are major bearers of information in text as they provide answers to the text representation questions *Who did What to Whom, Where and When.* For this reason, work on NER and Classification is abundant (Nadeau & Turney 2005) and NEs have been linked to knowledge bases (Rao et al. 2013; McNamee & Dang 2009). Major challenges are homographic entity names belonging to different classes or within the same class and the existence of variant spellings within the same or across different languages, as well as morphological inflection (Steinberger et al. 2013). An additional challenge for names of organisations and events is that they may be referred to as multi-word expressions or acronyms, e.g., *Economic Community of West African States* (abbreviated as ECOWAS), and that name parts are likely to be translated, e.g., the equivalent Portuguese *Comunidade Económica dos Estados da África Ocidental* (abbreviated as CEDEAO). Users searching for such an entity will want to retrieve all mentions, independently of their spelling or abbreviation or language.

Our interest in entity variants originally stems from our multiannual work on the *Europe Media Monitor* (EMM), which is a freely accessible meta-news web platform[1] that has been online since 2002 (Steinberger et al. 2009; 2015). EMM currently gathers an average of 300,000 news articles per day in about 70 languages from about 8,000 news websites (HTML pages and RSS feeds). News items are classified into thousands of categories and related news (e.g., from different news sources) are grouped into clusters. EMM-NewsBrief and the medical information system EMM-MediSys group the newest articles every ten minutes and show intra-day trends, while EMM-NewsExplorer groups related articles published on the same calendar day and follows trends over longer periods of time. For each news article and for each news cluster, the system displays extracted meta-information, which includes the news category, entity names found (persons, organisations and geo-locations), quotations by and about entities, as well as various types of statistics, trends and analysis results. Entity mentions are disambiguated according to entity types (e.g., *Paris Hilton* is a person) and geographical reference (e.g., there are about fifteen places world-wide called *Paris*). Spelling variants of the same person or organisation name are mostly recognised as belonging to the same real-world entity. For instance, the spellings *Jean-Claude Juncker, Jean Cloud Junker, Jean-Claude Juencker,* Жан-Клод Юнкер, *Ζαν Κλοντ Γιούνκερ,* جان كلود جونكر, *Ζαν Κλοντ Γιούνκερ,* 让-克洛 德 · 容克 and many

---

[1] See http://emm.newsbrief.eu/overview.html and http://emm.newsexplorer.eu/

others are all identified as referring to the 12th President of the European Commission. Such multilingual entity variants – and also disambiguated place names – are a major ingredient for the successful identification of related news across languages in EMM-NewsExplorer. The system was entirely developed by the European Commission's Joint Research Centre (JRC) with the purpose of providing media monitoring functionality for the European institutions, for national authorities of the European Union (EU) Member States, for international organisations such as the United Nations or the African Union, as well as for EU partner country organisations. However, the results are also freely accessible to the wider public through web pages and as customisable mobile applications.

Person name recognition is rather well-implemented in EMM, but the coverage of multi-word organisation and event names has traditionally been rather poor because they behave like free text, i.e. they may include lower-case words, prepositions, determiners, etc. Recognising such complex MWEntity types would benefit from using syntax parsers, part-of-speech taggers, morphological analysers and generic dictionaries, but EMM cannot use these because of its need to process very large volumes of text data in near-real time and because such resources are not easily available nor quick to develop (Steinberger et al. 2013). In response to this shortcoming, the EMM team has engaged in less knowledge-intensive ways of recognising multi-word entities such as those presented in this chapter. Our general idea is to collect large numbers of known entities using patterns to recognise acronyms and their long-forms (presented in Section 3) and then to use these to learn light-weight recognition patterns for such complex MWEntities (Section 4). In order to validate this last step independently of the quality of the initially automatically created resource, we did our first experiments using MWEntity lists derived from the BabelNet resource to learn recognition patterns in a couple of languages.

In the following sections, we will first summarise the state-of-the-art for the recognition of acronyms and other multi-word entities, as well as for the recognition of monolingual and cross-lingual entity variants (Section 2). Section 3 focuses on methods and results to recognise acronyms and their expansions (e.g., *EC – European Commission*) and to identify the variant spellings and translations. In Section 4, we present different pattern learning methods that will help with the recognition of multi-word entities that are not found next to their acronyms and we will compare their relative performance. We will conclude our chapter with a summary and with pointers to future work.

2 Related work

As mentioned in the introduction, multi-word entity recognition is strongly related to acronym recognition. This statement will be further developed in the following sections.

Work in the domain of abbreviation processing is abundant, but it mostly focuses on the biomedical domain and on the English language. Since the pioneer work of Taghva & Gilbreth (1999), research has developed into three main directions, namely acronym extraction and mapping to their expansions; acronym variant clustering; and, more recently, acronym disambiguation. While the extraction of acronym/expansion pairs corresponds to the primary stage of lexical unit acquisition, variant clustering resembles sense inventory organisation, which can eventually serve as reference for disambiguation. We report here on the first two aspects.

With regard to acronym extraction, existing work almost exclusively focuses on English biomedical literature (Schwartz & Hearst 2003; Okazaki & Ananiadou 2006; James et al. 2001; Wren & Garner 2002; Adar 2004; Chang et al. 2002; Nadeau & Turney 2005). Results are good and the extraction-recognition step can be considered a mature technology for this combination of domain and language. However, there is very little work on other languages: Kokkinakis & Dannélls (2006) investigate the specificity of Swedish, Siklósi et al. (2014) carry out Hungarian abbreviation processing, both on medical texts. Kompara (2010) and Hahn et al. (2005) seem to be the only ones to work with acronyms *across* languages, with preliminary work on Slovene, English and Italian for the former, and acronym alignment across English, German, Portuguese and Spanish based on an interlingua for the latter.

As mentioned previously, the variety and the number of acronyms is very large so that it is useful to organise the acronym dataset on a semantic basis by grouping related variants under the same acronym identifier. The aim is thus – for each set of expansions having the same acronym – to identify those which are conceptually related. Previous related work focused mainly, anew, on biomedical literature in English. Adar (2004) experimented with k-means clustering based on an n-gram similarity measure and on a MeSH term similarity measure. Results showed that the n-gram based clustering performs actually better than that based on the MeSH resource. Okazaki et al. (2010) designed a more complex clustering approach, using a similarity metric based on a mixture of several features. Once the best feature setting has been acquired (by supervised machine learning), hierarchical clustering is used to induce the final variant grouping. The features used to build the similarity metric are themselves similarity measures, such as character and word n-gram similarity. The outcome of these experiments on English abbreviations showed that character and word n-gram features contribute the most to the final result. Work on monolingual clustering of acronym variants outside the biomedical domain and for altogether 22 different languages was carried out in Ehrmann et al. (2013). Ehrmann's approach is based on hierarchical group-average clustering, where cluster homogeneity is set using an empirically determined threshold. The clustering depends on a pair-wise string similarity between expansions, using a normalised Levenshtein edit distance.

To the best of our knowledge, no work has been carried out for acronym clustering across languages. What comes closest to this or, more exactly, to its result, are multilingual lexical resources such as BabelNet (Navigli & Ponzetto 2012) or YAGO (Hoffart et al. 2013). Automatically built based on the mapping between WordNet and Wikipedia (and other resources), these resources provide (among others) multilingual variants of expansions for specific acronyms. They are inherited from cross-lingual and cross-script links provided in Wikipedia. In contrast, the work presented here starts from raw data extracted from real-life texts.

As regards learning resources for the recognition and classification of named entities and domain-specific multi-word expressions, a vast bulk of research has been reported on using weakly-supervised approaches. These are based, in particular, on the bootstrapping paradigm in which, starting from an initial set of annotated examples (or seeds), the learning process proceeds without further supervision, until a convergence criterion is reached. Some examples of the work in this field is presented in Riloff (1996); Collins & Singer (1999), and Yangarber et al. (2002).

With the emergence of large-scale knowledge bases and the availability of web-scale corpora, numerous efforts on exploiting such resources for developping named entity recognition and classification tools have been reported. For instance, Nothman et al. (2013) reports on a multilingual NER approach based on using Wikipedia links for automatically annotating a huge corpus for training purposes, whereas Downey et al. (2007) presents a novel method for detecting complex (multi-word) named entities using solely capitalisation information and n-gram statistics over a Web corpus. This approach outperformed standard supervised and semi-supervised approaches for named-entity recognition in cases of complex names of types not known in advance.

Our contribution complements prior work and focuses on exploiting the vast number of named entities contained in BabelNet (Navigli & Ponzetto 2012) for learning structurally simple and linguistically unsophisticated patterns for the recognition of multi-word named entities in various languages.

3 Creation of the multilingual MWEntity resource

In this section, we describe completed work (Jacquet et al. 2016) on recognising MWEntities and their corresponding acronyms in large volumes of text in 22 different languages, on identifying monolingual variants for the same entity and on linking the equivalent groups of variants across all languages. Figure 1 illustrates that task with an example of cross-lingual linking, which shows that we can neither assume that entities across languages have the same acronym, nor can we assume that the same acronym (within the same or across languages) refers to only one entity. The result of this work is a collection of currently 64,000 MWEntities plus their 600,000 multilingual lexical variants.

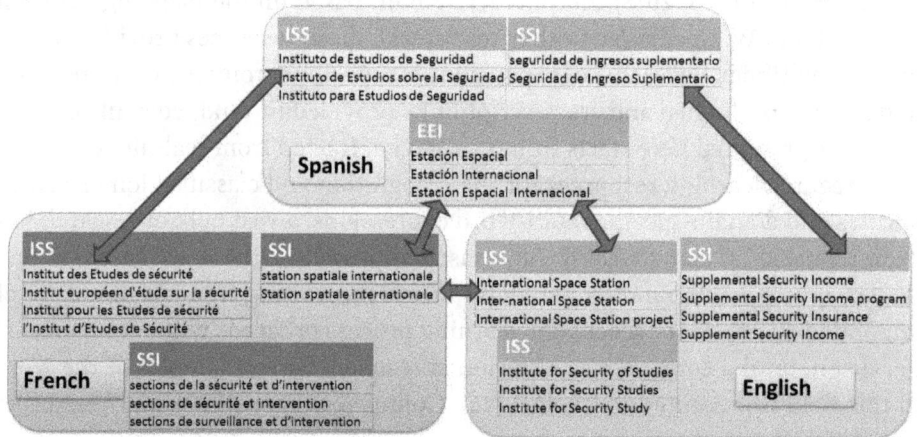

Figure 1: Example of multilingual MWEntity linking

3.1 Starting point

The starting point of our work is a large set of multi-word entities and their corresponding acronyms in 22 Roman-script languages (Ehrmann et al. 2013). These acronym/expansion pairs were extracted from the news stream analysed by the EMM processing chain by applying patterns similar to those proposed by Schwartz & Hearst (2003). In a nutshell, the algorithm collects acronym/expansion pairs (such as *expansion (acronym)* and *acronym (expansion)*) by identifying short strings within parenthesis, along with candidate expansions in a side-window of a limited length. A filtering step is then applied, with the following main constraints: the first letter of the acronym must be upper-cased, and the length of the expansion must be smaller than (a) twice as many words as there are characters in the acronym, or (b) the number of characters in the acronym plus five words, whichever is the smaller (i.e. min($|A| + 5, |A| * 2$) words, with $|A|$ being the number of characters of the acronym). We refer the reader to Schwartz & Hearst (2003) for more details. This process resulted in the extraction of 1.7 million expansions for 0.4 million different acronyms.

Applied on news articles, this method identified acronym/expansion pairs referring mostly to organisation names (e.g., *CP – Communist Party*), but also events (*WW2 – World War II*), names of drugs or of vaccines (*MMR – measles, mumps, rubella*), organisation types (*NGO – non-governmental organisation*), job titles (*MEP – Member of Parliament*), physical measurement units (*kmh – kilometres per hour*), and more. As one of the next steps, we will work on categorising the acronym/expansion pairs into various semantic categories.

To automatically determine which of the expansions are lexical variants of the same conceptual entity, a clustering step was carried out, on the basis of expansions having the same language and the same acronym. This monolingual clustering, based on a pair-wise string similarity, allowed to distinguish between sets of conceptually related expansions, such as those referring to the *International Space Station* and those referring to the *Institute for Security of Studies*, both clusters having the acronym *ISS* (cf. English part of Figure 1). Evaluated over the 10 most covered languages, this monolingual clustering has a micro-average precision of 95.2% (Jacquet et al. 2014).

Out of this monolingual clustering step, we selected only clusters having at least four expansions, resulting in 81,000 monolingual clusters with an average of 7.5 expansions per cluster, the biggest one having 232 expansions.

Based on this data, the objective is to go a step further by identifying cross-lingual multi-word entity lexical variants. More specifically, the goal is to link multilingual expansions referring to the same entity across languages and regardless of their acronyms. To this end, we leverage the previously computed monolingual clusters and attempt to link them across languages. Considering the previous example with the entity *International Space Station* (cf. Figure 1), this results in aggregating the monolingual clusters *SSI – Station spatiale internationale* (French), *ISS – International Space Station* (English) and *EEI – Estación Espacial* (Spanish). Additionally to linking expansions across languages and independently from their acronym, cross-lingual cluster aggregation can also revise monolingual clusters by aggregating those conceptually related but isolated because of their acronyms (both pairs *IMF – International Monetary Fund* and *FMI – Fondo Monetario Internazionale* occur in Italian texts).

3.2 Approach

Cluster aggregation can be cast as the problem of identifying connected components of a graph, where monolingual clusters represent vertices and where edges need to be computed. This section describes different cross-lingual aggregation strategies tested in our experiments (cf. Section 3.3) to link sets of monolingual clusters across languages.

3.2.1 Cluster aggregation based on common expansions

The most straightforward solution to link related acronyms in different languages (hereafter *ExpAgg*) is to merge those clusters that have more than n expansion forms in common, independently of whether their acronyms are identical or not (in our experiments, n was set to 1). This aggregation has been applied both to improve monolingual clusters (cf. IMF vs FMI case mentioned at the end of Section 3.1) and to aggregate clusters across languages.

3.2.2 Cluster aggregation based on tokens

3.2.2.1 Cluster representation

For the two following aggregation strategies, monolingual clusters are no longer represented by vectors of expansions, but by a vector of all individual tokens appearing in the expansions.

C is the resulting ($|\mathbb{C}| \times |\mathbb{T}|$) cluster-token matrix where $c_i : i = 1, \ldots, |\mathbb{C}|$ is a monolingual cluster, and $t_j : j = 1, \ldots, |\mathbb{T}|$ is a token. $\mathbb{T}$ contains all the tokens across languages which appear at least once in an expansion. If a token is present in different languages, such as *place* in English and *place* in French, it corresponds to different tokens in $\mathbb{T}$.

Each token has its own importance to describe a cluster. In order to compare two clusters on the basis of their most relevant tokens, we consider the tf-idf value of each token t_j where, in our context, each cluster c_i is seen as a document and the whole set of clusters $\mathbb{C}$ as a corpus:

(1)
$$C(c_i, t_j) = \mathrm{tf}(t_j, c_i) \times \mathrm{idf}(t_j, \mathbb{C})$$

3.2.2.2 Cluster aggregation based on similar tokens

This aggregation (hereafter *TokAgg*) addresses cases where monolingual clusters do not have identical expansions across languages, but they have a significant amount of highly similar tokens.

Table 1: Example of clusters aggregated on the basis of similar tokens

Clusters	Expansion	Acronym	Language
cluster 1	*Social-Democratic Party*	*SDP*	en
	Social Democratic Party		
cluster 2	*Partito Social-Democratico*	*PSD*	it
	Partito di socialdemocratico		
	Partito socialdemocratico		

We compute the matrix ($|\mathbb{T}| \times |\mathbb{T}|$), hereafter *InvEdit*, which corresponds to the inverse of the normalised Levenshtein edit distance where $t_i : i = 1, \ldots, |\mathbb{T}|$ and $t_j : j = 1, \ldots, |\mathbb{T}|$ are tokens from all the addressed languages:

$$(2) \qquad \text{InvEdit}(t_i, t_j) = 1 - \frac{\text{Lev}(t_i, t_j)}{\max(|t_i|, |t_j|)}$$

$\text{Lev}(t_i, t_j)$ is the Levenshtein edit-distance between t_i and t_j, and $|t_i|$ and $|t_j|$ are respectively the length of the tokens t_i and t_j. We filter InvEdit using a threshold δ as follows:

$$(3) \qquad \text{InvEdit}(t_i, t_j, \delta) = \begin{cases} \text{InvEdit}(t_i, t_j) & : \text{InvEdit}(t_i, t_j) \geq \delta \\ 0 & : \text{InvEdit}(t_i, t_j) < \delta \end{cases}$$

In this case, if $\delta = 1$, InvEdit only contains values for exact matching tokens. This matrix is then used to enrich the monolingual cluster representation. Given two languages l_1 and l_2, the corresponding monolingual clusters C_{l_1} and C_{l_2} do not have common tokens since in $\mathbb{T}$ tokens are language-dependent. The InvEdit matrix is used to identify common or similar tokens. We convert the obtained matrix $C\_\text{Tok}_{l_1}$ to a binary matrix:

$$(4) \qquad C\_\text{Tok}_{l_1}(c_i, t_j) = \begin{cases} 1 & : C_{l_1}(c_i, t_j) \times \text{InvEdit}(c_i, t_j, \delta) > 0 \\ 0 & : \text{otherwise} \end{cases}$$

This aggregation is particularly useful when comparing clusters from similar languages. Table 1 illustrates such cases, with the English-Italian tokens *Party/Partito* and *Democratic/Democratico*. This representation can also benefit from the fact that it is possible to find multi-word entities of a given language in texts in another language (especially with names of international organisations such as *European Space Agency* which can be found in German text).

3.2.2.3 Cluster aggregation based on translated tokens

Table 2: Example of clusters aggregated on the basis of translated tokens

Clusters	Expansion	Acronym	Language
cluster 1	*Russian Academy of Sciences* *Russian of Academy of Sciences*	*RAS*	en
cluster 2	*russischen Akademie der Wissenschaften* *Russischen Akademie für Wissenschaften* *Russische Akademie der Wissenschaften*	*RAW*	de

However, many entities have different written forms across languages so that a string-based comparison of tokens is not successful. We therefore complement the cluster aggregation by using token translation probabilities (hereafter *TransTokAgg*).

They are produced using statistical translation models trained on parallel corpora built from Wikipedia, by making use of redirection tables (i.e. several written forms redirecting to a specific page/entity) and of interlingual links between pages (implementation details of translation models are provided in Section 3.3.3). In order to separate training and test data, any variant name from these Wikipedia tables matching with one of the 1.7 million expansions or 0.4 million acronyms is removed from the parallel corpora (see Section 3.3).

Let TransMod be the resulting ($|\mathbb{T}| \times |\mathbb{T}|$) translation model matrix where t_i : $i = 1, \ldots, |\mathbb{T}|$ and t_j : $j = 1, \ldots, |\mathbb{T}|$ are tokens. As for InvEdit matrix, we filter TransMod using a threshold β:

$$(5) \quad \text{TransMod}(t_i, t_j, \beta) = \begin{cases} \text{TransMod}(t_i, t_j) & : \text{TransMod}(t_i, t_j) \geq \beta \\ 0 & : \text{TransMod}(t_i, t_j) < \beta \end{cases}$$

This matrix is then used to enrich the monolingual cluster representation. Given a language l and its corresponding monolingual clusters C_l, C_TransTok_l corresponds to the binary extended matrix based on a given translation model:

$$(6) \qquad C\_\text{TransTok}_l(c_i, t_j) = \begin{cases} 1 : C_l(c_i, t_j) \times \text{TransMod}(c_i, t_j, \beta) > 0 \\ 0 : \text{otherwise} \end{cases}$$

Table 2 illustrates a case of such cluster aggregation, thanks to a high score in the TransMod matrix between tokens *Science* in English and *Wissenschaften* in German.

3.2.3 Aggregation strategies

We formulate cluster linking as the task of identifying connected components in a graph, where monolingual clusters are vertices and where edges represent links of related clusters across languages. Clusters are linked if their similarity is above a certain threshold α. During preliminary experiments, we had also tested *pure* clustering algorithms, but it turned out that the graph approach was more efficient.

For the last two cluster aggregation methods (TokAgg and TransTokAgg), we applied two similarity measures: cosine and ComMNZ. The latter is actually a data fusion algorithm (Fox & Shaw 1994) which we assimilate, in this context, to a similarity measure. This algorithm aims at measuring the similarity between two objects having multiple comparison criteria. Specifically, the overall similarity score between two objects is better when those objects have reasonable similarity scores for all criteria than when they have a very good similarity score for one criterion, and less good or no value for the others. In our case, it would promote the similarity between two clusters c_i and c_j if they have many similar or translated tokens t_k with a reasonable similarity score, and it would decrease the similarity between two clusters c_i and c_j if they have few similar or translated tokens t_k with a very high similarity score:

$$(7) \qquad \text{CombMNZ}(c_i, c_j) = \sum_{t_k \in c_j} \frac{C(c_i, t_k)}{\sum_{t_l \in c_i} C(c_i, t_l)} \times \sum_{t_k \in c_j} 1_{\{C(c_i, t_k) \neq 0\}}$$

3.3 Evaluation

3.3.1 Evaluation dataset

As described in Section 3.1, the starting point of our experiments is a set of 81,000 monolingual clusters with one acronym per cluster, an average of 7.5 expansions per cluster, many of them having few expansions, and the biggest 232 expansions.

We evaluate cross-lingual cluster aggregation against Wikipedia data excluding the part used for the translations models (see previous section). The gold standard corresponds to a set of Wikipedia redirection tables and interlingual linking tables, where we consider Wikipedia entities/pages as cross-lingual classes. Each class contains all the expressions listed in the redirection tables in all the languages linked via the interlingual linking tables. Only classes having at least two expansions were selected, resulting in a gold standard of 10,000 classes. Considering Wikipedia information as a gold standard is disputable. The interlingual linkings should be reliable but this is less the case for the redirection tables. However, a manual evaluation of the redirection table quality shows that, in over 160 randomly extracted classes in 4 different languages (fr, en, de, it), 93.4% of the forms were correct (Jacquet et al. 2014).

3.3.2 Parameters

Parameters have to be set with regards to, first, the thresholds δ and β applied to filter out some similarity values in the above-mentioned token matrices (C_Tok_l and C_TransTok_l) and, second, the threshold α applied to the aggregation strategies, i.e. the one above which clusters are aggregated.

With respect to cluster representations based on similar tokens C_Tok_l, the threshold δ should be high in order to consider two tokens as similar only if they are close in terms of edit distance. Regarding representations based on translated tokens C_TransTok_l, the threshold β can be low since even a weak token similarity could be a relevant indicator at the cluster level. For our experiments, the values of δ and β were fixed to 0.7 and 0.3 respectively.

Cluster aggregation is allowed when the cluster similarity (either in terms of cosine or CombMNZ) is above a certain threshold α. We experimented with different values for α, ranging from 0.7 to 1 (cf. Section 3.3.5).

This aggregation step is further regulated with the addition of the following constraints: two clusters c_1 and c_2 are linked if their similarity is above α and if c_1 is in the k most similar clusters of c_2 or c_2 is in the k most similar clusters of c_1. This additional constraints allow to rule out clusters having a high similarity with a lot of other clusters. This is the case for short and frequent expansions, e.g., *Olympic Committee* which is highly similar to a cluster containing expansions such as *Olympic Organizing Committee* or to another containing *games organising committee*, but as well to clusters containing more specific expansions such as *Vancouver Olympic Committee*. In our experiments, k equals 3.

3.3.3 Translation models

Cluster representations based on translated tokens correspond to lexical conditional translation probabilities computed for three language pairs, between English and French, German and Italian. The translation models were trained on parallel corpora built from Wikipedia, by making use of redirection tables (i.e. several written forms redirecting to a specific page/entity) and of interlingual links between pages. More specifically, given an entity/page p and two redirection tables rt_1 and rt_2 in languages l_1 and l_2, each written form from rt_1 can be seen as a translation t of each written form from rt_2. For a given language pair, the corresponding parallel corpus is the concatenation of all translations t from all the entities/pages p.

These Wikipedia tables are also used for evaluation purposes (see Section 3.3.1). As a consequence, the 1.7 million expansions and 0.4 million acronyms on which the approach is applied were removed from the parallel corpora.

There were about 300,000 training examples for German–English and French–English, and about 170,000 for Italian–English. Word alignments with many-to-one links were generated using the unsupervised fast_align tool (Dyer et al. 2013) in both directions and combined with the grow-diag-final-and symmetrisation heuristic (Koehn et al. 2003). Lexical translation tables for the three language pairs in both directions where extracted with a tool from the Moses translation toolkit (Koehn et al. 2007). Tables contain maximum likelihood probability estimated for the conditional word translation probabilities $p(\text{En}|\{\text{Fr, De, It}\})$ and $p(\{\text{Fr, De, It}\}|\text{En})$. Our TransMod matrix is constructed based on the concatenation of these tables.

3.3.4 Evaluation measures

Clusters are evaluated against the gold standard using micro-average precision and recall, adopting the mapping between identified clusters and gold standard clusters which maximised the F_1 measure. Micro-average precision (MAV-P) and recall (MAV-R) are defined as follows:

$$(8) \qquad \text{MAV-P}(C) = \frac{\sum_{c \in C} \text{EXP}(c)_{\text{true}}}{\sum_{c \in C} \text{EXP}(c)_{\text{true}} + \sum_{c \in C} \text{EXP}(c)_{\text{false}}}$$

$$(9) \qquad \text{MAV-R}(C) = \frac{\sum_{c \in C} \text{EXP}(c)_{\text{true}}}{\sum_{c \in C} \text{EXP}(c)_{\text{true}} + \sum_{c \in C} \text{EXP}(c)_{\text{miss}}}$$

where C is the set of produced clusters, $\text{EXP}(c)_{\text{true}}$ is the set of expansions in a cluster c which also appear in the corresponding class of the gold standard, and $\text{EXP}(c)_{\text{false}}$ is the set of expansions in a cluster c which do not appear in the gold standard.[2]

3.3.5 Results and discussion

Table 3: Cluster aggregation strategies for 3 language pairs

	MAV-P	MAV-R	F1
Baseline	97.7%	51.5%	67.4%
Monolingual ExpAgg	96.8%	54.8%	69.4%
Multilingual ExpAgg	96.9%	65.7%	78.2%
Cosine measure			
TokAgg	97.7%	52.5%	68.3%
TransTokAgg	97.6%	51.8%	67.7%
All aggregations	**95.5%**	**71.4%**	**81.6%**
ComMNZ measure			
TokAgg	97.7%	52.5%	68.3%
TransTokAgg	97.7%	51.6%	67.6%
All aggregations	**95.8%**	**71.2%**	**81.6%**

Table 3 reports the results obtained for the three language pairs for which we have a translation model, and Table 4 reports on a global evaluation for 22 languages. In both cases, values were computed with the aggregation similarity threshold α set to 0.9.

We defined the baseline as the concatenation of all monolingual clusters from all languages under consideration. It has a high precision (97.7% and 98.2% in Table 3 and 4 resp.) and a poor recall (51.5% and 40.5%) since none of the clusters is cross-lingual. The challenge is thus to improve the recall without affecting the precision too much.

In Tables 3 and 4, *monolingual ExpAgg* corresponds to the expansion aggregation strategy applied at the monolingual level, and *multilingual ExpAgg* at the multilingual level. The TokAgg and TransTokAgg lines correspond to results

---

[2]We tried two other metrics: macro-average and B-cubed measure (Bagga & Baldwin 1998) but since results are comparable we do not report them.

Table 4: Cluster aggregation strategies on 22 languages

	MAV-P	MAV-R	F1
Baseline	98.2%	40.5%	57.4%
Monolingual ExpAgg	97.0%	44.9%	60.5%
Multilingual ExpAgg	97.4%	54.6%	70.0%
Cosine measure			
TokAgg	98.2%	45.3%	62.0%
TransTokAgg	97.7%	41.1%	57.9%
All aggregations	**93.1%**	**65.9%**	77.2%
ComMNZ measure			
TokAgg	98.2%	45.3%	62.0%
TransTokAgg	98.2%	40.8%	57.6%
All aggregations	**95.8%**	**65.5%**	77.8%

with the corresponding token aggregation strategies using cosine similarity and CombMNZ fusion, and *All aggregations* to the ones obtained when using the four aggregation strategies in a joint way.

It can be observed that each aggregation strategy contributes to improving the quality of cross-lingual cluster aggregation, with multilingual ExpAgg providing the best improvement (+10.8 points for the 3 language pairs and +12.6 points for the 22 languages). The contribution of the TransTokAgg aggregation is slightly disappointing; it improves the baseline in both language configurations, but not significantly. Nevertheless, when all the aggregations are applied (bold lines), results are better than the addition of each single aggregation. It could mean that the TransTokAgg aggregation provides links between clusters which are not useful in isolation, but adds relevant bridges between sets of clusters when combined with other aggregations. Besides, one should notice that between the three language pairs and the 22 languages, improvements per aggregation strategy are comparable. Similarly, results obtained based on cosine similarity and CombMNZ fusion are comparable. This strengthens the reliability of the obtained results.

Figure 2 shows the impact of the threshold α. When too low (0.7), the F1 measure can be below the baseline because too many links are established between clusters; when too high (1.0), aggregations based on similar and translated tokens are reduced to values close to zero. In between, it has a clear improvement impact.

Overall, all aggregations strongly improve the baseline by increasing the recall (+19.7 and +23.4 points resp.) with a small loss in precision (−1.9 and −2.4 points resp.). Eventually, there are 64,000 cross-lingual connected clusters across languages instead of 81,000 monolingual ones for the 22 languages.

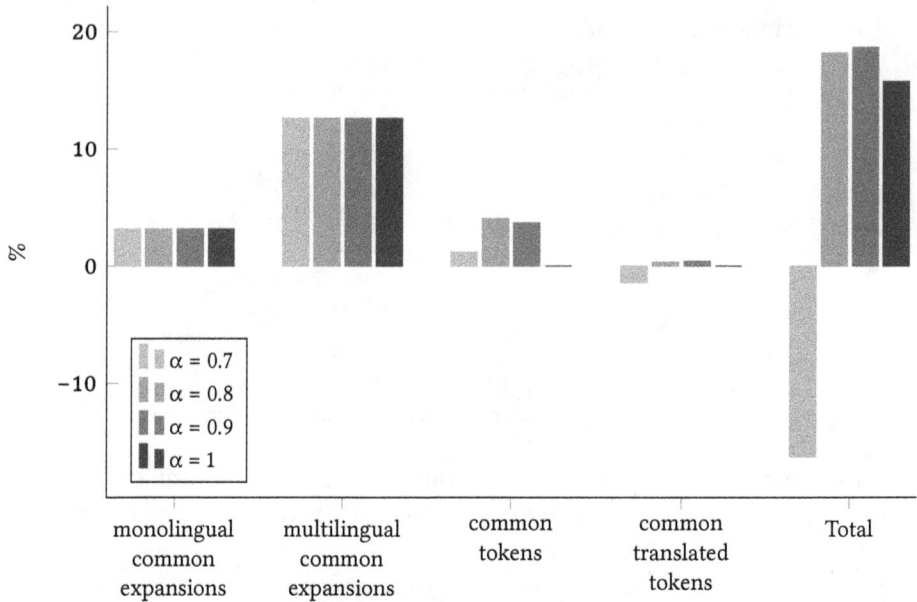

Figure 2: F1 improvement per aggregation type on 22 languages given α, using cosine similarity

4 Multi-word entity pattern learning

The previous section describes an approach which is useful to recognise frequently mentioned MWEntities and cluster them across languages, but it is limited to MWEntities mentioned at least once followed or preceded by its corresponding acronym. In this section we focus on a complementary approach to address the MWEntity recognition task. From the automatically obtained resource composed of 64,000 entities and their 600,000 multilingual lexical variants, we aim at learning MWEntity patterns in order to recognise new and not previously mentioned MWEntities. The described approach is ongoing work. Consequently, if the final goal is to learn these MWEntity patterns from the automatically extracted MWEntity resource, we must first control that our learning approach is reliable independently of the used MWEntity resource's quality. This section describes the use of an existing and reliable resource to evaluate our pattern learning approach.

4.1 Extraction of organisation names from BabelNet

For the sake of learning multi-word entity extraction patterns we have exploited BabelNet (Navigli & Ponzetto 2012), a large multilingual encyclopedic dictionary and semantic network, created by merging various publicly available linguistic resources, e.g., WordNet and Wikipedia. In particular, BabelNet contains circa 7.7 millions of named entity-related (NE-related) synsets. We used the BabelNet API[3] to extract organisation names for English and Spanish, which were then used in the process of learning patterns in various ways. Since the NE-related BabelNet synsets are not tagged with a specific NE tag, the NE type was inferred through utilisation of the hypernym information provided in BabelNet (i.e., using WordNet hypernyms and Wikipedia categories). To be more precise, based on hypernym frequency information for the entire set of named entities a list of *positive* (circa 200) and *negative* (circa 20) hypernyms was manually created. These lists were subsequently used to extract organisation names, i.e., a given synset was extracted if: (a) there was at least one hypernym for the main sense of the synset in the list of positive hypernyms, and (b) no hypernym for the main sense of the synset was on the list of negative hypernyms. For instance, the list of positive hypernyms for extracting organisations includes terms like: *airline, enterprise, corporation, bank, local_government, political_organisation, law_enforcement_agency*, whereas the list of negative hypernyms includes terms like *person* and *human*. The main drive behind the usage of negative hypernym list was to filter out potentially ambiguous named entity candidates. In total, we have extracted 647,898 and 127,264 organisation names for English and Spanish respectively. We exploited only names that consisted of at least two tokens for the multi-word organisation name pattern learning, which resulted in maintaining only 87.0% (557,841) of the English and 86.1% (127,264) of the Spanish organisation names extracted. Noteworthy, the resource for English obtained in this manner includes a portion of organisation names in foreign languages, which is most likely due to the fact that some non-English name variants have been tagged in BabelNet as variants in English. Since the entire procedure for pulling out organisation names from BabelNet is automated such language-specific name variants have not been manually removed.

---

[3]http://babelnet.org/guide

4.2 Learning multi-word entity patterns based solely on BabelNet resources

The first approach to learning multi-word organisation name extraction patterns exploits as the only resource the organisation names extracted from BabelNet (see Section 4.1). Therefrom, simple linear patterns are learned that consist of two types of elements, namely, surface forms (as they appear in the organisation names) and generic token classes, which will be referred to as token class elements. Example (10) illustrates the syntax of the patterns.

(10) University [] of [] the [] [UPP_W] [] in [] [UPP_W]
      [ALLCAP] [] [UPP_W] [] Construction [] Group
      The [] [NUM_LET] [] Company
      [UPP_W] [DASH] Institute

[] denotes a whitespace (not necessarily required to be included in the pattern as illustrated by the last pattern), whereas other token classes are delimited using square brackets. There are 28 generic token classes, out of which 8 cover natural language words (e.g., [UPP_W] – uppercase word, [LOW_W] – lowercase word, [ALLCAP] – all capital words), letters (e.g., [SINGCAP] – single capital letter), numbers (e.g., [NUM]) and combinations thereof (e.g., [NUM_LET] – sequence of digits followed by a sequence of letters, etc.), whereas the remaining 20 classes are used to denote specific symbols (e.g., brackets, commas, dots, colons, etc.).

The pattern learning process consists of three main steps: (a) acquisition of candidate patterns, (b) filtering unreliable and ambiguous candidate patterns, and (c) ranking patterns. These are described in more detail below.

4.2.1 Acquisition of candidate patterns

First, each organisation name is transformed into a candidate pattern, i.e., each token which can be found in a set of predefined surface forms (consisting of keywords that trigger organisation names, e.g., *University*, and frequently occurring word forms, e.g., prepositions) remains unchanged, whereas all other tokens are mapped into a corresponding generic token class. Each candidate pattern must contain at least one surface form and at least one token-class element, otherwise it is discarded.

The set of predefined surface forms has been computed automatically and consists of word uni-grams that fulfill the following criteria: (a) it appears more than $\phi = 20$ times as part of an organisation name, (b) it does not appear on a list of known toponyms,[4] (c) it does not appear on the list of known first names and

---

[4]We used GeoNames resource at: http://www.geonames.org for this purpose.

surnames,[5] and (d) it is not an adjective (unless it appears very frequently). For instance, for the subset of English organisation names consisting solely of company names, the 10 top-most frequent word uni-grams that fulfill the aforementioned criteria are: *Company, and, of, The, Group, Corporation, Bank, de, Limited* and *Air.*

4.2.2 Filtering candidate patterns

In the subsequent step, a candidate pattern is discarded if:

1. its final element is the token class [LOW_W] (any lowercase word), or

2. it contains only surface forms which are single uppercase letters and it does not contain any token-class element representing words starting with an uppercase letter (e.g., [UPP_W], [ALLCAP]), or

3. it starts with an initial uppercase letter, followed by an optional dot and a sequence of token classes corresponding to words starting with uppercase letters (and variations of this pattern), e.g., the following candidate pattern would be discarded: A [] [DOT] [] [UPP_W] [] [ALLCAP]

The filtering rules 1–2 are used in order to eliminate unreliable patterns, i.e., ones that are likely to overgenerate, whereas the filtering rule 3 aims at eliminating candidate patterns that are likely to match person names. The application of the filtering resulted in maintaining 47,496 (12,966) extraction patterns for English (Spanish), where 32.3% (41.9%) of these patterns were observed more than once. Interestingly, only 0.57% of English and 0.35% of the Spanish patterns occur more than 100 times.

4.2.3 Ranking patterns

In the final step candidate patterns are ranked with respect to their reliability based on the following general assumptions related to their structure:

- a pattern that contains either: (a) a larger fraction of surface forms vis-a-vis token-class elements, or (b) longer sequences of consecutive surface forms is deemed more reliable,

- a pattern whose final element is a lowercase surface form is deemed less reliable,

---

[5]We used for this purpose the *JRC Name Variant Database* and a huge list of first names extracted from Piskorski et al. (2011).

- a pattern that contains either: (a) a larger fraction of token-class elements representing single capital letters and lowercase words, or (b) longer sequences of consecutive token-class elements representing lowercase words is deemed less reliable.

The formal definition of the reliability score (Rel(p)) for a pattern p is given below, where the expressions starting with # denote the number of elements in the pattern of a specific type[6] and $\alpha = 0.2$, $\beta = 0.2$, $\gamma = 0.2$, $\delta = 0.15$, $\lambda = 0.1$ and $\kappa = 0.15$ are weighting coefficients for the various criteria used in the reliability ranking, whose values have been set based on empirical observations.

$$
\begin{aligned}
\text{Rel}(p) \;=\; & \frac{\#\text{SurfaceForms}(p) \cdot \alpha + \#\text{ConsecutiveSurfaceForms}(p) \cdot \beta}{\#\text{NonWhitespaces}(p)} \\
& - \frac{(\#\text{LowerCTokens}(p) \cdot \gamma + \#\text{ConsecutiveLowerCTokens}(p) \cdot \delta)}{\#\text{NonWhitespaces}(p)} \\
& - \frac{\#\text{SingleCapitalLetterTokens}(p) \cdot \lambda}{\#\text{NonWhitespaces}(p)} \\
& + \gamma + \delta + \lambda + (1 - \text{LastElementIsLowerCToken}(p)) \cdot \kappa
\end{aligned}
$$

A few examples of patterns with various reliability scores (provided in brackets) are given in (11).

```
(11)  Ministry [] of [] Foreign [] Affairs [] of [] [UPP_W]         (0.97)
      Institute [] of [] [UPP_W] [] Studies                         (0.95)
      [UPP_W] [] [UPP_W] [] [ALLCAP] [] at [] [UPP_W] [] University  (0.67)
      St [DOT] [] [LOW_W] [] [LOW_W] [] [LOW_W] [] [LOW_W] [] school (0.24)
      [UPP_W] [] [LOW_W] [] [LOW_W] [] [LOW_W] [] committee          (0.22)
```

Figure 3 depicts the distribution of patterns with respect to their reliability scores.

---

[6]#LowerCTokens(p) denotes the number of lowercase tokens, while #NonWhitespaces(p) denotes the number of elements in the pattern which are not whitespaces, i.e., it is a count of surface forms and token-class elements. LastElementIsLowercaseToken(p) denotes a function which returns 1 in case the last element of the pattern is a lowercase token class or 0 otherwise.

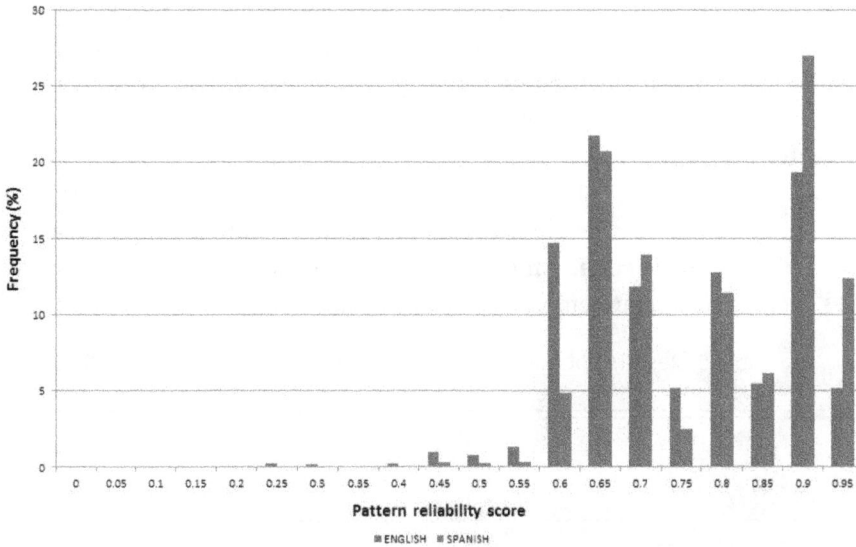

Figure 3: Distribution of patterns with respect to their reliability score for English and Spanish. Each of the bars represents the fraction of patterns, whose reliability score is within the range $(x, x + 0.5)$, where $x \in \{0, 0.5, \dots, 0.95\}$.

4.3 Evaluation

In order to evaluate the quality of the learned patterns we used two NE annotated corpora from the CoNLL shared task for English and Spanish[7], which contains respectively 6,300 and 7,389 organisation occurrences, and tested the performance using different settings. In particular, we compared three settings: (a) using only BabelNet-derived patterns (denoted in the figures with PATTERNS), (b) using only an existing rule-based NER system as a baseline (denoted RULES), (c) combining rule-based NER system and BabelNet-derived patterns (denoted in the figures with RULES+PATTERNS). In our experiments, we used an in-house rule based NER system (Steinberger et al. 2011; Ehrmann et al. 2015) that is geared towards high precision. The choice of a specific NER system is not decisive for these experiments, but by combining an existing NER system with our BabelNet-derived patterns, we aim at testing how our automatically created patterns could be useful to improve the quality of the NER recognition.

Figures 4, 5, 6 and 7 depict the performance of applying the BabelNet-derived patterns for English and Spanish in terms of precision and recall. The precision

---

[7]https://www.clips.uantwerpen.be/conll2002/ner/   and   https://www.clips.uantwerpen.be/conll2003/ner/

and recall values were computed for the varying minimum pattern reliability threshold in the range of {0.10, 0.15, ... , 0.95}, i.e., patterns below the minimum reliability threshold were discarded. The figures are showing the results obtained for exact matching (denoted with EXACT-PATTERNS or EXACT-RULES+PATTERNS) and for fuzzy matching, e.g., when there is a matching but with a left or right boundary mismatch (denoted with FUZZY-PATTERNS or FUZZY-RULES+PATTERNS). We did not visualise the results corresponding to the RULE setting in the figures because they do not depend on the reliability threshold. However, the obtained scores for this setting are embraced in Table 5.

Table 5: Results obtained with pattern reliability threshold = 0.60

	EXACT matching			FUZZY matching		
	P	**R**	**F1**	**P**	**R**	**F1**
Spanish						
PATTERNS	63.1%	10.2%	17.6%	81.4%	13.2%	22.8%
RULES	**79.8%**	24.2%	37.1%	**91.3%**	27.6%	42.4%
RULES+PATTERNS	73.5%	**31.0%**	**43.6%**	84.2%	**35.5%**	**50.0%**
English						
PATTERNS	48.5%	11.4%	18.5%	69.2%	16.3%	26.4%
RULES	**69.0%**	25.5%	37.3%	**80.4%**	29.7%	43.4%
RULES+PATTERNS	55.9%	**28.7%**	**37.9%**	65.6%	**33.6%**	**44.5%**

Table 5 provides the results obtained with a pattern-reliability threshold equal to 0.60, which corresponds to the best results obtained in both languages. For the EXACT evaluation, an improvement in terms of F1 of 6.5 points for Spanish could be observed with the setting RULES+PATTERNS versus the baseline RULES. As regards FUZZY evaluation, one could observe an improvement of F1 of 7.6 and 1.1 points for Spanish and English respectively when comparing RULES+PATTERNS versus the baseline RULES setting.

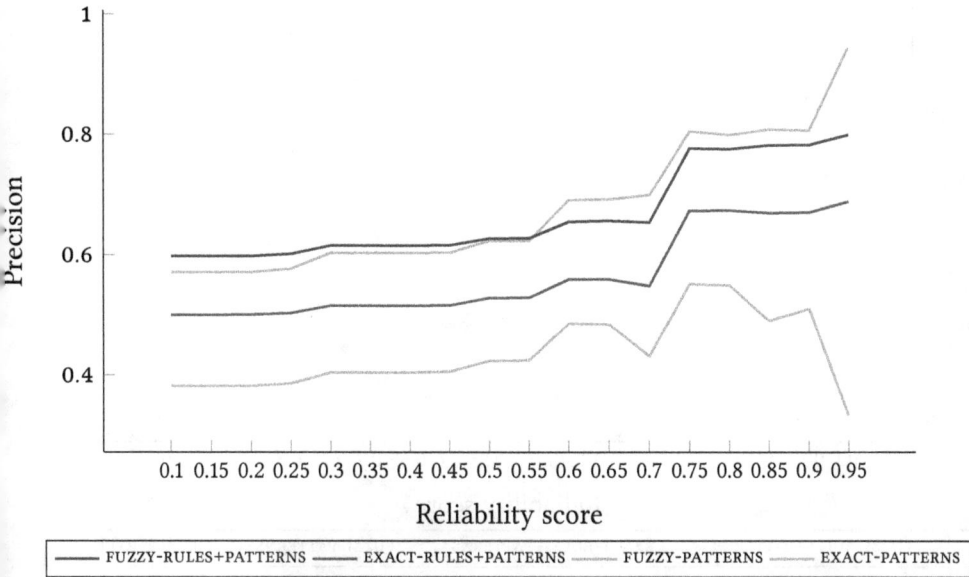

Figure 4: Experiments on English: Precision curves reflecting the performance of applying BabelNet-derived patterns and combining them with a rule-based NER system

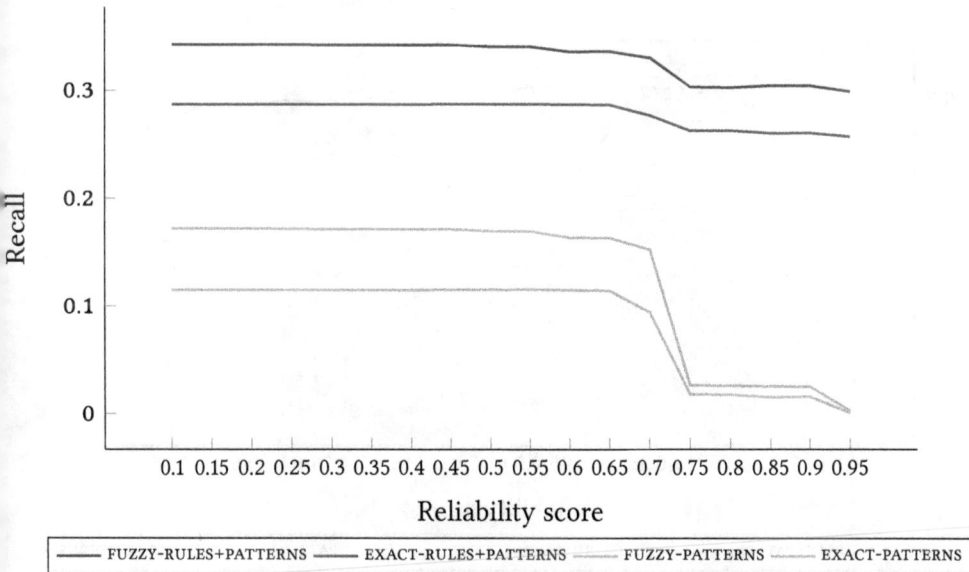

Figure 5: Experiments on English: Recall curves reflecting the performance of applying BabelNet-derived patterns and combining them with a rule-based NER system

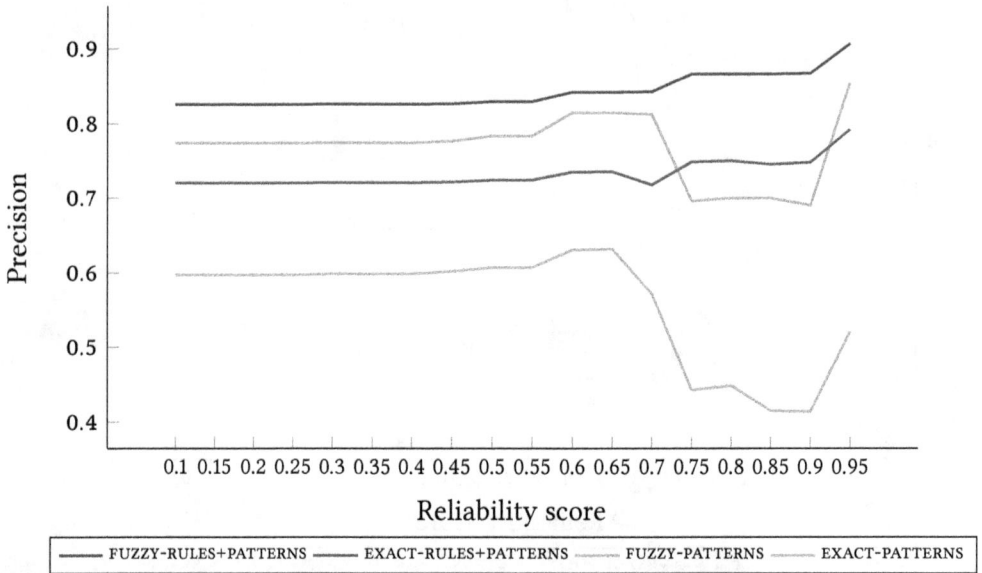

Figure 6: Experiments on Spanish: Precision curves reflecting the performance of applying BabelNet-derived patterns and combining them with a rule-based NER system

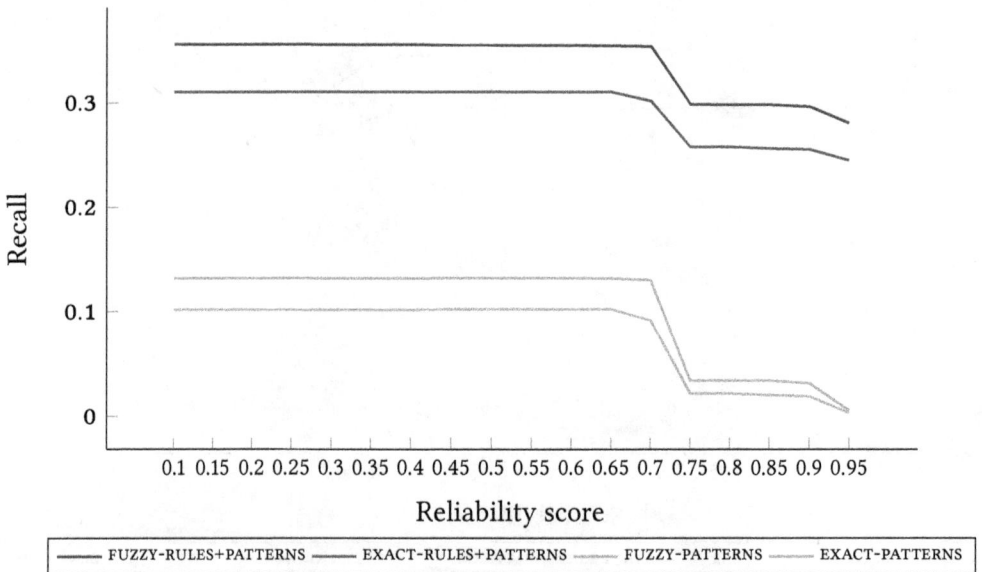

Figure 7: Experiments on Spanish: Recall curves reflecting the performance of applying BabelNet-derived patterns and combining them with a rule-based NER system

4.4 Mistakes and fuzzy matchings

Using existing NE annotated corpora for our preliminary experiments was the most obvious choice to measure the quality of our patterns. Nevertheless, it appears that some MWEntities recognised by the BabelNet-derived patterns considered as incorrectly extracted according to the annotated corpora, could still be considered as correct extractions. Figure 8 provides the complete list of "wrong" MWEntities (first column) recognised by our patterns when pattern reliability threshold equals 0.90. Even if some cases are clear mistakes, like *Results of European Super* or *Bank on Thursday*, a large fraction of the extractions could be considered as valid organisation names. The two other columns show the partial matches with the same reliability threshold, which are considered as incorrect in the *Exact matching* evaluation, and correct in the *Fuzzy matching* evaluation. Again, if some of them are clear mismatches, like *European Commission on Wednesday* or *NATO and the European Union*, most of the extractions appear to be consistent entities.

We expect to achieve higher precision of the learned patterns through embracing in the computation of the reliability score additional external evidence, i.e., exploiting contextual information obtained from pattern matchings in a web-scale corpus to judge the correctness.

"Wrong" patterns	LEFT boundary problems	RIGHT boundary problems
Major League Baseball	Brazilian Foreign Ministry	American University in Washington
Union National Bank	Chong Hing Investment Ltd	Association for Relations Across
Bank on Thursday	County Board of Education	Association of Lloyd
Results of European Super	Court of Appeals for the Fourth Circuit	Awami League of Prime
Sachs and Co.	Court of Appeals for the Ninth Circuit	Bosnian Association for Refugees
Results of European Cup	Credit Corp of USDA	British Securities and Investments
Bank of Pakistan	Democratic Party of Iran	Bureau of Alcohol
Foreign and Commonwealth Affairs	Department of Humanitarian Affairs	Department of Humanitarian
The News Agency	Gas Chemical Co Ltd	DLJ Merchant Banking Partners
Hospital School of Medicine	Illinois University at Carbondale	Economic Community of West
Police in Malta	Information Systems Co Ltd	European Commission on Wednesday
Brooks Investment Corp.	Life Insurance Co	European Union and the United States
Venture Partners of Menlo	Lodge of the University of the Witwatersrand	Government of National Unity
Department of Health	NATO and the European Union	Institute for Human Gene
Bank on Monday	Patriotic Union of Kurdistan	Irish Department of Enterprise
New England Telecommunications Corp	Rangoon Karen National Union	Kingston Technology Co.
Scottish League Cup	Rights Action League	Life Insurance Co
Police in Berovo	Staff Union of Universities	Lockhart Industries Inc.
Legislative Council on Wednesday	Taylor Made Co Ltd	Mallinckrodt Group Inc.
Yemeni Ministry of Petroleum	The Bank of Finland	Morgan Stanley and Co
	The Bank of France	National Council of Christian Churches
	The Foreign Ministry	NATO and the European Union
	The Lebanese Association for the Democracy of Elections	Security Council on Friday
	The National Basketball Association	Security Dynamics Technologies Inc
	The Republican Party	Shanghai Posts and Telecommunications
	Turkish Foreign Ministry	State National Bank
		Ukrainian Academy of Agrarian
		United in Turin
		University of Oklahoma.
		University of Pennsylvania Medical

Figure 8: Complete list of "wrong" MWEntities and left or right boundary mismatching with pattern reliability threshold = 0.90

5 Conclusion and future work

The methods described in this chapter have produced a large 22-language resource containing multi-word entities of different types and a number of automatically learned patterns to recognise newly occurring MWEntities. We intend to integrate these recognition patterns, together with the variant matching techniques, into the workflow of the *Europe Media Monitor*. An interesting feature of this collection and the patterns is that all MWEntity forms were found in real-world text and that large numbers of variants were identified, including typos, simplifications of longer names, syntactic and morphological variants and translational equivalences.

The results obtained in MWEntity recognition with the patterns automatically derived from BabelNet are promising when applied to English and Spanish, although the reported approach and evaluation figures reflect only our preliminary research in this area. Expanding the pattern learning to other languages is part of our future work. We also envisage applying the same pattern learning approach from the automatically created MWEntity resource. This would require to categorise the MWEntity sets into some broad semantic classes (e.g., organisations, events, measurements, and others) which is a task we are currently working on.

Furthermore, we are also working on expanding the patterns we learned based on a distributional approach. It consists of replacing meaningful surface forms from each pattern by a cluster of surface forms that would belong to the same semantic class. In such a way, similar words like *company, firm, corporation*, etc., will be part of the same cluster because they have a high distributional similarity. Finally, the pattern reliability scoring could be extended through inclusion of additional statistics when applying the patterns on web-scale corpora.

References

Adar, E. 2004. SaRAD: A simple and robust abbreviation dictionary. *Bioinformatics* 20. 527–533.

Bagga, Amit & Breck Baldwin. 1998. Algorithms for scoring coreference chains. *Proceedings of the First International Conference on Language Resources and Evaluation, Workshop on Linguistic Coreference.* 563–566.

Chang, Jeffrey T., Hinrich Schütze & Russ B. Altman. 2002. Creating an online dictionary of abbreviations from MEDLINE. *Journal of the American Medical Informatics Association* 9(6). 612–620.

Collins, Michael & Yoram Singer. 1999. Unsupervised models for named entity classification. In *Proceedings of the joint SIGDAT conference on Empirical Methods in Natural Language Processing and Very Large Corpora (EMNLP-VLC)*, 100–110. College Park, MD: University of Maryland.

Downey, Doug, Matthew Broadhead & Oren Etzioni. 2007. Locating complex named entities in web text. In *Proceedings of the 20th International Joint Conference on Artifical Intelligence* (IJCAI'07), 2733–2739. Hyderabad, India: Morgan Kaufmann Publishers Inc. http://dl.acm.org/citation.cfm?id=1625275.1625715.

Dyer, Chris, Victor Chahuneau & Noah A. Smith. 2013. A simple, fast, and effective reparameterization of IBM model 2. In *Proceedings of the 2013 conference of the North American chapter of the Association for Computational Linguistics: Human Language Technologies (NAACL-HLT)*, 644–648.

Ehrmann, Maud, Guillaume Jacquet & Ralf Steinberger. 2015. JRC-Names: Multilingual entity name variants and titles as linked data. *Semantic Web* (Preprint). 1–13.

Ehrmann, Maud, Leo D. Rocca, Ralf Steinberger & Hristo Tanev. 2013. Acronym recognition and processing in 22 languages. In *Proceedings of the 9th conference on Recent Advances in Natural Language Processing (RANLP)*, 237–244. Hissar, Bulgaria.

Fox, Edward A. & Joseph A. Shaw. 1994. Combination of multiple searches. *NIST Special Publication*. 243–243.

Hahn, Udo, Philipp Daumke, Stefan Schulz & Kornél Markó. 2005. Cross-language mining for acronyms and their completions from the web. *Proceedings of the 8th international conference on Discovery Science (DS'05)* 9. 113–123.

Hoffart, Johannes, Fabian M Suchanek, Klaus Berberich & Gerhard Weikum. 2013. YAGO2: A spatially and temporally enhanced knowledge base from Wikipedia. In *Proceedings of the twenty-third international joint conference on Artificial Intelligence*, 3161–3165.

Jacquet, Guillaume, Maud Ehrmann & Ralf Steinberger. 2014. Clustering of multi-word named entity variants: Multilingual evaluation. In *Proceedings of the 9th Language Resources and Evaluation conference (LREC 2014)*, 2548–2553. Reykjavik, Iceland.

Jacquet, Guillaume, Maud Ehrmann, Ralf Steinberger & Jaakko Väyrynen. 2016. Cross-lingual linking of multi-word entities and their corresponding acronyms. In *Proceedings of the 10th Language Resources and Evaluation Conference (LREC 2016)*, 528–535. Portorož, Slovenia.

James, J. Pustejovsky, José Castano, Brent Cochran, Maciej Kotecki & Michael Morrell. 2001. Automatic extraction of acronym-meaning pairs from MEDLINE databases. *Studies in health technology and informatics* 1. 371–375.

Koehn, Philipp, Hieu Hoang, Alexandra Birch, Chris Callison-Burch, Marcello Federico, Nicola Bertoldi, Brooke Cowan, Wade Shen, Christine Moran, Richard Zens, Chris Dyer, Ondrej Bojar, Alexandra Constantin & Eva Herbst. 2007. Moses: Open source toolkit for statistical machine translation. In *Proceedings of the 45th annual meeting of the ACL on interactive poster and demonstration sessions*, 177–180. Prague, Czech Republic.

Koehn, Philipp, Franz J. Och & Daniel Marcu. 2003. Statistical phrase-based translation. In *Proceedings of the 2003 conference of the North American chapter of the Association for Computational Linguistics on Human Language Technology*, vol. 1, 48–54.

Kokkinakis, Dimitrios & Dana Dannélls. 2006. Recognizing acronyms and their definitions in Swedish medical texts. In *Proceedings of the 5th conference on Language Resources and Evaluation (LREC)*, 1971–1974. Genoa, Italy.

Kompara, Mojca. 2010. Automatic recognition of abbreviations and abbreviations' expansions in multilingual electronic texts. In Chris Cummins, Chi-Hé Elder, Thomas Godard, Morgan Macleod, Elaine Schmidt & George Walkden (eds.), *Proceedings of the sixth Cambridge postgraduate conference in language research (CAMLing)*, 82–91.

McNamee, Paul & Hoa T. Dang. 2009. Overview of the TAC 2009 knowledge base population track. In *Text Analysis Conference (TAC)*, vol. 17, 111–113.

Nadeau, David & Peter D. Turney. 2005. A supervised learning approach to acronym identification. In Balázs Kégl & Guy Lapalme (eds.), *Advances in artificial intelligence: Canadian AI 2005* (Lecture Notes in Computer Science 3501), 319–329. Berlin & Heidelberg: Springer.

Navigli, Roberto & Simone Paolo Ponzetto. 2012. BabelNet: The automatic construction, evaluation and application of a wide-coverage multilingual semantic network. *Artificial Intelligence* 193. 217–250. DOI:10.1016/j.artint.2012.07.001

Nothman, Joel, Nicky Ringland, Will Radford, Tara Murphy & James Curran. 2013. Learning multilingual named entity recognition from Wikipedia. *Artificial Intelligence* 194. 151–175. DOI:10.1016/j.artint.2012.03.006

Okazaki, Naoaki & Sophia Ananiadou. 2006. Building an abbreviation dictionary using a term recognition approach. *Bioinformatics* 22. 3089–3095.

Okazaki, Naoaki, Sophia Ananiadou & Jun'ichi Tsujii. 2010. Building a high-quality sense inventory for improved abbreviation disambiguation. *Bioinformatics* 26. 1246–1253.

Piskorski, Jakub, Martin Atkinson & Jenya Belyaeva. 2011. Exploring the usefulness of cross-lingual information fusion for refining real-time news event extraction: A preliminary study. In *Proceedings of the conference Recent Advances in Natural Language Processing*, 210–217. Hissar, Bulgaria.

Rao, D., P. McNamee & M. Dredze. 2013. Entity linking: Finding extracted entities in a knowledge base. In *Multi-source, multilingual information extraction and summarization*, 93–115. Springer.

Riloff, Ellen. 1996. Automatically generating extraction patterns from untagged text. In *Proceedings of thirteenth National Conference on Artificial Intelligence (AAAI-96)*, 1044–1049. The AAAI Press/MIT Press.

Schwartz, Ariel S. & Marti A. Hearst. 2003. A simple algorithm for identifying abbreviation definitions in biomedical text. In *Proceedings of the PAC on Biocomputing*, 451–462.

Siklósi, Borbála, Attila Novák & Gábor Prószéky. 2014. Resolving abbreviations in clinical texts without pre-existing structured resources. In *4th workshop on Building and Evaluating Resources for Health and Biomedical Text Processing (BioTxtM), LREC*, 69–75. Reykjavik, Iceland.

Steinberger, Ralf, Maud Ehrmann, Júlia Pajzs, Mohamed Ebrahim, Josef Steinberger & Marco Turchi. 2013. Multilingual media monitoring and text analysis–Challenges for highly inflected languages. In *International conference on Text, Speech and Dialogue*, 22–33.

Steinberger, Ralf, Aldo Podavini, Alexandra Balahur, Guillaume Jacquet, Hristo Tanev, Jens Linge, Martin Atkinson, Michele Chinosiand, Vanni Zavarella, Yaniv Steiner & Erik van der Goot. 2015. Observing trends in automated multilingual media analysis. In *Proceedings of the symposium on New Frontiers of Automated Content Analysis in the Social Sciences (ACA'2015)*, 1–8.

Steinberger, Ralf, Bruno Pouliquen, Mijail Kabadjov & Erik van der Goot. 2011. JRC-Names: A freely available, highly multilingual named entity resource. In *Proceedings of the 8th International Conference Recent Advances in Natural Language Processing (RANLP'2011)*, 104–110. Hissar, Bulgaria.

Steinberger, Ralf, Bruno Pouliquen & Erik van der Goot. 2009. An introduction to the Europe Media Monitor family of applications. In *Proceedings of the SIGIR 2009 workshop (SIGIR-CLIR'2009)*, 1–8. Boston, USA.

Taghva, Kazen & Jeff Gilbreth. 1999. Recognizing acronyms and their definitions. *International Journal on Document Analysis and Recognition* 1(4). 191–198.

Wren, Jonathan D. & Harold R. Garner. 2002. Heuristics for identification of acronym-definition patterns within text: Towards an automated construction of comprehensive acronym-definition dictionaries. *Methods of Information in Medicine* 41(5). 426–434.

Yangarber, Roman, Winston Lin & Ralph Grishman. 2002. Unsupervised learning of generalized names. In *Proceedings of COLING: The 19th international conference on Computational Linguistics*. Taipei, Taiwan.

Name index

Language index

Subject index

www.ingramcontent.com/pod-product-compliance
Lightning Source LLC
Chambersburg PA
CBHW050925150426
42812CB00051B/2299